DEMOCRACY GOES TO WAR

Democracy Goes to War

*British Military Deployments under
International Law*

NIGEL D. WHITE

*Professor of International Law at
the University of Sheffield*

OXFORD
UNIVERSITY PRESS

OXFORD
UNIVERSITY PRESS

Great Clarendon Street, Oxford OX2 6DP

Oxford University Press is a department of the University of Oxford.
It furthers the University's objective of excellence in research, scholarship,
and education by publishing worldwide in

Oxford New York

Auckland Cape Town Dar es Salaam Hong Kong Karachi
Kuala Lumpur Madrid Melbourne Mexico City Nairobi
New Delhi Shanghai Taipei Toronto

With offices in

Argentina Austria Brazil Chile Czech Republic France Greece
Guatemala Hungary Italy Japan Poland Portugal Singapore
South Korea Switzerland Thailand Turkey Ukraine Vietnam

Oxford is a registered trade mark of Oxford University Press
in the UK and in certain other countries

Published in the United States
by Oxford University Press Inc., New York

British Library Cataloguing in Publication Data

Data available

Library of Congress Cataloging in Publication Data
White, N. D., 1961-
Democracy goes to war: British military deployments under
international law / Nigel D. White.
p. cm.
Includes bibliographical references and index.
ISBN 978-0-19-921859-2
1. Military law—Great Britain. 2. Great Britain—Foreign relations—
Law and legislation. 3. Peacekeeping forces, British. 4. War
(International law) I. Title.
KD6012.W48 2009
342.41'0412—dc22   2009011689

Typeset by Newgen Imaging Systems (P) Ltd., Chennai, India
Printed in Great Britain by the MPG Books Group, Bodmin and King's Lynn
on acid-free paper

ISBN 978-0-19-921859-2

1 3 5 7 9 10 8 6 4 2

Preface

At the end of the Second World War a new world order was crafted, based on the United Nations and the prohibition of military force in international relations. Despite these developments, British troops have been regularly deployed around the globe since 1945: most notably to Korea, the Suez Canal, Cyprus, and the Falklands during the Cold War; and Kuwait, Bosnia, Kosovo, Afghanistan and Iraq since the fall of the Berlin Wall. This book considers the different constitutional frameworks operating at national and international levels, within which troop deployments are made by the British government, and assesses whether mechanisms of democratic accountability can contribute to upholding international law.

The inspiration for this book came from the American Society of International Law project which led to the publication of a book in 2003, edited by the project leaders Charlotte Ku and the late Harold Jacobson, entitled *Democratic Accountability and the Use of Force in International Law*. In contributing to the project and writing a chapter on British doctrine and practice I realized that it was impossible to do justice in such a limited space to both legal and political debate on matters of great constitutional and international importance. Thus this work concentrates on the UK's involvement in shaping the world order after 1945, and its decisions to go to war, or otherwise become involved in conflict or post-conflict situations—some of which conform to the norms of that world order but others of which seek to challenge and change them. It aims to fill a gap in legal and political literature on the exercise of what are sometimes called 'war powers' by the British government, but also to place such decisions in the wider international context. The text was finished in December 2008, when the issue of reform of prerogative war powers was still finding its way through parliament.

The research for this book was partly funded by a Social Science Small Grant from the Nuffield Foundation, as well as the School of Law at Sheffield University. I would like to thank the following students from the School of Law who, at various times, acted as research assistants: Kate Bisset, Gabi Dwyer, Chamu Kuppuswamy, Djims Milius, Simon Newman, Lin Qi, Matthew Saul, Christy Shucksmith, and Rachel Thompson. Thanks as always goes to my family for their support, especially my wife Gill.

Nigel D. White

School of Law
University of Sheffield
December 2008

Contents

Table of Cases

List of Abbreviations

AC	Appeals Cases
AJIL	American Journal of International Law
All ER	All England Law Reports
ASIL	American Society of International Law
AU	African Union
BYBIL	British Yearbook of International Law
CFSP	Common Foreign and Security Policy
CND	Campaign for Nuclear Disarmament
CPA	Coalition Provisional Authority
CSCE	Conference on Security and Cooperation in Europe
DRC	Democratic Republic of the Congo
EC	European Community
ECHR	European Court of Human Rights
ECOWAS	Economic Community of West African States
ECR	European Court Reports
ECSC	European Coal and Steel Community
EDC	European Defence Community
EEC	European Economic Community
EFAR	European Foreign Affairs Review
EFTA	European Free Trade Association
EPC	European Political Cooperation
ESDP	European Security and Defence Policy
EU	European Union
EUFOR	European Union Force
EURATOM	European Atomic Energy Community
EWCA	England and Wales Court of Appeal Reports
EWHC	England and Wales High Court Reports
FRY	Federal Republic of Yugoslavia
G7/8	Group of Seven/Eight Industrialized Countries
G77	Group of Developing Countries
GA Res.	United Nations General Assembly Resolution
GCHQ	Government Communications Headquarters
GYBIL	German Yearbook of International Law
HC	House of Commons
HL	House of Lords
IAEA	International Atomic Energy Agency
ICC	International Criminal Court
ICJ	International Court of Justice
ICJ Rep.	International Court of Justice Reports
ICLQ	International and Comparative Law Quarterly
ICTY	International Criminal Tribunal for the Former Yugoslavia

IFOR	Implementation Force
IGC	Iraqi Governing Council
ILC	International Law Commission
ILM	International Legal Materials
INTERFET	International Force in East Timor
ISAF	International Security Assistance Force
JACL	Journal of Armed Conflict Law
JCSL	Journal of Conflict and Security Law
JIC	Joint Intelligence Committee
KB	King's Bench Division
KFOR	Kosovo Force
KLA	Kosovo Liberation Army
LJIL	Leiden Journal of International Law
MONUC	United Nations Mission in the Congo
MP	Member of Parliament
MPYBUNL	Max Planck Yearbook of UN Law
NATO	North Atlantic Treaty Organization
NGO	non-governmental organization
NYBIL	Netherlands Yearbook of International Law
OAS	Organization of American States
OEEC	Organization for European Economic Co-operation
OJ	Official Journal (European Communities)
ONUC	UN Operation in the Congo
OSCE	Organization for Security and Co-operation in Europe
P5	Five Permanent Members of the Security Council
PSO	Peace Support Operation
QB	Queen's Bench Division
RAF	Royal Air Force
RIAA	Reports of International Arbitral Awards
R2P	Responsibility to Protect
SC Res.	United Nations Security Council Resolution
SCOR	Security Council Official Records
SFOR	Stabilization Force
SFRY	Socialist Federal Republic of Yugoslavia
TCN	Troop Contributing Nation
TEU	Treaty on European Union
UKHL	United Kingdom House of Lords (law reports)
UKMIL	United Kingdom Materials on International Law
UN	United Nations
UN Doc. A/	United Nations General Assembly Document
UN Doc. S/	United Nations Security Council Document
UNAMET	United Nations Assistance Mission in East Timor
UNAMSIL	United Nations Assistance Mission in Sierra Leone
UNCIO	United Nations Conference on International Organization
UNEF	United Nations Emergency Force
UNFICYP	United Nations Force in Cyprus

UNITAF	Unified Task Force
UNMIK	United Nations Mission in Kosovo
UNMOVIC	United Nations Monitoring, Verification and Inspection Commission
UNPROFOR	United Nations Protection Force
UNSCR	United Nations Security Council Resolution
WEU	Western European Union
WLR	Weekly Law Reports
WMD	Weapons of Mass Destruction
WTO	World Trade Organization

Introduction

When Parliament met in the evening a short but very fierce debate occurred, in which the Prime Minister's [Mr. Chamberlain] temporising was ill-received by the House. When Mr. Greenwood rose to speak on behalf of the Labour Opposition Mr. Amery from the Conservatives benches cried out to him, 'Speak for England.' This was received with loud cheers. There was no doubt that the temper of the House [on 2 September 1939] was for war. I even deemed it more resolute and united than in the similar scene on August 3, 1914, in which I had also taken part. (Winston Churchill writing of events on the eve of Britain's declaration of war against Germany in 1939)[1]

Although the struggle would be long and hard, requiring the most strenuous effort from all, we had reached the top of the pass, and our road to victory was not only sure and certain, but accompanied by constant cheering events. I was not denied the right to share in this new phase of the war because of the unity and strength of the War Cabinet, the confidence which I preserved of my political and professional colleagues, the steadfast loyalty of Parliament, and the persisting goodwill of the nation. (Winston Churchill writing of the turning of the tide in the war in September 1942)[2]

When I hear people talking in an airy way of throwing modern armies ashore here and there as if they were bales of goods to be dumped on the beach and forgotten I really marvel at the lack of knowledge which still prevails of the conditions of modern war. (Winston Churchill writing about complaints in Parliament made in September 1943 over the delay in attacking Naples)[3]

Britain's democracy stood firm during the Second World War. Winston Churchill's history of this period reveals the importance of the relationship between the government, in particular the Prime Minister, and parliament. In 1939 Prime Minister Neville Chamberlain seemed to lack the same political will for war as shown by parliament. As the war became one of survival for Britain, Churchill as Prime Minister relied heavily on the support of his executive as well as parliament and the country, but even as the war turned in favour of the Allies, criticism of specific policy and tactics could still be found in the House of Commons. However, the justness and legality of the cause against the Axis powers meant that on the big issue of the overall prosecution of the war there was limited criticism of Churchill's leadership.

---

[1] W.S. Churchill, *The Second World War: Volume I The Gathering Storm* (London: Cassell, 1949) 362.
[2] W.S. Churchill, *The Second World War: Volume IV The Hinge of Fate* (London: Cassell, 1951) 494.
[3] W.S. Churchill, *The Second World War: Volume V Closing the Ring* (London: Cassell, 1952) 138.

With the end of the Second World War there came the United Nations and a new world order based on the prohibition of military force in international relations, and yet since 1945 British troops have been regularly deployed around the globe: most notably to Korea, Suez, Cyprus, and the Falklands during the Cold War; and Kuwait, Bosnia, Kosovo, Afghanistan and Iraq since the fall of the Berlin Wall. The decisions to deploy forces are political ones made within several constitutional frameworks, national, regional, and international. After considering the various legal and institutional regimes applicable to such deployments, the main purpose of this book is to examine the decision to deploy troops from the perspective of international law.

In its military interventions since 1945 Britain has consistently tried to utilize international law to justify its actions, though often it argues against orthodox interpretation of the laws. In an area of law that is notoriously open-ended and contested, caution must be observed and the simple application of rules to the facts avoided. However, the inherent fluidity of international law must be balanced against the fact that there is consensus among states on certain fundamental rules, though that consensus must be constantly reappraised. In gauging whether Britain's actions are in breach of international law we can make judgements at different levels using various forms of accountability: from judicial fora (for example the International Court of Justice in the Hague or the European Court of Human Rights in Strasbourg), to political ones (the UN General Assembly in New York or the House of Commons in Westminster), though political ones dominate. While this book examines international and regional mechanisms, tumultuous debates on Suez, Afghanistan, Iraq and others in the House of Commons and its Committees are highlighted to show how international law impacts upon domestic politics. In considering whether democratic accountability is effective in upholding the principles of international law, this book throws new light on an old democracy, and thereby makes a contribution to current reform proposals that are aimed at improving democratic decision-making.

The book places domestic political decision-making within the international, as well as domestic, legal orders. In considering whether governmental actions are compatible with international law, the main points of reference are the international rules governing the use of force in international relations (known as the *jus ad bellum*). These rules define the circumstances under which a use of military force by a state is lawful, whether it be to claim or reclaim territory, to protect its nationals or its homeland, to remove an unpopular government or rout a terrorist group from some remote location within another country. Decisions to deploy troops to conflicts in other countries are judged by reference to these rules since they are directly applicable. Other international laws that may be applicable once a deployment has been made, such as international humanitarian law (part of the *jus in bello*) or human rights law, are not directly the subject matter of the book, though they are referred to. Given that the book follows the duration of the deployments of British troops in the main post-Second World War conflicts, issues of humanitarian law may arise, but the focus of these discussions remains an examination of the reasons for their deployment. What is the legal basis of the continuing presence of British troops in Afghanistan long after the events of 9/11 of 2001; and in Iraq, over five years after the invasion of that country? These are still issues concerning the justification for armed force and therefore are to be judged by the principles of the *jus ad bellum*.

A subsidiary purpose of the book is to consider the functions of the UK democratic system in times of war and foreign crises, when British troops are deployed to conflict and post-conflict zones around the world. From the outset it engages in the debate surrounding the balance between democracy and the necessities of war, and considers whether the British constitutional system is sufficiently democratic in taking decisions on military intervention. It places that decision-making process within the wider international context, in particular by considering the impact of international law and international legal debate upon the British political and legal systems.

British troops can be sent to operate in many different capacities: as military observers, peacekeepers, peace-enforcers, state-builders, and war-fighters. Sometimes they have authority from parliament as a whole and sometimes just from the executive, sometimes they operate under the mandate of an international organization, other times not. Often they fight alongside troops from allied states, occasionally by themselves. Advice on the legality of war and deployment of troops is occasionally clear, other times not. The book examines how these different factors can influence decisions to deploy and increases or decreases their legality and legitimacy.

In overview, the book first of all considers the domestic and then the international legal and institutional regimes within which decisions to go to war or more generally to deploy troops are made. Then, by taking the international legal framework for military operations, a number of case studies reveal how the international legal basis of military action impacts on the national political debate, and serve to illustrate the role international law plays in the domestic legal and political orders. With recent interventions being based on controversial international legal bases there has been increased pressure for greater accountability, especially to parliament. The reform debate that this has sparked gives the book a contemporary political relevance.

These chapters also consider how the domestic debate may help to re-shape international law and institutions. The international legal system does not simply consist of a set of fixed rules that must be followed by states, but is in a process of change and development since it is primarily made by governments and institutions. In essence the relationship between the international legal and political order and, with focus on Britain, the domestic legal and political orders on the issue of using military force are the questions addressed in this book.

The first half of the book is mainly concerned with developing the constitutional, institutional and legal contexts at both the domestic and international levels. The relationships between the national and international regimes are developed in this part, but detailed analysis follows in the second half of the book by taking examples of different types of military operations in which British troops have been deployed: under UN mandates, self-defence, collective-defence, humanitarian intervention, and in the case of enforcement operations without an international mandate. The order is thus not a chronological one but is primarily dictated by the legal basis upon which the deployment is made and ranges from consensual peacekeeping (Bosnia in the 1990s), through self-defence (Falklands in 1982 and Afghanistan in 2001), to humanitarian intervention (Kosovo in 1999), and intervention on the basis of UN Resolutions (Iraq 2003). The latter is the most controversial intervention in that there was no clear mandate to use force, and can be contrasted with instances of clear authorization to use force (in Korea in 1950 and Iraq in 1991) dealt with in the earlier part of the book.

More specifically, chapter one contains an historical account of the origins of the Crown's authority in military matters and its continuation in modern times in the shape of executive prerogative powers. Historical developments are considered but more attention is paid to the Second World War, the end of which ushered in a new order in international relations, one based around the United Nations and international law, though traditional balance of power politics prevailed during the Cold War.

After considering the post-1945 international legal regime and Britain's attitude towards it in chapter two, the importance of the UN and NATO to the UK is discussed in chapter three by considering the parliamentary and wider political and legal debates that led to the UK's membership and subsequent contributions to these organizations. At this point consideration is given in chapter four to the development of the UN collective security system, and Britain's role in it by tracing the development of coalitions of the willing acting under UN authority. The actions in Korea in the 1950s and Iraq in 1991, both involving significant British contributions, are analysed. In the post-Cold War era the EU has taken on an increased foreign and security profile resulting in British troops being committed to European operations, as well as NATO and UN forces. The development of the European dimension of collective security is considered in chapter five. On other occasions though Britain acts alone or in collaboration with its allies without any institutional mandate. Practice is brought into the discussions in the first half of the book, but more detailed analysis is left until later. Coverage of the main instances of post-1945 British military deployment will be ensured to give a complete modern account of such practice, and the legal problems it raises.

In taking a number of conflicts and explaining the political and legal background to decisions to send troops, and ultimately addressing the questions of whether the deployment was justified legally and politically, the complex interplay of domestic and international legal and political factors becomes clearer. The inadequate international response, in which Britain played an influential role, to the conflict and atrocities in Bosnia in the 1990s is reviewed in chapter six. The resolute action to recover the Falklands from Argentinian attack and occupation is considered in chapter seven, while the decision to join the US in responding to the terrorist attacks of September 2001 is discussed in chapter eight. Chapter nine looks at the controversial decision to bomb Serbia to stop its repressive actions in Kosovo in 1999. Chapter ten considers the hugely divisive decision to join the US in invading Iraq in 2003, the repercussions of which are still being felt today. Each of these chapters examines in detail the international legal framework and rules applicable to such operations. Throughout, the relationship between parliamentary involvement and the international legal and institutional basis of the military operation is discussed. Parliamentary debates are examined to consider the relevance of the international legality and institutional legitimacy of the intervention in evaluating executive decision-making. Would greater accountability be achieved by requiring prior parliamentary approval of the operation, or does the dominance of party politics in the Westminster system mean that this would make little difference?

The book concludes with a chapter that considers the complex interplay of democracy with international law. Different mechanisms of legal and political accountability both at the domestic and international levels are considered with a view to their application in cases where decisions to deploy troops are politically or legally controversial. The role of Select Committees of the House of Commons, of domestic courts (including courts-martial), of (public) inquiries, and their equivalent at the international level including cases before the International Court of Justice and the International Criminal Court, give the conclusions a practical perspective. Pressure for the strengthening of mechanisms of accountability at the domestic and international level, and the practical reforms called for as a result of this pressure are analysed in full. At the domestic level, for instance, this has led to calls for prior parliamentary approval of military actions.

In order to place the interplay of democracy and war in a wider context, some comparisons are made in the final chapter to other countries, especially when they form part of a coalition with Britain. While Britain is the focus of the study, reference to other countries facilitates a better understanding of this complex issue. This in turn will provide some comparative analysis within which to place the current debate within parliament and elsewhere on the issue of whether prior parliamentary approval should be necessary before decisions on foreign deployment of British forces are made.

1

The British Constitution and Military Action

1. Introduction

When a country decides to go to war, there are many political, economic, and of course, military considerations that enter into the decision-making process. This complex matrix will be shown throughout this book, but the main purpose of looking at these factors in decision-making is to put the legal frameworks that seek to regulate war-making within a wider context. When a government decides to deploy troops to combat zones around the world there will be two main types of law seeking to both regulate and empower that choice[1]—the constitutional law of the country in question and the norms and customs of international law (within which we include the notion of regional law). The law seeks to regulate the decision by positing certain rules and procedures that should be followed if the decision is to avoid charges of illegality. It will also empower the government to make decisions that have the most serious consequences for the country it represents, and for the country to which troops are dispatched.

This chapter focuses on the British constitution and considers the origins and application of prerogative powers in decisions to deploy British forces to conflict and post-conflict zones. The roles of the executive, legislative and judicial branches of government are outlined. The traditional dominance of the executive (in reality smaller groupings of the Cabinet in formal committees or informal arrangements) is considered, as is the role of parliament, which appears to have increased in recent years. The current discussion as to whether this should culminate in parliamentary approval being given before the deployment of troops will be outlined at this stage, and the reasons for it returned to in later chapters, before being fully debated and concluded on in chapter eleven. The slow encroachment of the judiciary into other aspects of the royal prerogative is be contrasted with the reserved domain of foreign affairs and the deployment of troops.

---

[1] L.F. Damrosch, 'Trends in Executive and Legislative Powers', in C. Ku and H.K. Jacobson (eds), *Democratic Accountability and the Use of Force in International Law* (Cambridge: Cambridge University Press, 2003) 39 at 40.

2. The Sovereign's Army

In matters of deploying troops and waging war, the Prime Minister has quite startling 'prerogative' powers under British constitutional law. The Prime Minister has at his or her disposal a highly trained army, navy and air force, currently numbering about 200,000.[2] The constitutional framework within which the prerogative is operated in modern times will be reviewed more fully below. The purpose of this section is to trace the origins of this power to the medieval monarchs of England. Michael Prestwich describes the English army of over 10,000 men led into Scotland by Edward I in 1300:

The army was commanded by the king himself, and some of the cavalry were paid regular members of the royal household. Others were present because landowners had been requested to provide military service under the terms by which they held their land. Yet others served voluntarily at their own expense. Many knights and men-at-arms had entered into contracts to serve a magnate as part of his retinue. There were even a few foreign mercenaries. The infantry were mostly there unwillingly, recruited by royal commissioners. They were paid for their service, but their columns were diminished daily by desertion.[3]

The only standing element of this army, one that was always in the king's service and at his disposal, was the royal household, which in general terms provided several hundred knights. This was clearly inadequate for most of the military operations undertaken by the Crown.[4] The demise of feudal service in the fourteenth century, was replaced by an 'obligation on all free men to bear arms in defence of their country', an obligation that can be traced back to Anglo-Saxon times. It is clear that the 'military obligation was to . . . defend the land; it would not apply to offensive expeditions'.[5]

While the knights and nobles fought for glory, position and reward, the ordinary men in the infantry 'faced a dismal prospect of discomfort and exhaustion, dysentery and sickness. If they were captured, they were not worth ransoming, and so were far more likely to be killed in battle than the knights'.

---

[2] C. Heyman, *The British Army: A Pocket Guide 2006–2007* (Barnsley: Pen and Sword Books, 2005) 9.

[3] M. Prestwich, 'The English Medieval Army to 1485', in D.G. Chandler and I. Beckett (eds), *The Oxford History of the British Army* (Oxford: Oxford University Press, 1994) 1. For the development of the navy and RAF see J.R. Hill, *The Oxford Illustrated History of the Royal Navy* (Oxford: Oxford University Press, 1995); J. Rawlings, *History of the Royal Air Force* (London: Random House, 1985).

[4] Prestwich 'The English Medieval Army', 3–4.

[5] Ibid., 6. See further A. Lyon, *Constitutional History of the United Kingdom* (London: Cavendish, 2003) 102–3. Compulsory military service was introduced during the First World War in 1916: P. Simkins, 'The Four Armies 1914–1918', in Chandler and Beckett (eds), *History of the British Army*, 235 at 235. Conscription was again introduced in 1939 after the outbreak of the Second World War: A. Danchev, 'The Army and the Home Front 1939–1945', in Chandler and Beckett (eds), *History of the British Army*, 298 at 300.

Furthermore, the 'only group which received a significant favour from the Crown in exchange for fighting were criminals', who were promised pardons in return for service.[6]

While the medieval king had complete constitutional power to wage war, he was faced with considerable practical limitations on that power especially when raising an army. The lack of a standing army meant that 'war was the most complex enterprise in which the medieval English state was involved'.[7] Furthermore, since the signing of the Magna Carta in 1215, the monarch could not levy the taxes necessary to wage expensive wars without the then rudimentary parliament's approval.[8] Another limitation that did not seem to prevent the raising of armies for foreign war, but an interesting one nonetheless, was that the obligation on free men to serve in the army was confined to actions in defence of the realm. Early examples of debates about the line between defensive and offensive wars can be found with F.W. Maitland who wrote that 'the Welsh and Scottish Wars of Henry VI were regarded as defensive, resistances on invasion, and the county forces could lawfully be called to meet them'.[9]

By the outset of the sixteenth century, the core armed force at Henry VII's disposal consisted of 2,000–3,000 men in arms. This force was supplemented in the main by the obligation of all men to defend the realm which in the sixteenth century was 'modernized and made the backbone of the nation's defences on land'.[10] Further troops consisted of foreign mercenaries. In Henry VIII's wars against France, out of a force of 44,000—'the largest army ever seen under English command on the Continent until the late seventeenth century'—a quarter were foreign troops.[11] The effects of war, especially for the many wounded and disabled men returning from Henry's and Elizabeth I's wars, caused 'a growing war weariness' so that 'MPs, JPs, and local communities alike became less co-operative towards the demands of government'.[12] This discontent was exacerbated with the onset of the Thirty Years War and the military expeditions ordered by Charles I.

---

[6] Prestwich, 'The English Medieval Army', 20.

[7] Ibid., 23.

[8] I. Loveland, *Constitutional Law, Administrative Law and Human Rights* (3rd edn, London: Butterworths, 2003) 23.

[9] F.W. Maitland, *The Constitutional History of England* (Cambridge: Cambridge University Press, 1931) 278.

[10] I. Roy, 'Towards the Standing Army 1485–1660', in Chandler and Beckett (eds), *History of the British Army,* 23 at 26.

[11] Ibid., 27. During the Napoleonic wars in 1813, the British army numbered over 250,000 troops: D. Gates, 'The Transformation of the Army 1783–1815', in Chandler and Beckett(eds), *History of the British Army*, 132 at 139. Though the numbers varied, by 1914 at the outbreak of the First World War the army stood at just under 250,000, but by 1918 it had risen to 3,458,586, one and a half million of whom were in France: T. Travers, 'The Army and the Challenge of War 1914–1918', in Chandler and Beckett (eds), *History of the British Army*, 211 at 211. At the end of the Second World War the British Army stood at 2,920,000: A. Danchev, 'The Army and the Home Front 1939–1945', in Chandler and Beckett (eds), *History of the British Army*, 298 at 302.

[12] I. Roy, 'Towards the Standing Army', 39.

The loss of life in these expeditions was very great: Members of Parliament were shocked by the sight of discharged sailors and soldiers dying in the streets of west country ports. Parliament made it plain its discontent in the Petition of Right in 1628, which placed severe restraints on the demands which the Crown could make on the subject in time of War.[13]

As Ian Loveland states, 'by the seventeenth century the Commons and Lords had become increasingly reluctant to give approval for the levying of taxes without a guarantee that the Monarch accepted certain limits on his personal powers'.[14] The monarch could try to by-pass parliament by relying on his prerogative powers but 'the difficulty arose whenever the Crown needed money above and beyond its own resources—whenever it wanted to go to war for example'.[15] The power struggle between parliament and the Sovereign culminated in a number of con-stitutional 'moments' in history, moments when the balance of power changed significantly. The Magna Carta of 1215 was an early example,[16] and the Bill of Rights of 1689 a later one. In 1642, the struggle between Charles I and parlia-ment produced internal conflict. The civil war in England, 1642–8, led to the two sides creating 'war machines comparable to those...laying waste [to] whole areas of the Continent'.[17] Control of the warring armies reflects, in a way, the current debate about who should control military operations, with the Cavaliers under the control of the King and the New Model Army or Roundheads under the control of parliament, though considerable discretion was left to the com-manders on the ground.[18]

Although the standing army was reduced by half during the Protectorate of Oliver Cromwell (1653–1658) neither he, nor his regime's successors, resolved the dilemma of maintaining a still large standing army with the low taxes enjoyed by the gentry before the Civil War.[19] Though Charles II and his successors were aware of this, Cromwell laid the foundations, not only for a standing army but also for Britain's subsequent 'great power status'.[20]

Despite the Civil War and the growth in power of parliament, it was true to say that up until the intervention of William of Orange in the so-called 'Glorious Revolution' of 1688, 'the army belonged to the king. In peacetime, a standing army was unknown to English statute law and the army was not knowingly rec-ognized by parliament. The army was commanded by the king and ranked as a department of the royal household'.[21] Parliament did, however, control the purse strings more tightly, thus restricting the monarch's ability to create a powerful army, at least without parliamentary support. 'It was arguably James II's per-sistent disregard of parliamentary authority that eventually triggered the 1688

---

[13] Ibid., 42.   [14] Loveland, *Constitutional Law*, 23.
[15] Ibid., 23.   [16] Lyon, *Constitutional History*, 39–40.
[17] Roy, 'Towards the Standing Army', 42.
[18] Ibid., 43.   [19] Ibid., 45.   [20] Ibid., 45.
[21] J. Childs, 'The Restoration Army 1660–1702', in Chandler and Beckett(eds), *History of the British Army*, 46 at 52.

revolution'.[22] The intervention of William of Orange in England in the Glorious Revolution, 'motivated by European rather than English concerns', 'brought a profound and lasting alteration in the relations between Crown, parliament, and the army'.[23] William's war against France meant that his desire for more troops led to his willingness to restrict the Crown's prerogative power in military matters.

The 1688 revolution, like Magna Carta and the Civil War before it, marked the crossing of a political watershed. A new political 'contract' was struck between Parliament and the Monarchy, and consequently a new constitutional foundation was laid. In return for the throne, William and Mary accepted that the Crown's ability to govern the English nation through its prerogative powers would be severely limited in future. The Monarch might still be responsible for governing the country, and she/he could appoint the Ministers who would do the job, but those Ministers would govern the country according to laws defined by Parliament.[24]

The Bill of Rights produced by parliament in 1689 declared that 'levying of money for and to the use of the Crown by pretence of prerogative without grant of Parliament is illegal', which re-iterated the Magna Carta, but also 'that the raising or keeping of a standing army within the kingdom in time of peace unless it be with the consent of Parliament is against the law'. The latter clause 'removed the standing army from the royal household and placed it firmly under the control of parliament making it a national institution'. Further, it meant that 'both constitutionally and financially, the Crown could no longer employ the army as its own political tool'; the British army was now destined to be the servant of parliament.[25]

   Though constitutionally control of the army passed from the king to parliament, the gradual transference of power to parliament from 1689 onwards did not mean the disappearance of the prerogative nor the monarch's involvement in decision-making and war-making.[26] But the extent of the Sovereign's prerogative powers was limited, and the remaining prerogative could be amended or abolished by legislation.[27] Since the Revolution of 1688 there has been a decline in the practical significance of the Sovereign's powers. By the mid-eighteenth century the relationship between the Sovereign and his Ministers had changed so that neither George I nor George II were involved to any great degree in government affairs. By 1740 the 'Prime Minster'—the first one being Sir Robert Walpole—was practically in control of the Cabinet. Though progress towards the modern constitutional monarchy was by no means smooth, the trend was towards Cabinet government, which was 'pretty much in place by 1810'.[28] In

---

[22] Loveland, *Constitutional Law*, 87.   [23] Childs, 'The Restoration Army', 57.
[24] Loveland, *Constitutional Law*, 25.   [25] Childs, 'The Restoration Army', 57.
[26] 'King George II was the last British monarch to lead his troops into action, at Dettimngen on 27 June 1743', A.J. Guy, 'The Army of the Georges 1714–1783', in Chandler and Beckett(eds), *History of the British Army*, 92 at 98.
[27] Loveland, *Constitutional Law*, 87–8.
[28] R.A. Dahl, *On Democracy* (New Haven: Yale University Press, 1998) 123.

the modern age the 'Queen is now largely just a figurehead, performing cere-
monial and symbolic functions' within the current constitutional framework.[29]
The prerogative powers have been eroded but they have not gone. 'For most practical purposes, prerogative powers are exercised on the monarch's behalf by the
government'.[30] Such powers remain in areas as important as the conduct of foreign affairs, including the signing of treaties and the decisions to go to war or to
otherwise deploy troops.

Though the waging of war and the deployment of troops came within the remit
of the emerging democracy in England, it was not exercised by parliament, but
by Ministers using powers formerly possessed by the Sovereign. Ministers were
accountable to parliament for such decisions, but the beginning of the end of the
Sovereign's concern for government in the eighteenth century 'coincided with the
emergence of a sophisticated system of party political organisation'.[31] This meant
that the levels of accountability for decisions to go to war were limited, for in general terms the electoral system in the UK ensured that the executive dominated
parliament, as will be explained in the next section.

3. Democracy and War

Historically, as democracy has grown in the UK, we have seen the power to wage
war being transferred from the monarch to the government, which in turn is
accountable to parliament. In a democratic system it might be expected that political pressure from MPs and the electorate would prevent the country from going
to war too readily. Indeed, in 1795 Immanuel Kant put forward a theory for
democratic peace on the premise that democracies are far less likely to wage war.

> If...the consent of the citizenry is required in order to determine whether or not there
> will be war, it is natural that they consider all its calamities before committing themselves
> to so risky a game...By contrast, under a nonrepublican constitution where subjects are
> not citizens, the easiest thing in the world is to declare war. Here the ruler is not a fellow
> citizen, but the nation's owner, and war does not affect his table, his hunt, his places of
> pleasure...Thus he can decide to go to war for the most meaningless of reasons, as if it
> were a kind of pleasure party, and he can blithely leave its justification to his diplomatic
> corps, who are always prepared for such exercises.[32]

The proposition that democracies do not readily wage war, a proposition usually
confined to explain the absence of war between democracies,[33] is premised on

---

[29] Loveland, *Constitutional Law*, 88.
[30] Ibid., 88.   [31] Ibid., 88.
[32] I. Kant, *Perpetual Peace, and Other Essays on History and Morals* (Indianapolis: Hackett
Publishing, 1983, T. Humphrey Trans.) 113.
[33] See for example T.M. Franck, 'The Emerging Right to Democratic Governance' (1992) 86
AJIL 82; S.R. Weart, *Never at War: Why Democracies Will Not Fight One Another* (New Haven: Yale
University Press, 1998); B. Russett, *Grasping the Democratic Peace: Principles for a Post-Cold War*

the Kantian assumption that the electorate, or their elected representatives, control belligerent decision-making. However, as has been seen in the above section, the modern reality is that in the UK, the executive, in the form of the Cabinet or a sub-group of that body, makes the decision to commit military forces. The House of Commons, representing the electorate, then has a chance to debate the matter. As will be seen in this book, in recent times parliament, mainly through the House of Commons, has acted as a more significant control on the actions of the executive, in the sense that the military action is subject to questioning and debate in the House of Commons and in its relevant Select Committees, though this has not been a consistent practice.

Although not playing a major role in parliament's scrutiny of the executive's actions in times of conflict, the unelected upper house, the House of Lords, can play a subsidiary role principally in seeking information from the government. This can be explained by the 'intensity of party discipline and paucity of investigatory resources in the lower house [that] places stringent restrictions on the effectiveness of MPs' supervisory capacities. Consequently, there is appreciable scope for the Lords to complement and reinforce the Commons in this respect',[34] although this supporting role is less pronounced in the field of foreign affairs.

One of the questions this book wants to consider is whether prior parliamentary approval should be required before troops could be deployed. This might seem to be a quick and easy solution to the problem but there are a number of issues associated with this possible change that need to be addressed. First, would this reduce the effectiveness of the government in responding to aggression against Britain or its allies and threats to the peace arising from crises around the world, perhaps prompted by humanitarian concerns? Second, might the reduction in inefficiency be justified by the relative increase in democracy that such a reform would bring? Third, would parliamentary approval be a real check on the power of the executive?

Historically, 'the Glorious Revolution of 1689 was about subjecting executive power—the king—to a range of limitations that secured that certain laws could not be changed, and things could not be done without the consent of the Commons and Lords in Parliament assembled'.[35] As we have seen, this left certain powers, those of concerning the royal prerogative, including decisions to wage war and deploying troops, largely untouched by the requirement of the consent of parliament. Parliament annually consents to the presence of a standing army, but it is not required to approve of each deployment of those troops.

World (Princeton: Princeton University Press, 1993). For further international relations perspectives on the relationship between democracy and war, see D. Reiter and A.C. Stam, *Democracies at War* (Princeton: Princeton University Press, 2002). For a comparative political analysis of democracy and terrorism see S. Cohen (ed), *Democracies at War Against Terrorism* (London: Palgrave, 2008).

34 Loveland, *Constitutional Law*, 177.
35 D. Oliver, *Constitutional Reform in the UK* (Oxford: Oxford University Press, 2003) 31.

From 1689 to the constitutional reforms in the nineteenth and twentieth centuries by which the right to vote was made universal, parliamentary sovereignty, signifying parliament's supreme legislative capacity,[36] was not reflecting democracy but was developed to 'secure government by consent', namely of the Commons and the Lords.[37] With the widening of the franchise the concept of representative democracy developed whereby, with the exception of the prerogative powers, parliament, representing the electorate, controlled the government. At some point though, in the post-1945 period, through a combination of ruthless control of the political parties, the first-past-the-post electoral system that ensures that one party usually dominates parliament, and the ever increasing often technical legislative burden, parliament no longer controlled the government. The reality became that 'the executive governs through Parliament'.[38]

Thus with the concepts of representative democracy and parliamentary sovereignty being undermined (the latter by other external factors as well such as the impact of European Community legislation), one might question whether the solution to the perceived lack of democracy in the areas of the prerogative, such as the decision to deploy troops, is to bring it within the remit of parliamentary control. This issue will be returned to in later chapters, and concluded upon in chapter eleven. In this chapter the debate will be put within the context of different visions of democracy that might be used to control the executive, both in terms of its core competence and its prerogative powers.

Lessons might be learnt from other countries. In other parliamentary democracies there is a spectrum from the executive having almost complete dominance in the UK, towards the other end, for example in Germany, which requires advanced parliamentary approval for decisions to commit military power.[39] Even within countries with established constitutions the pendulum might swing between the executive and parliament in different cases though in general there has been what has been labelled a 'parliamentarization' of the decision-making process,[40] with debate and approval within parliaments increasing, in recognition that within democracies 'it is only when military policies are fully debated and understood through the constitutional processes of democratic societies [that] there will be sufficient assurance of public support for them'.[41]

A similar pendulum effect can be seen within Presidential systems such as the United States where there has been a 'long-running and fundamentally irresolvable controversy over the allocation of domestic authority to decide upon the external uses of military force'.[42] The President, on the one hand, has asserted

---

[36] See generally J. Goldsworthy, *The Sovereignty of Parliament: History and Philosophy* (Oxford: Oxford University Press, 2002).

[37] Oliver, *Constitutional Reform*, 32.   [38] Ibid., 33.

[39] Damrosch, 'Trends in Legislative and Executive Powers', 59.

[40] Ibid., 54.   [41] Ibid., 60.

[42] Ibid., 48. See further M. Glennon, 'The United States: Democracy, Hegemony and Accountability', in Ku and Jacobson (eds), *Democratic Accountability*, 323.

sole constitutional authority to commit US troops, but on the other, in the War Powers Resolution of 1973, Congress has claimed a share in decisions to commit troops to hostilities.[43] The President might not recognize the legality of Congress' position, but sometimes he will have to recognize the political necessity of Congressional approval:

In the Gulf War [of 1991], although President Bush insisted that he did not need the approval of 'some old goat in the United States Congress to kick Saddam Hussein out of Kuwait', he did request and receive congressional authorization under the War Powers Resolution, thereby significantly enhancing the legitimacy of the military effort in the eyes of the public.[44]

The need for that legitimacy was also evidenced by the fact that President George W. Bush secured Congressional approval for launching wars in Afghanistan in 2001 and Iraq in 2003.[45]

Lessons might be learnt as well from democratic and constitutional theory. In answer to the question of what is democracy, Robert Dahl argues that it is about providing opportunities for members of any association, namely: for effective participation, equality in voting, gaining enlightened understanding, exercising final control over the agenda, and for the inclusion of all adults.[46] Clearly democracy at the level of the state is almost always deficient when tested against these standards. It cannot be said that representative democracy normally allows all citizens 'effective participation' in the sense that 'before a policy is adopted' all the citizens 'must have equal and effective opportunities for making their views known to the other' citizens 'as to what the policy should be'; nor that the citizens have final control of the agenda to be debated; nor do they normally have enlightened understanding 'about the relevant alternative policies and their likely consequences'.[47]

The paradox is that the larger an organization or institution becomes the less practical full participatory democracy becomes. John Stuart Mill recognized this in 1861—'since all cannot, in a community exceeding a small single town, participate personally in any but some very small portions of the public business, it follows that the ideal type of perfect government must be representative'.[48] The advent of dominant political parties must, however, call into question the ideal. Furthermore, the origins of representative democracy are far from ideal: 'representative government originated not as a democratic practice but as a device by which nondemocratic governments—monarchs, mainly—could lay their hands on precious revenues and other resources they wanted, particularly for fighting wars'.[49] Though generally defending representative democracy, Dahl recognizes

[43] Damrosch, 'Trends in Legislative and Executive Powers', 48.   [44] Ibid., 49.
[45] See generally J. Yoo, *The Powers of War and Peace: The Constitution and Foreign Affairs After 9/11* (Chicago: University of Chicago Press, 2006).
[46] Dahl, *On Democracy*, 38.   [47] Ibid., 37.
[48] J.S. Mill, *Considerations on Representative Democracy* (New York: Liberal Arts Press, 1958) 55. See also Dahl, *On Democracy,* 110.
[49] Dahl, *On Democracy*, 103.

its 'dark side' whereby citizens 'delegate enormous discretionary authority over decisions of extraordinary importance'.[50]

Attempts have been made in recent years to remedy the deficiencies of representative democracy with elements of 'participatory' democracy, but, in the UK they have focused on trying to improve the model that assumes that 'the electorate participates in government primarily through voting and holding ministers to account via MPs in Parliament'. To improve this there has been some move towards proportional representation (at least in the devolved Scottish and Welsh electoral processes), and improved rights of access to information so that more informed electoral choices can be made, enhanced by the protection of freedom of information under the Human Rights Act 1998. However, that does not go as far as allowing the full participation of citizens in the democratic process which could, for example, be achieved through giving 'opportunities to put forward one's views for consideration by officials', giving 'rights to be consulted and have one's representations responded to', and 'rights to vote on decisions'. A variation would be to improve 'deliberative' democracy which envisages citizens discussing 'together and with officials the solutions to problems'.[51] The latter could be achieved by an active civil society—'the professions, pressure groups, trade unions, the voluntary sector . . . spontaneously engaging in discussion and consultation with a receptive government about policy and administration',[52] and thus providing a balance to the dominance of the political parties. In the UK, there is an absence of any participation by civil society in decisions to deploy troops, although there have been consultations in the recent process of reviewing prerogative powers reviewed in chapter eleven.

Furthermore, decisions about war and the deployment of troops are regularly made on the international stage, for example by the UN Security Council deciding that a peacekeeping force will be sent to a particular country. Though the UK, in general terms, has no international legal obligation to provide troops, it may well commit them in negotiations with the UN Secretary General without any reference to parliament let alone wider society. The lack of democracy in such decisions at the national level is more evident at the international level. Though there is a strong trend towards international organizations supporting the spread of democracy within nation states, combined with a trend towards international law recognizing democratic rights as part of the internal aspect of the right to self-determination,[53] there is limited evidence of democracy within international organizations themselves, though international civil society in the form of

---

[50] Ibid., 113.

[51] Oliver, *Constitutional Reform*, 34–5. See generally, A. Weale, 'Contractarian Theory, Deliberative Democracy and General Agreement', in K. Dowling, R.E. Goodin and C. Pateman (eds), *Justice and Democracy* (Cambridge: Cambridge University Press, 2004) 79.

[52] Oliver, *Constitutional Reform*, 37.

[53] D.J. Harris, *Cases and Materials on International Law* (6th edn, London: Sweet and Maxwell, 2004) 112.

non-governmental organizations (NGOs) have made an impact in certain specific areas.[54] Theorists such as David Held have advocated global or 'cosmopolitan
democracy' which involves the 'creation of a democratic community which both
involves and cuts across democratic states'.[55] Following from this, Susan Marks
advocates the recognition of a principle of 'democratic inclusion', which is the
'idea that all should have a right to a say in decision-making which affects them,
and that systematic barriers to the exercise of that right should be acknowledged
and removed. For this purpose, the relevant processes of decision-making and
barriers to participation include not only those operating within nation-states,
but also those operating among nation-states and in transnational arenas'.[56]

In general terms, though, there is little democratic input, certainly in a participatory sense, nationally or internationally, into executive decisions to deploy troops.
It would be unjust though to say that such decisions were totally undemocratic
as the executive is, in a very basic sense, the 'elected' government of the UK, and
furthermore it represents the UK at international level. There is still democratic
accountability of the government to the electorate. The government may become
increasingly unpopular if it sends troops to conflicts with consequent heavy
loss of life to British service personnel and with no real prospect of withdrawal.
Democratic accountability means that the electorate can judge the record of those
holding political power in the UK.[57] However, given the number of factors that
the electorate has to take into account, and given that the main concern of electors
is the next five years not so much the previous five years, democratic accountability, at least as operated in the UK, is not generally going to be precise enough to
act as a check on individual decisions to go to war. The prosecution of the war in
Iraq in 2003 and the consequent on-going commitment of troops to that increasingly violent country was unpopular with the electorate, but that did not stop the
Labour government keeping its hold on power in the 2005 elections. The issue of
democratic accountability will be returned to in chapter eleven where the question
will be asked whether there are other forms of accountability, political and perhaps
legal, that should be developed to scrutinize decisions to deploy troops.

The presence of other checks and balances, for instance through parliamentary
Select Committees, will become apparent in this book,[58] but in general controls

---

[54] C. Wartentin and K. Mingst, 'International Institutions, the State, and Global Civil
Society in an Age of the World Wide Web' (2000) 6 Global Governance 237; P. Willetts, 'From
Consultative Arrangements to Partnership: The Changing Status of NGOs in Diplomacy at the
UN' (2000) 6 Global Governance 191.
[55] D. Archbugi and D. Held, 'Introduction', in D. Archbugi and D. Held (eds), *Cosmopolitan
Democracy: An Agenda for a New World Global Order* (Cambridge: Polity Press, 1995) 1 at 13.
[56] S. Marks, *The Riddle of All Constitutions* (Oxford: Oxford University Press, 2000) 119.
[57] For definition see C. Harlow, *Accountability in the European Union* (Oxford: Oxford
University Press, 2002) 8.
[58] See for example the Foreign Affairs Select Committee's report of 7 June 2000 (HC 28-I) into
the Kosovo campaign. A much earlier example was the select committee established in 1855 to look
into the Crimean war: P. Burroughs, 'An Unreformed Army? 1815–1868', in Chandler and Beckett
(eds), *History of the British Army*, 161 at 183.

are quite limited, whether political, legal or financial. Political and legal methods of accountability will be a theme throughout the book. In general, financial checks do not prevent such decisions from being made in that the funding of each operation does not need the sanction of parliament, with at least initial finances being taken by the government out of the already approved Defence budget.[59]

Democratic or political control or even criticism within parliament is in reality limited since dissent about UK military action is often seen as unpatriotic. Bipartisanship, whereby there is agreement between government and the opposition within parliament, is the norm. Confidential discussions between the leaders of the parties may well be held before parliamentary debates on the deployment of military forces. For instance, this appeared to be the case before the UK's military response to the events of 11 September 2001 when terrorists attacked the United States. Prior to the American and British military response against the Taliban and Al-Qaeda in Afghanistan on 7 October 2001, Prime Minister Blair made it clear in the House of Commons that the leaders of the other main parties had been consulted, and further he made it clear that the British would fight alongside the United States in Afghanistan.[60] With party leaders on board, party discipline and the sense of patriotism that surrounds these issues ensures that criticism is usually from a small number of 'maverick' MPs. Thereafter, the main concern of the government is to keep public opinion on board. It is only in this diluted sense that the electorate can influence decision-making. Government, often assisted by large sections of the media, normally successfully maintains public support for the military operation. In 1999 at the outset of the Kosovo campaign, the headline of *The Sun*, the most popular newspaper in Britain, ran 'Clobba Slobba. Our Boys batter Serb butcher in NATO Bomb Blitz'.[61] In 2003, at the outset of the invasion of Iraq, the same newspaper declared, in slightly more muted terms, 'Wanted Dead or Alive: 100,000 Allies move to front line for invasion as Saddam stands defiant'.[62]

In internationally sanctioned operations a high level of popular support for military actions is often sustained even though it is not British territory or interests that are under direct attack. It is still seen as somewhat subversive if criticism is made of British forces while engaged in dangerous military operations. Indeed, this is perhaps strengthened by the change in emphasis away from wars of national interest (Suez in 1956 and the Falklands in 1982), to wars of international concern (the Gulf in 1991 and Kosovo in 1999). The imprimatur of an international

---

[59] A. McSmith and P. Beaver, 'Commander Blair Goes it Alone', *The Observer*, 18 April 1999, 14. On financial controls see S. de Smith and R. Brazier, *Constitutional and Administrative Law* (8th edn, London: Penguin, 1998). Any review of expenditures on armed conflicts is normally retrospective by the Public Accounts Committee, and the Comptroller and Auditor General. In the case of Kosovo the initial expenditure of the bombing (about £2m a day) was met out of contingency reserves.

[60] *Hansard*, HC vol 372, col 671, 4 Oct. 2001.   [61] *The Sun*, 25 March 1999, 1.

[62] *The Sun*, 20 March 2003, 2. See generally H.J. Gans, *Democracy and the News* (Oxford: Oxford University Press, 2003).

organization gives the government the necessary legitimacy to take military action. The invasion of Iraq in 2003, was markedly more unilateral (or bilateral) in nature, and seemed to mark the development of a more critical attitude from the electorate, and to a lesser extent, their representatives in parliament.

4. The Modern Constitution and Military Action

The prerogative powers of the Crown still prevail on the issue of troop deployment, and wider constitutional theory about the nature of statehood reflects this. From the perspective of international law the UK is undoubtedly a state,[63] but in UK constitutional theory it is not. The UK has been described as a 'stateless society',[64] since its 'constitutional system has been constructed largely without the use of the concept of the state'.[65] UK legislation rarely refers to the concept of 'state'. In one rare instance of usage, in the Official Secrets Act of 1911, s 1 of which makes it an offence to enter any prohibited place 'for any purpose prejudicial to the safety and interests of the State', the UK's highest court, the House of Lords, struggled to define its meaning. Lord Devlin stated in 1964:

What is meant by 'the State'? Is it the same thing as what I have just called 'the country'? Mr Foster, for the appellants, submits that it means the inhabitants of a particular geographical area. I doubt if it ever has as wide a meaning as that...the more precise use of the word 'State', the use to be expected in a legal context, and the one which I am quite satisfied ... was intended in this statute, is to denote the organs of government of a national community. In the United Kingdom, in relation at any rate to the armed forces and to the defence of the realm, that organ is the Crown...[66]

The state is not defined in terms of the People but in terms of the Crown. As we have seen in this chapter, the 'Crown' has evolved from a person—the monarch—to an organ or institution—the government.[67] In the modern era 'it is usual to refer to "the Sovereign" in matters concerning the personal conduct or decisions of the monarch, and to "the Crown" as the collective entity which in law may stand for central government'.[68] Central government is largely coterminous with 'the Executive'. Executive functions include 'the execution of law and policy,

---

[63] It has territory, population, effective government and has the capacity to engage in international relations; for criteria of statehood see M.N. Shaw, *International Law* (5th edn, Cambridge: Cambridge University Press, 2003) 178.

[64] K.H.F. Dyson, *The State Tradition in Western Europe* (Oxford: Robertson, 1980) 19.

[65] C. Turpin, *British Government and the Constitution* (5th edn, London: Butterworths, 2002) 11.

[66] *Chandler v Director of Public Prosecutions* [1964] AC 763 at 807.

[67] But see J. Austin, *The Province of Jurisprudence Determined* (London: John Murray, 1833) 193, where he stated that during prorogation sovereignty lies with the People not the Crown. This may be a result of a mistaken identification of the Crown with individuals as opposed to the institutions 'the Crown' encompasses.

[68] A.W. Bradley and K.D. Ewing, *Constitutional and Administrative Law* (12th edn, London: Longman, 1997) 253.

the maintenance of public order ... the direction of foreign policy, the conduct of military operations'.[69] The fulcrum of the executive is the Cabinet, headed by the Prime Minister. In theory, major policy, and in the case of military operations and foreign policy, decision-making, is hammered out in the Cabinet and in various standing and *ad hoc* Cabinet committees. Decision-making on issues of foreign affairs and the deployment of armed forces are within the prerogative power of the Crown.[70]

A.V. Dicey defined prerogative powers as follows:

The prerogative appears to be both historically and as a matter of actual fact nothing else than the residue of discretionary or arbitrary authority, which at any given time is legally left in the hands of the Crown ... From the time of the Norman conquest down to the Revolution of 1688, the Crown possessed in reality many of the attributes of sovereignty. The prerogative is the name for the Crown's original authority ... Every act which the executive government can lawfully do without the authority of the Act of Parliament is done in virtue of this prerogative.[71]

Though Dicey's constitutional theory, first expounded in the late nineteenth century, has been criticized,[72] his definition of the prerogative remains useful. As prerogative powers, both foreign affairs and the placement of armed forces are exercised on the authority of the Cabinet or of Ministers, particularly the Prime Minister, the Secretary of State for Foreign and Commonwealth Affairs, and the Secretary of State for Defence.

The presence and exercise of prerogative power has two serious consequences for the rule of law and democratic accountability. First: 'while Parliamentary approval is not generally needed before action is taken, Ministers are responsible to Parliament for their policies and decisions'.[73] Second, the courts have no power to review the decisions of the Crown on the disposition and use of the UK's armed forces.[74] Given that prerogative powers by-pass normal methods of democratic control and accountability, it is necessary to re-evaluate the balance between necessity and democracy. There is certainly a strong view that the deployment of troops and the waging of war, or more generally 'the exercise of the physical might of the modern state' *should* be subject to democratic control.[75]

---

[69] *Halbury's Laws of England* (4th edn, London: HMSO, 1973), col 8(2), para 9.

[70] Lord Lester and D. Oliver (eds), *Constitutional Law and Human Rights* (London: Butterworths, 1997) 465–6, 476.

[71] A.V. Dicey, *Introduction to the Study of the Law of the Constitution* (10th edn, London: Macmillan, 1959) 424–5. For a modern definition see Lester and Oliver, *Constitutional Law*, 244.

[72] See for instance Loveland, *Constitutional Law*, 21.

[73] Bradley and Ewing, *Constitutional and Administrative Law*, 352.

[74] *China Navigation Co. Ltd v Attorney General* [1932] 2 KB 197 (Court of Appeal). *Chandler v Director of Public Prosecutions* [1964] AC 736 (House of Lords). P. Rowe, *Defence: The Legal Implications* (London: Brassey's, 1987) 3. There is a discernible trend to review the prerogative in other areas: Lester and Oliver, *Constitutional Law*, 250.

[75] Bradley and Ewing, *Constitutional and Administrative Law*, 373.

It is true that the Bill of Rights of 1689 asserted constitutional superiority over the armed forces when it declared that the raising or keeping of a standing army within the Kingdom in time of peace, unless it be with the consent of parliament, is against the law. However, the purpose of this part of the Bill was to prevent the King establishing his own army. Parliamentary authority was asserted over the standing army, not over each deployment of troops. The parliamentary power to withdraw authority for the maintenance of an army is not a realistic control in the modern age. Although regular (annual) legislation is required to renew parliamentary authority, it is adopted as a matter of course.[76]

The reality of the exercise of prerogative powers in the areas of foreign affairs and the disposition of armed forces is shown by the exchange in the House of Commons in 1982 when negotiations were taking place for the settlement of the Falklands conflict in the period between the Argentinian invasion and the arrival of the British task force to defend the islands.[77] The Leader of the Opposition, Neil Kinnock, claimed that 'the House of Commons has the right to make judgment on this matter before any decision is taken by the government that would enlarge the conflict'. In response, the Prime Minister, Margaret Thatcher, declared that 'it is an inherent jurisdiction of the government to negotiate and reach decisions. Afterwards the House of Commons can pass judgment on the government'.[78]

The method by which the lower house passes judgment on the government can vary. As the Foreign Affairs Select Committee noted in its report on Kosovo produced on 7 June 2000:

…the British Government commits our armed forces to any conflict by exercise of the Royal Prerogative. For that reason, it has become normal for Governments to rely on motions for the adjournment to debate the United Kingdom's involvement in a conflict. These procedural motions are unamendable. This is a traditional means of preventing an alternative proposition to that of the Government being offered to the House. Governments have not always shied away from substantive motions. The Korean War and the Suez intervention were both approved by substantial resolution of the House. The Falklands War was, however, only debated on the adjournment, and the Gulf War was also debated in the adjournment on four occasions before a substantive motion was moved. All the debates on the Kosovo conflict were held on the adjournment.[79]

Only substantive motions truly enable the lower house to to challenge the government's decision.[80] The vote has traditionally been one of approval, but it does put the government more firmly under the spotlight. It is interesting though that

[76] de Smith and Brazier, *Constitutional and Administrative Law*, 217.
[77] Reviewed more fully in chapter seven.
[78] *Hansard,* HC vol 23, cols 597–8, 11 May 1982.
[79] HC Foreign Affairs Committee, Fourth Report, 7 June 2000 (HC 28-I), para 166.
[80] According to Erskine May, while a substantive motion 'is a proposal for the purpose of eliciting a decision of the House', to which amendments 'may be tabled as soon as the motions have been tabled'. Motions for the adjournment are in fact 'technical' forms 'devised for the purpose of enabling the House to discuss matters without recording a decision in terms. It is, therefore, not subject to amendment' (21st edn, 1989) 625, 321, and 325.

while the Kosovo conflict of 1999 was the subject of much more debate in the lower house, it was not subject to a substantive vote, thereby reducing the chances of the government's decisions being challenged. The debates prior to the invasion of Iraq in 2003 did, however, culminate in a substantive vote in the House of Commons on 18 March, two days before the invasion.

In theory the legislature controls the executive since a government can be ousted by a vote of no-confidence in parliament. However, the often decisive majorities commanded by the government of the day in the House of Commons, produced by the first-past-the-post electoral system, signify that any control exerted is limited. A government with a large majority in the House of Commons has been described as an 'elective dictatorship' by the most conservative of commentators[81] even in matters requiring legislation; this is clearly more so in the case of prerogative powers. There may often be quite lively debates in parliament, primarily in the House of Commons, though limited discussion may also be found in the House of Lords. Furthermore, there may be the questioning of Ministers before the Defence Select Committee or the Select Committee on Foreign Affairs of the House of Commons.[82] However, it is questionable whether these operate as robust controls on Cabinet decision-making. Crucial decisions have already been made, making the controls appear, at best, retrospective. Nevertheless, Ministers may curtail their decisions when considering the possible adverse reaction of the House of Commons or the relevant Select Committee in the near future.

5. War Before the Courts

In addition to this possibility of political accountability, there are possible avenues for the government to be held legally accountable. At national level the prerogative has been gradually opened up to judicial review. Lord Roskill declared in the *GCHQ* case in the House of Lords in 1985 that he could not see:

Any logical reason why the fact that the source of the power is the prerogative and not statute should today deprive the citizen of that right of challenge to the manner of its exercise which he would possess were the source of power statutory. In either case that act in question is the act of the executive. To talk of that act as the act of the sovereign savours of the archaism of past centuries.[83]

However, this was not a green light to signal that all prerogative powers were to be reviewable; it also depended on whether they were justiciable, in other words whether the dispute was suitable to resolution by judicial decision. If the dispute

---

[81] Turpin, *British Government*, 393 citing the former Lord Chancellor, Lord Hailsham.

[82] For example the Foreign Affairs Committee examined the sinking of the *General Belgrano* during the Falklands conflict, HC 11 (1984–85).

[83] *Council of Civil Service Unions v Minister for the Civil Service* [1985] AC 374 at 417 (hereinafter *GCHQ* case).

involves 'a great many points of view all of which have to be weighed and balanced in the search for an overall political solution',[84] such as national security,[85] the making of treaties, the defence of the realm, the prerogative of mercy, the grant of honours, the dissolution of parliament and the appointment of Ministers,[86] then 'judicial process is totally inept to deal with the sort of problems' raised.[87] While currently excluding decisions to deploy troops from judicial review, the question remains though as to whether this is a fixed list, or whether the overriding concept of justiciability is 'like other common law principles...prone to sudden and substantial change'.[88] Some acts of foreign affairs such as the making of treaties have been held to be non-justiciable.[89] On the other hand the issue and renewal of passports, although an exercise of prerogative power, was held to be justiciable in the case where an individual's passport was not renewed.[90] Taylor LJ suggested that foreign relations issues that involved matters of 'high policy' were non-justiciable, and that the granting of passports did not fall into this category.

On this basis the decision of government to go to war or otherwise to commit troops overseas would appear to be an issue of 'high policy' and therefore non-justiciable and non-reviewable. Thus while not reviewing government decisions to go to war or to deploy troops, the judiciary will hear cases brought against soldiers for breaches of military law and international humanitarian law before military courts (courts martial), and more recently by civilian courts under the Human Rights Act 1998.

There have been a spate of recent cases arising out of the Iraq war that will be returned to in more detail in chapter eleven. There was the court martial of soldiers for abuse of Iraqi prisoners at 'Camp Breadbasket' in Basra in May 2003.[91] The death of Baha Mousa, an Iraqi civilian who died after suffering ninety-three separate injuries while in detention in Basra in September 2003, led to a largely unsuccessful prosecution of a number of British soldiers by court martial,[92] a decision by the House of Lords that the Human Rights Act did apply to Iraqis held in places of detention under the authority and control of British forces,[93] and a public inquiry announced by the government on 14 May 2008.[94] In the

---

[84] Loveland, *Constitutional Law*, 104–5.   [85] *GCHQ* case, Lord Diplock at 412.
[86] *GCHQ* case, Lord Roskill at 418.   [87] *GCHQ* case, Lord Diplock at 412.
[88] Loveland, *Constitutional Law*, 105.   [89] *Ex parte Molyneaux* [1986] 1 WLR 331.
[90] *R v Secretary of State for Foreign and Commonwealth Affairs, ex parte Everett* [1989] QB 811, CA.
[91] Three soldiers were convicted by court martial sitting in Germany in 2005. The soldier who had taken 'trophy' photographs of the abuse was also convicted in a separate trial <http://news.bbc.co.uk/1/hi/uk/4296511.stm>, 25 Feb. 2005.
[92] Seven members of the Queen's Lancashire Regiment faced a court martial. Six were acquitted and one was jailed for a year after admitting committing a war crime under the International Criminal Court Act 2001 <http://news.bbc.co.uk/1/hi/uk/6609237.stm>, 30 April 2007 (accessed 26 Jan. 2009).
[93] *R (Al-Skeini) v Secretary of State for Defence* [2007] UKHL 26.
[94] The inquiry is chaired by a retired Court of Appeal Judge (Sir William Gage) and its terms of reference are 'to investigate and report on the circumstances surrounding the death of Baha Mousa and the treatment of those detained with him, taking into account the investigations which have already taken place, in particular where responsibility lay for approving the practice of conditioning

Al-Jedda case decided by the House of Lords in 2007, the Court found that the appellant's right to liberty under Article 5 of the European Convention on Human Rights had been violated by his detention in Iraq since 2004 without charge or trial, but that those rights had been overridden by a Security Council resolution (1546 of 2004) which authorized the detention of suspected terrorists; in effect upholding the government's argument to the effect that the security concerns embodied in the Security Council decision should prevail over human rights.[95]

The position of the judiciary in matters of war will be returned to in chapter eleven, where the question of why issues of 'high policy' should be excluded from the courts will be re-considered. Though the recent cases coming out of the brutal conflict in Iraq after the invasion of 2003 show an increasing juridification of war,[96] attempts to question the legality of the war have thus far failed. Cases brought against the Prime Minister by the CND and Rose Gentle (the mother of a soldier killed by a roadside bomb in Iraq) failed because the courts refused to confront the use of prerogative powers by the government.[97] Similarly in a criminal case (for criminal damage of military equipment in protest at the Iraq war), the courts (ultimately the House of Lords) refused to be drawn on the legality of the war in Iraq.[98] Finally the attempted defence of Flight Lieutenant Malcolm Kendall-Smith for disobeying orders to serve in Iraq on the basis that the war was illegal was dismissed by the judge at his court martial.[99] Though the courts are willing to exercise jurisdiction over soldiers for crimes committed in war, and, in certain circumstances, recognize that there has been a violation of the human rights of civilians in combat zones by UK forces, attempts to make military and political leaders legally accountable for their decisions, especially the ultimate decision—to go to war—have failed.

On the issue of the individual responsibility of politicians for decisions to use force, in extreme cases, for example where a Minister has sanctioned a war crime or a crime against humanity, that person could be forced from office, although there has been no instance of this occurring in the UK. As shall be seen, issues of troop deployment and going to war have led on occasions to the resignation of senior politicians but this has largely been due to them taking responsibility for failures of policy. In Israel the Minster of Defence, and future Prime Minister, Ariel Sharon, was forced to resign for having indirect responsibility for the Sabra and Shatila Palestinian camp massacres in 1982, following a report by an

---

detainees by any members of the 1st Battalion, The Queen's Lancashire Regiment in Iraq, and to make recommendations' <http://www.bahamousainquiry.org>, accessed 26 Jan. 2009.

[95] *R (on the application of Al-Jedda) v Secretary of State for Defence* [2007] UKHL 58.

[96] G. Simpson, 'The Death of Baha Mousa' (2007) 8 Melbourne J Intl L 19.

[97] *Campaign for Nuclear Disarmament v The Prime Minister of the United Kingdom* [2002] EWHC 2777; *R (Gentle) v Prime Minister* [2008] UKHL 20.

[98] *R v Jones* [2006] UKHL 16.

[99] <http://news.bbc.co.uk/2/hi/uk_news/4905672.stm>, 18 Oct. 2007 (accessed 26 Jan. 2009).

independent commission of inquiry into the episode.[100] Independent commissions of inquiry are to be found within the UK system in instances of internal violence committed by UK troops (the Widgery Inquiry of 1972 into the Bloody Sunday Massacres in Belfast, now re-opened with the current Saville Inquiry), on issues of foreign affairs (the Scott inquiry into arms to Iraq),[101] and on issues connected to military actions (the Hutton inquiry into the death of Dr David Kelly 2004).[102]

The main international court that could play a role in apportioning individual criminal responsibility is the International Criminal Court (ICC) whose Statute was agreed in 1998, though it did not come into force until 1 July 2002. The UK is a party to the Statute, having signed the Statute in 1998 and having ratified it on 4 October 2001. The potential impact of this Statute as a means of attributing individual criminal responsibility to politicians, military commanders and soldiers is limited, bearing in mind that the Statute is not retrospective, though Corporal Payne was convicted of committing a war crime for his acts at Camp Breadbasket under the International Criminal Court Act 2001. Subject to the limited impact of the ICC and other *ad hoc* international criminal tribunals, military discipline and punishment for unlawful conduct by British troops is in practice normally under the control of the British contingent's commander and British Courts Martial operating under UK legislation, principally the Armed Forces Act 2006, which replaced three separate discipline acts of the 1950s.

6. The War Cabinet

With the slow and as yet unfulfilled encroachment of mechanisms of judicial accountability on the decision to go to war, we must return to the issue of political accountability, and consider the way such decisions are made. In general terms the gap between accountability to parliament and the reality of government is shown by the committal of armed forces to combat. Bradley and Ewing state that '[l]ike other branches of central government, the armed forces are placed under the control of the ministers of the Crown, who are in turn responsible to Parliament'.[103] The authorization and control of military operations are the province of the Cabinet. Indeed, normally military operations are run by an inner War Cabinet known as the War Cabinet, a mechanism that seems to have been accepted in UK constitutional practice. In relation to the prosecution of wars, the chain of political authority runs from the inner Cabinet to the Cabinet, then to the party, parliament and the public at large. In times of conflict, it has

---

[100] Final Report of the Commission of Inquiry Into the Events at the Refugee Camps in Beirut, *Final Report* (1983) 22 ILM 473 ('the Kahan Report').
[101] *Hansard* HC 115 (1995–6). See D. Oliver, 'The Scott Report' (1996) Public Law 357.
[102] *Hansard* HC 247, 28 Jan. 2004. Reviewed in chapter ten.
[103] Bradley and Ewing, *Constitutional and Administrative Law*, 375.

been said that the main concern of the Prime Minister is keeping 'the Cabinet happy'. The Party is 'important; Parliament as a whole, [is] useful but not essential; and the public? Well, the day of reckoning at the next general election [is] some way off'.[104]

These inner War Cabinets are almost always *ad hoc* arrangements established at the behest of the Prime Minister, by-passing the standing Cabinet committees whose structure and role has been predetermined. The only exception to this practice in the post Second World War period was the Korean War, when the existing Cabinet Defence Committee ran the British contribution to the war. It has been suggested that Prime Minister Attlee 'had least need to consider forming an ad hoc committee', one reason being that the UK was not 'running' the Korean War, given that the Korean military action was a UN sanctioned operation under Unified (US) command.[105] However, a suggestion that in UN authorized operations the existing institutions of government will be respected is not borne out by subsequent UK involvement in such operations. For instance the British involvement in the Gulf War of 1991 was coordinated by an *ad hoc* War Cabinet consisting of the Prime Minister, the Chancellor of the Exchequer, and the Secretaries of State for Foreign Affairs, Defence and Energy. The British contribution to the NATO sanctioned Kosovo operation in 1999 was directed by an even looser inner cabinet. Prime Minister 'Blair ha[d] no formal War Cabinet, but supervise[d] the campaign through daily face-to-face meetings with Chief of Defence Staff, General Sir Charles Guthrie, [Defence Secretary] Robertson, Foreign Secretary Robin Cook and trusted officials'.[106]

However, the difference between the Cabinet Defence Committee and the various *ad hoc* War Cabinets is not that great, both are small committees with specialist membership, normally attended by all the Chiefs of Staff headed by the Chief of Defence Staff, whose decisions tend to be rubber stamped by the full cabinet. The reason for having such a small body directing the UK's forces appears to be the need to remove political debate from the running of an efficient military operation.[107] The danger of this is clear—the military operation can simply become the domain of a few people—indeed in extreme cases can become the Prime Minister's war, as with Anthony Eden in Suez, to a lesser extent Margaret Thatcher in the Falklands,[108] and Tony Blair in relation to Kosovo. In the latter case, this is still true even though the operation was not a British one but a NATO one, with the Prime Minister being referred to quite regularly as the 'NATO leader'.[109]

[104] C. Seymour-Ure, 'British "War Cabinets" in Limited Wars: Korea, Suez and the Falklands' (1984) 62 Public Administration 182.

[105] Ibid., 188.

[106] McSmith and Beaver, 'Commander Blair Goes it Alone', 14.

[107] Seymour-Ure, 'War Cabinets', 181–2.

[108] Ibid., 185–7.

[109] E.Vulliamy and P. Wintour, 'The Pentagon Prepares to Put its Trust in Blair', *The Observer*, 25 April 1999, 14.

The deployment and use of military forces are clearly the gravest issues in politics and therefore to exclude wider political debate and input seems perverse. Indeed, the emergence of War Cabinets has two consequences which increase the democratic deficit in these situations—'[t]he dangers of *tunnel vision* among the decision-makers, and the dangers of *military professionals dominating the politicians'*. By excluding all 'extraneous' political factors from their decision-making the War Cabinet is in danger of becoming obsessed with the successful prosecution of the war—in effect this becomes the War Cabinet's *raison d'être*. This is compounded by the fact that they are only receiving input from the military in the shape of the Chiefs of Staff under the Chief of Defence Staff.[110]

This mechanism, at least in the modern sense, originates from the world wars. During the First World War, 'authority was concentrated in an inner War Cabinet', led by Prime Minister Lloyd-George, 'detached from administrative routine and charged with the framing of a policy to which the action of every department was related'.[111] Prime Minister Churchill formed a War Cabinet during the Second World War. In such total wars, by necessity of survival, 'politics generally is subordinated to military considerations'.[112] Though Churchill did engage with parliament during the Second World War, democratic accountability to the electorate was suspended.[113] However, in the case of more limited wars, in which Korea, the Gulf, Kosovo, and Afghanistan must be included, the government should be considering the war in relation to all its other policies and goals.

It seems at least questionable whether the War Cabinet system provides a good method of resolving this. The basic dilemma is that the War Cabinet tends to become fixated on the war and is quite unsuited to achieving an overview; while the full Cabinet is likely to be progressively less in touch and equally ill-equipped to take a balanced view. The system is in disequilibrium. The consequence of this situation may be that the War Cabinet gets more and more involved in short term goals, and with means more than ends.[114]

The effective by-passing of the Cabinet and parliament obviously is a serious shortcoming when looking at the accountability of the Ministers prosecuting the war.

In the Korean War, for instance, Prime Minister Attlee had approved of British support in the Security Council for a resolution of 25 June 1950 condemning the North Korean attack.[115] The Cabinet then responded on 27 June 1950 to the US draft circulated to Security Council members recommending assistance be given

---

[110] Seymour-Ure, 'War Cabinets', 194–5.

[111] D.L. Keir, *The Constitutional History of Modern Britain 1485–1937* (3rd edn, London: Blacks, 1938) 458.

[112] Seymour-Ure, 'War Cabinets', 198.

[113] R. Hardin, *Liberalism, Constitutionalism and Democracy* (Oxford: Oxford University Press, 2003) 276.

[114] Seymour-Ure, 'War Cabinets', 198.

[115] SC Res. 82, 25 June 1950. A. Farrar-Hockley, *The British Part in the Korean War: Volume 1—A Distant Obligation* (London: HMSO, 1990) 31.

to repel the North Korean armed attack.[116] As well as supporting this resolution, the Cabinet directed the Minister of Defence to organize a report from the Chiefs of Staff to the Defence Committee on the logistics of military assistance. Within a day of the Security Council resolution being adopted, on 28 June the Defence Committee met, approved of the recommendations of the Chiefs of Staff that naval forces be put at the disposal of the US Naval Commander, and authorized instructions be given to that effect. Thus the decision to commit UK forces to the UN authorized operation under US command was made, 'without any reference to the Cabinet'.[117] Thereafter the main decisions about the British commitment to the conflict were taken by the Defence Committee of the Cabinet, including, on 24 July the deployment of land forces under US command.[118] The Defence Committee made this decision and put it into effect, it was then 'endorsed' by the Cabinet, and made public in a House of Commons debate two days later.[119] Although the Cabinet was kept informed by the Minister of Defence during the conflict, its main concern was managing the debates within parliament, and keeping public opinion on board.[120]

The absence of Cabinet papers in relation to more recent conflicts makes detailed analyses of the inner workings of the executive more difficult. Focusing on the Kosovo conflict of 1999 for a moment though, it is interesting to note how the actual conduct of military operations was in the hands of Prime Minister Blair and Secretary of State for Defence Robertson. As was reported in *The Observer*, during the bombing campaign of 1999:

In the early stages of the [bombing] campaign—when most of the targets were large, fixed installations—virtually every [RAF] bomb that landed had the personal approval of either Blair or...Robertson. Now that the Harriers and Tornados are circling over Kosovo hunting moving targets, orders are more general—but still ultimately come from Downing Street.[121]

In relation to the UK's contribution to the war fought against the Taliban and Al-Qaeda in Afghanistan from October 2001, in response to the attacks against the United States of 11 September 2001, a War Cabinet met on 9 October, two days after the hostilities had started. This body consisting of Prime Minister Tony Blair, his Deputy John Prescott, Chancellor Gordon Brown, Foreign Secretary Jack Straw, Defence Secretary Geoff Hoon, Leader of the House Robin Cook, International Development Secretary Claire Short and the Chief of Defence Staff replaced the *ad hoc* arrangements of Ministers and advisers who had been in charge of planning the UK's role since 11 September.[122]

---

[116] See SC Res. 83, 27 June 1950.   [117] Seymour-Ure, 'War Cabinets', 189.
[118] Ibid., 188–9.   [119] Ibid., 190.
[120] Ibid., 190–1. See chapter four for a fuller discussion of Korea.
[121] McSmith and Beaver, 'Commander Blair Goes it Alone', 14.
[122] Prime Minister's Official Spokesman, Press Briefing, 8 Oct. 2001 <http://www.number10.gov.uk/Page2169> (accessed 26 Jan. 2009).

Prior to the invasion of Iraq by the US and UK in March 2003, there were a number of meetings of a rolling group of Ministers and advisers to plan the British involvement.[123] These meetings continued after the outbreak of hostilities and although there was no official reference to a War Cabinet,[124] the press did describe it in those terms, saying it was drawn from a group of Ministers and advisers including Prime Minister Tony Blair, his Deputy John Prescott, Chancellor Gordon Brown, Foreign Secretary Jack Straw, Defence Secretary Geoff Hoon, the Attorney General Lord Goldsmith, International Development Secretary Clare Short, Chief of Defence Staff, and the Head of MI6.[125]

The role of the War Cabinet, the executive as a whole, and parliament will be the subject of greater analysis when individual conflicts are looked at in greater detail in chapters four, six, eight, nine, and ten. While the theory of Cabinet government still persists, as a matter of practice, it appears that the role of the Cabinet as a whole has declined, so that executive decisions are very rarely made by this body any more. In tracing the historical development of Cabinet government from 1900, Anthony Seldon identifies that in the period 1900–1914 the Cabinet was the sole decision-making body. From 1914–1945 the Cabinet became the principal decision-making body, since decisions were increasingly taken in standing cabinet committees and, in times of conflict, the War Cabinet. From 1945–1979, 'the Cabinet committee system came of age'. 'Decisions were taken mainly in Cabinet committees, but important decisions would always be presented for ratification (if not always discussion) by Ministers to full Cabinet which could very occasionally reverse those decisions'. From 1979–1987, the Cabinet was the supreme discussion and information-giving body, but executive decision-making lay elsewhere, some still in the committees but increasingly outside that system, in small groups of ministers, sometimes just the Prime Minister and one other Minister. The Labour government from 1997 resulted in what Seddon calls a 'personal system', whereby Prime Minister Blair had an even more 'informal system of conducting business at the heart of government, so that principal decision-making is neither with the Cabinet or established committees. Cabinet has become a place for a "weekly exchange of views", no more'.[126]

Thus in terms of executive decision-making on something as profoundly significant for Britain and its service personnel (not to mention the people of the country subject to military intervention) as the deployment of troops to conflict and post-conflict situations, there are a number of warning signs that even the limited democratic and constitutional checks and balances that have emerged

---

[123] Prime Minister's Official Spokesman, Press Briefing, 18 Mar. 2003 <http://www.number10.gov.uk/Page3299>.

[124] Prime Minister's Official Spokesman, Press Briefing, 20 Mar. 2003 <http://www.number10.gov.uk/Page3321> (accessed 26 Jan. 2009).

[125] 'Blair's War Cabinet' <http://news.bbc.co.uk/1/hi/uk_politics/2866043.stm>, 19 Mar. 2003 (accessed 26 Jan. 2009).

[126] A. Seddon, 'The Cabinet System', in V. Bogdanor (ed), *The British Constitution in the Twentieth Century* (Oxford: Oxford University Press, 2003) 97 at 123, 129–30.

over the centuries are being eroded. Parliamentary debate of the executive decision to deploy might be more lively and protracted than ever before but party
control of parliament renders it of reduced value as a means of accountability. The
electorate has an increasing number of domestic and global issues to concern it
so that decisions to deploy troops rarely come under the spotlight in elections to
make that aspect of democratic accountability a true check on executive power.
And finally the doctrine of collective Cabinet responsibility that ensured that
at least all Ministers of State were behind decisions to deploy troops has been
reduced as a check, as executive decision-making has largely moved outside of the
cabinet, and even beyond the established cabinet system of committees.

As pointed out by Daintith and Page, there may be as much, if not more, value
in looking at remedying the lack of 'internal' controls within the executive as in
looking at increasing the effectiveness of 'external' controls by parliament and
the courts.[127] Daintith and Page are critical of the traditional constitutional analysis that applies the doctrine of separation of powers, and concentrates on the
relations between the executive, legislative and judicial branches of government.
The doctrine of separation of powers is the orthodox way of trying to ensure a
democratic system of government is in balance, with no organ dominating and
with checks and balances between the different organs. The doctrine provides a
limited critical analysis of the actual and possible controls over each branch:

> While the trinity of executive, legislative and judicial functions may be the most power-
> ful rationalization of the specialization process that has yet been offered, it cannot by
> itself capture the overall significance of any given structure of government for constitu-
> tional values such as democracy and accountability.[128]

The authors warn us to 'resist the easy assumption that the allocations of powers
and functions *within* each of the organizational blocs identified by separation
of powers doctrine are less significant to the protection of constitutional values
than are the relations *between* those blocs'.[129] Most significant organizations rely
on 'internal' as well as 'external' audit to identify weakness, whether in finance,
management or other aspects of accountability.

7. Conclusions

Following from this review of the elements of the UK's political system as it
relates to decisions to deploy troops, the democratic deficit is so severe that we
might question whether we have a system that is little different from that which
surrounded the king in the fourteenth and fifteenth centuries. F.W. Maitland

---

[127] T. Daintith and A. Page, *The Executive in the Constitution: Structure, Autonomy, and Internal Control* (Oxford: Oxford University Press, 1999) 8–9.
[128] Daintith and Page, *The Executive*, 12.   [129] Ibid., 12.

portrays the monarch of that time as 'the ruler of the nation, the commander of its armies and its fleets', advised not by parliament (which did exist in a very early form) but by the king's council, the members of which 'can be dismissed by the king whenever he pleases; they are sworn to advise the king according to the best of their cunning and discretion'. 'The function of the council . . . is to advise the king upon every exercise of the royal power'.[130] It would be easy to compare the modern Prime Minister and his ministerial colleagues to the king and his council, but it is not necessarily as straightforward as that. Indeed, although the medieval king had untrammelled power on paper, there were increasing pressures from parliament, from his subjects (soldiers and civilians), and from his treasury that meant that in political terms waging war was not as simple as might appear from the constitutional framework.[131] In modern times, there are similar pressures, and although the British constitutional legal framework is still limited, there is increasing pressure for reform—an issue that will be returned to in chapter eleven.

Furthermore, in the era of globalization it is true to say that 'national democratic politics cannot be understood without reference to international forces'.[132] It must not be forgotten that Britain has since 1945 become part of a wider international institutional and legal order, which may affect its ability to wage war. In different areas of decision-making, sovereignty has been limited by European law, both of an economic nature from the EC and of a human rights kind from the Council of Europe. The question of whether these and other international legal frameworks and institutions have restricted the government's prerogative powers in military matters is the issue to be considered in the next chapter.

---

[130] Maitland, *Constitutional History*, 197–9.
[131] Ibid., 324–9.
[132] Marks, *The Riddle*, 100.

2

Lawbreaker or Lawmaker? Britain and International Law on the Use of Force

1. Introduction

From the domestic constitutional framework reviewed in chapter one the analysis moves on to the international context, with this chapter considering international law, while chapters three, four, and five focus on international institutions (the UN, NATO, and the EU). This chapter gives an account of the current debate on the international rules governing the use of military force, but will differ from the normal approach that seeks to discern the rules accepted by the international community,[1] by viewing international law from the perspective of the British government. In recent years the perception is that Britain is more willing to challenge—arguably flout—international law, with its actions in Kosovo (1999) and Iraq (2003) in particular. However, this chapter will show that British practice has, on a number of occasions, since the new world order introduced by the UN Charter of 1945, been problematic from an orthodox international legal perspective. The UK's arguments before the International Court in the *Corfu Channel* case of 1949, its initiatives in creating the first UN sponsored coalition of the willing in Korea in 1950, its military venture to secure the Suez Canal in 1956, are examples drawn from earlier times that, together with recent practice in Kosovo, Afghanistan (2001) and Iraq, all raise the question of whether Britain is a law-abiding state.

More fundamentally the choice in these cases appears to be between Britain being a lawbreaker or an enlightened lawmaker. To be the latter, the British arguments for variations in the established laws must be supported and accepted by the international community. International law can be developed by practice as long as that practice is accepted as law. In the two main sources of international law, custom and treaty, custom is a 'general practice accepted as law',[2] while in

---

[1] See for example I. Brownlie, *International Law and the Use of Force by States* (Oxford: Oxford University Press, 1963); Y. Dinstein, *War, Aggression and Self-Defence* (4th edn, Cambridge: Cambridge University Press, 2005); C. Gray, *International Law and the Use of Force* (2nd edn, Oxford: Oxford University Press, 2004).

[2] Art 38(1)(b) of the Statute of the International Court of Justice 1945.

treaty law the text of the treaty can be interpreted and developed by subsequent practice.[3] It may be of course that an examination of British practice on war and other uses of force indicates that its record is mixed—in some instances it may have contributed to the development of the law, in other cases it has breached international law. It is to that record that the chapter turns, but in order to understand post-1945 practice, it is necessary briefly to consider the development of international law on war and the use of force in international relations.

2. The Just War

Chapter one contained a number of instances of English monarchs invoking various justifications for going to war, from defence of the realm to a just war. In the latter case, mention ought also to be made of the crusades of Richard I in the Holy Land in the twelfth century. Richard was so often fighting in the Middle East doing 'God's work' that he only spent less than one year out of his nine and a half year reign in England.[4] The 'just war' doctrine predated Richard the Lionheart, with an elaborate, but basically procedural doctrine being found in the Roman period. According to the Roman approach, a just war was commenced in accordance with the law by approval of the college of *fetiales*, 'the view of the majority of writers being that the *fetiales* were not concerned with the intrinsic justice of the war but only with the correct observance of formalities'.[5] In the fourth century St Augustine incorporated the just war doctrine into Christianity, giving a number of just causes of war including avenging injuries, but moreover declaring that war was just if it were one which 'God himself ordains'.[6]

Whilst Augustine in the fourth century, and much later, St Thomas Aquinas in the thirteenth century, wrote in terms of war being just only if the other party was at fault, and that the attacking sovereign intended the 'advancement of good, or the avoidance of evil',[7] the principles appeared too broad to offer any precise rules as to permissible uses of force. Indeed, they seemed to advance the appalling religious wars that regularly occurred in the medieval period, culminating in the Thirty Years War that was ended by the Peace of Westphalia of 1648.

3. Westphalian Order

The period following the Peace of Westphalia marked the emergence of modern nation states in Europe, each with 'internal' sovereignty over their own territories,

---

[3] Art 31(3)(b) of the Vienna Convention on the Law of Treaties 1969.
[4] S. Schama, *A History of Britain: At the Edge of the World?* (London: BBC, 2000) 154, 157.
[5] Brownlie, *International Law and the Use of Force by States*, 4.
[6] Ibid., 5.   [7] Ibid., 6.

and each being free 'externally' to deal with sovereign powers of other states. Thus international law moved away from being dominated by the justice discourse of the medieval period, towards a more formal or 'positivistic' international law created by the practice of sovereign European states either by treaty or by the formation of customary rules. As regards the freedom to wage war, Machiavelli, writing in the early part of the sixteenth century, seemed to anticipate the philosophy that was to become entrenched for the next four centuries, when he wrote that the sovereign power within a state had the absolute right to wage war whenever it was felt necessary.[8]

However, the just war doctrine did not just quietly disappear; it still competed with the emerging positivist approach. Indeed, the influence of the oft-labelled 'father' of international law, Hugo Grotius, writing in the period of warfare leading up to the Peace of Westphalia, was still felt for a long period. Writing in 1625, Grotius compiled a list of just and unjust causes of war, always admitting the exception for honest belief in the justice of war.[9] Other jurists took a more state-based approach, such as Gentili who stated that war was permitted in cases of necessity and expediency as well as in self-defence.[10]

The natural law-motivated theories of Aquinas and Grotius eventually gave way to a significant extent to the positivist notions of state sovereignty and freedom to contract or otherwise deal with other sovereigns, which eventually took its purest form in a period of 'political absolutism'[11] dominant in international relations until the League of Nations' Covenant in 1919. Just war doctrine did not disappear completely, with limited state practice in favour of a doctrine of humanitarian intervention. In this period the task of the international lawyer changed. No longer would the jurist have so much direct influence on the development of international law. Jurists tried to capture and analyse state practice, though in so doing, by virtue of their choice and emphasis, they could still influence evolution of international law. The primary sources of international law became treaty and custom, reflecting the law's consensual nature,[12] with the writings of jurists still playing a role, but a subsidiary one.[13]

The absolute sovereignty of states removed all but limited procedural constraints on the initiation of war. Brownlie reports that in the period between the Final Act of the Congress of Vienna in 1815 and the creation of the League of Nations in 1919 state practice reflected an almost unlimited right for states to wage war.[14] Britain, being a major colonial power, was not averse to using force to pursue its national interests. For example, in the nineteenth and early twentieth

---

[8] *The Prince*, ch 3.

[9] *The Classics of International Law* (London: Oxford University Press, 1923) No 3, 565.

[10] *The Classics of International Law* (London: Oxford University Press, 1933) No 16, 17–18.

[11] Q. Wright, *A Study of War* (2nd edn, Chicago: University of Chicago Press, 1967) 335–8.

[12] See *'Lotus'*, *Judgment No 9*, 1927 PCJIJ Ser A, No 10 at p 18.

[13] Art 38(1)(d) of the Statute of the International Court of Justice 1945.

[14] Brownlie, *International Law and the Use of Force by States*, 22–3.

centuries Britain intervened militarily in Afghanistan on several occasions from its colony in India, first in 1839–1842 to re-instate a deposed ruler, again in 1879 as part of the 'great game' being played out by the Russian and British empires, and again in 1919 when the newly installed king of Afghanistan declared full independence and sympathy for those seeking the independence of India.[15] Military interventions were seen as part and parcel of international relations.

Some limited restrictions on the right to go to war did emerge in the decades before 1914. Peaceful methods of settling the underlying dispute should be tried, a rule that was incorporated into the 1907 Hague Convention for the Pacific Settlement of International Disputes, and later in the Covenant of the League in 1919.[16] The machinery for the pacific settlement of disputes also developed in this period with, for example, the establishment of the Permanent Court of Arbitration in 1899.

Another, more established procedural limitation was that there had to be a declaration of war, at least for a formal 'state of war' to exist. However, this was not a real limitation for full-scale armed conflict could still occur without either state being at 'war' with the other in the absence of any formal declarations. States' reasons for not declaring war were mainly internal, since going to war might attract constitutional constraints, and would also require the 'preparation of public opinion'.[17] In order to avoid these constraints, states develop a variety of 'restricted forms of coercion ... reprisals, pacific blockade, and intervention to protect nationals and their property in foreign states'.[18]

It will be seen that some of these forms of use of force, or variations on them have been practiced by the UK in more recent times. It is worth outlining the doctrine of reprisals as developed in the nineteenth century, and contrast it with the doctrine of self-defence. It must be remembered though at this stage of the development of the *jus ad bellum* these were only two of a number of legitimate justifications for using force.

4. Armed Reprisals

In the period prior to the establishment of the League, states developed the practice of armed reprisals usually in the form of bombardments or military expeditions, as well as other forms of gun boat diplomacy, whereby states would seek to punish wrongful acts committed against them by other states. Often these expeditions served to punish states or other entities and also to protect the intervening state's interests.

---

[15] T.A. Heathcote, 'The Army of British India', in D.G. Chandler and I. Beckett (eds), *The Oxford History of the British Army* (Oxford: University Press, 1994) 374–7.
[16] Brownlie, *International Law and the Use of Force by States*, 22–3.
[17] Ibid., 27.   [18] Ibid., 28.

An example drawn from British history was the decision by the government of William Gladstone in 1882 to punish the new nationalist government in Egypt whose anti-European sentiment was threatening the lives and property of European nationals. The arrival of a combined French and British fleet off the port of Alexandria led to the murder of a number of Europeans. The French withdrew but the British fleet bombarded the forts of Alexandria and landed marines to protect the Europeans. With Egypt falling into a state of anarchy the British army intervened to restore order by defeating the nationalist leader and occupying Cairo.[19]

The *Naulilaa* arbitration of 1928 between Germany and Portugal provided a clearer instance of a reprisal, as well as a judicial opinion on the legal content of the doctrine. It involved a German armed reprisal from its colony in South-West Africa (now Namibia) against the Portuguese colony of Angola in 1914. The initial injury to Germany arose out of a border incident which resulted in the death of three German soldiers. The German army responded by launching a military expedition into Angola which resulted in considerable damage and loss of life. These hostilities were not formally part of the First World War since Portugal was, at the time, a neutral power. The arbitral tribunal agreed to by the parties accepted that armed reprisals could be a lawful response to a prior international wrong, but Germany had not satisfied the two conditions attaching to lawful reprisals: first that it should have made a demand for reparation that had not been met; and secondly that the armed response should be proportionate to the original wrong.[20]

5. Self-Defence

Reprisals were different to action taken in self-defence. The aim of reprisals was punitive not defensive—the aim was not to repel the border attack but to punish Portugal for its wrongful act at a time and in a manner of Germany's choosing. In a time of an unlimited right to wage war, there was no need to define self-defence with any great precision, though it was still used as one of a number of justifications for the use of force. Classically, the *Caroline* incident of 1837 is cited as authority for a definition of self-defence in that period.[21] In the incident, the British authorities authorized the burning of a ship while it was in a US port, the ship allegedly being used to further the armed insurrection taking place in the British colony of Canada at the time.

---

[19] R. Muir, *British History* (London: George Philip and Son, 1936) 637–9.
[20] (1928) 2 RIAA 1012.
[21] 30 British and Foreign State Papers, 1137–8; 30 British and State Papers, 195–6. See I. Brownlie, 'Non-Use of Force in Contemporary International Law', in R. Butler (ed), *The Non-Use of Force in International Relations* (The Hague: Kluwer, 1989) 19; C.H.M. Waldock, 'The Regulation of the Use of Force by Individual States in International Law' (1952) 81 Recueil des Cours 455; D.W. Bowett, *Self-Defence in International Law* (Manchester: Manchester University Press, 1958) 188–9.

Both the British and American governments agreed during the course of diplomatic exchanges over the incident that the British would have 'to show a necessity of self-defence, instant, overwhelming, leaving no choice of means and no moment for deliberation', in order to legitimate the action. Often cited as authority for anticipatory self-defence,[22] in other words as allowing a threatened state to strike first in expectation of an imminent attack, the phrase clearly allows for some degree of anticipation but not a great deal, and it may be doubted whether the British action actually met those requirements. Moreover as Ian Brownlie relates 'self-defence was regarded as synonymous with self-preservation or as a particular instance of it', so that it is not possible to draw out a general doctrine of self-defence from this incident, it was simply an attempt to proscribe self-preservation in relation to the particular facts.[23]

6. Humanitarian Intervention

To this list of justifications for using force, there must be added the development of a nineteenth century version of the just war doctrine, namely the claimed right of humanitarian intervention. Ian Brownlie summarizes the right in the following terms:

A state which had abused its sovereignty by brutal and excessively cruel treatment of those within its power, whether nationals or not, was regarded as having made itself liable to action by any state which was prepared to intervene.[24]

He further states the weakness that has always undermined this and older versions of the just war:

Operation of the doctrine was open to abuse since only powerful states could undertake police measures of this sort; and when military operations were justified as 'humanitarian intervention', this was only one of several characterizations offered and circumstances frequently indicated the presence of selfish motives.[25]

Within a legal regime that allowed for force, humanitarian intervention was just one of many justifications that could be put forward, but the practice of states reveals very few instances of genuine interventions on humanitarian grounds.[26] Stowell cites the British, French, and Russian intervention in the revolt against Turkey by Greek insurgents fighting for independence.[27] In 1821 English and French volunteers, including Lord Byron, who lost his life in the struggle, had gone to help the

---

[22] R.Y. Jennings, 'The Caroline and McLeod Cases' (1938) 32 AJIL 82 at 92; T.M. Franck, *Recourse to Force: State Action against Threats and Armed Attacks* (Oxford: Oxford University Press, 2002), 97. But see Dinstein, *War, Aggression and Self-Defence*, 184–5.

[23] Brownlie, *International Law and the Use of Force by States*, 43.

[24] Ibid., 338.   [25] Ibid., 338–9.   [26] Ibid., 340.

[27] E.C. Stowell, *Intervention in International Law* (Washington DC: John Byrne & Co, 1921) 126, 389, cited by Brownlie, *International Law and the Use of Force by States*, 339.

Greeks in their fight. These fighters and the Greek insurgents were on the brink of total defeat at the hands of an Egyptian fleet and army when a joint British, French and Russian fleet was sent to enforce demands for Greek autonomy. The decisive naval battle at Navarino in 1827 saw the defeat of the Egyptian fleet and the path was cleared to Greek independence in 1829 under the protection of Britain, France and Russia.[28] Though there may have been some humanitarian considerations in this intervention, it seems more in support of the achievement of independence, an early instance of force being used in support of the self-determination of a people. Of course policies such as the weakening of Turkey were, more than likely, the real motivating factors in this British inspired military intervention.

7. The Inter-War Period

The limited constraints on 'war' and other uses of force identified earlier in this chapter were clearly insufficient to prevent the outbreak of the First World War. The total nature of the 1914–8 hostilities had profound effects on public and governmental thinking. The British military alone lost over 700,000 men, while over 1.6 million were wounded. The creation of a universal organization with powers to secure international peace and security was a radical development in international relations. However, the influence of state sovereignty was too strong, both on the constitution of the organization itself, especially in the unanimity requirement,[29] and ultimately on the willingness of states to join the League and follow its strictures.[30] The United States failed to join the League, and other powerful states were outside the League at crucial times.

The Covenant did oblige members to 'respect and preserve as against external aggression the territorial integrity and existing political independence of all Members of the League',[31] and it did emphasize the need for collective action by declaring that 'any war or threat of war . . . is hereby declared a matter of concern for the whole League, and the League shall take any action that may be deemed wise and effectual to safeguard the peace of nations'.[32] However, these provisions were outweighed by a series of procedures that effectively allowed war or other uses of force. One provision, for instance, obliged member states to submit their disputes to arbitration or to the Council of the League and not to 'resort to war until three months after the award by the arbitrators or the report by the Council'.[33]

While the League's Covenant and machinery was defective, the lack of a substantive and clear prohibitory norm appeared to have been remedied by the 1928 Treaty for the Renunciation of War as an Instrument of National Policy

---

[28] Muir, *British History*, 528.
[29] Art 5(1) of the Covenant of the League of Nations 1919.
[30] P. Kennedy, *The Parliament of Man* (Toronto: HarperCollins, 2006) 13.
[31] Art 10 of the Covenant of the League of Nations 1919.
[32] Art 11(1).   [33] Art 12(1). See also arts 13, 15 and 16.

(also known as the Pact of Paris or Kellogg-Briand Pact), by which state parties condemned 'recourse to war for the solution of international controversies', and renounced war 'as an instrument of national policy'. The treaty then obligated the parties to settle their disputes by peaceful means.[34] Parallels with the norm prohibiting the use of force in the UN Charter will be seen.[35] The Pact of Paris appeared to represent international law on the use of force by 1939 in that most states were parties, including Germany, Japan and Italy, and it was used as the basis for prosecuting crimes against peace at both the Tokyo and Nuremberg trials in which the surviving war leaders of Germany and Japan were tried in the immediate aftermath of the war.[36] The Pact though was weak in that it only addressed 'war' and not 'use of force' more generally, and it lacked clarity on what was meant by 'national policy'.[37] Furthermore, it is important to note that neither Covenant nor Pact contained any definition of self-defence, though this was clearly recognized as an inherent right of a sovereign state in reservations made to the 1928 Treaty.[38]

8. UN Order

In the brief overview of the development of the *jus ad bellum* given above, a number of justifications for using force have emerged: the just war (including humanitarian intervention); the right of self-defence; and the armed reprisal. These lacked great legal clarity especially as the right to wage war became increasingly recognized, at least until the formation of the League of Nations. With the advent of the UN Charter it appeared that a new world order was brought in whereby threat or use of force by states against other states was prohibited,[39] except in the case of a defined right of individual and collective self-defence in response to an armed attack,[40] or in the case of a Security Council sanctioned military action in response to a threat to the peace, breach of the peace or act of aggression.[41] The scheme looked straightforward and appeared to remove the doctrines of war, just war and armed reprisal, and wider doctrines of self-preservation beyond a defined right of self-defence, from the lexicon of lawful action. In fact the only just wars were those sanctioned under the UN Charter. For example states could legitimately come to the aid of a state-victim of aggression under the right of collective self-defence, and the Security Council could authorize humanitarian

---

[34] Arts 1 and 2.   [35] Arts 2(3) and 2(4) of the UN Charter 1945.
[36] R. Cryer, *Prosecuting International Crimes: Selectivity and the International Criminal Law Regime* (Cambridge: Cambridge University Press, 2005) 36–48.
[37] See for example J.H.W. Verzijl, *International Law in Historical Perspective* (Leiden: Sijthoff, 1976) vol 8, 109.
[38] Brownlie, *International Law and the Use of Force by States*, 90, 235–7.
[39] Art 2(4) of the UN Charter 1945.   [40] Art 51 of the UN Charter 1945.
[41] Arts 39, 42 and 53 of the UN Charter 1945.

intervention to stop genocide within a state if it deemed it to be a threat to the peace. However, there was no mention in the Charter of states or other international actors having the right of humanitarian intervention in another state to stop widespread violation of basic human rights. In fact that sort of unilateral action seemed to be prohibited by the ban on the use of force.

It is important to relate more precisely the content of the Charter rules prohibiting the use of force and the exceptions to it, since their meaning and application come into focus in the military actions examined below and in later chapters. Article 2(4) contains the prohibition and states that:

All Members shall refrain in their international relations from the threat or use of force against the territorial integrity or political independence of any state, or in any other manner inconsistent with the Purposes of the United Nations.[42]

One ambiguity in this provision contained in the words 'against the territorial integrity or political independence', was argued by Britain in the *Corfu Channel* case, examined below, as permitting for other limited uses of force not encapsulated in the exceptions contained in the Charter. Further, arguments that the final phrase, 'in any other manner inconsistent with the Purposes of the United Nations' somehow allows for force undertaken in pursuit of the UN's purposes, including the protection of human rights, seems to be stretching the provision beyond recognition.[43] It does illustrate though that the 'just war' doctrine still has its advocates in the modern age, including Britain, despite the fact that as recently as 1984 the UK Foreign and Commonwealth Office stated that the 'best case that can be made in support of humanitarian intervention is that it cannot be said to be unambiguously illegal'.[44] The British reliance on humanitarian motives in the 1990s in relation to interventions in both Northern Iraq 1991 and Kosovo 1999, reviewed more fully in chapter nine, represented a hardening-up of a more unequivocal doctrine of humanitarian intervention. In the light of this practice, in 2000 Britain was proposing guidelines on humanitarian intervention to the UN under which the international community should intervene 'when faced with an overwhelming humanitarian catastrophe, which a government has shown it is unwilling or unable to prevent or is actively promoting'. That intervention should be 'proportionate to achieving the humanitarian purpose', should be collective, and 'wherever possible' should have the authority of the Security Council.[45]

Article 51 of the Charter contains the right to self-defence and reads:

Nothing in the present Charter shall impair the inherent right of individual or collective self-defence if an armed attack occurs against a Member of the United Nations, until

---

[42] For discussion see A. Randelzhofer, 'Article 2(4)', in B. Simma (ed), *The Charter of the United Nations* (2nd edn, Oxford: Oxford University Press, 2002) 117–25.

[43] Dinstein, *War, Aggression and Self-Defence*, 88–91.

[44] (1975–2001) UKMIL Part Sixteen. I, item 70, para 22 (1986 Foreign Policy Document No 148).

[45] (2000) UKMIL Part Sixteen: IV, item 16/9.

the Security Council has taken measures necessary to maintain international peace and security. Measures taken by Members in the exercise of this right of self-defence shall be immediately reported to the Security Council and shall not in any way affect the authority and responsibility of the Security Council under the present Charter to take at any time such action as it deems necessary in order to maintain or restore international peace and security.[46]

Self-defence in this provision is limited to responding to an armed attack, which will inevitably cause problems for states wishing to try and deal with threats to them, especially given the devastating potential of (nuclear) missile attack developed during the Cold War, and the growing threat of international terrorism first emerging out of the Middle East Crisis in the mid 1960s. Should states have to wait for an attack to be able to take military force in self-defence? Bearing in mind that the *Caroline* incident of 1837 seemed to allow anticipatory action, the question is whether this is still good law after 1945. The British position on this will be explored in later chapters.

The right of self-defence is not dependent on the express approval of the Security Council, although if the Council takes 'measures necessary' to restore peace and security then article 51 suggests that the right might then cease. Arguments of what constitute such measures will be considered in later chapters. If states want to take military action that is not a response to an armed attack, the Charter does not leave them without any avenues, but they must persuade the Security Council to first of all make a determination under chapter VII, article 39 of which provides:

The Security Council shall determine the existence of any threat to the peace, breach of the peace, or act of aggression and shall make recommendations, or decide what measures shall be taken in accordance with Articles 41 and 42, to maintain or restore international peace and security.

While there is an overlap between the concept of armed attack in article 51 and 'act of aggression' in article 39, and between 'threat or use of force' in article 2(4) and 'threat to the peace' and 'breach of the peace' in article 39, practice has shown that article 39, especially the term 'threat to the peace', is not confined to breaches or indeed potential breaches of article 2(4), so that the Council can take action under chapter VII to deal with threats or acts of violence within countries as well as between countries.[47] While article 41 permits the Council to take non-forcible measures such as economic sanctions, article 42 covers the use of military force under Security Council auspices. Article 42 states:

Should the Security Council consider that measures provided for in Article 41 would be inadequate or have provided to be inadequate, it may take such action by air, sea, or land forces as may be necessary to maintain or restore international peace and security. Such

---

[46] See further A. Randelzhofer, 'Article 51', in Simma (ed), *The Charter*, 789–806.
[47] J. Frowein and N. Krisch, 'Article 39', in Simma (ed), *The Charter*, 723.

action may include demonstrations, blockade, and other operations by air, sea, or land forces of Members of the United Nations.

Members of the UN were meant to contribute troops to UN operations by virtue of pre-existing agreements and under the direction of the UN's Military Staff Committee,[48] but this proved impossible to achieve in the Cold War. Instead, as we shall see in chapter four, Britain was instrumental in developing a new method of fulfilling article 42, namely the development of coalitions of volunteer states (known as 'coalitions of the willing'). The legal and practical weaknesses of such a system will be returned to in that chapter.

9. The Cold War

The Cold War period saw frequent and flagrant violations of the prohibition on the use of force, with very little enforcement action being taken against transgressors. The executive organ's principal weakness—that of the veto belonging to each of the five permanent members (P5)—meant that it was largely inactive. Article 27(3) of the UN Charter contains the right of veto when it states that 'decisions of the Security Council on all other matters shall be made by an affirmative vote of nine members including the concurring votes of the permanent members ...'.

The content of article 27(2) shows that the veto does not apply to procedural matters such as the inclusion of items on the agenda,[49] such decisions can be adopted by a majority of nine out of the fifteen members (originally seven out of eleven). However, on all other matters, in other words matters of substance, article 27(3) gives each of the P5 (France, UK, US, the Soviet Union (Russia) and China) a veto by requiring the concurrence of each of them. Practice has interpreted this provision to exclude abstention by a permanent member from being considered as a veto.[50] Though abstention does not seem to be either 'concurring' or 'affirmative' as required by the terms of article 27(3), it has not been viewed as a veto for the simple reason that such an interpretation has been agreed by the P5 themselves and in fact does not restrict their right of veto. A permanent member simply has to cast a negative vote to block a resolution proposed under chapter VII which contains the enforcement powers (both non-forcible and forcible) of the Security Council.

However, if the resolution is proposed under chapter VI, which contains the consensual, and therefore more traditional, powers of the Council to promote the peaceful settlement of disputes, then article 27(3) of the Charter obliges a permanent member or any other member of the Security Council to abstain from the vote if they are a party to a dispute. While this principle was respected in the

---

[48] See arts 43–7 of the UN Charter 1945.

[49] S.D. Bailey and S. Daws, *The Procedure of the UN Security Council* (3rd edn, Oxford: Clarendon Press, 1998) 225–6.

[50] This development is supported by the International Court's advisory opinion in the *Namibia* case of 1971. See *Legal Consequences for States of the Continued Presence of South Africa in Namibia (South West Africa) Notwithstanding Security Council Resolution 276 (1970)* 1971 ICJ Rep. 16.

early years (witness below the UK's abstention on the Security Council resolution which recommended that the Corfu Channel incident of 1946 be referred to the International Court), its impact was very much reduced during the Cold War period (witness below the British and French willingness to veto proposed resolutions in the Security Council during the Suez crisis of 1956).

The veto prevented significant enforcement action being taken by the Security Council during the Cold War period. There were limited exceptions such as the US-led, UN-endorsed response to the North Korean invasion of South Korea in 1950,[51] but most military interventions went unpunished. The reaction to the North Korea invasion by the Security Council was only made possible by the Soviet Union's absence from the chamber, which was rather controversially treated as a case of abstention.[52] The Korean War involved significant British political and military involvement and will be reviewed more fully in chapter four.

The only other occasion that military force was authorized by the Security Council during the Cold War also involved the British military, in this case the Royal Navy in the Beira Patrol of 1966–75 on station off the coast of Mozambique. The aim of the patrol as authorized by the UN Security Council was to 'prevent by the use of force if necessary the arrival at Beira of vessels reasonably believed to be carrying oil destined for Rhodesia'.[53] An oil embargo had been placed on Rhodesia following its unilateral declaration of independence from Britain in 1965,[54] yet the colonial power in Mozambique (Portugal) had permitted oil tankers to dock at Beira and oil to be piped across its colony to Rhodesia. In requesting Security Council authority to use force if necessary to stop the embargo from being breached, the British representative Lord Caradon stated in the Council chamber:

Without that authority, the United Kingdom Government has to face the defiance of the United Nations with its hands tied. The Royal Navy undoubtedly had the physical power to prevent the *Joanna V*, for instance, from entering Beira. But in this matter my Government has been anxious that at all times its actions should be lawful actions and that it should not risk acting in breach of the law of nations. One of the very purposes of the action we are . . . taking against the illegal regime in Southern Rhodesia is to assert the rule of law and the principles of the United Nations Charter. I therefore ask the Council now . . . . To enable the United Kingdom to carry out without fear of illegality the responsibilities which in the Rhodesian situations are ours.[55]

In 1969 the Under Secretary of State for Defence, Dr David Owen stated in the House of Commons that 'the patrol has been fully effective in cutting off the most direct route for the supply of oil to Rhodesia'.[56] However, alternative oil supplies were found by Rhodesia, leading to critical questioning in the House of Commons of the value of the patrol over the following years.[57]

---

[51] SC Res. 83, 27 June 1950.   [52] Bailey and Daws, *Procedure*, 257.
[53] SC Res. 221, 9 April 1966.   [54] SC Res. 217, 20 Nov. 1965.
[55] SC 1276th mtg, 9 April 1966.   [56] *Hansard* HC vol 788, col 382, 15 Oct. 1969.
[57] For example *Hansard* HC vol 847, cols 607–8, 30 Nov. 1972; *Hansard* HC vol 866, cols 1117–8, 18 Dec. 1973.

In contrast to the clear illegality of its intervention in the Suez Crisis of 1956 (reviewed below), the United Kingdom acted within the bounds of the UN Charter ten years later in undertaking the Beira Patrol. In so doing it helped to develop further the idea that willing states could be authorized to use force under article 42, in the absence of any earmarked UN forces as originally foreseen in the UN Charter. Despite the high sounding words of Lord Caradon, this did not mark an enduring commitment to the rule of law in international relations, rather on this occasion the UK's and Security Council's interests coincided sufficiently for it to receive authority. This did not constitute a guarantee that the UK would not act unilaterally in the face of the UN Charter. Though Suez might have marked the end of Britain's imperial ambitions, the 1990s would witness a resurgence in Britain's propensity to use force to solve pressing problems.

Southern Rhodesia was deemed to be a threat to the peace by the Security Council by virtue of its denial of self-determination by the white racist regime.[58] During the Cold War, only the Korean War involved the enforcement of the prohibition on the use of force, North Korea having committed an armed aggression against the South. In many other cases, the Council was inherently incapable of enforcing the prohibition on the use of force. This was especially so in the case of superpower interventions in their respective spheres of influence—for instance by the United States in Guatemala (1954), Cuba (1961), the Dominican Republic (1965), Grenada (1983) and Panama (1989), and the Soviet Union in Hungary (1956), Czechoslovakia (1968), and Afghanistan (1979).

However, the rule prohibiting the use of force seemed to survive intact because these violations were still recognized as violations not as permissible uses of force, both by the rest of the international community, and often by the violators themselves evidenced in their attempts to argue that their actions came within the exceptions to the prohibition, or that there were in fact further exceptions to the ban on the use of force other than those allowed in the Charter.[59] For instance the Soviet Union argued that its intervention in Afghanistan in 1979 was justifiable collective defence of the country at the request of the Afghan government. The falsity of this contention was not lost on the international community when it regularly condemned the Soviet Union for its invasion at each UN session up until the Soviet withdrawal in 1989.[60] The reality of the Cold War period when power often prevailed over law was shown by the comment by Dean Acheson in relation to the situating of Soviet made missiles in Cuba leading to the missile crisis of 1962:

---

[58] See further SC Res. 232, 16 Dec. 1966; SC Res. 235, 29 May 1968, imposing wider mandatory sanctions against Rhodesia.

[59] See statement of the International Court in *Case Concerning Military and Paramilitary Activities in and Against Nicaragua* 1986 ICJ Rep. 14 at 98.

[60] Starting with GA Res. ES-6/2, 14 Jan. 1980.

The power, position and prestige of the United States had been challenged by another state: and law does not deal with such questions of ultimate power—power that comes close to the sources of sovereignty.[61]

For powerful states power and prestige were more important on occasions than any notion of the rule of law. Whether middle ranking military powers like the United Kingdom also saw fit on occasions to ride roughshod over the rules on the use of force during this period needs consideration.

10. The UK and the Use of Force in the Cold War

Before reviewing the post-Cold War period, it is interesting to evaluate some of the British arguments for using force during the Cold War. Like the superpowers, the UK was not averse to using military force. Its involvement in the Korean War (1950–3), peacekeeping in Cyprus (1964 to the present day), and its defence of the Falklands (1982) will be returned to in later chapters. Furthermore, it was involved in quelling insurgencies in Malaya and Kenya in the 1950s.[62] In this section consideration will be given to two episodes in recent British military history, one minor involving the Royal Navy (the Corfu Channel incident 1946) and the other more significant (Suez 1956), but both representing uses of force that did not fit easily within the framework of the UN Charter.

10.1 The Corfu Channel 1946

With the United Nations barely established and the Cold War looming, Britain was involved in a minor clash with the Communist People's Republic of Albania led by Enver Hoxha. On 22 October 1946 a squadron of four British warships was sailing through the Straits of Corfu. Their passage was 'intended as a warning to Albania not to flex its muscles in sight of the Royal Navy'.[63] When passing through the northern part of the channel, with Albania to the west, two of the ships, *Saumarez* and *Volage*, were struck by mines with resulting loss of life and injury to their crews. Three weeks later on 13 November 1946, the North Corfu Channel was swept for mines by British minesweepers and twenty-two moored mines were cut.

At this time the Cold War stalemate in the Security Council had not yet hardened into the almost automatic use of the veto in disputes between East and West, and so the Council was able to recommend that the governments of the United Kingdom

---

[61] D. Acheson, 'Response to Panel: The Cuban Quarantine—Implications for the Future' (1963) 14 ASIL Proceedings 14–15.

[62] A. Farrar-Hockley, 'The Post-War Army 1945–1963', in D.G. Chandler and I. Beckett (eds), *The Oxford History of the British Army* (Oxford: Oxford University Press, 1994) 329–33.

[63] J.R. Hill, 'The Realities of Medium Power, 1946 to the Present', in J.R. Hill (ed), *The Oxford Illustrated History of the Royal Navy* (Oxford: Oxford University Press, 1995) 381 at 383.

and Albania refer their dispute to the International Court of Justice in its first contentious case.[64] Following this recommendation, both parties agreed to submit two questions to the Court. First the parties asked the Court whether Albania was liable under international law for the damage and loss of life caused by the mine explosions. Secondly, they asked the Court whether the UK had violated the sovereignty of Albania by its naval operations of 22 October and 13 November.[65]

In answering the first question, the Court acknowledged that, given the evidence, it was not possible to establish that Albania had laid the mines that the British ships had struck. There were suggestions that Albania's then close ally, Yugoslavia, led by President Tito, had laid them, though the Court could not entertain these contentions. Despite that, the International Court thought that Albanian liability would be established if knowledge of the minelaying could be imputed to it. The principle established by the Court referring to 'every State's obligation not to allow knowingly its territory to be used for acts contrary to the rights of other States', is still seen as good law and the *Corfu Channel* case was cited widely in the International Law Commission's Commentary on its Articles on State Responsibility of 2001.[66] The Court was satisfied that Albanian knowledge had been established by the fact that it constantly kept a close watch over the waters of the North Corfu Channel, and by the fact that the geography of the Albanian coast made it easy to maintain such a close watch. The Court concluded that 'the laying of a minefield in these waters could hardly fail to have been observed by the Albanian coastal defences'.[67]

Having found Albania liable in international law for the explosions of 22 October, which gave rise to a duty on Albania to pay compensation to the UK,[68] the Court then considered the second question in two parts by looking at each of the naval operations of 22 October and 13 November. The Court related the background to both naval actions by recounting the fact that Albania had fired upon British naval vessels in the North Corfu Channel in May 1946, which led to the UK protesting to the Albanian government that its right of innocent passage had been violated. The British government warned that if firing continued then that fire would be returned by British warships. It was in such circumstances that the squadron of four warships sailed through the North Corfu Strait on 22 October.

---

[64] SC Res. 22, 9 April 1947. The Soviet Union and Poland abstained on the vote and the UK did not vote as it was a party to the dispute, so complying with the requirements of art 27(3) of the UN Charter which provides in part that 'a party to a dispute shall abstain from voting'. Chapter VI of the Charter empowers the Council to recommend procedures or methods for the settlement of disputes, including referring the case to the International Court of Justice: see art 36(3). Such resolutions are recommendatory only see *obiter* statement in *Corfu Channel Case (Preliminary Objections)* 1947–8 ICJ Rep. 15 at 31–2 (joint separate opinion).

[65] *Corfu Channel Case (Merits)* 1949 ICJ Rep. 4 at 6.

[66] See for example the commentary on art 2 of the Articles: J. Crawford, *The International Law Commission's Articles on State Responsibility* (Cambridge: Cambridge University Press, 2002) 82.

[67] 1949 ICJ Rep. 17–22.

[68] See *Corfu Channel Case (Assessment of the Amount of Compensation)* 1949 ICJ Rep. 244.

The Court considered that the Corfu Channel was an international strait through which passage could not be denied in times of peace, and therefore the UK had not violated Albanian sovereignty by sending the warships through. It also found that the manner in which the British warships sailed through the straits did not violate the principle that the passage should be innocent, even though the warships were at action stations ready to respond if they had been fired upon, and that the British action was not simply for navigation purposes but was really to test Albania's attitude and 'demonstrate such force' that Albania 'would abstain from firing on passing ships'.[69] Though the Court did not expressly say so, by acknowledging that the British warships exercising their right of passage had the right to fire-back if fired upon, it seemed to be accepting that the manner in which the passage was undertaken was not a threat of force contrary to article 2(4) of the UN Charter, but legitimate preparation to act in self-defence if attacked by Albania.[70]

Thus it would appear that the British, while engaging in a limited form of gunboat diplomacy on 22 October 1946, had kept within the bounds of international law. However, by characterizing the passage of British warships as innocent, the Court did seem to be allowing this concept to cover the forceful exercise of the right.[71] The British were, after all, intent on using force if necessary to keep the Straits open. However, somewhat paradoxically, the Court was far more critical of the second naval operation of 12–13 November 1946, known as 'Operation Retail'.

In response to the explosions of 22 October, the British government informed its Albanian counterpart of its intention to sweep the Corfu Channel for mines. The Albanian government refused to give its consent to minesweeping in its waters. The Court found that the minesweeping operation could not be justified as the exercise of the right of innocent passage, and that 'international law does not allow a State to assemble a large number of warships in the territorial waters of another State and to carry out minesweeping in those waters'.[72]

Furthermore, the Court took the opportunity to balance its rather lenient approach to the passage of 22 October by dismissing two British arguments for allowing a limited use of force in the form of Operation Retail on 13 November. First of all the British argued that limited intervention was allowed to secure evidence of wrongdoing (in this case the mines) in the territory or territorial waters of another state. The Court rejected this argument in language that was rather sweeping when compared to its analysis of the incident on 22 October:

The Court cannot accept such a line of defence. The Court can only regard the alleged right of intervention as the manifestation of a policy of force, such as has, in the past, given rise to most serious abuses and such as cannot, whatever be the defects in international organization, find a place in international law. Intervention is perhaps still less admissible in the particular form it would take here; for, from the nature of things, it

[69] 1949 ICJ Rep. at 26–32.   [70] Dinstein, *War, Aggression and Self-Defence*, 233.
[71] Brownlie, *International Law and the Use of Force by States*, 283–9.
[72] 1949 ICJ Rep. at 33–4.

would be reserved for the most powerful States, and might easily lead to perverting the administration of international justice itself.[73]

The Court does not mention article 2(4) but the subliminal message is clear. Forceful interventions, no matter how limited, are not permitted, and it is no excuse to argue that the Security Council has been unable to take effective action to deal with the dispute. A strict approach to the rules prohibiting forceful action was reinforced by the Court's response to the second line of argument put forward by Sir Ian Beckett on behalf of the UK, namely that the action of 13 November 'threatened neither the territorial integrity nor the political independence of Albania. Albania suffered thereby neither territorial loss nor any part of its political independence'.[74] The Court again responded in broad condemnatory terms:

> The United Kingdom Agent, in his reply, has further classified 'Operation Retail' among methods of self-protection or self-help. The Court cannot accept this line of defence either. Between independent States, respect for territorial sovereignty is an essential foundation of international relations.... [T]o ensure respect for international law ... the Court must declare that the action of the British navy constituted a violation of Albanian sovereignty.[75]

What the *Corfu Channel* case of 1949 shows is an early attempt by the British government to test the limits of the rules governing the use of force, in particular by trying to establish that article 2(4) does not contain an absolute ban on the threat or use of force, so that certain limited uses of force, not taken in self-defence, may be allowed. Although the Court almost seemed to allow this argument to succeed in relation to the events of 22 October by virtue of a very lenient definition of innocent passage through the territorial waters of another state, its conclusions on the minesweeping 'Operation Retail' of 13 November make clear that article 2(4) is to be read as protecting the sovereignty of all states from forceful interventions no matter how limited. For a country used to asserting its rights and interests by forcible means, this represented a blow, though there was very little discussion of the incident or the case in parliament.[76] It did not, however,

---

[73] Ibid., at 35.
[74] ICJ Pleadings, *Corfu Channel Case*, iii, 295–6 cited in Brownlie, *International Law and the Use of Force by States*, 266.
[75] 1949 ICJ Rep. 35.
[76] A brief written answer was given on the mining of the two destroyers on 22 October 1946: *Hansard* HC vol 430, col 133w, 20 Nov. 1946. A fuller explanation of the incident in the form of a written note was introduced into the House on 11 December 1946: *Hansard* HC vol 431, cols 1168–75, 11 Dec. 1946. Even in February 1947 the government dismissed the idea of taking the case before the International Court of Justice: *Hansard* HC vol 433, col 1151, 19 Feb. 1947. The House of Commons was kept informed of the proceedings before the Court from November 1947 until the Court decided in December 1949 that Albania should pay nearly £850,000 in damages for the sinking of October 1946: see *Hansard* HC vol 472, col 750, 13 March 1950. Negotiations with Albania regarding payment of the compensation dragged on throughout 1950 and the government reported that they had led to no result in January 1951: *Hansard* HC vol 483, col 570, 29 Jan. 1951 (Ernest Davies). Suggestions were made in a fuller discussion in the House of Commons in March 1951 that Albanian assets be seized but the government minister said that such assets were

stop it from using military means to secure its interests when in 1956 it played a leading role in the Suez Crisis.

10.2 The Suez Crisis 1956

The Anglo-Egyptian Agreement of 1954 had guaranteed the international status of the Suez Canal. In July 1956 President Nasser of Egypt, who had recently come to power, nationalized the Suez Canal Company, a company in which Britain and France had significant holdings. As part of a co-ordinated plan by France, Britain and Israel, on 29 October 1956 Israel invaded Egypt in the area of the Suez Canal.[77] A cease-fire resolution proposed by the United States was vetoed by Britain and France in the Security Council.[78] Instead, France and Britain issued an ultimatum to Egypt and Israel demanding that they agree a cease-fire and withdraw their troops from the Suez Canal and allow French and British troops to police the area around the Canal. The ultimatum was not heeded and on 31 October French and British troops landed in the Suez Canal area.

The period between the Egyptian nationalization of July 1956 and the use of force by Britain and France at the end of October, reveals both political and legal tensions. Politically, the Suez intervention ('Operation Musketeer') proved extremely difficult for the Conservative government, particularly its Prime Minister, Sir Anthony Eden. 'Eden was aware that he was coming perilously close to the limits of what a statesman in a democracy can do'.[79] Public support for a military operation quickly fell away in the weeks following the nationalization of July 1956. Furthermore Eden's cabinet reflected that opinion and ceased to be united after the initial decision to use force.[80] The planning and running of the operation was handled on a day to day basis by an *ad hoc* Egypt Committee, under Eden's chairmanship. 'At its first meeting the committee identified the overthrow of Nasser as the prime objective, to be followed by the international takeover of the management of the canal'.[81]

In parliament the government put forward legal arguments to justify its actions. Shortly after the nationalization in July 1956 Sir Anthony Eden spoke briefly in the House of Commons of Egypt's 'unilateral decision . . . to expropriate the Suez Canal Company, without notice and in breach of the Concession Agreements',

negligible and that the Albanian government had offered only £40,000 in settlement. The Minister stated that the 'Albanian government happen to be a Communist Government who do not respect the rule of law or the principles of international law as do Western democracies': *Hansard* HC vol 484, col 2513, 1 March 1951 (Davies). Questions were still asked on the matter until May 1955: *Hansard* HC vol 540, col 1344, 2 May 1955.

[77] See generally K. Scott, 'Commentary on Suez: Forty Years on' (1996) 1 JACL 205.
[78] UN Doc. S/3710, 1956.
[79] D. Carlton, *Britain and the Suez Crisis* (London: Basil Blackwell, 1988) 59.
[80] K. Kyle, 'Britain's Slow March to Suez', in D. Tal (ed), *The 1956 War: Collusion and Rivalry in the Middle East* (London: Frank Cass, 2001) 95 at 99.
[81] Ibid.

and that the government was considering a number of options after evaluating its international rights.[82] In a full debate on 2 August he spoke of the Egyptian action breaching the 1888 Suez Canal Convention, particularly the principle of free navigation of the waterway, and how the treatment of the Suez Canal Company's employees by the Egyptian authorities in forcing them to remain at their posts under threat of imprisonment, was a violation of their human rights. After stating that the government could not accept a position whereby the Canal was in the 'unfettered control of a single power', he announced that 'certain precautionary measures of a military nature', in the shape of movement of armed forces, were being taken.[83]

Such initial steps were supported by the opposition. Hugh Gaitskell, however, warned that 'while force cannot be excluded, we must be sure that the circumstances justify it and that it is, if used, consistent with our belief in, and our pledges to, the Charter of the United Nations and not in conflict with them'.[84] Full-scale intervention was being planned by the government but this was not made clear to parliament. Legal advice, which was not made public, was against military intervention made clear by the Foreign Secretary's memorandum to the Egypt Committee of the Cabinet on 20 August, which read in part 'however illegal the Egyptian action in purporting to nationalize the Suez Canal Company may be, it is not, in itself as things stand at present, of such a character as would, under international law, afford a justification for armed intervention'.[85] This may explain why when the intervention was imminent Eden was reputed to have declared that the 'lawyers are always against our doing anything. For God's sake keep them out of it. This is a political affair'.[86]

The parliamentary consensus of early August seems to have disappeared in the next full debate on the matter on 12 September, when the Prime Minister was constantly interrupted and again only hinted at the use of force. He denied the charge of 'sabre rattling' and stated that it was Egypt that had first used force by seizing the assets of the Suez Canal Company by armed agents.[87] Hugh Gaitskell spoke of the debate in the country where there was a wide difference of opinion, and stated that, in the absence of any act of aggression by Colonel Nasser, if the government contemplated 'the use of force to impose a solution' then it would not have the support of the opposition, and he accused the government of having a joint plan with the French even before the earlier debate in August. Such 'sabre-rattling' he stated had undermined any attempt to settle the dispute peacefully.

---

[82] *Hansard* HC vol 557, col 778, 27 July 1956.

[83] *Hansard* HC vol 557, cols 1603–6, 2 Aug. 1956.

[84] Ibid., col 1617.

[85] CAB 134/1217, 136–7 in G. Marston, 'Armed Intervention in the 1956 Suez Canal Crisis: Legal Advice Tendered to the British Government' (1988) 37 ICLQ 773 at 782.

[86] On 16 October 1956 at a small meeting of ministers: A. Nutting, *No End of a Lesson: The Story of Suez* (London: Constable, 1967) 95.

[87] *Hansard* HC vol 558, cols 13–14, 12 Sept. 1956.

He urged the government to go to the Security Council to seek a solution.[88] Another Labour MP stated that if the Security Council was blocked by the veto then the authority of the General Assembly should be sought, as recognized by the Assembly's own Uniting for Peace Resolution of 1950.[89] The opposition's mood was that Britain should not go it alone, but should act through the United Nations and thus comply with its international legal obligations. The division in the House of Commons was made clear by the fact that a vote endorsing the government's policy was only won by 319 votes to 248.[90]

The excuse to intervene that the British and French governments had been looking for was conveniently provided by the Israeli invasion of Egypt on 30 October 1956. In the House of Commons Eden issued the ultimatum to withdraw and allow British and French troops into the Canal Zone, and concluded that if either Israel or Egypt did not comply then 'British and French forces will intervene in whatever strength may be necessary to secure compliance'. Gaitskell immediately asked 'under what authority and with what right, he believes the British and French forces are justified in armed intervention in this matter'? The Prime Minister stated that there was nothing in the Charter 'which abrogates the right of a Government to take such steps as are essential to protect the lives of their citizens' and vital international 'rights such as here at stake'.[91] In response to calls from the opposition benches that action should be delayed, the Foreign Secretary, Selwyn Lloyd, dismissed the idea that the government needed the agreement of the opposition before taking action.[92] The government accordingly won the vote on adjournment but the House was deeply divided.[93]

On 31 October the Prime Minister announced the British and French military intervention to the House of Commons,[94] and it won a further vote endorsing its action,[95] but it was in the House of Lords that a full legal justification was given by the Lord Chancellor, Viscount Kilmuir, during a lengthy debate on the British and French military action. He stated that force may only be used lawfully either with the express authority of the Security Council, or in self-defence, 'but self-defence includes a situation in which the lives of a State's national's abroad are threatened and it is necessary to intervene on that territory for their protection'. He further stretched this principle to include the protection of 'valuable and internationally important foreign property' which was in danger of 'irreparable injury'.[96]

Though there has been a significant amount of state practice before and after 1945 to support limited interventions to evacuate or rescue nationals whose

[88] Ibid., cols 15–31.   [89] Ibid., cols 44–5 (Henderson). See GA Res. 377, 3 Nov. 1950.
[90] *Hansard* HC vol 558, cols 311–12, 13 Sept. 1956.
[91] *Hansard* HC vol 558, cols 1275–7, 30 Oct. 1956.   [92] Ibid., cols 1372–3.
[93] Ibid., col 1378.   [94] *Hansard* HC vol 558, cols 1446–9, 31 Oct. 1956.
[95] *Hansard* HC vol 558, col 1743, 1 Nov. 1956, by 320 votes to 253.
[96] *Hansard* HL vol 199, cols 1349–50, 1 Nov. 1956. See full argument in memorandum to the Cabinet of 29 Oct. 1956, PREM 11/1129, in Marston, 'Armed Intervention', 800.

lives are in serious danger in a foreign state,[97] the Suez action was designed to secure wider aims—the Canal itself and to undermine the Egyptian government. Contrary to the Lord Chancellor's opinion, the Law Officers—the Attorney General (Sir Reginald Manningham-Buller), the Solicitor General (Sir Harry Hylton-Foster)—had stated in a letter to Lord Kilmuir on 12 October that it was 'difficult if not impossible to establish that such use of force by us came within the doctrine of self-defence'. The failure of the Security Council to act did not somehow free the UK from legal obligation since the 'doctrine of self-help was condemned by the International Court in the Corfu case'.[98] Neither the Law Officers nor the Foreign Office Legal Advisers (Sir Gerald Fitzmaurice and Francis Vallat) knew about the British, French and Israeli plan, and were not consulted about the legality of the British element of that plan ('Operation Musketeer'). The exchange of views between these advisors and the government clearly showed that the decision was taken on grounds of policy not of law, and that none of the advisors would have supported the Lord Chancellor's view that the intervention was legal. They also criticized the Cabinet and Prime Minister for taking the action solely on the advice of the Lord Chancellor.[99]

The lack of convincing legal argument reflecting the wider lack of legitimacy underlying the Suez campaign seems to have undermined support in parliament and in the country. Kyle also considers the level of international protests to be significant, especially by the United States which viewed Suez as an unnecessary distraction from the concerns of the Cold War.

The volume of world protest at British and French action continued to be turned up, all the more in that it was being orchestrated by the United States and that the Suez War coincided with the savage repression of the Hungarian rising against Soviet imperialism. The yearning, as the United States prepared to go to the polls on 6 November, was for the world scene to be transformed into a morality play in which communism, caught in the beam of a searchlight resting unblinkingly on what was occurring in Budapest, would be forever damned. Thanks to the Suez campaign the moral absolutes seemed confused.[100]

For the United States, the confrontations of the Cold War were far more important than the dwindling imperial ambitions of Britain and France. 'So ended Britain's last serious effort to play the Great Power in the Middle East and its last effort to carry out on the ground a foreign policy in the face of US dissent'.[101] Its inability to carry public opinion and world opinion led to the ignominious withdrawal of British and French troops and their replacement by the first UN peacekeeping force (UNEF I) authorized not by the Security

---

[97] See generally N. Ronzitti, *Rescuing Nationals Abroad through Military Coercion and Intervention on the Grounds of Humanity* (Dordrecht: Martinus Nijhoff, 1985).

[98] LCO 2/5760, in Marston, 'Armed Intervention', 792.

[99] Marston, 'Armed Intervention', 803–9.   [100] Kyle, 'Britain's Slow March to Suez', 111.

[101] Ibid., 115.

Council, but by the General Assembly,[102] due to the fact that the matter had been passed from the Security Council to the Assembly under the Uniting for Peace Resolution following the British and French vetoes of early cease-fire proposals.[103]

A further interesting feature of the Suez intervention was the criticism it received at the hands of the military, who were concerned about the unclear aims of the operation. 'The armed services felt that they had achieved what had been asked of them and been exposed to ridicule by indecisive political leadership'.[104] The criticism from the military was about the 'lack of a clear political aim', not any perceived lack of legality and legitimacy of the operation.[105] Of course it would be extremely difficult for the military establishment to question the overall legality of an operation since that might undermine the soldier's obligation to obey 'lawful' commands. As Tony Rogers clearly states 'soldiers have a duty to obey lawful orders and a duty not to comply with unlawful orders'.[106] Although this is written in the context of superior orders not being a defence to a specific war crime committed by a soldier, it can be seen how a war that was recognized as unlawful under the *jus ad bellum* could undermine the whole command structure of the armed services.

11. Post-Cold War and Post-9/11

The rule prohibiting the use of force certainly seemed to receive very robust support in 1990–1, literally at the beginning of the post-Cold War period, when the aggression committed by Iraq against Kuwait was repulsed by a coalition of states, including the UK, acting under a UN mandate.[107] The 'relative indelibility' of the rules on the use of force in the Charter reflects their peremptory status in international law—they are widely viewed as fundamental rules or '*jus cogens*'—from which no derogation is allowed and which are very difficult to modify.[108] Although the rules governing the use of force survived the intense power pressures of the Cold War, it might be questioned whether the post-Cold War period, in combination with the post-9/11 era, have led to the re-emergence of

---

[102] GA Res. 1001, 5 Nov. 1956. Adopted by 57 votes to 0, with 19 abstentions (including France and Britain).

[103] UN Doc. S/3710, 1956 (US); UN Doc. S/3713/Rev 1, 1956 (USSR).

[104] Kyle, 'Britain's Slow March to Suez', 115.

[105] General Hugh Stockwell (British commander of the Suez operation) in J. Riley, *The Life and Campaigns of General Hughie Stockwell* (London: Pen and Sword, 2006) 255.

[106] A. Rogers, *Law on the Battlefield* (2nd edn, Manchester: Manchester University Press, 2004) 211.

[107] SC Res. 678, 29 Nov. 1990.

[108] I. Brownlie, *Principles of Public International Law* (6th edn, Oxford: Oxford University Press, 2003) 488–9.

older doctrines of just war, reprisals—uses of force not contemplated by the UN Charter—as well as a wider right of self-defence than recognized by article 51.

With the defeat of Iraq in 1991, the Iraqi army was turned upon the Kurds and the Shias within Iraq who had revolted against Saddam Hussein. Unable to secure any clear authority to intervene from the Security Council,[109] Western states intervened by briefly sending troops to northern Iraq to protect the Kurds, and then by imposing no-fly zones in the north again to protect the Kurds and in the south to protect the Marsh Arabs. In defending the second of these no-fly zones in the absence of an express Security Council mandate, the British Foreign Secretary Douglas Hurd stated that 'not every action that a British Government...takes has to be underwritten by a specific provision in a UN resolution provided that we comply with international law', and 'international law recognises extreme humanitarian need'.[110] As shall be detailed in chapter nine, this argument was developed in 1999 by the UK when it contributed to the NATO air campaign directed at stopping the crimes being committed by Serb forces against the Albanian majority in the Serbian province of Kosovo in defiance of Security Council resolutions.[111]

Such post-Cold War, post-modern interventions which disregard the strong concept of state sovereignty found, for example, in the International Court's judgment in the *Corfu Channel* case, cause problems for the rules on the use of force since they appear to be a violation of them yet in their pure 'just' form they seem necessary to prevent gross violations of human rights. In essence a fundamental norm of international law (that prohibiting the use of force) is being breached in order to uphold other fundamental norms (such as those prohibiting genocide and other crimes against humanity). Such a challenge to the orthodox rules on the use of force has been supported in recent years by the United Kingdom, a full analysis of which is given in chapter nine.

Somewhat differently, the post 9/11 interventions in Afghanistan in 2001 and Iraq in 2003 were attempts to expand the two recognized Charter exceptions to the ban on the use of force—the exercise of the right of self-defence (in the case of Afghanistan) and military action taken under the authority of the Security Council (in the case of Iraq). While the underlying concerns that are driving these types of intervention are the need to combat global terrorism and the spread of weapons of mass destruction (WMD), made clear in President Bush's National Security Strategy of 2002,[112] the 'just war' rhetoric found in the Kosovo campaign was also found in relation to the response of the US and its allies to

---

[109] SC Res. 688, 5 April 1991.

[110] In M. Weller (ed), *Iraq and Kuwait: The Hostilities and Their Aftermath* (Cambridge: Cambridge University Press, 1993) 723–4.

[111] SC Res. 1199, 28 Sept. 1998, SC Res. 1203, 24 Oct. 1999.

[112] See N.D. White, 'Self-Defence, Security Council Authority and Iraq', in R. Burchill, N.D. White and J. Morris (eds), *International Conflict and Security Law* (Cambridge: Cambridge University Press, 2005) 235 at 236–40.

9/11 as regards their campaign in Afghanistan. For instance, on 8 October 2001, the day after force was used by the United States and the United Kingdom in Afghanistan, Prime Minister Tony Blair declared that 'we will see this struggle through to the end and to the victory that would mark the victory not of revenge but of justice over the evil of terrorism'.[113] The British involvement in Afghanistan will be considered in more detail in chapter eight below.

In the case of Iraq in 2003, Iraq's failure to fulfil the disarmament agenda set by the Security Council in 1991,[114] frustrated the US and the UK to the extent that they intervened ostensibly on the basis of this failure. Ultimately as shall be seen in chapter ten the British justifications for the invasion of Iraq were based on an interpretation of Security Council resolutions.[115] Furthermore, just war rhetoric was less evident and even less convincing in the invasion of Iraq, though before the invasion President Bush did try to link the proposed action to the war on terrorism and the idea of defending the nation:

The danger is clear. Using chemical, biological or, one day, nuclear weapons obtained with the help of Iraq, the terrorists could fulfil their stated ambitions and kill thousands or hundreds of thousands of innocent people in our country or any other.[116]

Again the rhetoric is wider than the formal rules on the use of force, where defence is only allowed in response to an armed attack, and it is wider than the customary law of self-defence said to be contained in the *Caroline* incident of 1837, which permits defensive force in response to an imminent attack. While the current consensus seems to be that the *Caroline* incident still represents (or has come to represent) good law, the doctrine of pre-emption found in American claims has not been accepted.[117] The issue of whether the British and American action in Iraq has contributed to the stretching of the two exceptions to the ban on the use of force—namely the right of self-defence, and the right to use force under the authority of the Security Council—will be considered in greater detail in chapter ten.

Interestingly, as with the unpopular Suez campaign of 1956, the current military operations in Afghanistan and Iraq have come under criticism from senior military commanders as well as politicians, not only in terms of the clarity of the aims of the operations, but also in terms of the pressure placed on the armed forces caused by overstretch. As well as significant military presences in Iraq and Afghanistan in 2008, British troops are deployed to a number of countries including Cyprus, the Falklands, and Kosovo. Charges that the troops are under-equipped for the job have been combined with even more serious allegations that the unwritten covenant that binds soldiers to the country is in danger of being

---

[113] *Hansard* HC vol 372, col 814, 8 Oct. 2001 (Blair).
[114] SC Res. 687, 3 April 1991.
[115] SC Res. 678, 29 Nov. 1990; SC Res. 687, 3 April 1991; SC Res. 1441, 8 Nov. 2002.
[116] <http://news.bbc.co.uk/1/hi/world/middle_east/2948068.stm> (accessed 26 Jan. 2009).
[117] E. Wilmshurst, 'The Chatham House Principles of International Law on the Use of Force in Self-Defence' (2006) 55 ICLQ 963.

breached. The covenant has been 'codified' (in the sense of being written down) in an army publication in 2000, which explains that 'the Military Covenant is the mutual obligation between the Nation, the Army and each individual soldier; an unbreakable common bond of identity, loyalty and responsibility which has sustained the Army throughout its history'. More specifically it states that in return for the personal sacrifices made by soldiers, including the ultimate sacrifice, 'British soldiers must always be able to expect fair treatment, to be valued and respected as individuals, and that they (and their families) will be sustained and rewarded by commensurate terms and conditions of service'.[118]

While not legally binding, the fact that senior politicians and military commanders view that covenant under threat seriously undermines the legitimacy of existing and any further controversial deployments of troops to conflict and post-conflict zones. For example, in March 2008 the leader of the Conservative Party, David Cameron, declared that the military covenant had been broken in particular by the poor treatment of the wounded;[119] in July 2008, General Sir Richard Dannatt, the head of the British Army, described the covenant as out of balance caused by lack of resources;[120] and in September 2008 Sir Menzies Campbell of the Liberal Democrats stated that the operational strain placed on the forces in recent years had breached the covenant.[121]

12. Conclusion

The purpose of this chapter is to show that in the most recent period of history around the turn of the twenty-first century we are seeing liberal democratic countries willing to use force in circumstances that are not reconcilable with the rules contained in the UN Charter. This does not simply represent a continuation of the Cold War approach of the superpowers who tended to disingenuously state that they were operating within the bounds of international law, while at the same time putting power above the law. Rather it represents a concerted attempt by these countries to develop the recognized exceptions as well as additional exceptions to the ban on the use of force. The British government, though, has something of a track record of attempting to develop the law in this area. Sometimes its approach is viewed as a breach of international law as in the Corfu Channel incident in 1946 and ten years later in the disastrous Suez campaign, and sometimes it is seen as a development of the law as with the idea that the Security Council can simply authorize volunteer states to undertake military

---

[118] <http://www.army.mod.uk/join/terms/3111.aspx> (accessed 26 Jan. 2009).
[119] <http://news.bbc.co.uk/1/hi/uk_politics/7276924.stm>, 4 March 2008 (accessed 26 Jan. 2009).
[120] <http://news.bbc.co.uk/1/hi/uk/7510490.stm>, 17 July 2008 (accessed 26 Jan. 2009).
[121] <http://news.bbc.co.uk/1/hi/uk_politics/7636990.stm>, 26 Sept. 2008 (accessed 26 Jan. 2009).

action under its authority, as shown by the Korean War (reviewed more fully in chapter four) and the Beira Patrol. It remains to be seen whether the just war rhetoric behind the Kosovo and Afghan campaigns, and the technical arguments about breach of Security Council resolutions relayed by Britain in the Iraq war of 2003, have become, or will become, part of a growing lexicon of legitimate uses of force in international relations.

However, the lessons of history drawn from earlier British practice show that there are a number of significant hurdles that have to be overcome to develop a legal doctrine that is not simply a clear application of the rules contained in the UN Charter. The first is legal and found in the nature of the rules themselves. As peremptory rules or *jus cogens* these rules reflect the basic values of the international system as created in 1945. The rule prohibiting the use of force has been fought for by leaders, politicians, states and many other interest groups and individuals over the centuries. Its embodiment in the UN Charter represented the climax of that struggle and it is something that will not be given up easily. For a start, world opinion must come behind any attempted change to the rules.

Political, military and general public opinion also form political obstacles to the legitimacy of military operations that have a controversial pedigree. A British government will struggle, as happened in the Suez Crisis of 1956, to maintain a military campaign unless it has the support of the opposition and the general public as well as its own party. While the government of the day might be able to win narrow votes in parliament in the short-term, the longer-term consequences for its credibility and its electability will be serious if it continues to prosecute an unpopular war. Admittedly, there is no direct correlation between the illegality of a war and its unpopularity, but it is apparent that while politicians and the public will generally support a war that is in defence of the nation, or in furtherance of clearly stated universal values, wars that fall short of these requirements will usually be unpopular.

Thus it is argued the axioms of international law try to reflect in their admittedly imperfect way the values of the international community. There may be hard cases, where the laws seemed to prevent the achievement of justice, when opinion might either lead to a change in the law or a recognition that such cases do not necessarily make good law in the sense of establishing clear general rules for the future. These are issues that we will come back to in chapters four to ten when considering the main post-1945 instances of the use of force by the UK. Before that, though, it is necessary to consider the British attitude towards the international organizations which it helped establish in order to provide for international peace and security in the aftermath of the Second World War.

3

Between Idealism and Realism: Britain, the UN, and NATO

1. Introduction

Since 1945, the UK government's decisions to deploy troops have increasingly been made within international institutional frameworks. The UK, as a permanent member of the UN Security Council, and as an original party to the NATO Treaty of 1949, is both a member of a deficient—arguably idealist—global security system (the UN), and party to a discretionary realist regional defence alliance (NATO) that has its historical roots in the nineteenth century balance of power system. The end of the Cold War saw both the re-vitalization of the UN system and the reinvention of NATO, so that both organizations now claim to operate within similar legal and political contexts. The changing functions of both organizations and Britain's role within them will be the key features of this chapter, in that they are essential for understanding the decisions to go to war or to deploy troops under international authority.

2. Britain and the Creation of the UN

During the early years of the Second World War, there were some intriguing debates in parliament relating to the idea of international organization, as the number and coordination of the Allies increased and improved. In 1941, the British government expressed satisfaction at the way the then nine Allies were working to fight Germany, but rejected the idea that a Joint Allied Council was necessary, dismissing the idea as an issue of method. The questioner responded by rhetorically asking 'is there not a further question beyond that of method, the question of an international symbol—so many nations working together for a common object?'[1] Later in that year, the Prime Minister, Winston Churchill,

---

[1] *Hansard* HC vol 371, cols 827–8, 7 May 1941 (Mander).

spoke about a joint British and American declaration, known as the Atlantic Charter, made by the Prime Minister and President Roosevelt, the purpose of which (as reflected in the preamble) was to 'make known certain common principles in the national policies of our respective countries on which they base their hopes for a better future'.

The Atlantic Charter was made on 14 August 1941 a few months before the United States was to enter the Second World War. It contained the two leaders' vision for the post-war world. The principles included the right of peoples to self-government, increased economic collaboration, economic advancement and social security; issues which would require a high degree of collaboration. Furthermore, the abandonment of the use of force was declared as the final principle, which was accompanied by the statement that 'pending the establishment of a wider and permanent system of general security', the disarmament of potential aggressors would be necessary.

There was no real mention in the Atlantic Charter of any new institution or international legal order, though it was suggested in the debate. One member, Seymour Cocks, Labour MP for Broxtowe, said that there was a need for a 'new order' after the war aims of the Allies had been achieved and the peace aims had been formulated, on the basis that 'this is no ordinary war, and the settlement must not be an ordinary one either'. He stated that the 'design of the temple of peace depended on the area of ground cleared for its erection, as well as upon the materials available for its building'. However, he did suggest that 'nations should be bound in some federation, or political union, or in several federations, closer in texture than anything contemplated in the Covenant of the League of Nations'.[2] Most contributors to the debate though were concerned with the immediate plight of the Soviet Union, under attack from Nazi Germany. The Prime Minister himself concentrated on the more traditional principles contained in the Atlantic Charter designed to achieve the 'restoration of the sovereignty, self-government and national life of the States and nations now under the Nazi yoke'.[3]

By January 1942 it was reported to the House of Commons that twenty-six nations had accepted the principles of the Atlantic Charter,[4] in fact a later brief explanation to the House made it clear that the representatives of those nations had gathered in Washington on 1 January 1942 to sign the 'Declaration by the United Nations'.[5] In adhering to the Atlantic Charter principles and pledging to use their resources to defeat the Axis Powers, these states were 'convinced that complete victory over their enemies is essential to defend life, liberty, independence and religious freedom and to preserve human rights and justice in their own lands as well as in other lands'. The grim reality of nations united in a common war effort seemed a long way from the prospect of a global security organization,

[2] *Hansard* HC vol 374, cols 130–1, 9 Sept. 1941 (Cocks).
[3] Ibid., col 69 (Churchill).
[4] *Hansard* HC vol 377, col 83, 8 Jan. 1942 (Attlee).
[5] *Hansard* HC vol 377, col 241, 20 Jan. 1942 (Law).

but the seeds had been sown. Interestingly, the Foreign Secretary, Anthony Eden, was soon referring to the 'establishment of the United Nations', which signified that the Allied aims could not be declared by any one state.[6] The idea of a collective approach had taken hold, and in the aftermath of Allied victories in North Africa in November 1942, King George VI spoke to both the Houses, stating that 'the declaration of the United Nations endorsing the principles of the Atlantic Charter provides a foundation on which international society can be built after the war', mentioning that his government had entered into consultations with the governments of the United Nations about post-war reconstruction.[7] Government ministers were soon mentioning a 'future world organisation'.[8]

A year later following the Tehran Conference ending on 1 December 1943 between Stalin, Roosevelt, and Churchill, there appeared to be no further development in planning the peace, at least none such was evident from the conference declaration which was mainly concerned with the prosecution of the war. There was recognition of a responsibility on the three governments and the United Nations to make a peace that would 'banish the scourge and terror of war for generations'. In the House, although the Foreign Secretary declared that the foundations of peace had been laid at Tehran, there was no indication of any detail. There were calls for more concrete planning for 'a new chapter of permanent international co-operation', and criticisms of the 'lack of [any] pattern' emerging from the series of conferences between the Big Three, which culminated with Tehran.[9] The fact that the whole of the United Nations had not been involved in the discussions was also pointed to, in an echo of the criticisms that are often levelled at the permanent members of the Security Council today.[10]

In response to parliamentary pressure to reveal the plans for world peace, Prime Minister Churchill was moved to make the following statement in May 1944:

Scarred and armed with experience we intend to take better measures this time than could ever previously have been conceived in order to prevent a renewal, in the lifetime of our children or grandchildren at least, of the horrible destruction of human values which has marked the last and present world wars. We intend to set up a world order and organisations, equipped with all the necessary attributes of power, in order to prevent the breaking out of future wars, or the long planning of them in advance, by restless and ambitious nations. For this purpose there must be a World Council, a controlling Council, comprising the greatest States which emerge victorious from this war, who will be obligated to keep in being a certain minimum standard of armaments for the purpose of preserving peace. There must be a World Assembly of all Powers, whose relation to the world Executive . . . for the purpose of maintaining peace I am in no position to define.[11]

6 *Hansard* HC vol 377, col 326, 21 Jan. 1942 (Eden).
7 *Hansard* HC vol 385, cols 6–7, 11 Nov. 1942.
8 *Hansard* HC vol 385, col 156, 12 Nov. 1942 (Law).
9 *Hansard* HC vol 395, col 1442, 1495, 14 Dec. 1942 (Greenwood, Thomas).
10 *Hansard* HC vol 397, col 789, 22 Feb. 1944 (Guest).
11 *Hansard* HC vol 400, col 784, 24 May 1944 (Churchill).

Churchill declared that this new world order 'must be based upon a reign of law which upholds the principles of justice and fair play and which protects the weak against the strong if the weak have justice on their side'. In order to deter aggressors 'we must arm our world organisation and make sure that, within the limits assigned to it, it has overwhelming military power'. He saw no incompatibility between existing relationships and arrangements such as the Commonwealth and the special relationship with the United States, as well as 'the conception of a Europe truly united', and the world organization.[12] Yet major enduring tensions in the post-1945 world order are between unilateralism (or bilateralism in the case of the invasion of Iraq in 2003) and multilateralism; and between universalism and regionalism, as shown in the uncertain legal basis of the NATO bombing of Serbia over Kosovo in 1999. There was some scepticism in the House in 1944 when one speaker warned against 'paper theorising'. He went on to state that a 'great deal of harm can be done by beautiful paper constitutions, for which there is no backing in reality'.[13]

There was a high degree of realism in the negotiations leading up to the San Francisco Conference where the UN Charter was adopted in June 1945. Meetings between the major powers characterized the process of negotiation that led to the San Francisco Conference in 1945 at which over forty nations were present. A first draft of what was to become the UN Charter was negotiated by the US, UK, and the USSR, plus the Republic of China, at Dumbarton Oaks in August and October 1944. The detailed proposals for a general international organization as well as the basic principles that would govern post-war international relations adopted at Dumbarton Oaks included the prohibition on the threat or use of force, a re-affirmation of the sovereign equality of states, a weak General Assembly and Economic and Social Council, an International Court of Justice based on the Permanent Court of International Justice (and therefore based on the need for the consent of both parties), and a powerful Security Council with the competence to impose sanctions, and to take military action to maintain or restore international peace and security. It also included a provision for the Security Council to authorize any enforcement action by regional arrangements. The Security Council would have eleven members including five permanent members. The right of veto was refined at the Yalta Conference in February 1945, after a series of exchanges between the Soviet Union and the United States,[14] at which Stalin, Churchill, and Roosevelt agreed on the formulation that is now contained in article 27(3) of the UN Charter, including the need to have the 'concurring votes of the permanent members', for all important resolutions of the Security Council.

In fact, as related by Paul Kennedy, most of the key provisions of the Charter were drafted by 'American, British and Soviet policy makers' in 1944–5 who

---

[12] Ibid., cols 784–6 (Churchill). [13] Ibid., col 802 (Thomas).
[14] S.C. Schlesinger, *Act of Creation: The Founding of the United Nations* (Boulder: Westview, 2003) 55–7.

were 'intent upon fashioning the world order' not on the basis of 'flaccid well-meaning declarations that, they suspected, had given the League of Nations such weak legs', but on the basis that the 'new security system had to have teeth'.[15] The Foreign Secretary, Anthony Eden, made this clear in the House of Commons in May 1944 when he stated that the 'responsibility in any future world organisa-tion must be related to power, and consequently the world organisation should be constructed around the four great Powers'—the United States, the Soviet Union, Britain, and China.[16] There was very little discussion of the Dumbarton Oaks proposals in the House of Commons during the period of their negotiation, despite the Prime Minister and Foreign Secretary being asked questions about them.[17] The Deputy Prime Minister, Clement Attlee, defended the government from criticism about its reluctance to reveal any details of post-war institutions by stating in January 1945 that the 'foreign policy of this Government is not a matter that is left to the impulse of the Prime Minister or to the sole discre-tion of a Foreign Secretary. These matters are debated and discussed very fully in Cabinet'.[18] It was in February 1945 that the Prime Minister outlined to parlia-ment the Dumbarton Oaks proposals as modified by the Yalta agreement. From his speech it was clear that the sticking issue, and one that probably prevented greater openness in parliament, had been the voting procedures in the Security Council. Without explaining the content of the agreement reached at Yalta, he justified the voting arrangements by saying:

It is on the Great Powers that the chief burden of maintaining peace and security will fall. The new world organisation must take into account this special responsibility of the Great Powers, and so must be framed as not to compromise their unity or their cap-acity for effective action if it is called for at short notice. At the same time, the world organisation cannot be based upon a dictatorship of the Great Powers. It is their duty to serve the world and not to rule it. We trust that the voting procedure on which we agreed at Yalta meets these two essential points and provides a system which is fair and acceptable . . . [19]

The vision of a Council united in effective action with each permanent member under a duty to serve seems a long way from the veto-ridden inactive Cold War body, and even the selective, sometimes effective post-Cold War body. The truth is that the introduction of the veto was more likely to lead to the Council being a forum for diplomacy rather than one for action.[20]

---

[15] P. Kennedy, *The Parliament of Man: The Past, Present and Future of the United Nations* (Toronto: HarperCollins, 2006) 27.

[16] *Hansard* HC vol 400, col 1055, 25 May 1944 (Eden).

[17] *Hansard* HC vol 403, cols 24–5, 26 Sept. 1944 (Churchill); vol 403, cols 213–4, 27 Sept. 1944 (Eden). See also debate of 17 April 1945, vol 410, col 127.

[18] *Hansard* HC vol 407, col 488, 18 Jan. 1945 (Attlee).

[19] *Hansard* HC vol 408, col 1272, 27 Feb. 1945 (Churchill).

[20] I.L. Claude, 'The Security Council', in E. Luard (ed), *The Evolution of International Organizations* (London: Thames and Hudson, 1966) 68 at 72.

On 26 June 1945 the UK became an original signatory at San Francisco to the UN Charter. Indeed, along with the Soviet Union, the United States, and China, it was one of the sponsoring powers at the conference, attended by forty-six other states. The UK was a major force in the drafting of the Charter, during which there emerged different visions for collective security arrangements. Prime Minister Winston Churchill supported greater regionalism within a universal framework. His belief was that 'it was only the countries whose interests were directly affected by a dispute [that] could be expected to apply themselves with sufficient vigour to secure a settlement'. He envisaged three regional Councils, but he also emphasized that 'the last word would remain with the Supreme World Council'.[21] Although there was no recognition of specific regional structures in the Charter, a relationship between regionalism and universalism was built into chapter VIII of that treaty, with the UN Security Council having ultimate authority over enforcement action.[22] This limitation on regional autonomy has been tested on many occasions, possibly most significantly by the NATO bombing of the Federal Republic of Yugoslavia in 1999. Britain's involvement in the NATO operation will receive separate analysis in chapter nine; suffice it to say at this juncture that on occasions Britain has regretted tying the right to take military enforcement action to the Security Council.

3. Britain and the Veto

The right of veto had its genesis in the desire to prevent the permanent members from being the potential objects of collective measures. However, article 27(3) was drafted on a much wider basis after the Yalta Conference of 1945. It was clear after Yalta that great power unity was destined to be an unachieved ideal with the veto extending beyond the enforcement provisions of chapter VII, to chapter VI, which granted the Council general, recommendatory powers for pacific settlement, unless one of the permanent members was a party to the dispute.

Indeed, the Yalta formula, presented to the San Francisco conference in explanation of the right of veto, illustrated the permanent members' desire to leave no loopholes to prevent their use of the veto. The Yalta formula introduced the prospect of the 'double veto', which meant that any decision regarding the 'preliminary question' as to whether a proposed resolution was important enough to be subject to the veto required the 'concurring votes of the permanent members'.[23]

However, the smaller powers' objections at San Francisco were not directed at the double veto, but at the 'chain of events' theory outlined in the Yalta formula.

---

[21] R.B. Russell and J.B. Muther, *A History of the United Nations Charter* (Washington: Brookings Institute, 1958) 107. See further G.L. Goodwin, *Britain and the United Nations* (Oxford: Oxford University Press, 1957) 10–11.

[22] Art 53 of the UN Charter.

[23] UN Conference on International Organization (UNCIO), vol 11, 713.

The smaller powers demanded that the veto should be confined to questions concerning enforcement action. The Australian delegate argued that 'the Council has the duty rather than a right to conciliate disputants' and that it was essential that no member should have the right to veto resolutions aimed solely at pacific settlement of disputes.[24] The major powers stuck to the somewhat fallacious argument presented in the Yalta formula that any pacific measures 'may initiate a chain of events which might in the end require the Council under its responsibilities to invoke measures of enforcement'.[25] It might well be that such a chain of events could occur, but it did not appear necessary to allow the veto to occur at the pacific settlement stage as long as the permanent members could operate it at the enforcement stage. The 'chain of events' theory was, in reality, a mechanism whereby the whole field of Council action would be the subject of the veto. The smaller powers continued to object, but it became clear that an expansive right of veto would have to be accepted as the 'Big Five decided to let it be known that unless the voting provision was accepted, there would be no Organisation'.[26] It was no longer a question of preserving great power unanimity but of preserving the organization.

The applicability of the double veto and the chain of events theory peppered exchanges in the Council during its first decade. These have been thoroughly reviewed elsewhere.[27] Such debates petered out in the face of the permanent members developing a practice which enabled them to use the veto to defeat any sort of proposal under chapter VI or chapter VII, unless it was clearly procedural.

In accordance with UK constitutional practice,[28] the UN Charter was presented to the House of Commons for approval on 22 August 1945. In introducing it to the House, Prime Minister Attlee stated that 'the Charter was voted and discussed in accordance with the best traditions of democracy'.[29] It was clear that he was referring to the debates between states at the drafting conference at San Francisco earlier that year, not the debate he was opening in parliament where formal approval for ratification was sought and duly granted.[30] The Prime Minister outlined the 'outstanding points' of the Charter. First, the position of the great powers in the Charter was 'commensurate with their importance and with the responsibilities they had to assume', and that the smaller states had accepted the veto in a Charter that 'corresponded to the realities of the situation that exists in the world to-day'. Remarkably, in anticipation of the more expansive powers of the Council witnessed since the end of the Cold War during which it has acted not simply as an executive body but also in a legislative sense, the Prime Minister

[24] H.V. Evatt, *The United Nations* (London: Oxford University Press, 1948) 53.
[25] UNCIO, vol 11, 714.
[26] Russell and Muther, *A History of the United Nations Charter*, 766.
[27] S.D. Bailey, *Voting in the Security Council* (Oxford: Clarendon, 1969) 18–25, 33–7.
[28] Lord Lester and D. Oliver, *Constitutional Law and Human Rights* (London: Butterworths, 1997) 466.
[29] *Hansard* HC vol 413, col 660, 22 Aug. 1945 (Attlee).   [30] Ibid., col 950.

stated that the 'British delegation took a foremost part in seeking to make the Security Council something more than a policeman' who is called in when there is already a danger of a breach of the peace.

We sought, and sought successfully, to make it a place where the policies of the States, and especially the greater States, could be discussed and reconsidered for the time, especially when they showed signs of such divergencies as to threaten the harmony of international relations. Collective security is not merely a promise to act when an emergency occurs, but it is active co-operation to prevent emergencies occurring.[31]

It is clear from this that the British government had realized that the idea of collective security as embodied in the UN Charter was much wider than the balance of power system that had dominated much of international relations in the eighteenth and nineteenth centuries. Though he did not point to any Charter provisions, the fact that the Security Council was 'organized so as to be able to function continuously', and could address disputes and situations that were 'likely to endanger the maintenance of international peace and security' under chapter VI of the Charter (dealing with the pacific settlement of disputes), and threats to the peace under chapter VII of the Charter (providing for action with respect to such threats or breaches of the peace),[32] gave support to the Prime Minister's contention, even though today it is sometimes still argued that the Council cannot step beyond an executive role.[33]

The Prime Minister stressed that the General Assembly would be of 'immense value in focusing public opinion on the great issues that arise between nations'. Attlee was also prescient in anticipating the flexibility in the Charter stating that 'the success of the new organisation will not depend so much on the exact provisions' of the treaty 'as on the spirit in which they are worked'. This was made even more so by the wide purposes and principles upon which the UN was founded in comparison to the more limited version in the Dumbarton Oaks proposals; even the principle of non-intervention by the UN was qualified to allow for Security Council enforcement action.[34] In any case Attlee declared that there could be no doubt 'that the kind of treatment that was meted out by Hitler and the Nazis to the Jews is a matter that far transcends a question of mere domestic jurisdiction',[35] thus anticipating collective humanitarian action by the UN, and more controversially by others.

As for a definition of collective security, Anthony Eden, who had negotiated at San Francisco as Foreign Secretary, but who spoke in the House as Deputy Leader of the opposition after Labour's 1945 victory, described it as a method 'under which most of the nations of the world would band themselves together

---

[31] Ibid., cols 659–63 (Attlee).   [32] Arts 28(1), 34, 39 of the UN Charter.
[33] See for example M. Happold, 'Security Council Resolution 1373 and the Constitution of the United Nations' (2003) 16 LJIL 593.
[34] Art 2(7) of the UN Charter.
[35] *Hansard* HC vol 413, cols 663–6, 22 Aug. 1945 (Attlee).

and would have sufficient power to prevent any nation that wished to disrupt the peace, or any other nation that wished to work with it, from being successful'. He also decried any criticism of the Charter as a product of big power diplomacy saying that each provision was discussed in commissions or committees and that every item had to be carried by two-thirds majority—'if . . . there was ever an international document which represented the consensus of opinion of nations in conference, I claim this Charter is in fact such a document'.[36] While this appears to have vastly downplayed the influence of the major powers on the Charter, the fact is that the document has lasted, and has maintained its position as the most important treaty—some would argue international constitution[37]—of the international community. While MPs welcomed the Charter and approved without dissent its ratification,[38] a number were critical of the veto. For instance, Evan Durbin, Labour MP for Edmonton, spoke in the following terms:

Yet all this powerful apparatus of force, all this machinery of coercion, more ambitious than anything ever conceived in the League of Nations, rests upon the extremely insecure foundation of unanimity amongst the great Powers—the permanent members of the Security Council.[39]

Others though were more concerned with the threats that would arise out of the extreme poverty many countries were experiencing in the immediate postwar period, but above all with the threat of the atomic bomb, the destructive power of which had been witnessed a few weeks earlier in Japan. Above all a number of speakers warned that the idealism of the Charter as expressed in the preamble, which flew in the face of a state-based system of international relations in declaring 'we the peoples of the United Nations determined to save succeeding generations from the scourge of war', was going to have to be balanced against the realism of a world dominated by those powerful states possessing the most destructive weapons known to mankind.[40]

By October 1946 the tide of realism had risen to the extent that Prime Minister Attlee declared that:

At San Francisco we agreed to the creation of the veto, but I am quite certain that we all regarded this as something to be used only in the last resort in extreme cases where the five Great Powers might be involved in conflict. We never perceived it as a device to be used constantly whenever a particular power was not in full agreement with the others. Yet that is what has happened recently. The veto was used for very trifling things and that is reducing to a nullity the usefulness of the Security Council. What is more it is leading to disrespect, whereas the Security Council was created in order to create confidence, to

    [36] Ibid., cols 674–9 (Eden).
    [37] C. Tomuschat (ed), *The United Nations at Fifty: A Legal Perspective* (The Hague: Kluwer, 1995) ix.
    [38] *Hansard* HC vol 413, col 950, 23 Aug. 1945 (Bevin).
    [39] *Hansard* HC vol 413, col 708, 22 Aug. 1945 (Durbin).
    [40] See for example *Hansard* HC vol 413, col 872 (Beamish) and cols 890–1 (Davies), 23 Aug. 1945.

command confidence as a quasi-judicial body in matters of differences between States which involved the danger of war.[41]

By this time the Soviet Union had used its veto in the Security Council seven times and France once. But in the first ten years of the UN's existence, the Soviet Union used its veto on forty-two occasions, France used it twice, and China once.[42] While the UN was western dominated in this period, the defensive use of the veto by the Soviet Union to block applications for membership, but also to stop any progress being made on difficult issues such as the remaining Fascist regime in Spain and the Greek civil war, seriously undermined the credibility of the Security Council, as predicted by the Prime Minister. Such arguments still plague the Security Council after the end of the period of the superpower veto (1945–89), because although the veto is no longer regularly cast, it still shapes all negotiations in the Council, leading to a collective security system that while more active, is inevitably inconsistent and selective.

In 1946 the Prime Minister bemoaned the failure of the Military Staff Committee, and by implication the demise of any binding agreements on the provision of troops to the UN as required by article 43 of the UN Charter. It is interesting to note that the enabling legislation adopted by the UK Parliament (the United Nations Act of 1946) was a limited statute enabling effect to be given to non-forcible measures ordered by the Security Council under article 41 of the UN Charter. In effect this represented the only practical intrusion into British sovereignty; that non-forcible measures should bind individuals and companies and require them not to trade with states targeted by Security Council sanctions. British freedom of action on decisions to deploy troops was in effect unimpaired by the UN Charter. As shall be seen in the next chapter it became accepted practice that decisions to deploy troops under Security Council mandated operations were to be made by the government on the basis of political, military, moral, and legal considerations, but those legal considerations would not include any international *obligation* to contribute troops to the operation.

Though there were plenty of questions in the first decade in the House of Commons about reform of the UN Charter by means of a review conference,[43] it was not until 1965 that there was any significant change of the United Nations, with the Security Council being increased from eleven to fifteen members, in effect from 1 January 1966. There was no debate on this matter in the House of Commons, it being made clear on a number of occasions that there would be no reform of the veto.[44]

---

[41] *Hansard* HC vol 427, col 1674, 23 Oct. 1946 (Attlee).
[42] S.D. Bailey and S. Daws, *The Procedure of the UN Security Council* (3rd edn, Oxford: Clarendon Press, 1998) 231–2.
[43] As provided by art 109(3) of the UN Charter. See for example *Hansard* HC vol 561, col 1005, 3 Dec. 1956 (Rippon).
[44] See for example *Hansard* HC vol 717, col 1031, 2 Aug. 1965 (Thomson); *Hansard* HC vol 741, col 203w, 20 Feb. 1967 (Thomson).

4. Britain, the UN, and Collective Security

Britain's record at the UN has been fashioned by its permanent seat in the Security Council, and, within the context of a reform debate re-started in the UN in the 1990s, its express desire to maintain that status despite its world position as a middle ranking power. The reform debate has stalled over the issue of the size and composition of any new executive body, and the inevitable disagreements about the value of the veto.[45] The fact that the permanent members control the reform debate, and that any amendment to the Charter must be agreed to by all these members,[46] makes any drastic changes to the veto, or to those states that hold it, very unlikely. In 2004 the British government made its position on the veto clear. The government was asked 'whether they will review the criteria governing the use of veto power by the permanent members of the United Nations Security Council; and whether they consider that these criteria should be re-defined and narrowed'. The government responded that there were 'no criteria governing the use of the veto', though 'the UK encourages all permanent members of the Security Council to use the veto with restraint and only in accordance with the values of the United Nations'. The government noted that the UK had not used the veto since 1989 and stated that any formal change to the scope of the application of it would require an amendment to the Charter, something that that government would not be pursuing.[47] This rather benign picture of the veto, as something rarely used in the modern era, and then only used responsibly, paints over the many possibilities that might have been explored further by the Security Council if it were not for the fact that they were threatened with the veto. The public use of the veto during the Cold War has been replaced by private debate that is still shaped by the veto. Britain values its permanent membership and the power this gives it to block any actions, though it has tried to justify its status as one of the five privileged members of the Council.

An example of Britain's perception of the duties of permanent membership is drawn from the crisis in the Great Lakes region of Africa in the mid-1990s, in the aftermath of the Rwandan genocide of 1994. In 1996 the Security Council had authorized a coalition of the willing built around Canadian and British contingents to intervene in the humanitarian and refugee crisis in eastern Zaire.[48] In a Commons debate, faced with questions about British military involvement in a country far from British shores, the Conservative Defence Secretary, Michael Portillo stated:

---

[45] See Y. Blum, 'Proposals for UN Security Council Reform' (2005) 99 AJIL 632; B. Fassbender, 'All Illusions Shattered? Looking Back on a Decade of Failed Attempts to Reform the UN Security Council' (2003) 7 MPYBUNL 183; J. Morris, 'UN Security Council Reform: A Counsel for the 21st Century' (2000) 31(3) Security Dialogue 265.

[46] Arts 108, 109(2) UN Charter.   [47] *Hansard* HL vol 657, col 72w, 2 Feb. 2004.

[48] SC Res. 1078, 9 Nov. 1996.

The House will rightly ask why Britain should become involved in a place far from our country and where no vital interest is engaged. It is because we are a civilized nation. We can see that people are about to die in their thousands, and we are one of the few nations on earth that has the military capability to help at least some of them. We recognise our humanitarian obligation. We take pride in our permanent membership of the United Nations Security Council, but it carries with it clear duties. Some of our leading allies in NATO are willing to assist, and our place is with them.[49]

In fact the force was not deployed following a decision of the contributing states that the crisis had receded, illustrating the level of control that states have over their deployments under UN mandates.

The operation in Zaire would have been a chapter VII military operation with robust rules of engagement, in contrast to the consensual peacekeeping operations under the UNEF I model (created in the aftermath of the Suez Crisis of 1956). Such blue-helmeted peacekeeping operations normally have more restricted rules of engagement, centred around defence of the force. The UK has not, until recently, been a significant contributor to consensual peacekeeping operations, although ironically, it was the French and British flawed military action in Suez that precipitated the development of such forces. The British and French vetoes in the Security Council did not prevent the invocation of the Uniting for Peace procedure transferring the matter to the General Assembly,[50] where UNEF I was duly authorized.[51] The UK abstained on the vote on the crucial Assembly resolution establishing UNEF I, reluctantly conceding that what it called its 'police' action was to be replaced by an international one.[52]

The UK's grudging acceptance of UN peacekeeping, combined with the tacit agreement during the Cold War that largely ruled out permanent member participation in consensual peacekeeping operations, restricted UK involvement mainly to the occasional logistical support operation such as an airlift of Ghanaian troops at the beginning of the UN operation in the Congo in 1960. The one exception to this non-involvement, in the case of the UK, was in Cyprus in 1964 when intercommunal violence led to debate about the need for British intervention.

Though there was a good deal of discussion about British involvement in Cyprus there was no full debate nor any vote. The initial British position, revealed to the House of Commons in response to questions,[53] was for a joint British/Turkish/Greek 'peacemaking' force to be interposed between the two warring communities.[54] Conservative Prime Minister, Sir Alec Douglas-Home, declared the Treaty of Guarantee between Britain, Turkey, Greece, and Cyprus to be a regional arrangement under chapter VIII of the UN Charter in answering a question on the matter in the House.[55] The Foreign Secretary, Rab Butler, was

---

[49] *Hansard* HC vol 285, cols 487–9, 14 Nov. 1996 (Portillo).
[50] SC Res. 119, 31 Oct. 1956.   [51] GA Res. 998–1001 (1956).
[52] GA 563rd plen. mtg, 3 Nov. 1956, paras 292–3.
[53] *Hansard* HC vol 688, col 815, 3 Feb. 1964 (Butler).   [54] UN Doc. S/5508 (1964).
[55] *Hansard* HC vol 688, col 530, 30 Jan. 1964 (Douglas-Home)

asked by Konni Zilliacus (Labour MP for Manchester Gorton) to recognize that article 53 of the UN Charter signified that 'no international force or individual forces may be used for any purpose except defence against armed attack without the authority of the Security Council'. Butler refused to acknowledge this.[56] The proposed force also met with Soviet criticism that it constituted NATO enforcement action,[57] which combined with the desire of the Cypriot government to have a UN presence,[58] led to the UK agreeing to a UN peacekeeping force and, moreover, contributing to it.

The participation of the United Kingdom was at the time without precedent in the history of UN peacekeeping...Although the initial Charter intention had been to involve the permanent members of the Security Council in the establishment of UN forces, the path that UN peacekeeping had in fact followed (away from enforcement towards peacekeeping by consent) had led to a consistent practice of excluding them. British participation in UNFICYP had to be seen as stemming from the singular historical circumstances of the Cyprus case. Before the UN was called in British forces had, for three months, exercised powers under the Treaty of Guarantee and had sought impartially to restore peace in the island. The British Sovereign Bases on the island would clearly be also of the greatest importance to the United Nations for logistical support. Britain therefore provided some forces for the UN command.[59]

Moreover, the UK submitted its troops to UN command as noted by the Secretary General when establishing the Force. 'The Force is under the exclusive command of the United Nations at all times. The Commander of the Force is appointed by and exclusively responsible to the Secretary General. The contingents comprising the Force are integral parts of it and take their orders exclusively from the Force Commander'.[60]

The Cold War limited UK involvement in peacekeeping. The post-Cold War period is characterized by an increased level of UK contributions to observation, monitoring and traditional peacekeeping, as well as more widely drawn peace operations with a peacebuilding element. Generally, consensual peacekeeping operations consisted of contributing states' military contingents under UN command and control—specifically the Secretary General acting under delegated authority from the Security Council, exceptionally the General Assembly. This should be contrasted with the enforcement model that emerged out of chapter VII of the Charter under which a coalition of the willing is authorized by the

---

[56] *Hansard* HC vol 688, col 816, 3 Feb. 1964 (Zilliacus). See also vol 689, cols 11–12, 10 Feb. 1964 (Zilliacus).

[57] See letter from Khrushchev to the Prime Minister Douglas-Home produced in Written Answers in the House of Commons: *Hansard* HC vol 690, col 108w, 13 Feb. 1964.

[58] UN Doc. S/5488 (1963). SC 1095th mtg, 18 Feb. 1964.

[59] R. Higgins, *United Nations Peacekeeping: Documents and Commentary: Volume 4 Europe 1946–1979* (Oxford: Oxford University Press, 1981) 161.

[60] UN Doc. S/5950 (1964). See also HC *Hansard* HC vol 690, col 1528w, 5 March 1964 (Thomas).

Security Council with command and control being vested in the contributing state(s) or organization.[61]

The Brahimi Report of 2000 both recognized and developed the change that had occurred in peacekeeping in the late 1990s, by using the term 'peace operation' to reflect the more typical UN operation, which combines peacekeeping and peacebuilding.[62] The UK has generally contributed only small number of troops to modern peace operations, such as UNAMSIL in Sierra Leone emplaced between 1999–2005,[63] and MONUC in the Democratic Republic of the Congo *in situ* since 1999.[64] The latter force was emplaced in a civil war situation that had claimed a minimum of two million lives, a situation in which MONUC struggled to uphold the 1999 Lusaka Peace Accords, though elections were eventually successfully held in 2006. From a limited force of 5,500 with a limited mandate,[65] MONUC was built into a more effective peace operation of nearly 17,000 with a broader chapter VII mandate to deter violence and protect civilians.[66]

The UK has also been at the forefront of contributions to several UN authorized enforcement operations both to combat aggression and to enforce international mandates—principally Korea (1950), the Gulf (1991), the aborted mission in Zaire (1996), IFOR/SFOR/EUFOR in Bosnia (1995–), KFOR in Kosovo (1999–), and the multi-national force sent to East Timor in September 1999. While a number of these will be returned to in later chapters, it is interesting to note that the level of parliamentary debate and discussion regarding some of these deployments appeared to be inadequate.

When Indonesian inspired violence broke out in East Timor following the independence vote in that country in 1999, Britain contributed to the Australian-led INTERFET force deployed to the island in September 1999. The UK had previously contributed to the small UNAMET team, which organized and conducted the referendum on the independence of East Timor under a Security Council mandate;[67] notably by providing the head of mission. Despite the precarious position of the mission, there was very little parliamentary discussion of the continuing violence in the lead up to the referendum. The government simply expressed 'cause for concern' at the security situation in East Timor, and then only in a written answer in the House of Lords.[68]

The entirely predictable collapse of security that followed the referendum in East Timor of 30 August 1999 when a large majority voted for independence, eventually led to the establishment of a coalition of the willing which arrived in East Timor on 20 September 1999. The force was established under chapter VII of

---

[61] See chapter four.
[62] Report of the Panel on United Nations Peace Operations, UN Doc. A/55/305, S/2000/809, 21 Aug. 2000.
[63] SG's report, UN Doc. S/2004/965, 10 Dec. 2004.
[64] SG's report, UN Doc. S/2007/156, 20 Mar. 2007.
[65] SC Res. 1291, 24 Feb. 2000.   [66] SC Res. 1565, 1 Oct. 2004.
[67] SC Res. 1246, 11 June, 1999.   [68] *Hansard* HL vol 604, col 118w, 22 July 1999.

the UN Charter, though it also had the consent of the Indonesian government. Its main function was to secure peace and security in East Timor.[69] With the various armed groups on the island this was clearly an extremely dangerous operation.

In these circumstances it is surprising that the Labour government's decision to send 275 troops (mainly Gurkhas based in Brunei) in the first wave was subject to no discernible parliamentary scrutiny. There were written and oral questions and answers in the upper house in October and November, and in the lower house in November and December 1999. The questions and answers were perfunctory and related to the cost (£7.5m compared to over £100m for the Kosovo operation), the duration, level of contribution, and date of Gurkha withdrawal from the operation (which occurred on 8 December 1999).[70] The minimal amount of scrutiny of this operation cannot simply be explained by the much lower level of UK contribution—it was still disproportionately low. The lack of valuable parliamentary time dedicated to East Timor is more a reflection of both the lack of public concern on the issue, and also by the fact that parliament was content with the government's decision. The presence of a clear Security Council mandate, combined with the consent of the Indonesian government, may well have persuaded parliament that there was no need for the type of scrutiny achieved in the Kosovo campaign.

A contrast can be drawn with the UK's response to the escalating crisis in Sierra Leone in May 2000. The lack of a clear Security Council mandate for the Labour government's despatch of 700 troops to the country on 8 May appears to have led to a higher level of debate in parliament. The initial lack of clarity as to the function of the military operation, in particular whether it was intended to shore up the ailing UN peacekeeping operation (UNAMSIL), or whether it was merely to evacuate British nationals, led to a sharp exchange in the Commons, with the opposition making clear its objections to a wider use of the troops and claiming that the British public would only support a rescue of nationals.[71] Mission creep did occur, however, despite continued criticism in parliament.[72] With the public largely indifferent, the government's large majority again enabled it to withstand the protests of the opposition.

With chapter VII operations authorized by the UN Security Council being in essence the delegation of power to states to take military action,[73] the Security Council debates, level of Council control, and accountability of those states acting under UN authority to the Security Council, are limited.[74] This must be

---

[69] SC Res. 1264, 15 Sept. 1999.

[70] *Hansard* HL vol 605 col 127w, 21 Oct. 1999; vol 606, col 1252, 9 Nov. 1999. *Hansard* HC vol 339, col 115w, 24 Nov. 1999; vol 340, col 284w, 2 Dec. 1999.

[71] M. Evans, 'Forces Pull Out all Stops to Clear Freetown', *The Times*, 9 May 2000, 1, 4. *Hansard* HC vol 349, col 250, 8 May 2000 (Maples).

[72] *Hansard* HL vol 349, col 1890, 12 May 2000 (Attlee).

[73] D. Sarooshi, *The United Nations and the Development of Collective Security* (Oxford: Oxford University Press, 1999) 167–74.

[74] N.D. White, *Keeping the Peace: The United Nations and the Maintenance of International Peace and Security* (2nd edn, Manchester: Manchester University Press, 1997) 115–128.

contrasted with consensual UN peacekeeping forces and most peace operations where command and control is normally with the UN, and the force is kept within a more tightly controlled renewable mandate. Under the non-consensual chapter VII provisions, with no agreements arrived at under article 43 of the Charter, there is no question of the Security Council obliging member states to supply troops for military operations. Instead, as the Korean operation reviewed in chapter four established, states in essence volunteer for such operations, and command and control is vested in the states or state according to political and military considerations.

It follows that an important element in considering the legitimacy of chapter VII operations is the enabling resolution and the debate surrounding it. It is at this stage that the other members of the Security Council can challenge the legality and necessity of the proposed military action and can block it, if either a sufficient number vote against or a permanent member casts its veto. Once the resolution has been secured there is very little member states can do to halt the prosecution of the war. There is no requirement that approval be sought from the General Assembly, although the legitimacy of the operation would be increased immensely if such approval was achieved. In many of the chapter VII operations to date the General Assembly has adopted a supportive resolution, but normally only after the use of force has commenced.[75]

Parallels can be drawn between the international decision-making processes and those on the domestic stage. In the UK the executive, or rather a small part of it, makes the decisions committing British forces to combat; Cabinet and parliamentary support need only be sought after that. At UN level, the executive organ, the Security Council, or rather the P3 or P5, will make a decision on the deployment of forces, which will, unless blocked, later be endorsed by the full Security Council and then possibly by the plenary body—the General Assembly. The latter though will normally only endorse after the operation has started.[76] Lack of accountability to the more representative body seems to exist both at the international level and the domestic level. At the international level there is the possibility of veto in the executive body, which is not present at the domestic level. Increased control of the executive, both at the national and international levels may be desirable. At the moment, decisions to go to war appear to suffer from a democratic deficit. Against this must be balanced the requirements of acting quickly and effectively to deploy troops, not only in defence of the nation but in order to prevent humanitarian catastrophes in other countries.

The UK's contribution in a wider sense to military operations authorized by the UN has been considerable. In the case of UN peacekeeping this was perhaps

[75] N.D. White, 'From Korea to Kuwait: The Legal Basis of United Nations' Military Action' (1998) XX International History Review 600.

[76] For enforcement operations there is no funding issue either, since in general the operations are funded by contributing States rather than the UN. This can be contrasted with the case of UN peacekeeping.

unintended in the case of Suez in 1956. Nevertheless, the UK's contribution to observation, monitoring, traditional peacekeeping and complex peacekeeping operations has grown. This culminated in June 1999 with the Labour government signing a memorandum of understanding with the UN Secretary General, giving the UN access to rapidly deployable troops. This represented an addition to the UK's commitments under the UN standby arrangements made in 1994. However, the final decision to commit UK troops to UK operations remains with the government.[77]

In the case of enforcement action, the UK shares responsibility for the shaping of a decentralized military option in the Security Council, quite different from that intended in the Charter. Indeed, dissatisfaction with the deadlocked Security Council led to the UK sponsoring, along with other states, the Uniting for Peace resolution of 1950,[78] in which the General Assembly claimed recommendatory military enforcement powers. The UK government regretted this decision at a later date[79] (in the Suez crisis for instance), and certainly seemed to ignore the possibility of using the General Assembly for much of the Cold War period and thereafter. However, there it can strongly be argued that Uniting for Peace is still a valid legal precedent, indeed in many ways it can be argued that it simply recognized powers already possessed by the Assembly.[80] Its practical impact has been limited, though it may be argued that in extreme circumstances (arguably in the case of the NATO bombing of the FRY in 1999), it should be reactivated.[81] Surprisingly this was the conclusion of the House of Commons Foreign Affairs Select Committee in its report on the Kosovo crisis produced on 7 June 2000, considered further in chapter nine.

5. Britain and the Founding of NATO

As well as supporting a strengthened world security organization, Britain was also forcefully behind the development of a strong collective defence entity. Indeed, the formation of NATO in 1949 'was a response to the demonstrated incapacity of the United Nations to deal with the fundamental cleavage of the post-war period, and that NATO rather than the United Nations had become the hub of British foreign policy'.[82] The need for NATO was made clear in the House of Commons when in reply to a rather mischievous question as to whether

[77] See 2002 Memorandum of Understanding with the UN at <http://www.fco.gov.uk/en/newsroom/latest-news/?view=PressR&id=2030014> (accessed 6 Feb. 2009).

[78] GA Res. 377, 3 Nov. 1950.

[79] See Goodwin, *Britain and the United Nations*, 249–50.

[80] Bailey and Daws, *The Procedure of the UN Security Council*, 296. This was in essence the UK government's position when informing the House of Commons of the resolution: *Hansard* HC vol 480, cols 328–9, 5 Nov. 1950 (Davies).

[81] N.D. White, 'The Legality of Bombing in the Name of Humanity' (2000) 5 JCSL 27.

[82] Goodwin, *Britain and the United Nations*, 57.

the Soviet Union would be invited to join the proposed North Atlantic Pact, the government minister stated:

No, Sir, and for this reason. The negotiation of a North Atlantic Pact would never have been necessary had not all the attempts to organise collective security directly under the United Nations been made impossible (temporarily it is to be hoped) by the obstruction, suspicion and non-co-operation of the Soviet Government.[83]

Despite this significant shift in foreign policy, it is accurate to state that while 'the United Nations was, and is, a tribute to the ideal and NATO a response to reality, the ideal lived on',[84] in the hope that the restrictions in the UN were only temporary. Indeed the issue in the post-Cold War era is to re-define the relationship between the ideal and the real, between the UN and NATO.

The post-Second World War debate in the UK was between a Western European entity and one that involved the United States. While the Foreign Office preferred the former, which would enable Britain to play a leading 'Third Force' role, the Chiefs of Staff argued for a close military relationship with the United States in view of the already perceived post-war threat from the Soviet Union.[85] Post-war reality led to the negotiation and signing of the North Atlantic Pact in Washington on 4 April 1949.

Britain was not able to provide the resources to pursue a global strategy and at the same time back up its aspirations to play a leading role in Europe ... it gradually became clear to the Foreign Office that a much more substantial American role would be necessary to match the power of the Soviet Union. As a result the 'Third Force' idea gave way to the search for an Atlantic Alliance and a 'special relationship' with the United States.[86]

There was no opportunity to debate the proposed North Atlantic Pact in the House of Commons before the Foreign Secretary signed it in Washington on 4 April 1949.[87] The twelve original parties to the North Atlantic Treaty,[88] 'reaffirmed their faith in the purposes and principles' of the UN Charter and stated their determination to 'safeguard the freedom, common heritage and civilisations of their peoples, founded on the principles of democracy, individual liberty and the rule of law'. From this it is clear that NATO's purpose is to protect Western civilization and values from attack, not to export those values (at least by military means). Article 1 supports the principles of the UN Charter committing states to settle their disputes by peaceful means and to refrain from the

---

[83] *Hansard* HC vol 461, col 15, 7 Feb 1949 (McNeil).

[84] Goodwin, *Britain and the United Nations*, 58.

[85] J. Baylis, *The Diplomacy of Pragmatism: Britain and the Formation of NATO 1942–1950* (Basingstoke: Macmillan, 1993) 116.

[86] Ibid., 124.

[87] *Hansard* HC vol 461, col 538, 10 Feb. 1949 (Warbey); vol 462, col 1400, 10 March 1949 (Chamberlain).

[88] Belgium, Canada, Denmark, France, Iceland, Italy, Luxembourg, Netherlands, Norway, Portugal, UK, US. There are currently twenty-six state parties.

threat or use of force. Article 4 provides for consultations between the parties if any of them feels their security is threatened, and article 9 establishes the North Atlantic Council consisting of all parties to facilitate effective decision-making, though in the absence of any voting provisions, decisions must be made with the consent of all parties.

This very traditional form of consensus organization is finally reflected in the key obligation in article 5 under which each party agrees to come to the assistance of any party attacked in Europe or the North Atlantic area. In essence the North Atlantic Treaty embodies a precise contractual obligation under which each party pledges to come to the defence of an attacked state in exchange for protection and assistance if it is itself attacked. This also constitutes a promise to the attacking state or organization that NATO states will come to the aid of an attacked member. It is also interesting to see how article 5 rests very clearly on the UN Charter by stating that it is based on article 51 and further that any collective defensive measures will be reported to the Security Council and will be 'terminated when the Security Council has taken the measures necessary for the maintenance of international peace and security'.

It was not until 12 May 1949 that the House of Commons had the opportunity to debate the Treaty, when the Foreign Secretary, Ernest Bevin, moved 'that this House approves the North Atlantic Treaty signed in Washington on 4th April, 1949, relating to the promotion of stability and wellbeing in the North Atlantic area and to collective defence for the preservation of peace and security'.[89] He clearly re-stated that the need for a defensive pact was due to the failure of the Security Council because of the extensive (ab)use of the Soviet veto, and the growing threat from the Soviet Union. Further, he argued that a guarantee that NATO members would come together in defence of Western Europe and North America was needed to prevent another world war breaking out due to the calculations of an aggressor that democracies would prevaricate when faced with an attack. He denied that the NATO treaty abandoned 'the idea of world security system' by declaring that the treaty was 'fully in conformity with the United Nations'. As to the international legal basis of NATO Bevin stated:

The Treaty is not a regional arrangement under Chapter VIII of the Charter. The action which it envisages is not enforcement action in the sense of Article 53 at all. The Treaty is an arrangement between certain States for collective self-defence as foreseen by Article 51 of the Charter. It is designed to secure parties against aggression from outside until such time as the Security Council has taken the necessary measures. Enforcement action by a regional group is something quite different.[90]

The Foreign Secretary accurately analysed the position of collective self-defence pacts under the UN Charter. The right of self-defence in response to an armed

---

[89] *Hansard* HC vol 464, col 2011, 12 May 1949 (Bevin).
[90] Ibid., col 2018.

attack does not require Security Council authority, while a regional arrangement proposing to deal with a threat to the peace by taking action that is not defensive but constitutes enforcement action against a state, must gain the authorization of the Security Council under article 53. By being founded squarely on article 51 NATO retained the freedom of action inherent in the sovereign right of self-defence. That the sovereignty of the parties to the treaty was unimpaired was made clear by the Foreign Secretary at the end of his speech when he states that 'the constitutional rights of the individual Parliaments' of each state party were 'preserved' despite the obligation to come to the aid of an attacked state party.[91] By this he meant that decisions to deploy troops were still subject to the approval of each state according to their constitutions.

The pact was welcomed by the vast majority of the House in essence because it was about the defence of the nation, an issue around which people with different views can unite. As was stated by one Member: 'free peoples will unite in a war of defence, but of defence only; not in a war of aggression'.[92] The North Atlantic Treaty was approved by the House of Commons by 333 votes in favour to 6 against.[93]

6. Britain and the Evolution of NATO

While NATO arguably was fundamental in maintaining a level of global peace and security during the Cold War, its *raison-d'être*—the defence of Western Europe from Soviet attack—seemed to have been lost when the Eastern bloc collapsed and the Soviet Union disintegrated in the period 1989–91. In the instability arising out of the collapse of the Berlin Wall it was unsurprising that the British government was concerned that NATO continue to exist,[94] despite the collapse in 1991 of its mirror organization in the Eastern bloc (the Warsaw Pact). However, it became clear that NATO would have to adapt and adapt quickly to the changing circumstances. The Alliance reacted speedily enough in a meeting of heads of state and government held in Rome in November 1991, where the parties agreed to adopt a Strategic Concept to reflect the changing global conditions. This did not take the form of a new or amended treaty but was more akin to a policy document.

The 1991 Strategic Concept recognized that 'risks to Allied security' were 'less likely to result from calculated aggression against the territory of the Allies, but rather from the adverse consequences of instabilities that may arise from the serious economic, social and political difficulties, which are faced by many countries

---

[91] Ibid., col 2021.
[92] Ibid., col 2032 (Clement Davies). For criticism of the Treaty see col 2073 (Zilliacus).
[93] Ibid., col 2128. See also approval in the House of Lords: *Hansard* HL vol 162, cols 804–34, 18 May 1949.
[94] *Hansard* HC vol 162, col 347, 24 Nov. 1989 (Hurd).

in central and eastern Europe'. Such concerns underlined the need to retain NATO but to 'frame its strategy within a broad approach to security'. However, the document still reiterated the 'purely defensive' purpose of the Alliance, even going so far as to state that 'none of its weapons will be used except in self-defence'. It did, however, recognize a non-defensive role by stating that the Allies could 'be called upon to contribute to global stability and peace by providing forces for United Nations missions'.[95]

By the time of its 50th anniversary in 1999, Alliance Heads of State and Government were much bolder in declaring a new Strategic Concept on 24 April 1999. Adopted amidst the NATO air campaign against Serbia to try to prevent the repression occurring in Kosovo, the Strategy developed the functions of NATO within a broader notion of security to include the possibility of it taking action other than of a defensive nature under article 5 of the North Atlantic Treaty, namely in crisis management tasks which would require NATO 'to stand ready, case-by-case and by consensus to contribute to effective conflict prevention and to engage actively in crisis management, including crisis response situations'. The document points to the risks of a 'wider nature' than just the threat of attack, to include 'acts of terrorism, sabotage and organised crime' as well as the disruption of vital resources and massive flows of refugees. In the light of these threats the Strategy declares that NATO 'will seek, in cooperation with other organizations, to prevent conflict, or, should a crisis arise, to contribute to its effective management, consistent with international law, including through the possibility of conducting non-Article 5 crisis response operations'.[96]

While the 1999 Strategic Concept refers to acting in conformity with international law, and states that the development of NATO is consistent with article 7 of the NATO treaty which refers to the primary responsibility of the Security Council for peace and security, the very idea of a 'non-article 5 operation' appears both to contradict the NATO treaty itself and the UN Charter, unless approval is given by the Security Council for enforcement actions either under chapter VII or chapter VIII of the Charter.

Unlike the 1991 Strategic Concept, the 1999 version was discussed in the House of Commons, with Prime Minister Tony Blair stating that it depicted the 'fundamental security tasks of the alliance and how we intend to fulfil them'.[97] Inevitably the debate was dominated by the Kosovo campaign, though the Prime Minister seemed to accept that NATO was a regional alliance, but that did not mean it needed the authority of the Security Council to act although it would be desirable.[98]

The Kosovo air campaign of March–June 1999 witnessed an overt move by NATO from article 5 (mutual defence) action to non-article 5 operations to

---

[95] <http://www.nato.int/docu/basictxt/b911108a.htm>, paras 9, 14, 35, 41 (accessed 26 Jan. 2009).

[96] NATO Press Release NAC-S(99)65, 24 April 1999, paras 10, 24, 31, and 41.

[97] *Hansard* HC vol 330, col 22, 26 April 1999 (Blair).

[98] Ibid., col 35, 26 April 1999 (Blair). See also *Hansard* HL vol 600, col 29, 26 April 1999.

combat threats to the peace.[99] Bruno Simma points to a problem of 'democratic legitimacy of such re-invention' in relation to Germany, where parliamentary consent was given to the 1949 treaty but not to its radical development by subsequent practice.[100]

It is doubtful whether this is such a great problem for the UK, with its more fluid constitution. The UK government made it clear in March 1949 that it did not need the prior consent of parliament before signing the Atlantic Treaty. In response to a request for a debate before the Pact was signed, the government minister stated that 'proper British Parliamentary practice' would be followed, namely 'that the Government take their responsibility in entering into a treaty and the House of Commons has its perfectly free responsibility to approve or not approve of what the Government has done'.[101]

Given the legality of the government undertaking these international obligations without prior parliamentary approval, there appears little doubt that the government could agree with its other NATO partners to expand the nature of NATO, without seeking prior parliamentary approval. Of course, the House of Commons can express its disapproval retrospectively of what the government has done, but this is unlikely since 'the House of Commons is enmeshed with and supports the Government of the day'.[102] Even if such an event were to occur, the legal obligations undertaken by the UK on the international plane would not be undone, unless it led to the government withdrawing from the treaty.[103]

Despite the limitations of the NATO treaty of 1949, limitations made clear by the Foreign Secretary Ernest Bevin when opening the debate in the House of Commons in that year, the constitutional practice in the UK does not prevent the government of the day agreeing to a re-interpretation of treaties without any prior approval by parliament. Thus there appears to be no incompatibility in British constitutional law between the British involvement in NATO actions in Bosnia and Kosovo in the 1990s and the statement made by Bevin in 1949 that the treaty only envisaged collective self-defence under article 51, and was not creating a regional arrangement empowered to take enforcement action under chapter VIII.

Subsequent parliamentary disapproval of such developments remains a possibility, though a theoretical one. In effect the House of Commons debates on Kosovo in 1999 after the launching of the NATO bombing operations, amounted to approval of non-article 5 operations. Further approval was given by the House of Commons Defence Select Committee in its Third Report of 31 March 1999

[99] B. Simma, 'NATO, the UN and the Use of Force: Legal Aspects' (1999) 10 EJIL 14–21.

[100] Ibid., 18–19.

[101] *Hansard* HC vol 464, col 2292, 17 March 1949 (Morrison).

[102] J.P. Mackintosh, *People and Parliament* (Farnborough: Saxon House, 1978) 210.

[103] S. de Smith and R. Brazier, *Constitutional and Administrative Law* (8th edn, London: Penguin, 1998), 147.

on the challenges facing NATO at the forthcoming Washington Summit. The report produced, soon after the bombings had started, supported non-article 5 action dismissing argument that NATO was in need of reform as 'theological debate'; and furthermore declared that insisting Security Council authority be sought for such operations would 'covertly' give 'Russia a veto over Alliance action'. The Committee was confident that a decision arrived at by consensus in the NATO Council would be in accordance with international law.[104]

In the light of this it is somewhat surprising that the Foreign Affairs Committee in its review of the Kosovo crisis published on 7 June 2000, took the position that 'the North Atlantic Treaty gives NATO no authority to act for humanitarian purposes'. The Committee strongly recommended the adoption of a new legal instrument by NATO.[105] The 1999 Strategic Concept was very much wrapped up in the immediacy of the Kosovo action. In the cold light of day, as reflected in the report of the Foreign Affairs Committee, the future of non-Article 5 operations seems a great deal less clear at least from Britain's perspective than it was during the bombings and in their immediate aftermath.

7. Conclusion

Britain has played a central role in the shaping of both the United Nations and NATO. It is a sad fact that the idealism found in Parliament during the dark years of the Second World War, when the form of the future world organization was debated with such enthusiasm, largely gave way in the face of the reality of the looming veto in the Security Council, effectively agreed by Churchill, Roosevelt and Stalin at Yalta in February 1945. The idealism remaining at the end of the war quickly dissipated in the face of the Soviet veto which led Britain and its allies to revert to a fully realist approach to international relations, falling back on tried and tested notions of balance of power reflected in a strong defensive alliance.

That realism was continued in the Security Council where Britain used its veto when it needed to protect its interests or actions, and it shows no willingness to give up this privilege. With a veto-locked Security Council and a purely defensive NATO, the Cold War did not produce conflicting practices between the two organizations. Indeed, with NATO being based squarely on article 51 of the UN Charter, there appeared to be no real conflict between them, though they did represent different visions of collective security. NATO was there to protect its members from attack in the certain knowledge that the Security Council would be unable to take action, and furthermore it had the clear right in international law to do so.

---

[104] Select Committee on Defence, Third Report, 13 April 1999, paras 176–80 (HC 39).
[105] HC Foreign Affairs Select Committee Fourth Report, 7 June 2000, para 135 (HC 28-I).

However, the end of the Cold War has put NATO and the UN on a collision course, with NATO showing signs of a willingness to take enforcement action without Security Council approval if necessary, a scenario that finally materialized in the Kosovo air campaign of 1999, reviewed more fully in chapter nine. With both organizations focusing on security in a much broader sense than just defence in the face of attacks, the potential exists for further confrontation as well as co-operation.

4

From Korea to Kuwait: Britain and Coalitions of the Willing

1. Introduction

The deployment of large numbers of British troops to both Korea in 1950 and to Kuwait in 1990 followed similar domestic and international legal paths, though the political contexts were quite different, one occurring at the outset of the Cold War and the other at its end. Britain was instrumental in shaping the idea of coalitions acting under the authority of the UN as an alternative to the more centralized application of military force envisaged under the UN Charter. The parliamentary and international political debates that led to the development of this as a form of lawful military action will be traced in this chapter. In particular, the chapter will concentrate on why it was necessary to obtain UN authority for these actions when they could readily be justified as the exercise of the right of collective defence.

2. Coalitions of the Willing in International Law

Before looking at the parliamentary debates during the Korean and Gulf conflicts, it is necessary to review the international legal basis of UN military actions. This will set the framework within which to analyse the justifications of the British government and the debates that occurred in parliament.

Under international law as established by the UN Charter of 1945, a state, or group of states, is allowed to use military force in only three situations: self-defence (the sovereign right being embodied in article 51); if authorized by the Security Council itself under article 42; or acting through a regional agency authorized by the Security Council under article 53. There is disagreement about the legal basis of the only two operations authorized by the Security Council to combat aggression; Korea in 1950 and Kuwait in 1990. It has been claimed that states responding to aggression were simply exercising, with the encouragement of the Security Council, their inherent right of self-defence. This explanation is incorrect, however, as the actions taken against North Korea and Iraq were *United Nations*' operations empowered under article 42. Such an explanation is not only a more accurate analysis of the doctrinal law, but is also evidenced by the attitude of governments contributing to such operations, Britain being no exception. Indeed, the significant British role in each operation meant that its views were instrumental in helping to shape the future of coalitions of the willing designed to deal with threats to the peace as well as aggressions.

Although Security Council authorized military actions have not followed the text of the Charter, UN practice, and its acceptance by members, has created an alternative system more reflective of a world in which powerful states jealously guard their military strength and only allow its collective use within a system that protects their interests. Furthermore, the decentralized security system— one relying on volunteers—that has emerged has been used not only to combat aggression but also to address threats to the peace arising out of events within states.[1] Thus, it is no longer possible to view the UN's involvement in military enforcement operations as aberrant or *ad hoc*. Paradoxical though this statement may seem, the decentralized military option has been institutionalized.

If the legal basis for the interventions in Korea and Kuwait was provided by article 51 of the Charter, authorization by the Security Council would become legally superfluous, as the military action would be founded upon the right of self-defence. It would simply take the form of collective defence as other states co-operated with the victim to repel the attack.[2] It is argued here that those states participating in the Korean and Kuwait conflicts, and the UN itself were all of the legal opinion that they were taking part in UN military operations, not traditional actions taken in self-defence. Denying that article 42 provided the legal basis for these actions ignores the political pressures that have limited the application of chapter VII of the Charter, by preventing the development of mechanisms to make its operation more effective, and obliging the UN to adopt a decentralized security system in place of the collective system envisaged by the drafters of the Charter in 1945.

The application of the decentralized military model to intra-state as well as inter-state conflicts weakens the claim that article 51 provides the legal basis of UN-sanctioned military operations. Such conflicts rarely derive from claims of self-defence because, according to article 51, the right of self-defence is only triggered by an 'armed attack' by one state on another. The only alternative for those who might argue that the legal basis of such operations is not the UN but

---

[1] T. Stein, 'Decentralized International Law Enforcement: The Changing Role of the State as Law Enforcement Agent, in J. Delbruck (ed), *Allocation of Law Enforcement Authority in the International System* (Berlin: Duncker and Humblot, 1995) 107.

[2] For this argument see J. Stone, *Legal Controls of International Conflict* (London: Stevens, 1954) 234–7; J. Stone, *Aggression and World Order* (London: Stevens, 1958); E.V. Rostow, 'Until What? Enforcement Action or Collective Self-Defense?' (1991) 85 AJIL 506–10; O. Schachter, 'United Nations Law in the Gulf Conflict' (1991) 85 AJIL 459–60; R. Lavalle, 'The Law of the United Nations and the Use of Force under the Relevant Security Council Resolutions of 1990 and 1991 to Resolve the Persian Gulf Crisis' (1992) 23 NYBIL 3, 62.

customary law independent of the Charter is to contend that they are applications of the doubtful doctrine of humanitarian intervention, that is, foreign military intervention to protect the lives of an endangered population. Even the most fervent advocates of unilateral humanitarian intervention admit that, when authorized by the Security Council under chapter VII, the operation becomes a UN military operation and not one based on the alleged customary right of humanitarian intervention.[3] The same model of UN resolution has been used to deal with aggression and with threats to the peace. In other words, plenty of examples can be found of military measures taken by the UN in which the constitutional link between the operation and the Charter is either article 42, in the case of multilateral military operations (coalitions of the willing), or article 53, in the case of regional organizations taking military action.

Indeed, the existence of article 53 supports the decentralized model: if the Security Council may authorize a regional organization under chapter VIII of the Charter, it should be entitled under chapter VII to authorize a group of states, or indeed a single state, to act. Authorizing just a solitary state may undermine the legitimacy of the operation, as such delegation is more readily abused than in a multilateral or regional response in the current loose and voluntary collective security system. Abuse by a military or regional superpower—seen for example in Nigerian domination of the ECOWAS force in Liberia retrospectively endorsed by the Security Council in 1992[4]—can be anticipated and reduced, however, by greater precision in the formulation of the mandate in the enabling resolution.

The decentralized security model, though far from perfect, is evolving piecemeal in dealing with threats to the peace as well as breaches of article 2(4) of the Charter that prohibits states from using force. The military responses authorized to date by the United Nations lie between 'multilateral' and 'collective'. Collective responses involve a collective military operation under the Charter as well as collective authorization by the Security Council: multilateral responses are simply those undertaken by a group of states outside the UN's security system. Under the system developed by the Council, it gives collective authorization, but does not insist on truly collective command, control, and composition of the force. That the system falls short of the Charter or indeed, collective security ideal, however, does not make it unconstitutional.[5]

---

[3] F.R. Teson, *Humanitarian Intervention: An Inquiry into Law and Morality* (3rd edn, New York: Transnational, 2005) 125–8; R.B. Lillich, 'Humanitarian Intervention through the United Nations: Towards the Development of Criteria' (1993) 17 Heidelberg Law Review 563–9. For an argument that self-defence includes a right to protect others (states and individuals) see G.P. Fletcher and F.D. Ohlin, *Defending Humanity: When Force is Justified and Why* (Oxford: Oxford University Press, 2008) 63–85.

[4] SC Res. 788, 19 Nov. 1992.

[5] T.D. Gill, 'Legal and Political Limitations on the Power of the UN Security Council to Exercise Its Enforcement Powers under Chapter VII of the Charter' (1995) 26 NYBIL 57.

3. Collective Security and Collective Defence

Collective security has been defined as 'the proposition that aggressive and unlawful use of force by one nation against another will be met by the combined strength of all other nations. All will co-operate in controlling a disturber of the peace. They will act as one for all and all for one. Their combined strength will serve as a guarantee for the security of each'.[6]

A truly collective security system, whether international or national, demands the provision of a police force independent of any of the members or groups that make up the society. No state or small group of states should be able to dominate the system. Seen in this light, the UN-sponsored actions against North Korea and Iraq were defective in that the United States dominated them, both militarily and politically. However, there are degrees of collective security and a system is not ruled out because it does not match the ideal. Indeed, there is disagreement about what constitutes an ideal collective security system.[7] The greater the multilateral component of a UN force, the greater its legitimacy, even if it would be unrealistic to expect to mount a major military operation without a contribution from one of the major military powers. However, if a military action dominated by one state is not only authorized by the Security Council but is also supported by the international community, it meets the requirements for collective security.

A collective security system is not normally designed merely to deploy defensive force on a par with collective defence pacts. 'Collective measures' or 'enforcement actions',[8] taken for the maintenance or restoration of peace, do not have to conform therefore to the principles limiting the right of self-defence, whether individual or collective. Enforcement action may not be unlimited in scope, but must be proportionate to the ends aimed at, namely the maintenance or restoration of peace.[9] Moreover, it must comply with the restrictions of international humanitarian law, protecting civilians and other non-combatants, as well as restricting the use of indiscriminate weapons and the types of target chosen.

Sometimes enforcement action may be limited to repelling an aggressor; at others, the removal of an aggressor, or of a situation that threatens international peace, may be required. Thus proportionality is a more flexible concept when applied to a collective security system than to self-defence. Self-defence is limited to repelling the attack, while enforcement action may be mandated to repel the

---

[6] K.P. Saksena, *The United Nations and Collective Security* (Delhi: Sage, 1974) 405.
[7] I.L. Claude, *Power and International Relations* (New York: Random House, 1962) 110–68; C.A. Kupchan, 'The Case for Collective Security', in G.W. Downs (ed), *Collective Security Beyond the Cold War* (New York: University of Michigan Press, 1995) 42–4.
[8] Arts 1(1), 2(5), 2(7), 50, 53 of the UN Charter.
[9] J.N. Singh, *Use of Force under International Law* (Delhi: Harnam, 1984) 82.

attack and remove the aggressor, or it may be given specific tasks such as removing weapons of mass destruction from a state, or dealing with terrorist training camps in another. Unlike peacekeeping forces, whose weaponry has traditionally been limited to personal defence, enforcement operations are limited only by the mandate.[10] The phrase 'necessary measures', used by the Council to mean military measures, allows the contributing states wide choices in selecting not only the weapons to be used but also the number of troops to be deployed subject, of course, to the limitations of international humanitarian law.[11]

In the Korean War, the initial authorization from the Security Council in Resolution 83 of 27 June 1950, not only mandated the pushing back of North Korea to the 38th parallel but also added an ambiguous phrase recommending the restoration of peace and security to the area. The General Assembly gave the mandate a potentially more offensive character by calling for steps to unify Korea,[12] and as shall be seen the UN forces did cross into North Korea.

By contrast the Coalition's military actions in the Gulf in 1991 appeared to be mainly defensive, despite an equally ambiguous Security Council mandate. Security Council Resolution 678 of 29 November 1990 authorized the enforcement of previous Council resolutions demanding the withdrawal of Iraq from Kuwait and requiring the restoration of international peace and security to the area. However, it will be seen in chapter ten that the UK argued in 2003 that Resolution 678 was still operative and legally justified the American and British invasion of that country. Whatever the basis of this argument both the Korean and Iraq mandates did not just condone collective defence; they were authorizing enforcement action. Clearly such ambiguity in the mandates gives the states taking military action on behalf of the UN too much discretion. Events in both Korea and the Gulf illustrate the lack of accountability to the UN and its lack of control over operations carried out in its name.

Not only is UN enforcement action potentially offensive, it can be taken in response to a greater variety of situations than aggression including the breach of fundamental human rights protecting life. The Council has authorized states to use force to prevent starvation (the initially effective US-led intervention in Somalia in 1993) and to stop genocide (the ineffective French intervention in Rwanda in 1994). It is recognized that the Security Council is not confined to authorizing military action to deal with violations of fundamental international laws,[13] it can authorize force to restore democracy (as with the US-led intervention in Haiti in 1994) or to deal with anarchy (as with the Italian-led intervention

---

[10] P.F. Diehl, *International Peacekeeping* (Baltimore: Johns Hopkins, 1994) 7.

[11] See generally Y. Dinstein, *The Conduct of Hostilities under the Law of International Armed Conflict* (Cambridge: Cambridge University Press, 2004).

[12] GA Res. 376, 7 Oct. 1950.

[13] H. Kelsen, *The Law of the United Nations* (London: Stevens, 1951) 727; R. Higgins, *The Development of International Law through the Political Organs of the United Nations* (Oxford: Oxford University Press, 1963) 226.

in Albania in 1997), or to provide post-conflict security (as with the EU force—EUFOR—in Bosnia since 2004).[14]

Despite the extension and institutionalization of UN military enforcement action, volunteer states will only normally step forward if it is in their interests to do so. The operations in North Korea and Iraq were a product of a confluence of the interests of the intervening states, especially the United States in confronting the expansion of communism in the case of Korea and the protection of an oil-rich and western friendly state in the case of Kuwait, and the violation of a fundamental rule of international law prohibiting aggression.[15] That Britain shared these concerns is not only shown by its decision to contribute to the operations, but by parliamentary support as the debates below show. This would suggest that a violation of a fundamental law would not by itself trigger a UN-sponsored military intervention, which considerably weakens the UN's military capability. However, it is not always the case that there must be a combination of self-interest and violation of basic laws, as shown by the US-led intervention in Somalia in 1992 when there was a singular lack of American self-interest. Such altruistic military interventions, though, are the exception rather than the norm.

4. The Failure of the UN Charter Scheme

The UN's collective security role was premised on the ability of the primary organ, the Security Council, to use military force to keep the peace. Though article 42 allows the Council to take action by air, sea or land forces as may be necessary to maintain or restore international peace and security, the mechanism envisaged for achieving this was not through coalitions of the willing assembled on an *ad hoc* basis to combat a threat to the peace or armed aggression. Article 43 provided that armed force were to be available to the Security Council under special agreements with member states to be arrived at as soon as possible; those agreements stipulating the numbers, location, and the state of readiness of their forces.

Although the onset of the Cold War forestalled the agreements stipulated by article 43, the Council did instruct the Military Staff Committee, set up under article 47 and composed of the chiefs of staff of the permanent members, to report by April 1947 on the principles that should govern the operation of the

---

[14] The main instances of post-Cold War military enforcement actions: SC Res. 678, 29 Nov. 1990 (Iraq); SC Res. 794, 2 Dec. 1992 (Somalia); SC Res. 940, 31 July 1994 (Haiti); SC Res. 929, 22 June 1994 (Rwanda); SC Res. 1031, 15 Dec. 1995 (Bosnia—IFOR); SC Res. 1080, 15 Nov. 1996 (Zaire); SC Res. 1088, 12 Dec. 1996 (Bosnia—SFOR); SC Res. 1101, 28 March 1997 (Albania); SC Res. 1244, 10 June 1999 (KFOR); SC Res. 1264, 15 Sept. 1999 (E. Timor); SC Res. 1386, 20 Dec. 2001 (Afghanistan—ISAF); SC Res. 1484, 30 May 2003 (Congo); SC Res. 1511, 16 Oct. 2003 (Iraq); SC Res. 1529, 29 Feb. 2004 (Haiti); SC Res. 1575, 22 Nov. 2004 (Bosnia—EUFOR).

[15] J. Quigley, 'The Privatization of Security Council Enforcement Action: A Threat to Unilateralism' (1996) 17 Michigan J of Intl L 271–2.

statutory UN forces.[16] Unfortunately, only half of the Committee's proposals were accepted by all the permanent members. The Security Council did agree that initially its permanent members should contribute armed forces to the UN, with other members contributing later. It also agreed that forces should remain under the command of the contributing state except when they were being deployed by the Council, when it would take political control and the Military Staff Committee would take operational and military control. Although these were significant steps towards the ideal of collective security in the control of UN forces (singularly lacking in UN military enforcement operations to date), the Council was divided on the size of the force and more particularly the size of the contribution from each of the permanent members.[17]

With no likelihood of consensus among the permanent members as long as the Cold War lasted, the idea of a UN force was shelved in 1948, although the Military Staff Committee continued and still continues to hold unproductive meetings. The collective security ideal, unachievable for military enforcement operations, has been realized to a greater extent in UN peacekeeping operations (in which control is exercised through the UN Secretary General rather than the Military Staff Committee). The less intrusive nature, at least traditionally, of UN peacekeeping, explains the greater centralization of command and control, though if the peacekeeping forces become engaged in combat, permanent members are less willing to contribute under UN command and control. In these circumstances they may still supply forces under national command to provide support for UN peacekeeping forces.

This was the situation as regards British forces in Sierra Leone in May 2000. The lack of a Security Council mandate for the government's decision to send 700 troops to the country on 8 May resulted in some discussion in Parliament. The lack of clarity as to the role of the military operation, especially whether it was meant to support the struggling UN peacekeeping operation (UNAMSiL), or whether it was in fact sent to rescue British nationals, led to sharp exchanges in the House, with the opposition objecting to the use of troops for wider purposes other than the protection of nationals.[18] Mission creep did occur, however, despite continued criticism in parliament. The Defence Secretary, Geoff Hoon, stated later in May that 'our aim is to help the UN create a more effective force in Sierra Leone, which had to restore peace and order to Sierra Leone and help the Government there re-establish security'.[19] The government's large majority enabled it to weather the protest put up by the opposition, and contribute to a successful international operation in Sierra Leone by bringing an end to the civil war.

---

[16] SC 105th mtg, 1947.
[17] SCOR 2nd sess., special supp. No 1, 1947.
[18] M. Evans, 'Forces Pull Out all Stops to Clear Freetown', *The Times*, 9 May 2000, 1, 4. *Hansard* HC vol 349, col 520, 8 May 2000 (Maude).
[19] *Hansard* HC vol 350, col 863, 23 May 2000 (Hoon).

The absence of article 43 agreements does not negate the Council power to authorize military action under article 42, though it does denude that power. This means that the Council cannot legally oblige states to contribute troops, it has to rely on volunteer states, making it thus dependent on willing states stepping forward. The absence of earmarked UN forces under international contract to the UN also has knock-on effects on the remainder of the Charter scheme for the application of military enforcement measures. The Charter provides that 'plans for the application of armed force shall be made by the Security Council with the assistance of the Military Staff Committee', and further that the 'Military Staff Committee shall be responsible under the Security Council for the strategic direction of any armed forces placed at the disposal of the Security Council'.[20] Without guaranteed involvement of all permanent members in enforcement actions, there would inevitably be no role for the Military Staff Committee, which consists of the military commanders (or their representatives) of the permanent members. No permanent member would step forward to lead a coalition if it knew that it would be subject to the command and control of a committee containing the other permanent members.

5. The Constitutionality of Coalitions

In the place of a centralized military enforcement option there has emerged coalitions of the willing, accepted as constitutional by the membership, and being compatible with the aims and objectives of the UN to prevent wars and maintain peace and security. The elements of the decentralized system are first a resolution authorizing 'necessary measures' (a UN euphemism for the use of armed force) under chapter VII after determining that there exists either a threat to or breach of the peace, or act of aggression. States taking action under this resolution report on their actions to the Security Council. Ideally the mandating resolution should specify the extent, nature, and objectives of the military action. Unfortunately, as has been seen, the mandates of the two UN coalitions of the willing authorized to combat the aggressions of North Korea in 1950 and Iraq in 1990 were ambiguous and this has led to continuing problems of (mis)interpretation in the case of Iraq. The mandates of enforcement actions tasked with dealing with threats to the peace have generally been more precise, though they often lack sunset clauses which give a date or event for the termination of the operation.

Such a denuded constitutional system produces a minimal level of Security Council control over military enforcement operations undertaken under its authority, and it is certainly not able to prevent dominant groups within the Council from using it to achieve the ends of that group, though as the failure to gain clear authority for the invasion of Iraq in 2003 shows, such dominance

---

[20] Arts 46 and 47(3) of the UN Charter.

does not guarantee a compliant Security Council. Use of centralized power to achieve the ends of a dominant group within any society is not necessarily unlawful however, if the power is channelled through the institutional structures and is approved by an organ with the necessary competence. The west's current dominance in the Council need not imply that the use of its power to protect and further western interests is automatically a misuse, provided that the military action achieves the collective security purposes of the UN.

The result is an unstable collective security system that does not automatically respond to every situation that constitutes a threat to or breach of the peace. However, coalitions might not be asking for authority out of national interests in every case. Sometimes, it appears at least, the interests of the international community provoke powerful states to step forward; as with the United States in Somalia in 1992–3, and with NATO states in Bosnia before and after the Dayton Peace Accords of 1995. The fact that the EU has now taken over NATO's security duties in Bosnia from December 2004 may be explained by the fact that the Union has a vested interest in containing the Yugoslav conflicts; but this rationale is not convincing when applied to the EU-led operation in Bunia in the Democratic Republic of the Congo in 2003. The voluntary nature of the military option, however, jeopardizes the collective security ideal that every aggression (and threats reaching a certain level, for instance genocide) is met with counterforce, because no state may volunteer, or those that do may withdraw without legal hindrance.[21]

6. The International Legal Basis of the Military Operations in Korea and Iraq

The three most important issues pertaining to the legal basis of decentralized military operations in Korea and Iraq were: first, whether the imposition of sanctions by the Security Council against Iraq meant that, in law, the right of self-defence no longer persisted; second, whether states viewed the operations in Korea and Iraq as UN operations or simply as multilateral defensive operations; and third, whether the mechanisms used to terminate the military operations in Korea (armistice) and Iraq (Security Council resolution) affected the identification of their legal basis.

According to article 51 of the Charter the right of self-defence persists until 'the Security Council has taken measures necessary to maintain international peace and security'. One issue that was raised during the Gulf War of 1990–1 was whether the imposition of non-forcible measures against Iraq, in the form of a comprehensive economic embargo, undermined the right of self-defence.

---

[21] But see D. Sarooshi, *The United Nations and the Development of Collective Security* (Oxford: Clarendon Press, 1999) 152.

Ultimately this issue remained undecided, as shall be seen. In the Korean War the Security Council did not first impose sanctions under article 41, which authorizes the adoption of measures other than the use of force. Although the operation was not simply an action in collective self-defence, the Cold War had weakened the collective security mechanisms at the disposal of the Council. The opportunity created between January and August 1950 by the Soviet Union's absence in protest at the failure to sit the Chinese Communist regime in the Council as opposed to the Nationalist Chinese government, allowed the Council to activate the collective security machinery.[22] However, the brief window of opportunity only allowed it to authorize military measures to combat North Korean aggression—it did not permit an incremental use of chapter VII powers, as with Iraq, nor to mark the termination of the conflict by Council resolution, again as with Iraq. The fact that, in the Gulf, the Council not only imposed sanctions against Iraq before authorizing military measures but also ended the conflict, illustrates a limited strengthening of the collective security system.[23]

In the case of Iraq, Security Council-imposed sanctions were implemented shortly after Iraq invaded Kuwait, thereby arguably denying the exercise of the right of self-defence in accordance with the terms of article 51. By Resolution 661 of 6 August 1990, the Council imposed mandatory economic sanctions against Iraq with the aim of forcing Iraq to comply with the terms of Resolution 660 of 2 August 1990, which had demanded Iraq's withdrawal from Kuwait. The 'measures' were imposed to remove Iraq from Kuwait, the objective of an action in self-defence of Kuwait. However, coalition forces from Western and Arab states and led by the United States were gathering in the Persian Gulf in August 1990 to act in collective self-defence of both occupied Kuwait and Saudi Arabia (should it be attacked), at the request of the rulers of these two states.[24]

The two leaders of the coalition, the United States and Britain, argued that their right of self-defence was not curtailed by a resolution imposing sanctions which itself affirmed 'the inherent right of individual or collective self-defence, in response to an armed attack by Iraq against Kuwait, in accordance with Article 51'.[25] The other permanent members of the Council, although less vociferous, seemed to hold the opinion that article 51 signified that the right of self-defence was lost as soon as the Council applied article 41, meaning that armed force could

---

[22] A. Farrar-Hockley, *The British Part in the Korea War: Volume I: A Distant Obligation* (London: HMSO, 1990) 57; S.D. Bailey, *Voting in the Security Council* (Oxford: Clarendon, 1969) 70; J. Quigley, 'The United States and the United Nations in the Persian Gulf War: New Order or Disorder' (1992) 25 Cornell Intl L J 28–32.

[23] Gill, 'Legal and Political Limitations', 58; Quigley, 'United States', 42; Lavalle, 'Law of the United Nations', 62–4.

[24] UN Docs. S/21492, S/21501 (1990).

[25] See Prime Minister Thatcher's House of Commons statement *Hansard* HC vol 177, cols 734–8. For the US position see statement in the Security Council (SC 2937th mtg, 1990). See also R. Jennings and A. Watts, *Oppenheim's International Law* (9th edn, London: Longman, 1992) 423; Schachter, 'United Nations Law', 458–9.

be used against Iraq only if the Council took the next step by authorizing military action.[26] Eventually, the United States sought authorization from the Council to use limited force against vessels suspected of breaching the embargo on trading with Iraq,[27] and later to use whatever force should prove necessary to evict the Iraqis from Kuwait.[28] The United States seemed to imply, however, that it sought UN authority to interdict suspected sanctions-busting ships to make the use of force in the Gulf acceptable internationally, not to satisfy the legal requirements of the Charter. Both Britain and the United States claimed that the authorization, although unnecessary, gave the operations an 'additional' legal basis.[29]

The Gulf crisis did not provide a definitive answer to the question of whether sanctions affect the right of self-defence, since the Security Council ultimately authorized the operation in Resolution 678, thereby placing the action under article 42 as a UN military enforcement action, not article 51 as an action in collective self-defence. In the light of the evidence that sanctions by themselves are unlikely to reverse aggression, it would not be wise or indeed acceptable to states for their inherent right of self-defence to be restricted by the imposition of sanctions.

The United States and Britain argued in the early stages of the Gulf crisis that the right of self-defence was the sole legal basis for military action. Although the argument challenges the need for participating states to view the action as an enforcement action under UN auspices, it was made primarily to counter the alternative argument that sanctions under article 41 removed the right of self-defence, not directly to challenge the authority of Resolution 678. Having made the argument on sanctions, and after securing Resolution 678, they acted under the authority of the United Nations, not under the right of self-defence embodied in article 51. The argument for self-defence was in effect a reservation that if no authorizing resolution were forthcoming, the imposition of sanctions under article 41 would not impinge on the right. Obviously, the reservation will affect responses to aggression on occasions when the Security Council will not agree to go beyond the imposition of economic sanctions. Once Resolution 678 had authorized the use of force, the reservation no longer applied in the Gulf.

7. The British Attitude in the UN

If military action were taken in the Gulf in collective self-defence, an enabling resolution would not have been needed. To argue that the purpose of the resolution was simply to make the operations more widely acceptable internationally

---

[26] *The Independent*, 9 Nov. 1990, USSR; *The Observer*, 11 Nov. 1990, France and China. See also the statement of the UN Secretary General Perez de Cuellar, *The Independent*, 9 Nov. 1990.

[27] SC Res. 665, 25 Aug. 1990.   [28] SC Res. 678, 29 Nov. 1990.

[29] SC 2938th mtg, 25 Aug. 1990. This, at least, appears to be incorrect in that enforcement of an embargo imposed by the Council is only possible by a further resolution of the Council. See Gill, 'Legal and Political Limitations', 99.

is to ignore the fact that it *authorized* action;[30] it did not simply endorse self-defence. This should be contrasted with the Security Council's response to the terrorist attacks on the United States of 9 September 2001, when the Security Council recognized the right of individual and collective defence but did not authorize military action,[31] and the United States and Britain took military action against al-Qaeda and the Taliban regime in Afghanistan on the basis of self-defence. Although the leading participating states may have initially based their preparations to liberate Kuwait in 1990 on the right of self-defence, once they sought the Security Council's authority, and the Council gave it on the basis of its collective security powers, their actions have to be evaluated as collective security operations not as action taken in collective self-defence. The participants referred to the enabling resolutions of the Council as the source of authority, as indeed did the target states and their supporters or opponents. The international consensus shows that both the Gulf and Korea were UN operations. As references to the authorizing resolutions far outweigh any to collective self-defence, the international legal discourse about the conflict recognized Council authority as the legal basis of the operations.

In the case of Korea, the US and UK initially appeared to base their actions on self-defence as they gathered forces to combat North Korean and Iraqi invasions, but they only did so until Security Council authority was gained. Once it was gained it was clear that the operation was viewed as a UN military enforcement action, albeit one dominated by one state—the US. In relation to Korea when Resolution 83 was adopted on 27 June 1950, the contributing states argued about the constitutional basis but only in terms of the collective security provisions of chapter VII. The resolution recommended 'that the Members of the United Nations furnish such assistance to the Republic of Korea as may be necessary to repel the armed attack and to restore international peace and security in the area'. The British representative, Sir Gladwyn Jebb, based the military action in Korea on article 39 of the Charter: in the absence of agreements made under article 43, the Council could not 'decide' on military action within the terms of article 42, but could call on states to volunteer to help.[32] France agreed and the United States, although it argued at first that the basis was article 42, eventually agreed with Britain.[33]

When describing the war effort in Korea, the British government constantly referred to 'UN action' and 'UN forces'. Furthermore, after the Soviet Union had returned to the Council in August 1950, the British sponsored the General Assembly resolution that authorized the crossing of the 38th parallel by UN forces.[34] The British Foreign Secretary, Ernest Bevin, commented on

---

[30] But see Schachter, 'United Nations Law', 460.
[31] SC Res. 1368, 12 Sept. 2001. See further chapter eight.
[32] SC 477th mtg, 25 July 1950.
[33] Farrar-Hockley, *Distant Obligation*, 83–4.
[34] GA Res. 376, 7 Oct. 1950; Farrar-Hockley, *Distant Obligation*, 100, 102, 191.

26 September 1950 that 'the resolution contemplates the contingency that the United Nations' forces may enter North Korea but ... it very carefully defines their functions there. I feel strongly that if the authority of the United Nations is to be established we cannot be content with restoring the *status quo*'.[35] Bevin helped to ensure that the Assembly enacted the resolution before the commander-in-chief of the UN command, US General Douglas MacArthur, crossed the 38th parallel, thus maintaining UN authority over the operation.

Later as the war was drawing towards a stalemate at the 38th parallel in 1953, the British supported a joint policy declaration by UN participants, which stated that:

We, the United Nations members whose military forces are participating in the Korean action, support the decision of the Commander-in-Chief of the United Nations Command to conclude an armistice agreement ... [and] we affirm, in the interests of world peace, that if there is a renewal of the armed attack, challenging again the principles of the United Nations, we should again be united and prompt to resist.[36]

Similar references to the military operation in Korea as a UN operation were made by the United States and the other contributors, as well as by opposing and non-aligned states.[37] Furthermore, the UN Secretary-General, Trygve Lie, although uncertain at first whether the force could be regarded as a UN force, given that it did not strictly follow the terms of chapter VII concerning command and control,[38] endorsed the operation in 1950 as a UN operation and thereafter consistently referred to it as one. And although similarly uncertain at first whether the United Nations could base an action on article 42 in the absence of agreements arrived at under article 43, Lie stated in his annual report of 1950 that, despite the lack of such agreements, the Security Council's recommendation to use military force meant that:

The United States of America, and other countries, are providing assistance to the Republic of Korea in the form of both military material and contingents of their armed forces. At this moment, as I complete my annual report, these forces are fighting on behalf of the United Nations to assist the Republic of Korea to repel the attack and to restore international peace and security in Korea.[39]

Lie repeated his view that the military operation came under the UN umbrella by referring to the 'United Nations collective security action' in Korea. 'For the first time in the history of the world', he remarked on 8 September 1950, 'the enforcement of peace has been undertaken by a world organization'. This unique

---

[35] Farrar-Hockley, *Distant Obligation*, 209.
[36] Ibid., 225, 402.
[37] D.W. Bowett, *United Nations Forces* (London: Stevens, 1964) 45–7.
[38] T. Lie, *In The Cause of Peace* (London: Macmillan, 1954) 334.
[39] UN Doc. A/1287 (1950). See also the transcript of a Radio Press Conference on the Korean War in A.W. Cordier and W. Foote (eds), *Public Papers of the Secretaries-General of the United Nations: Volume I Trygve Lie* (New York: Columbia University Press, 1969) 321–2.

occurrence had 'happened in response to a recommendation of the Security Council, rather than a command'. Furthermore, he pointed towards both the General Assembly resolution of October 1950, which authorized action for the unification of Korea, and the Uniting for Peace resolution of November 1950,[40] implying that such decision-making, whether by the Council or the General Assembly, constituted a new collective security system to replace the balance-of-power system based on defence pacts: '[e]ven if the Security had been blocked by the use of the veto, the General Assembly, where there is no veto, could have made the same recommendation'.[41]

Lie had no difficulty reconciling the cessation of hostilities in Korea negotiated by US commanders with his view that the operation was a UN operation. Security Council resolutions had authorized the creation of a Unified Command led by the United States, 'authorized ... to conduct such military negotiations on behalf of the United Nations'. With the armistice in sight in April 1953, Lie spoke of 'a great victory for collective security', and, as the truce was announced in July, added that 'collective security has been enforced for the first time in human history'.[42] In the three years since the North Korean invasion, Lie had moved from the view that no collective security system was in place to the view that the military action was taken on behalf of the UN, and then to describing it as a rudimentary form of collective security. At no time did Lie describe the operation as the collective self-defence of Korea.

Similarly, although Britain and the United States had claimed to be acting in self-defence in the Gulf prior to the adoption of Resolution 678 on 29 November 1990, they did not restate the claim afterwards. Like Resolution 83 on Korea, Resolution 678 gave ambiguous directions, appearing first to give an ultimatum to Iraq and only secondly authorizing the use of force. The delay was inserted at the insistence of the Soviet Union in the hope that the threat of force would compel Iraq to withdraw from Kuwait. The second operative paragraph of the resolution authorized 'Member States co-operating with the Government of Kuwait, unless Iraq on or before 15 January 1991 fully implements ... the foregoing resolutions [of the Council on the crisis], to use all necessary means to uphold and implement Security Council resolution 660 and all subsequent resolutions and to restore international peace and security in the area'.

Despite the unnecessarily ambiguous language, the Security Council treated the resolution, which required the coalition to report to the Council on the actions taken under the resolution, as the necessary constitutional link between the Council and the military operation. At the meeting of 29 November 1990 at which the resolution was adopted, both the US Secretary of State, James Baker, and the British Foreign Secretary, Douglas Hurd, emphasized the Council's

---

[40] GA Res. 377, 3 Nov. 1950.
[41] Cordier and Foote, *Public Papers*, 351.
[42] Ibid., 397, 519. See also S.D. Bailey, *The Korean Armistice* (London: Palgrave, 1992) chs 3 and 4.

decision to authorize the enforcement of its own resolutions.[43] Finland and even the Soviet Union referred to the exercise of collective security, thereby withdrawing the latter's objection to this type of operation lodged at the time of the operation in Korea.[44] Most of the members of the Council discussed the matter as an exercise of its authority, even though Cuba and Yemen claimed that the Council had exceeded it.

The level of legal debate was perfunctory when compared with the detailed legal expositions that occurred during the Korean War, perhaps because the legal arguments about the decentralized military option (with the exception of the question of whether sanctions affected the right of self-defence) were aired (and mostly resolved) at that time. Since the end of the Cold War, however, such issues are dealt with in informal discussions of key Council members, leaving public meetings for the formal adoption of decisions already made. Once the arguments for self-defence were discarded in Resolution 678, the Council debate on 3 April 1991 about the adoption of Resolution 687 was based on the Council's authority to bring an end to a war that it had legitimately sanctioned.[45] That the hostilities were formally terminated by Council resolution, and that the Council decided to continue the economic sanctions in order to achieve the objectives set out in Resolution 687, attests to collective security, not collective self-defence, being the basis for the military operation against Iraq.

8. Britain and the Korean War

Having considered the international legal basis of the two coalition actions in 1950 and 1991, we turn to parliament to see how the government's explanations of the necessity of contributing to such operations far from British shores were received by MPs, and in particular to consider the role of international law in that debate, especially the international legal basis of the military operation.

In responding to aggression under a UN mandate, the model has been for the executive to decide and for parliament to have several lengthy debates during the course of the operation, particularly after there has been a new development. Aggression is a clear breach of article 2(4) of the UN Charter and there is generally little doubt that it has occurred. To respond to such aggression is seen by the UK, as the following analysis will show, as a minimum condition for the continued existence of the UN.

On 25 June 1950, 100,000 North Korean soldiers crossed the 38th parallel, which had divided the two halves of Korea since the Japanese withdrawal at the end of the Second World War. The aim of Communist North Korea was to unite

---

[43] SC 2963rd mtg, 29 Nov. 1990.
[44] Bowett, *United Nations Forces*, 46.
[45] SC 2981st mtg, 3 April 1991.

the country by force. One aspect of the Security Council's action as regards Korea was that the USSR was absent from the Council when the relevant Council resolutions were adopted.

In parliament, on 26 June the Leader of the Opposition, Winston Churchill, asked the Labour Prime Minister, Clement Attlee, for a statement on the situation on Korea. The Prime Minister explained that in response to the invasion, the Security Council had been convened by the United States, and that a resolution had been passed that found that the invasion constituted a breach of the peace and called for a cessation of hostilities and a withdrawal of North Korean forces to the 38th parallel.[46] In a brief exchange, one member of the House caused uproar and was ruled out of order by the speaker when he suggested that if the North Korean government refused to comply with the resolution, the atomic bomb should be used against it.[47] Though this now appears to be a complete over-reaction, it was a refrain that was heard again during the Korean conflict, including comments made by President Truman following the Chinese intervention in the conflict later in 1950.[48]

On 27 June 1950, the Prime Minister was asked if the government would join the US is coming to the assistance of South Korea in an action in collective self-defence. Attlee answered that it was better to wait for the outcome of the Security Council debates before commenting on what the UK's response to the North Korean invasion would be.[49] Later in the day the Prime Minister interrupted a debate to state that the UK representative on the Security Council was 'authorised to support' the proposed Resolution (83) that recommended the furnishing of assistance to South Korea. The Prime Minister emphasized that effective measures would be taken through 'international machinery'. Mr Churchill thanked the Prime Minister for making the House acquainted with these matters and expressed the unity of the whole House.[50] On 28 June, Prime Minister Attlee informed the House of the resolution and was asked whether the UK intended to take action to support it. In a very brief exchange the Prime Minister stated that action was being considered and that it was left to the UK as to what assistance was provided. Mr Churchill had confidence that the government would 'act up to [its] supreme international obligations'.[51] Later on 28 June, the Prime Minister informed the House of the government's decision to place its naval forces in Japanese waters at the disposal of the United States. Subsequently the UK deployed up to 12,000 troops in the Korean conflict. Again the Leader of the Opposition expressed his full support. One MP did suggest that such matters of grave peril ought to be *fully* debated in the House of Commons.[52]

---

[46] SC Res. 82, 25 June 1950.
[47] *Hansard* HC vol 476, cols 1094–6, 26 June 1950 (Roberts).
[48] M. Hastings, *The Korean War* (London: Michael Joseph, 1987) 214.
[49] *Hansard* HC vol 476, col 2103, 27 June 1950 (Blackburn).
[50] Ibid., cols 2159–60.
[51] *Hansard* HC vol 476, cols 2291–3, 28 June 1950.
[52] Ibid., cols 2319–20, 28 June 1950 (Silverman).

The first full House of Commons debate on Korea was held on 5 July 1950, clearly after the decision to deploy troops and initial deployments had been made. The Prime Minister requested the support of the House for the action taken by the government under the United Nations Charter 'in helping to resist the unprovoked aggression against the Republic of Korea'.[53] The government position on the international legal basis was that it was a UN action, not an action in collective self-defence. This was made clear by the Prime Minister's heavy reliance on Resolution 83, and his explanation that Soviet absence at the time of its adoption did not invalidate it. He quoted article 27(3) of the Charter, which contains the veto power, and stated that although the Soviet Union had not indicated its concurrence with the resolution as seemingly required by article 27 a custom had emerged in the permanent membership to the effect that abstention did not invalidate a resolution:

If a member of the Security Council, and in particular a permanent member, chooses to refrain from exercising its right of voting, not by failing to vote when present, but by refraining from attending the meeting at all, that member must be regarded as having deliberately abstained from the vote.[54]

He supported this legal argument on the validity of Resolution 83 by citing article 28 of the Charter which provides that the Security Council should function continuously, a provision which made it clear that a permanent member could not prevent its functioning by being absent. The practice of abstention had not fully been accepted in 1950 though it certainly came to be, and was recognized as legitimate by the International Court of Justice in 1971.[55] The argument about a permanent member not being able to prevent the continuous functioning of the Council seemed to disregard the fact that a veto could do this anyway. Despite weaknesses in the argument the importance of the Prime Minister's explanation of the validity of Resolution 83 was that it showed the importance of this resolution and therefore UN authority to the government's case for going to war.

Furthermore, the Prime Minister stated that the United States' initial assistance to the Republic of Korea before Resolution 83 had been a justifiable action in collective self-defence in accordance with article 51 of the Charter, but 'after the passing of the resolution of the 27th, justification for the continued action of America and the United Kingdom and of other members is to be found in this resolution'. More widely the action in Korea was justified out of the need to combat aggression to prevent the UN collapsing in a similar manner to the League. Interestingly, the Prime Minister saw no need to seek public support for such operations when he stated 'if the peoples wish to avoid another world war they must support their governments in asserting the rule of law'. Mr Churchill's speech in reply was supportive, although he put greater emphasis on the need

[53] *Hansard* HC vol 477, col 485, 5 July 1950.
[54] Ibid., col 489.
[55] *Legal Consequences for States of the Continued Presence of South Africa in Namibia Notwithstanding Security Council Resolution 276 (1970)*, 1971 ICJ Rep. 16, paras 21–2.

to combat Communism, while the Liberal leader, Clement Davies, put more emphasis on the action of forty-one countries in support of the Security Council, though he would have preferred to see a truly international army.[56] Overall, there was very little critique of the international legal basis of the operation, in particular there was no highlighting of the fact that the military action being mounted under the auspices of the UN was a long way from that which was envisaged in the UN Charter of 1945. There was some dissent, but this was due to disagreement with the government's policy of siding with the United States, which could lead to world conflict with the Soviet Union.[57] The debate ended with the House supporting a substantive motion that 'this House fully supports the action taken by His Majesty's Government in conformity with their obligations under the United Nations Charter, in helping to resist the unprovoked aggression against the Republic of Korea'.[58]

The importance of the operation being a UN-authorized one is clear. Without that source of legality and legitimacy, it would have been more difficult to explain to parliament, but more particularly to the British public who had only five years previously come out of a devastating world conflict, to support such an action far away from British shores. Simply put it would have been much more difficult to make the case out for defending a distant state from attack than it was to be seen to be clearly acting in support of UN principles and under UN authority to preserve world peace. For all practical military purposes, the distinction between collective defence of Korea and collective security against aggression was at this stage a fine one, but legally and, more importantly, politically the difference was great.

With Resolution 83 secured, the UN force was established, it flew the UN flag, but it was not commanded and controlled by the UN. The fact is that the resolution was simply a delegation of authority to the US, which supplied ninety percent of the force. In Resolution 84, the Security Council recommended that contributing states make forces available to a unified command under the US, requested the US to designate the commander of such forces, and to report to the Security Council on the course of action taken by the unified command. The force's commander, General MacArthur, was appointed by the US and took his orders from Washington, not the UN in New York. When the Soviet representative returned to the Security Council at the beginning of August 1950, thereby preventing the Security Council from adopting any further resolutions, the military action was already underway and so did not require any further mandate until the US-led force had turned the war around and had pushed North Korea back to the 38th parallel. The United States decided to push over the 38th parallel, with a nod towards the ambiguous phrase in Resolution 83 which recommended the restoration of peace and security in the area.

[56] *Hansard* HC vol 477, col 503, 5 July 1950.
[57] Ibid., col 552 (Hughes).
[58] Ibid., cols 485–90, 492–3, 502, 596.

In any event the Western-dominated General Assembly obliged by adopting a resolution on 7 October that called for stability throughout Korea and for
steps to be taken for the establishment of a unified Korea.[59] This was the day
US troops crossed the 38th parallel. Furthermore, the resolution stated that UN
forces should stay in Korea to fulfil these objectives. This implicitly legitimated
that crossing into North Korea. The Assembly's resolution on Korea was adopted
nearly a month before the Assembly's Uniting for Peace Resolution, which clearly
stated that the Assembly could recommend enforcement measures in response to
breaches of the peace and acts of aggression, when the Council was deadlocked by
the veto.[60] MPs welcomed the development of the Uniting for Peace Resolution
in the General Assembly, seeing it as making the collective security machinery
fully effective, though not adding to the powers of the Assembly.[61] The idea was
that after Korea, the Assembly would be able to authorize military action in cases
where the Council was deadlocked by the veto, thus making the UN as a whole
more active and interventionist.

Unfortunately, the crossing of the 38th parallel and the subsequent pushing
of UN forces up towards the Chinese frontier did not restore peace and security
to the area; instead it provoked a massive military intervention by the Peoples'
Republic of China, an act characterized as 'aggression' by the General Assembly.[62]
By July 1951, the belligerents were in a stalemate around the 38th parallel and
truce negotiations eventually resulted in an armistice but not until July 1953,
negotiated, in effect, by the United States.

Beyond the full debate of 7 July 1950, which centred on Resolution 83, subsequent events were not always subject to scrutiny by parliament, notably the
decision to cross the 38th parallel, which was not debated at the time. There was
greater concern about the pressure on British forces necessitating amendments to
the National Service Acts,[63] though in King George VI's speech at the opening
of parliament on 31 October 1950, there was a strong restatement of the cause
underlying the military operation:

In Korea forces, for the first time under the flag of the United Nations, are overcoming
the invaders. The success of this historic action in which My Forces are playing their
part marks a decisive moment in world affairs, and is arousing fresh hopes of achieving a
united, free and democratic Korea. It has already given proof of the ability of the United
Nations to meet a threat to world peace.[64]

In debating this speech MPs seemed to think that the Korean War was drawing
to a successful conclusion with Winston Churchill stating that the 'successful

---

⁵⁹ GA Res. 376, 7 Oct. 1950.   ⁶⁰ GA Res. 377, 3 Nov. 1950.
⁶¹ *Hansard* HC vol 480, col 239 1 Nov. 1950 (Foot, Davies). See further the statement on
Uniting for Peace: vol 480, cols 328–9, 11 Nov. 1950 (Davies).
⁶² GA Res. 498, 1 Feb. 1950.
⁶³ See lengthy debate on defence starting with *Hansard* HC vol 479, col 951, 12 Sept. 1950
(Attlee).
⁶⁴ *Hansard* HC vol 480, col 6, 31 Oct. 1950.

intervention of the United Nations in Korea and General MacArthur's brilliant conduct' were 'things for general rejoicing', while the Prime Minister spoke of the 'success' of the operation,[65] though by late October Chinese forces had already been involved in skirmishes with the UN force.

China entered the war fully in late November 1950. On 16 November 1950, the government reported to the House of Commons the presence of Chinese troops in strength in Korea.[66] In a debate on foreign affairs on 29 November 1950, the Foreign Secretary, Ernest Bevin, restated that the primary aim of the British and UN policy was 'peace, our second a unified democratically governed Korea, and the third the rehabilitation of the country'. He dealt with criticism of the lee-way given to General MacArthur by saying that 'this is the first real effort at collective security in resistance to aggression, which came very suddenly, and much had to be improvised'. On the Chinese intervention, Bevin could only guess at their motives and stated that 'the first essential is to stabilise the military situations and then to explore a political settlement',[67] a hint perhaps that the UK might be willing to forgo the second of its policies (a unified Korea) in pursuance of the first—peace. Anthony Eden, speaking for the Conservative opposition, took this further and stated that the policy should be to hold the 'wasp waist' of Korea in the light of the aggressive Chinese government which has not only intervened in Korea but had also marched into Tibet in October 1950.[68] Criticisms were made in the House of the decision to cross the 38th parallel. With the US-led army in Korea in retreat in the face of the Chinese action, the House was less supportive of government policy. By December 1950 the situation had worsened but Prime Minister Attlee recognized that defeat could be disastrous not only for the fight against communism but for the UN:

Korea is essentially a United Nations problem. Its outcome will have an important effect on the authority and prestige of the United Nations. It is vital that that authority should be maintained, and it is therefore, of supreme importance that any settlement should be arrived at under United Nations auspices.[69]

Winston Churchill took the opportunity to criticize the government for not talking over the decision in October to cross the 38th parallel with the United States,[70] demonstrating some accountability for government policies but again as the great man himself recognized 'it is always easy to be wise after the event'. Accountability to parliament is retrospective and in matters of war this comes too late to make any difference. Had a debate been held in October and MPs expressed concern about heading into North Korea, the government might have

---

[65] Ibid., col 18 (Churchill), col 31 (Attlee).
[66] *Hansard* HC vol 480, col 1905 (Shinwell), 16 Nov. 1950.
[67] *Hansard* HC vol 481, cols 1161–6, 29 Nov. 1950 (Bevin).
[68] Ibid., cols 1177–8 (Eden).
[69] *Hansard* HC vol 481, col 1353, 14 Dec. 1950 (Attlee).
[70] Ibid., col 1364 (Churchill).

tried to influence the US command. The government's response to this criticism though was that the UN force had the authority of the General Assembly to cross into North Korea, and this certainly seemed to influence a number of MPs.[71]

By February 1951 it was clear that the government was in favour of seeking a cease-fire and that, as the Prime Minister put it, 'the 38th parallel ought not to be crossed again until there are full consultations with the United Nations'.[72] The government was questioned when the parallel was crossed again by the US.[73] As it was, the conflict in Korea ebbed and flowed around the 38th parallel, eventually resulting in a stalemate by May 1951. In June 1951, the Foreign Secretary, Herbert Morrison, made a statement on the first anniversary of the outbreak of the conflict:

The immediate objective of driving back the attacking forces to the general area from which the original act of aggression was launched has now largely been attained. Great credit is due to the United Nations Forces for the military success that has been achieved, in which our own Forces have played a gallant and distinguished part.

The longer term objectives were stated to be limiting the fighting to Korea, and to bring the fighting to an end so that peace may be restored and the task of repairing the damage could be started.[74] The government had clearly decided, along with its UN partners, that the war aims should be more realistic especially in the light of the fact that, as the Foreign Secretary indicated, the Soviet Union had indicated that the fighting should stop. China indicated its willingness to seek a cease-fire in early July 1951.[75] Peace negotiations started that month but a cease-fire was not agreed until July 1953, when an armistice was signed by the United States and North Korea. That the negotiations were being conducted by delegates of the Commander in Chief (General Ridgway who replaced General MacArthur in 1951) was made clear by the government,[76] with the new Prime Minister Winston Churchill stating that the US was negotiating on behalf of the United Nations.[77]

In the lengthy period of negotiations a number of debates were held, in which criticisms were levelled at the government for not seeking greater consultation with the United States on UN policy on Korea, and for the continued

---

[71] Ibid., col 1459 (Bevin).

[72] *Hansard* HC vol 484, col 62, 12 Feb. 1951 (Attlee). See also statement by the Defence Secretary, vol 484, col 1072, 20 Feb. 1951 (Shinwell), who related the improving situation.

[73] *Hansard* HC vol 484, col 1274, 21 Feb. 1951 (Brockway). See statement by government on its policy re the 38th parallel and the need to make small incursions: vol 484, col 1743, 26 Feb. 1951 (Davies). See also statement by Foreign Secretary Herbert Morrison regarding the UN policy in Korea when he stated that the real issue was not the re-crossing of the 38th parallel but whether the North Koreans and Chinese would agree to a cease-fire: vol 486, col 1025, 11 April 1951.

[74] *Hansard* HC vol 489, col 1006, 25 June 1951 (Morrison).

[75] *Hansard* HC vol 489, col 1902, 2 July 1951 (Morrison).

[76] *Hansard* HC vol 494, col 2363, 5 Dec. 1951 (Eden).

[77] *Hansard* HC vol 495, col 197, 30 Jan. 1952 (Churchill). He stated that British losses in the War were nearly 3,000 while US losses were over 105,000.

bombing campaigns of the US.[78] In defending the government's policy from a vote of censure in the House of Commons during July 1952, Prime Minister Churchill spoke about the huge burden and cost to the United States giving the example that the 'bickering on the front' during armistice negotiations had led to 32,000 US casualties while the UK had suffered 1,200.[79] Fighting continued, with regular reports to the House of Commons from the government on this and the continuing negotiations, until July 1953. In November 1952 the government reported that the one issue holding up armistice negotiations was that of repatriation of prisoners of war, with the communist side wanting assurances that prisoners would be returned to North Korea or China, and not be given freedom to choose whether to be repatriated.[80] The government reported that there were debates in the UN General Assembly on this matter, and the Assembly did adopt an Indian sponsored resolution which laid down the principles and process under which repatriation should be conducted,[81] though this was rejected by China and North Korea as well as the Soviet Union.[82] The government reported that there were 949 British PoWs in North Korea.[83]

On 1 April 1953 a breakthrough came when the Chinese accepted the proposals for repatriating prisoners,[84] a decision which eventually led to the armistice in July 1953 when a demilitarized zone was established around the front line at the time, which was close to the 38th parallel. The agreement was announced to the House of Commons on 27 July 1953, with the government minister stating that 'for the first time since the formation of the United Nations, member states have taken up arms in collective resistance to aggression, and the joint action has been successful' asserting that the 'forces of aggression have been driven back beyond the line from which they first started'.[85] Though it was the United States who signed the armistice, the British government and parliament were concerned that the matter go to the UN General Assembly,[86] which endorsed the armistice as a major step towards the restoration of peace and security in the area, but also stated that the UN's aims were to achieve by peaceful means a united, independent and democratic Korea.[87] The resolution

---

[78] *Hansard* HC vol 502, col 2353, 25 June 1952 (Shinwell); vol 503, col 255, 1 July 1952 (Noel-Baker).

[79] *Hansard* HC vol 503, col 270, 1 July 1952 (Churchill). The government narrowly survived the vote of censure by 300 votes to 270.

[80] *Hansard* HC vol 508, col 631, 27 Nov. 1952 (Eden).

[81] GA Res. 610 (VII), 3 Dec. 1952. See also Korea: The Indian Proposal for Resolving the Prisoners of War Problem, presented by the Secretary of State for Foreign Affairs to Parliament, December 1952 (Korea No 2 (1952)).

[82] *Hansard* HC vol 510, col 206, 21 Jan. 1953 (Eden).

[83] *Hansard* HC vol 511, col 1233, 18 Feb. 1953 (Birch).

[84] *Hansard* HC vol 513, col 1219, 1 April 1953 (Churchill).

[85] *Hansard* HC vol 518, col 894, 27 July 1953 (Lloyd). See also Special Report of the Unified Command on the Korean Armistice Agreement, presented by the Secretary of State for Foreign Affairs to Parliament, September 1953 (Korea No 2 (1953)).

[86] *Hansard* HC vol 518, col 1091, 28 July 1953 (Butler).

[87] GA Res. 711 (VII), 28 Aug. 1953.

envisaged a political conference of Korea to try and further these objectives, but the Geneva Conference of 1954 on Indo-China concentrated on the next battle-ground in that region—Vietnam.[88]

9. Britain and Iraq's invasion of Kuwait

The Korean model of security action, seemingly unique in the circumstances of the Cold War, appears to have influenced the action taken by an *ad hoc* coalition of forces under US command, but authorized by the Security Council in the Gulf Crisis of 1990–1. Following, the Iraqi invasion and subjugation of Kuwait on 2 August 1990, the Security Council, acting under articles 39 and 40 of the UN Charter, adopted Resolution 660 on the same day, condemning the Iraqi invasion and determining that it constituted a breach of the peace. When this was not heeded, the Security Council adopted mandatory, comprehensive economic sanctions under article 41 of the Charter in Resolution 661 of 6 August. The Council then adopted a series of resolutions either condemning Iraqi actions, such as the purported merger of Kuwait into Iraq,[89] and the taking hostage of foreign nationals in Iraq and Kuwait;[90] or fine-tuning the embargo, as with the authorization for states to use limited force to stop ships in the Gulf in Resolution 665, and clarification of the humanitarian exception to the embargo on food and medicine.[91] While there was only a brief opportunity to utilize the Council in the Korean conflict, the relaxation on the political constraints of the Council in the immediate post-Cold War period meant that it seemed to take charge of the situation with a series of detailed chapter VII resolutions.

Resolution 678 of 29 November 1990, which sanctioned the use of force, was a compromise between the permanent members, with the Soviet Union wishing to delay any military action, while the US and UK were pressing for it. The result that the Council imposed a fairly generous ultimatum to Iraq when it authorized 'member States co-operating with the Government of Kuwait, unless Iraq on or before 15 January 1991', fully implemented Resolution 660 and all subsequent resolutions, 'to use all means to uphold and implement Security Council resolutions and all subsequent resolutions and to restore international peace and security in the area'. Despite the appearance of permanent member consensus, pushing to one side the Chinese abstention, the driving force behind the resolution was the United States and in this respect the military action against Iraq was little different to that taken against Korea, with the United States commanding the

---

[88] See Documents Relating to the Discussion of Korea and Indo-China at the Geneva Conference, presented by the Secretary of State for Foreign Affairs to Parliament, June 1954 (Miscellaneous No 16 (1954)) 1–96.

[89] SC Res. 662, 9 Aug. 1990.

[90] SC Res. 664, 18 Aug. 1990.

[91] SC Res. 666, 13 Sept. 1990.

contributing half a million troops to the coalition force of 750,000 drawn from twenty-nine countries. Once the Security Council had adopted Resolution 678, and the deadline had passed, the coalition was free to prosecute the war and the only obligation *vis-à-vis* the UN being was to provide reports to the Security Council.

It was under the UN umbrella but not under the UN flag that a coalition of Western and Arab forces started their campaign on 16 January soon after the Security Council-imposed deadline had run out. The ground offensive for the liberation of Kuwait started on 24 February 1991 and was successful in achieving its objectives within five days. Despite the fact that Resolution 678 contained the nebulous phrase authorizing the use of force to 'restore international peace and security in the area', the coalition interpreted Resolution 678 restrictively as limiting military operations to the enforcement of Resolution 660 and other resolutions aimed at Iraqi withdrawal from Kuwait. Although the air campaign was directed at military and industrial sites in Iraq, and the ground offensive included southern Iraq within it, these actions appeared necessary to achieve the successful liberation of Kuwait. Overall the coalition kept within the mandate, as laid down in Resolution 678. Whether the mandate could have been interpreted to include the overthrow of the brutal regime of Saddam Hussein seemed a moot point in 1991, though it became all too real in 2003. Certainly when Resolution 678 was adopted by the Security Council, member states, including the UK and the US made it clear that they saw the resolution as enabling them to remove Iraq from Kuwait, no more.[92]

The defeat of Iraq enabled the coalition to impose very strict cease-fire terms, differing greatly from the protracted armistice agreement ending the Korean War. A temporary cease-fire was detailed in Security Council Resolution 686 of 2 March 1991, in which Iraq accepted liability for any damage caused by the invasion and agreed to rescind its annexation of Kuwait. A formal cease-fire was established by Resolution 687, adopted on 3 April 1991. This lengthy document also imposed further punishment and conditions upon Iraq, not least the destruction of its chemical biological and nuclear capability to be overseen by a Special Commission and the IAEA, with a Compensation Commission established to oversee the payment of compensation by Iraq. Although Resolution 687 allowed for the lifting of some sanctions, particularly on foodstuffs and other essential civilian requirements, sanctions were maintained to enforce the disarmament provisions of the resolution.

While the Korean War lasted for three years, the Gulf conflict lasted a few weeks, or at least that seemed to be the case in April 1991. However, the Korean War included not only the repulsion of aggression but also an attempted conquest of North Korea. In 1991 the UN-authorized operation stopped at expulsion of

---

[92] SC 2963rd mtg, 29 Nov. 1990, 78 (UK), 101 (US).

Iraq, though in a sense the second phase came twelve years later with the invasion and conquest of Iraq in 2003.

Considering the role of parliament in the UK it is worth recounting that UN authority for the use of military force was not forthcoming until several months after the Iraqi invasion of Kuwait of 2 August 1990. This period of time gave the House of Commons some room for debate on the question of whether there was a need for such authority, or whether, as the government insisted, the gathering of US and UK troops in the region and their future use against Iraq, was justifiable collective defence of Kuwait. British troops were deployed to the region before the debates occurred in the House of Commons on 6 and 7 September 1990, but there had been no final decision committing them to action. Thus there was a greater opportunity for parliamentary debate prior to military action than there was in Korea.

The Prime Minister, Margaret Thatcher, opened the debate in a parliament recalled from its summer recess, by expressing the UK's support for UN measures (demanding a cease-fire and imposing economic sanctions), while informing the House on the deployment of British troops at the request of various Gulf rulers. She condemned Iraq's actions as 'an outrageous breach of international law' and further:

Iraq's actions raise very important issues of principle as well as of law. There can be no conceivable justification for one country to march in and seize another, simply because it covets its neighbour's wealth and resources. If Iraq's aggression were allowed to succeed, no small state would ever feel safe again. At the very time when at last we can see the prospect of a world governed by the rule of law, a world in which the United Nations and the Security Council can play a role envisaged for them when they were founded, Iraq's actions go back to the law of the jungle.

As with Korea, the credibility of the UN was at stake. However, the Prime Minister made it absolutely clear that the Security Council resolutions adopted so far did not affect the right of the UK and its allies to take military action under the rubric of collective self-defence embodied in article 51 of the Charter (as recognized in the terms of Council Resolution 661). In response to some criticism that authority to take military action should be sought from the Security Council, the Prime Minister stated 'I have full legal authority for everything I say on these matters ... and I am not willing to limit our freedom of action'. While Iraq was vulnerable to sanctions, and the Prime Minister hoped that they would work, she made it clear that 'we are not precluded by reason of any of the Security Council resolutions from exercising our inherent right of collective self-defence in accordance with the rules of international law'.[93] Though the Prime Minister pointed to the new found harmony between the permanent members of

---

[93] *Hansard* HC vol 177, cols 734–8, 6 Sept. 1990 (Thatcher). Questions from Benn and Dalyell.

the Security Council, there was clearly insufficient confidence at this stage in the willingness of the Council to authorize the use of force.

The opposition used this period in the build up of forces to press for any future military response to be founded upon a Security Council resolution. While supporting the need for a firm response to Iraqi aggression, the Leader of the Opposition, Neil Kinnock, pressed the case for sanctions being allowed some time to work and then, if these failed, to seek a Security Council mandate for a forceful eviction of Iraq. To push ahead with an action in collective self-defence of Kuwait would potentially destroy the unanimity among the Council and shatter the prospects for a new world order.

We had better think very hard and politically before risking that potential on the basis of even the most distinguished and technically correct legal advice about the extent of article 51.

Thus while not disagreeing with the Prime Minister's 'technical' interpretation of the right of self-defence, he did think that it would be politically wiser to obtain Security Council authority. He pointed out the fact that the government seemed to accept the need for a Council Resolution (665) to legitimate the maritime blockade in the Gulf.[94] Though the government had stated in the Security Council that Resolution 665 simply provided an 'additional' legal basis for the maritime action,[95] it did seem to be the case that it had accepted the political case for Security Council authority for the enforcement of sanctions.

Neil Kinnock's speech was also interesting in that he saw beyond the attainment of the primary objectives of the UN—to remove Iraq from Kuwait— stating that there must then be an arms embargo on Iraq, its chemical weapons must be destroyed, there must be monitoring of its nuclear and weapons making capability, and finally there must be reparations by Iraq for its aggression.[96] These indeed formed the core elements of Resolution 687 that ended the 1991 conflict.

There was a view, by no means universal in the House of Commons, but shared by MPs from different parties, that it was essential, for political reasons, for UN Security Council authority to be sought and gained for any military action. Former Conservative Prime Minister Edward Heath said that while the right of self-defence under article 51 should not be ruled out if Iraq tried to invade another country such as Saudi Arabia, if there was no further expansion 'it is difficult to imagine a position in which we would launch a deliberate attack without at least having the authority of the United Nations'.[97] The leader of the Liberal Democrats, Paddy Ashdown, endorsed this view stating that in this political

---

[94] Ibid., cols. 746–9 (Kinnock).
[95] SC 2938th mtg, 25 Aug. 1990.
[96] *Hansard* HC vol 177, col 750, 6 Sept. 1990 (Kinnock).
[97] Ibid., col 752 (Heath).

phase of the crisis it was necessary to build the 'strongest international consensus'. He stated in the strongest terms that:

I believe that the Government would find it extremely difficult to carry public opinion in this country—and international opinion abroad—if they were to embark on such an adventure without the backing of the United Nations.

To shatter this consensus 'through impatience would be foolish, and even a successful military outcome could nevertheless represent a serious political failure'.[98]

Although the government, using its large majority and with considerable bipartisan support, won a vote supporting its action in the Gulf by 437 votes to 35, a number of members made it clear that their vote was contingent upon the 'widest possible international agreement' being achieved if the use of force proved necessary.[99]

Events show that the British government came round to the view that politically, at least, a UN resolution was necessary to sanction the use of force against Iraq. The Queen's prorogation speech of 1 November accurately reflects the delicate balance at that stage between taking any military action under UN authority and simply acting in collective self-defence of Kuwait. Queen Elizabeth II stated:

My Government has played a full and vigorous part in the actions taken by the United Nations and the international community to bring about the withdrawal of Iraqi forces from Kuwait and the restoration of that country's independence and legitimate government. They have responded quickly to requests by Kuwait, Saudi Arabia and other Governments of the region to contribute to their defence. They have made clear their determination that this act of aggression will not be allowed to succeed.[100]

Clearly the government did not want to jeopardize its freedom of action under article 51, though it was, with the United States, working towards a further Security Council resolution.[101]

On 28 November 1990, the day before Resolution 678 authorizing force was adopted by the Security Council, the government informed the House of Commons of the imminent resolution. The Foreign Secretary, Douglas Hurd, stated that the resolution was necessary for the 'military option to be fully credible'.[102] Though this represented a change in government policy, it did not amount to a concession that there was a legal need for such a resolution. Indeed, in the later debate of 11 December Douglas Hurd unequivocally stated that 'article 51 and the original request from the Kuwaitis provided a legal basis; the argument

[98] Ibid., col 756, 6 Sept. 1990. But see for example Dr David Owen stating that 'it is nonsense to rule out action under article 51': col 786.
[99] *Hansard* HC vol 177, col 883, 7 Sept. 1990 (Steel).
[100] *Hansard* HC vol 178, col 1088, 1 Nov. 1990.
[101] *Hansard* HC vol 178, col 339, 24 Oct. 1990 (Hurd).
[102] *Hansard* HC vol 181, col 869, 28 Nov. 1990.

was about whether there should be an additional political basis. This has been supplied by resolution 678'.[103] Though this might explain the British position leading up to and including the adoption of Resolution 678, as an explanation of the legal basis after that Resolution, it is unsustainable. After the resolution was secured, as with Korea, the military action, both legally and politically speaking, was a UN authorized operation, not one in collective self-defence. Once the Resolution was adopted it was under article 42 of the Charter, not article 51, that action was taken.

Thus the necessity for a Security Council resolution was fully debated in the House. In addition, there was a debate on 11 December 1990 on the timing of military action with some members wishing more time to be given for sanctions to work, and others opposing the use of force. The government's position was that time favoured Iraq, at least in its military preparations, and in its policy of subsuming Kuwait into Iraq, and that coalition forces would be ready to act within a few weeks.[104] With the political consensus in place, the question was now one of military timing. The government won a vote on the issue of the necessity of military action by 455 votes to 42.

Thus the government was pressed on both the need for a Security Council resolution and the necessity of military action in the build up to the conflict in January 1991. On the day given for withdrawal by Iraq—15 January 1991—with war looming, the new Conservative Prime Minister, John Major, updated the House. His main reason for calling for the debate was that it was 'acutely important that our forces in the Gulf should feel that they have the united support of the vast majority of the House and of the country'. He also used the occasion to reiterate the government's position, amidst some criticism from opposition members, that waiting longer for sanctions to work was not an option given the atrocities occurring in Kuwait.[105] He concluded his speech by declaring:

We do not want a conflict. We are not thirsting for war, but if it comes to it I believe that it would be a just war . . . From tomorrow, we are ready, with our allies, to do whatever is necessary to implement the resolutions of the United Nations in full to ensure that Iraqi forces leave Kuwait without condition, without delay and without reward.[106]

Despite the misgivings of a number of opposition MPs, the government defeated a vote opposing the use of force by 534 votes to 57. On 17 January 1991, Prime Minister Major made a statement to the House announcing the start of hostilities in the Gulf, and reiterating the aims of the operation: 'to get Iraq out of Kuwait— all of Kuwait; to restore the legitimate Government; to re-establish peace and security in the area; and to uphold the authority of the United Nations'.[107] When asked by Tony Benn MP 'what role he sees for the Security Council in monitoring the operation?', the Prime Minister stated that the action was taken 'under

---

[103] *Hansard* HC vol 182, col 824, 11 Dec. 1990 (Hurd).
[104] Ibid., cols 822–9.
[105] *Hansard* HC vol 183, cols 734–6, 15 Jan. 1991 (Major).
[106] Ibid., col 743.
[107] *Hansard* HC vol 183, col 979, 17 Jan. 1991 (Major).

the authority of the United Nations, freely given', and that there was 'no need to reconvene the United Nations Security Council', concluding that the UN was 'not directly involved in the conflict; its member states are, but under the authority of the United Nations'.[108] Carrying parliament with it, the government moved that the House fully support British forces in the Gulf and 'their contribution to the implementation of United Nations resolutions by the multinational force, as authorized by United Nations Security Council Resolution 678'.[109] This was supplemented by the Labour leader, Neil Kinnock, with the words: 'commends the instruction to minimise civilian casualties wherever possible; and expresses its determination that, once the aggression in Kuwait is reversed, the United Nations and the international community must return with renewed vigour to resolving the wider problems in the Middle East'.[110] The approval for the substantive amended motion was 563 to 34.

Thus with the House overwhelmingly behind it, the government subsequently reported on the state of hostilities to the House on 31 January, 18 February, 22 February, 25 February (just after the ground campaign had started), 26 February and 28 February (when the ground campaign ended). In the latter, the Prime Minister told the House that the Security Council would shortly discuss the 'necessary political arrangements for the war to end', though to all intents and purposes the 'war had been won'.[111]

Despite this high degree of accountability to parliament in the period leading up to the conflict and indeed during the war, there was no discussion of the settlement, in particular proposals for what were to become Security Council Resolutions 686 and 687. This is somewhat surprising given the problems of enforcing such an ambitious post-war settlement. It was a breach of the Resolution 687, in combination with the original mandate of Resolution 678, which was used to justify further uses of force against Iraq, most particularly in 1993, 1998 and finally with the invasion of Iraq in March 2003 reviewed in chapter ten.

There were detailed discussions in parliament on the plight of the parts of the Iraqi population who had rebelled against Saddam Hussein's regime in the wake of his defeat in Kuwait.[112] The repression of the Kurds and Shias by the still powerful Iraqi army led the Security Council to adopt Resolution 688 on 5 April which condemned Iraq's actions but did not authorize any military intervention within Iraq. The breach of this resolution was also used by western states as a reason for military action against Iraq, most especially in 1996. These actions, to protect the Kurds and Shias, as well as to enforce the disarmament provisions of

[108] Ibid., cols 980, 987 (Benn/Major).
[109] *Hansard* HC vol 184, col 24, 21 Jan. 1991 (Major).
[110] Ibid., col 31 (Kinnock).
[111] *Hansard* HC vol 186, col 1117, 28 Feb. 1991 (Major).
[112] *Hansard* HC vol 189, col 21, 15 April 1991; vol 189, col 419, 17 April 1991; vol 189, col 571, 18 April 1991.

Resolution 687, raise a new raft of legal and political problems, and will be subject to separate discussion in chapters nine and ten.

10. Conclusion

In a violent world dominated by sovereign states, aggression is bound to occur. Traditionally, the victim of aggression has acted in self-defence and, if fortunate, has been joined by its allies in collective defence. However, both individual self-defence and collective self-defence are often abused. Israel claimed to be acting in self-defence when it launched the Six Day War in 1967. When the Soviet Union claimed in 1968 to be defending Czechoslovakia, the West ignored the Czechs' plea for help against defenders who were actually aggressors.

The UN Charter was intended to provide for a collective response to aggression, as well as dealing with other threats to the peace. Although the system that has developed since 1945 does not match the ideal, the United Nations has established its authority over military responses to aggression by North Korea and Iraq, and has thereby removed some, if not all, of the subjectivity and abuse inherent in a system based on defence pacts. Though the legal and political links between the United Nations and the operation should have been stronger in both Korea and the Gulf, a line can be drawn linking the Cold War action in Korea and the coalition's post-Cold War action in the Gulf. Several systemic defects remain, in particular, lack of precision in the enabling resolutions and the dependence on voluntary rather than compulsory commitment, but they remain UN operations and form the basis upon which modern day coalitions of the willing are authorized by the UN and dispatched by contributing states. Ultimately by seeing the operations in their true UN colours, as opposed to viewing them in traditional self-defence terms, we can see the defects in the UN system, and work towards improvement of it.

It must be said that Britain, along with the United States, has been instrumental in creating a decentralized UN military option under which the UN Security Council authorizes coalitions of the willing. Indeed, the creativity shown as regards UN Charter law in the action against North Korea was taken further by attempting to extend the constitutional development of military enforcement to include occasions when the General Assembly authorizes such action in situations when the Council is deadlocked by the veto. Though the 'Uniting for Peace' procedure has been used, its sponsors in 1950, including the UK, have long distanced themselves from it because of the vast changes in composition of the General Assembly. Simply put, the Assembly was dominated by the West in 1950, but that majority was lost later in that decade, as the first swathe of newly independent states joined the organization.

It also appears to be the case that parliament (and the population) is more likely to support an action to reverse aggression against a distant country when the action is taken under UN authority, rather than under the more traditional right of self-defence. In trying to understand this, it is necessary to recognize that international law does not distinguish between a state's right to defend itself and its right to come to the aid of another state. Legally speaking there is a clear right of collective self-defence, whereby the UK can come to the aid of an attacked state if so requested by that state. However, the core of self-defence is deep within the sovereignty of state, and its moral duty to protect that state from invasion. While we might technically speak of the 'right' of self-defence, from the perspective of the attacked state it is more in the nature of a duty, which can be placed deep within British constitutional practice and law,[113] placed upon the government to protect the state, its territory, institutions and population from outside attack. Further discussion on the nature of the right of self-defence and collective self-defence will be left to chapters seven and eight, suffice it to say at this stage in Korea and Iraq there was no overwhelming sense that the UK was in danger from the acts of aggression in question, but the UN order was. As a member of the UN, more particularly a permanent member, the UK has a duty to uphold the principles of the UN Charter, which are most sharply challenged by acts of naked aggression. By taking the case for war to the Security Council and receiving the authority of that body, those states prosecuting the wars against Korea and Kuwait were able to present much more convincing cases to their parliaments and peoples.

---

[113] See for example the Defence of the Realm Act 1914 and the Emergency Powers (Defence) Act 1939.

5

A Role for Europe: Britain and the EU

1. Introduction

During the Cold War, the British government concentrated on developing the deterrent effect of NATO, recognizing that coalitions of the willing under UN authority such as that deployed to Korea in 1950 would be the exception rather than the rule. Consensual peacekeeping under the auspices of the UN developed as an alternative form of international military deployment and will be considered in the next chapter. During this period Britain had an uneasy and uneven relationship with, and eventually within, the growing European organization created by the Treaty of Rome signed in 1956. Though this organization did not claim competence in collective security matters at its inception, it did eventually step into that realm. Add to this growing network of security organizations the Helsinki process, which eventually led to the Organization on Security and Cooperation in Europe (OSCE), and there seems to be a surfeit of such bodies centred upon Europe. The reality, though, is very different, with European states manifesting a marked reluctance to co-operate in defence and security matters, in contrast to the relative speed with which economic integration was achieved.

The end of the Cold War saw NATO changing and adapting, but also European powers trying to distance themselves from the transatlantic relationship. The UK though remained committed to a special relationship with the United States. Within this complex political web, the member states of the European Community (EC) agreed in the Maastricht Treaty of 1992 to move the newly created European Union (EU) onto the international stage, not simply as an economic organization as had hitherto been the case, but as a security actor. By the end of 2008 the EU had been involved in significant military operations in Macedonia, the Congo, Bosnia, and Chad, as well as developing rapid reaction capability.

British troops are part of the EU military infrastructure that is being built up. This chapter will focus on the domestic, regional and international legal frameworks of this developing example of military action, while maintaining the book's focus on Britain. In so doing this chapter completes the account of the wider legal and institutional contexts. The following chapters focus on analysing a number of British operations in conflict zones in order to illustrate the application of the rules, principles and constitutional practices at the domestic and international levels, and to assess the impact of international law and institutions on the constitutional and political order of the UK.

2. Part of the Federal Dream

The idea of a European Union with centralized policing and military power is not just something that has been discussed since the advent of the Union in 1992 by the Maastricht Treaty, which contained provisions for a Common Foreign and Security Policy (CFSP). Indeed, as shall be seen, the idea of a common army was at the very heart of discussions that led to European integration starting in the 1950s. However, the rapid progress on economic integration thereafter can be contrasted starkly with the sluggish pace of co-operation and limited integration on regional defence and security matters. Why? In a nutshell, defence and control over the military are core aspects of a state, and European governments were not going to give up control of their armies or their national defence easily. In such issues of high politics there is inevitably going to be limited progress when it comes to co-operation, even less when the talk is of integration.

European countries though were torn between a desire to integrate and thereby remove any temptation for a powerful European state to wage war on its neighbours as had happened so often in the past, and fear of attack not just from within but from external forces, especially the Soviet Union, a fear which led to most European states each maintaining a small army. In addition, the benefits of moving towards a larger combined force, within which each state could provide specialist military forces, were outweighed by the fear that the decisions to deploy such a powerful force would be difficult to achieve if European governments were still going to have a say in issues of deployment.

The idea of a single unified European army is wrapped up in the federalist agenda. The dream of a 'United States of Europe' was not simply a post-Second World War phenomenon. After the Great War ended in 1918, Giovanni Agnelli, founder of the Italian FIAT company, and Attilio Cabiati, an economist, wrote:

> Without hesitation we believe that, if we really want to make war in Europe a phenomenon which cannot be repeated, there is only one way to do so and we must be outspoken enough to consider it: a federation of European states under a central power which governs them. Any other milder version is an illusion.[1]

The essential element of the federal ideal is the centralization of governmental power. Agnelli and Cabiati pointed to the two constitutions of the United States to illustrate their point that nothing short of a federal State in Europe would

---

[1] Extracted in D. Weigall and P. Stirk (eds), *The Origins and Development of the European Community* (Leicester: Leicester University Press, 1992) 6–7.

be sufficient. The first constitution of the United States of 1781 essentially created a league or confederation of sovereign independent states, an unworkable system according to Agnelli and Cabiati, since the 'essence of sovereignty is legal omnipotence...it cannot acknowledge a higher sovereignty without destroying itself'.[2] The 1788 US Constitution resolved this problem and replaced the old constitutional system with a central federal government with legislative and executive power.

With the Second World War drawing to a close, there were strong arguments within Europe for a federal Europe, even in Britain. R.W.G. MacKay, a Labour MP, wrote a book in 1940 entitled *Federal Europe* in which he argued for a Federation consisting of a minimum of Britain, France, and Germany, without which 'war in Europe will continue'. One of the conditions he identified for a successful federation was that 'each of the States joining the Federation should transfer to it a minimum number of powers, which shall give to the Federation exclusive power to legislate in four matters, namely external affairs, defence, customs and currency'.[3] Even Winston Churchill, the Conservative leader and Prime Minister during the war, suggested on a number of occasions the need for some form of post-war European unity.[4] Indeed his speech in Zurich in September 1946, when he spoke about the United States of Europe (though without any detail), 'helped revive the cause of European Union'.[5]

A group sharing a federal vision for Europe was the European Union of Federalists established in Paris in 1946. At its first conference held in Montreux in December 1947 the Union provided some detail as to what elements were needed for a federal system:

Federalists must declare firmly and without compromise that it is absolute national sovereignty that must be abated, that a part of that sovereignty must be entrusted to a federal authority assisted by all the functional bodies necessary to the accomplishment, on the federal plane, of its economic and cultural tasks, whether in whole or in part. In particular the authority must possess:

(a) a government responsible to the peoples and groups and not to the federated states;
(b) a Supreme Court capable of resolving possible disputes between state members of the Federation;
(c) an armed police force under its own control...[6]

A federal system entails not simply autonomy for the central body in certain areas, but entails full government, representing the people of Europe and not simply consisting of a Council of member states. The Supreme Court must not only adjudicate disputes between member states, as stated in this vision, but should also be able to review and declare unconstitutional any acts of the federal government that exceed the powers given to it in the founding treaty.

---

[2] Ibid., 7.   [3] Ibid., 18.
[4] See for example his note to President Roosevelt in February 1943, ibid., 33.
[5] Ibid., 40–1.   [6] Ibid., 42.

3. The Separation of Security

The ideal of a European federal union was tempered by the politicians of Europe who wanted greater co-operation in order to compete with the superpowers, but who were not ready for wholesale European integration, especially in matters of defence and security. The result was a gradual move towards greater centralization of powers; the first steps being the creation by 'the Six'—France, West Germany, Italy, Belgium, Netherlands, and Luxembourg—of the European Coal and Steel Community (ECSC) in 1952, with a consultative Assembly, High Authority, Council and a Court. It must be remembered as well that this was part of a wider process of institutionalization in Europe with the creation of the Organization for European Economic Co-operation (OEEC), a European defence pact, NATO, and the Council of Europe—all institutions separate from the Community.

Focusing on defence, it must be noted that neither the Brussels Treaty of 1948 providing for mutual defence in Europe (and the WEU that was built upon it in 1954), nor the Washington Treaty of 1949 that created NATO, envisaged defence integration along the lines of the European federalists. They were built on traditional conceptions of sovereign equality, where the armies of the state parties would be deployed in defence of any state party that had been subject to an external attack. These were the defence structures that finally emerged from the numerous discussions and proposals on European integration of this period. In these circumstances it is easy to overlook the fact that there was nearly a very different European defence project in the form of a European Defence Community (EDC), originally envisaged in the Pleven Plan of October 1950. The French Prime Minister Rene Pleven argued:

The setting up of a European Army cannot result from a mere grouping together of national military units, which would in reality only mask a coalition of the old sort. For tasks which are inevitably common ones, only common institutions will do. The army of a united Europe, composed of men coming from different European countries, must, so far as is possible, achieve a complete fusion of the human and material elements which make it up under a single European political and military authority.[7]

Six governments (Belgium, France, Germany, Italy, Luxembourg, and the Netherlands) signed the EDC Treaty in May 1952, and although four ratified it, it was ironically the French National Assembly's failure to ratify that ended the EDC. The EDC Treaty 'had envisaged nothing less than the creation of a supranational organization to supervise integrated European Defence Forces'.[8] Its failure led to a European version of NATO—the Western European Union

---

[7] Ibid., 75–7.
[8] M. Trybus, 'The Vision of the European Defence Community and a Common Defence for the European Union', in M. Trybus and N.D. White (eds), *European Security Law* (Oxford: Oxford University Press, 2007) 13.

(WEU)—being created in 1954, based on military co-operation not integration. The British response to the EDC proposal had been lukewarm. In a parliamentary debate held in response to the Pleven Plan in November 1950, Ernest Bevin, the Foreign Minister, stated the government's preference was for a strong NATO: 'Europe is not enough; it is not big enough, it is not strong enough and it is not able to stand by itself', he declared.[9] The conservative government of Winston Churchill was more positive about the EDC, but still refused to join.[10]

Though defence integration had been halted, the success of the common market in coal and steel led to the expansion of the idea of economic integration by the creation of the European Economic Community (EEC), and the European Atomic Energy Community (EURATOM) (governing the peaceful uses of nuclear power) in 1956—the purpose of these being largely about achieving European stability and security. Indeed, the preamble of the first treaty of 1952, establishing the coal and steel community, contained within it a resolve 'to substitute for age-old rivalries the merging' of member states' 'essential interests to create by establishing an economic community, the basis for broader and deeper community among peoples long divided by bloody conflicts'. Coal and steel are essential for the production of armaments: 'if production and distribution of these commodities could be controlled by a centralized authority it would be far less possible for any country to develop a war machine which could be used against its neighbours'.[11] So began a process of pacification by economic unification.

4. The Birth of an Economic Giant

The EEC was based on the idea of free trade within a large market, and although it created a 'new legal order'[12] independent of member states with centralized decision-making power having direct effect in national legal systems without the need for national parliamentary approval, its concern was with economic integration rather than a political union. Decision-making in the Community was a mixture of inter-governmental, in the Council of Ministers, and supranational in the independent but unelected Commission.[13] The Assembly, to which MEPs were elected for the first time in 1979, had limited advisory and supervisory powers under the 1956 Treaty,[14] not permitting it to represent the people of Europe in more than a token fashion. It can be seen therefore that under the 1956 treaties

[9] Weigall and Stirk, *Origins*, 78.
[10] Ibid., 80–2.
[11] P. Craig, 'Britain in the European Union', in J. Jowell and D. Oliver (eds), *The Changing Constitution* (5th edn, Oxford: Oxford University Press, 2004) 88 at 89.
[12] Case 26/62, *Van Gend en Loos v Netherlandse Administratie der Belastingen* [1963] ECR 1 at 12.
[13] Weigall and Stirk, *Origins*, 93.
[14] See D. Freestone and J.S. Davidson, *The Institutional Framework of the European Community* (London: Routledge, 1988) 76–84.

the EEC, although possessing international legal personality, had a limited competence with its concentration on the creation of a common market, and at the decision-making level it was primarily controlled by member governments.

Nevertheless, there was sufficient centralization in the Treaty of Rome, as enhanced by the 1965 Treaty Establishing a Single Council and a Single Commission of the European Communities (the Merger Treaty), to encourage those European states fearing a loss of sovereignty—the United Kingdom, Norway, Sweden, Denmark, Austria, Portugal, Iceland, and Switzerland—to form the separate European Free Trade Association (EFTA) in 1959, which was explicit about the protection of the sovereignty of its member states.[15] However, the success of the EEC/EC/EU led to the UK, Denmark and Ireland joining in 1972, Greece in 1981, Spain and Portugal in 1986, and Austria, Sweden, and Finland in 1995 bringing the membership to fifteen. Further expansion to twenty-five was achieved in 2004 with the accession of Cyprus, Czech Republic, Estonia, Hungary, Latvia, Lithuania, Malta, Poland, Slovakia, and Slovenia; and to twenty-seven in 2007 when Bulgaria and Romania joined.

The UK's road to European membership had been a rocky one. It had twice tried to join in the 1960s, once under a Conservative government and once under a Labour administration, but on both occasions the French government blocked entry. Even within the British political parties there was disunity on entry to the EC: 'both the Labour left and Conservative right wings opposed accession'.[16] Membership was achieved in 1972 under a Conservative government, but only with the help of Labour rebels, and a Labour election victory in 1974 led to the issue of membership being reconsidered by dint of an unprecedented referendum, held in 1975, which was won by the pro-EC supporters by 67.2 per cent to 32.8 per cent. This did not result in the British position within the EC/EU being a settled one. Each revision of the Treaty of Rome caused constitutional and political strife within the houses of parliament. The debates on these key events will be considered below, but it is worth noting at this point the major political turbulence caused by the Maastricht Treaty of 1992, which incorporated a common foreign and security policy into the newly created Union. The Conservative government of John Major survived, but only just. 'Given the small size of ... the [Conservative] government's Commons majority, and the presence of a dozen anti-EC backbenchers within Conservative ranks, it was not clear that the government could win Commons approval for the treaty', but the prospect of losing a vote of confidence and possibly losing their seats, persuaded the rebel MPs to vote in favour.[17]

As an international legal person, the EEC, by adopting a common external tariff, was able to negotiate as a single entity in the GATT (the precursor to the

---

[15] Weigall and Stirk, *Origins*, 94.
[16] I. Loveland, 'Britain and Europe', in V. Bogdanor (ed), *The British Constitution in the Twentieth Century* (Oxford: Oxford University Press, 2003) 663 at 672.
[17] Ibid., 684.

WTO) trade rounds. 'The Community was set to become a very important force in the global economy, an economic giant. But this did not, at this stage, extend to foreign or defence policy. She was not a political giant'.[18] The Community in effect served liberal economic purposes namely the 'removal of impediments to voluntary and hence mutually beneficial transactions between individuals who happen to live on different sides of a border'.[19] It did not as yet fulfil the liberal political vision of political integration with a central European government. The Single European Act of 1986 and, more particularly, the Treaty on European Union of 1992 (the Maastricht Treaty) can be said to have made tentative steps towards this aim with an increase in interventionist supranational activities, in the form of greater majority voting in the Council and a greater co-operative role for the Assembly, re-named the European Parliament. This occurred in the fields of economic, social and industrial policy, to be dealt with by the original EC itself (the so called first pillar of the Maastricht treaty). However, the Common Foreign and Security Policy (CFSP), and the areas of justice and home affairs (the second and third pillars), were to be left to inter-governmental co-operation, although the mechanisms for action in these areas were to be brought within the treaty framework for the first time.

5. The Common Foreign and Security Policy (CFSP)

Turning to look at the CFSP as introduced by the Maastricht Treaty of 1992, it can be seen that this built on the process of European Political Cooperation (EPC) started in the 1970s, whereby member states agreed on a common position, which to become Community Law had to be adopted by the Council of Ministers of the EC. This for example was used in relation to the economic measures taken by the Community in response to the Argentinian invasion of the Falklands in 1982.[20] The EPC process was formalized first by the 1986 Treaty and then by the Maastricht Treaty, but is still clearly separate from 'the supranational aspects of the European Community (such as majority voting, the role of the European Parliament and the European Court of Justice)'.[21] With the defence policy of the European Union being in the hands of the already established inter-governmental WEU created upon the failure of the EDC in 1954, and developed from the Brussels Treaty of 1948,[22] the separation of defence and foreign policy from the supranational activities of the EC appeared complete. In the area of economic integration the European Court of Justice adopted a strong,

---

[18] Weigall and Stirk, *Origins*, 115.

[19] H. Schmieding, *Europe after Maastricht* (London: Institute of Economic Affairs, 1993) 12.

[20] EC Regulation 8777/82, OJ L102/1.

[21] M. Cremona, 'The Common Foreign and Security Policy of the European Union and the External Relations Powers of the European Community', in D. O'Keefe and P.M. Twomey (eds), *Legal Issues of the Maastricht Treaty* (London: Chancery Law, 1994) 248.

[22] Recognized in art 17 Treaty on European Union, 1992.

policy based role, to the extent that it could be compared with the US Supreme Court even though the EC was not fully a federal system.[23] The Court's absence of competence in matters of foreign policy signifies that member states are not yet prepared wholeheartedly to follow a federal road. However, the absence of judicial competence over matters of foreign policy, particularly decisions to use force, is not unique to the EU; in many countries including the UK there is a marked reluctance for any judicial review of such issues of high policy.[24]

Nevertheless, the further development of the second pillar by the Treaties of Amsterdam (1997) and Nice (2001), the adoption of a European Security and Defence Policy (ESDP) in 1999, and the gradual subsuming of the WEU into the EU, suggests that progress, albeit slow, is being made under the second pillar.[25] Article 17(1) of the Treaty on European Union provided that 'the common foreign and security policy shall include all questions relating to the security of the Union, including the progressive framing of a common defence policy'. This provision also included the so-called Petersberg tasks adopted by the WEU in 1992 namely 'humanitarian and rescue tasks, peacekeeping tasks and tasks of combat forces in crisis management, including peacemaking'. The development of military capability, even though a limited one, with small forces deployed to Macedonia and the Congo in 2002–3, seem to indicate the coming of age of the EU as a serious security organization, enhanced by the EU's take over of Bosnian security from NATO in December 2004.

Though there have been many documents developing peace and security within the EU order, the European Security Strategy entitled 'A Secure Europe in a Better World' prepared by the EU's High Representative, Javier Solana, and approved by the European Council on 12 December 2003, is perhaps the most far-reaching, reflecting as it does the shift towards confronting terrorism that has occurred following the events of 11 September 2001. The Strategy commences by declaring that 'Europe has never been so prosperous, so secure nor so free', and asserts that the EU 'has been central to this development'. The link between democracy and peace is also strong with the introductory section stating that since the EU's creation 'the progressive spread of the rule of law and democracy has seen authoritarian regimes change into secure, stable and dynamic democracies'.[26]

6. The EU as a Regional Arrangement

A thorny issue to be considered in this section is whether the EU is a 'regional' collective security organization in the sense of chapter VIII of the UN Charter.

---

[23] Freestone and Davidson, *Institutional Framework*, 27.

[24] See chapter eleven.

[25] See generally R.A. Wessel, 'The State of Affairs in EU Security and Defence Policy: The Breakthrough in the Treaty of Nice' (2003) 8 JCSL 265.

[26] Approved by the European Council held in Brussels on 12 Dec. 2003.

Chapter VIII purports to govern the relationship between the UN and regional arrangements or agencies in issues of peace and security, and includes within it a provision that requires that 'enforcement' action by regional arrangements has to be taken under the authority of the UN Security Council.[27]

Henry Schermers and Niels Blokker, leading authorities on international institutional law, include regional organizations within a somewhat wider category of 'closed' organizations, which 'seek only membership from a closed group of states and no members from outside the group will be admitted'.[28] Of course there may be some debate about whether an applicant country is within the group or not, as with the case of Turkey and the EU, but the contrast with universal organizations, which are normally open to all states,[29] is clear. It would seem that attempts at further refinement of the concept of regional organization are fraught with difficulty. To define regionalism in terms of geographical proximity is immediately appealing but in practice very difficult to judge as the endless debates about where Europe ends in a geographical sense illustrate only too well. Furthermore, 'the criterion of common cultural, linguistic, or historical relations'[30] is also imprecise and likely to cause as many disputes as it solves.[31]

In reality, regional organizations are non-universal groupings of states that are essentially self-defining in terms of membership and objects and purposes, but generally have as their aim the protection or achievement of certain values, such as peace and security or economic prosperity among their membership. The principal ones often share similar goals and values to the UN, ranging across peace and security, human rights and justice, to economic and social well-being, but on a regional level. Thus the potential for overlap between the functions and activities of the UN and regional organizations such as the EU is considerable.

The EU is certainly a regional body in an economic sense having a well-developed level of integration between members under the first pillar (the EC). It is also developing its competence with regard to foreign and security policy. Unlike the established regional organizations of the Americas and Africa, which are concerned with regulating their own membership, the EU's security policy is principally external to its membership, relating to threats to or breaches of the peace within or by states that are not members of the EU. This, though, does not disqualify it as a regional organization. The relative harmonious state of European affairs means that its main concern in security matters is external, though one

---

[27] Art 53 of the UN Charter.

[28] H.G. Schermers and N.M. Blokker, *International Institutional Law* (4th edn, Leiden: Martinus Nijhoff, 2003) 42.

[29] See art 4 of the UN Charter.

[30] W. Hummer and M. Schweitzer, 'Article 52', in B. Simma (ed), *The Charter of the United Nations* (2nd edn, Oxford: Oxford University Press, 2004) 821.

[31] For further discussion see P. Taylor, *International Organizations in the Modern World* (London: Pinter, 1993) 7; A. Abass, *Regional Organizations in the Development of Collective Security* (Oxford: Hart, 2004) 1–26; E.D. Mansfield and H.V. Milner, 'The New Wave of Regionalism', in P.F. Diehl (ed), *The Politics of Global Governance* (Boulder Col: Lynne Rienner, 2001) 314–16.

should not underestimate the propensity of the continent towards violence as history shows. The election of an extreme right-wing government in Austria in 2000 and the reaction of the EU to it, as well as the threat from terrorism as illustrated by the Madrid bombings of 11 March 2004 and London of 7 July 2005, show that European security is as much an internal issue as an external one.

In general terms although the EU has not expressly stated that it comes within the framework of chapter VIII (unlike for instance the OAS and the OSCE),[32] it has not tried to opt out of the UN Charter system for collective security. Nevertheless, the proposition that the EU comes within chapter VIII of the UN Charter is not necessarily that clear cut. In the text of the Treaty on European Union (TEU), there is a clear statement that the Union, in defining and implementing a foreign and security policy, shall safeguard its values and preserve peace and security 'in conformity with' and 'in accordance with' the principles of the UN Charter.[33] Although there is no specific reference to chapter VIII of the Charter (articles 52 to 54) in the TEU, conformity with the principles of the Charter requires compliance with the rules governing the use of force, an integral element of which is the UN Security Council's power to authorize states to use force under chapter VII, or regional arrangements under chapter VIII (article 53).

Interestingly though, in the three Security Council authorizations to EU forces to date—Artemis in the Democratic Republic of Congo (2003), Althea in Bosnia (2004), and the European peace support operation for Chad deployed in 2008— the Security Council authorized the forces under chapter VII rather than chapter VIII of the UN Charter.[34] Such practice is not incompatible with the EU being a regional arrangement within the meaning of chapter VIII, for as shown by past Security Council resolutions of the mid-1990s authorizing NATO in Bosnia,[35] the important issue is gaining Security Council authority to use force, and chapter VII is the normal method of granting this. This may also be explicable given that both the Bosnian and Congolese forces contained troops from outside the EU, and it was therefore more sensible to direct authorization at the member states of the UN (including EU states) undertaking the military action.

Following the rejection in 2005 of the Treaty Establishing a Constitution for Europe in referenda in both France and the Netherlands, EU leaders agreed to the Treaty of Lisbon amending the Treaty on European Union and the Treaty Establishing the European Community, signed on 13 December 2007. The Treaty, which is yet to come into force,[36] has a more elaborate set of security

[32] OAS Charter art 1 reads in part: 'Within the United Nations, the Organization of American States is a regional agency'. In 1992, the member states of the OSCE (then CSCE) declared the organization to be a 'regional arrangement in the sense of Chapter VIII of the Charter of the United Nations', (1992) 31 ILM 976 and 1390.

[33] Art 11 TEU.

[34] SC Res. 1484, 30 May 2003 (DRC); SC Res. 1525, 22 Nov. 2004 (Bosnia); SC Res. 1778, 25 Sept. 2007 (Chad).

[35] SC Res. 770, 13 Aug. 1992.

[36] The Irish electorate rejected the Treaty in June 2008.

provisions, and also has an increased number of references to the EU acting in conformity with the principles of the UN Charter and international law. Article 2.5 states that:

In its relations with the wider world, the Union shall uphold and promote its values and interests and contribute to the protection of its citizens. It shall contribute to peace, security, the sustainable development of the Earth, solidarity and mutual respect among peoples, free and fair trade, eradication of poverty and the protection of human rights, in particular the rights of the child, as well as to the strict observance and development of international law, including respect for the principles of the United Nations Charter.[37]

Again though there are no specific references to chapter VIII of the UN Charter, the only Charter provision mentioned is article 51, which preserves the right of individual or collective self-defence in response to an armed attack, reference to which is found in the Treaty's mutual defence clause.[38] The Treaty does state that the Union 'shall promote multilateral solutions to common problems, in particular within the framework of the United Nations',[39] and that the Union 'shall establish all appropriate forms of cooperation with the organs of the United Nations and its specialised agencies',[40] but these are not specific enough obligations to expressly incorporate chapter VIII.

On balance though it is difficult for the EU to deny that it is subject to chapter VIII. Although it is clearly within the founding states' competence to establish a closed organization by delimiting membership in certain ways, once such an organization is created having as one of its objects and purposes the maintenance or restoration of peace and security, then it is subject to the principle of the non-use of force and the rules of international law governing the use of force, which include the provisions of chapter VIII of the UN Charter.

There may be greater leeway in the case of economic measures (where a state has some freedom on trading matters), allowing a collection of states in a region powers of coercion. The EU has utilized this power, for example in taking non-forcible sanctions against Burma starting in 2000 and against Zimbabwe commencing in 2002, for human rights violations by the governments of those countries.[41]

---

[37] OJ C306/10, 17 Dec. 2007. See also art 10A.1, 10A.2.c, 28A.
[38] Art 28A.7. In the preamble to the Protocol on Permanent Structured Co-operation there is a recognition that the UN 'may request the Union's assistance for the urgent implementation of missions undertaken under Chapters VI and VII of the United Nations Charter'.
[39] Art 10A.1.
[40] Art 188P.1.
[41] For Burma see Regulation 1081/2000, 22 May 2000 ([2000] OJ L122), covering equipment for suppression, freezing of funds of persons related to important government functions—due to human rights violations. For Zimbabwe see Regulation 310/02, 18 Feb. 2002, relating to the freezing of funds and assets of members of government and ban on export of suppression equipment—due to human rights violations ([2002] OJ L050); see also Council Regulation 313/2003, [2003] OJ L046). The measures against Zimbabwe were in addition to those taken under the Cotonou Agreement of 2000 regarding development aid, imposed in furtherance of the human rights clause in that agreement: see P. Eeckhout, *External Relations of the European Union* (Oxford: Oxford University Press, 2004) 481.

Although arguably enforcement action, and therefore subject to the requirement of article 53 of the Charter that Security Council authority be sought and gained, practice suggests otherwise.

When turning to consider the issue of whether regional organizations such as the EU have freedom of action in military matters, the debate is no longer about the interpretation of article 53. If 'enforcement action' has any meaning at all it must cover aggressive military action, action that would otherwise be unlawful if it were not permitted. The very idea of authorization in article 53 assumes that otherwise the action would be illegal, a situation which applies to military enforcement action which is prohibited by article 2(4) of the UN Charter, but not economic enforcement (or at least not all of it).[42] While enforcement action may have been interpreted more restrictively than the 1945 consensus to exclude (at least presumptively) economic sanctions, if it still retains its core meaning, it must cover military enforcement action.

The continued application of article 53 of the UN Charter to military enforcement action by regional organizations is not just a result of the terms of the provision itself, but is underpinned by the other hierarchy provisions of the Charter. More profoundly it is underpinned by the fundamental and peremptory nature of the prohibition on the threat or use of force. Some regional military enforcement (including robust peacekeeping) practice appears contrary to article 53, for example the action of the OAS in the Dominican Republic in 1965, the Arab League in Lebanon in 1976, and of ECOWAS in Liberia and Sierra Leone in the 1990s and beyond.[43] This might be argued to have undermined article 53 if it were not part of the more basic hierarchies of the UN Charter and international law. First, article 103, which states that UN Charter obligations prevail over inconsistent duties in other treaties, thereby including regional treaties. This signifies that the Charter obligation to refrain from the use of force prevails over any inconsistent regional treaty obligation. Second, there is the *jus cogens* obligation to refrain from the use of force, which cannot be derogated from by inconsistent treaties.[44]

7. Post-War Parliamentary Debates

The idea of European security was soon on the agenda of the House of Commons after the Second World War ended. As discussed in chapter four, though allegiance to the UN was still strong in the House, there was a sober realization of its limitations. In debates in 1948, MPs spoke about the need for a 'Western

---

[42] U. Villani, 'The Security Council's Authorization of Enforcement Action by Regional Organizations' (2002) 6 MPYBUNL 535 at 539.

[43] C. Gray, *International Law and the Use of Force* (2nd edn, Oxford: Oxford University Press, 2004) 282–327.

[44] See art 53 of the Vienna Convention on the Law of Treaties, 1969.

Union'.[45] That the House was not simply foreseeing a security organization was made clear by the Labour Foreign Secretary Ernest Bevin in 1948 when he declared that 'if anyone rushes off with the idea that we are going to build European Union or economic co-operation without mutual sacrifices he is suffering under a fatal delusion'. He spoke about the Brussels Treaty of 1948 providing for mutual defence in Western Europe, the machinery of which 'was working well', but made it clear that he desired a further integration of defence when he alluded to the inefficiencies of having a number of smaller national armies, which 'cost money, and if there can be a planned defence system for Western Union which makes the greatest contribution to security with a minimum of cost it will be of great advantage to the economies of all countries'.[46] The Labour Defence Minister, Albert Alexander, made it clear that the move towards regional actors was because of the political conditions in the UN, requiring 'less ambitious means, by attempting to build collective security through regional security, which is expressly contemplated under the Charter of the United Nations'. He spoke about the Western Union Five-Power Military Committee set up under the Brussels Treaty, concluded within the terms of article 51 of the Charter, being a 'development of first importance'. The Chiefs of Staff from the five State parties (Belgium, France, Luxembourg, the Netherlands, and the UK) to the treaty were joined by Canadian and American Chiefs of Staff as non-members.[47]

Caught between the realities of the Cold War and the memories of German aggression, passionate advocates of European security, such as Reginald Paget, MP for Northampton, were in the minority in the Commons:

Western Europe cannot be defended—and many of us have recognised it for a long time—by a number of independent armies. We must get a European army co-ordinated and commanded as a single army. In that army there must be German units, and those German units ought not to be a threat to anybody else; any more then French or British units. That army should be built up—as indeed any great army is—that no unit can exist independently of the others.[48]

Such advocates came under severe criticism from many MPs opposing German rearmament. West Germany eventually joined NATO in 1955 and the successor to the Brussels Treaty—the Western European Union (WEU)—a year earlier in 1954. That the debates in the Commons in the early 1950s were dominated by concerns to establish two strong defence organizations was made clear by Manny Shinwell (Labour Defence Minister) who spoke of the 'desirability of co-ordinating, or perhaps I had better use another term, associating the Brussels

---

[45] *Hansard* HC vol 456, cols 82–3, 15 Sept. 1948 (Eden).
[46] Ibid., cols 100–3 (Bevin).
[47] *Hansard* HC vol 456, col 1097, 23 Sept. 1948 (Alexander).
[48] *Hansard* HC vol 472, col 1320, 16 March 1950 (Paget).

Treaty Defence Organisation with the North Atlantic Treaty Organisation'.[49]
The Prime Minister, Clement Attlee, made it clear that European defence without US involvement was not achievable when he stated that 'what is being done
is only part of the general defence of the Atlantic area. The fullest co-operation
with our friends in the United States and Canada is essential'.[50] This presages
his remarks dismissing the European Defence Community made in November
1950 and discussed above. The UK was not ready for an organization that was
solely European and supranational in the area of defence and security. The Prime
Minister made it clear that:

We are, in fact, now seeing the coming into being of what we have been striving to create—a European Defence Force, made up of the forces of the Western Union and the
North Atlantic allies, fully knit together to defend the democracies.[51]

Despite the fact that the Leader of the Opposition, Winston Churchill, called
for a European army with integrated German units,[52] the collective defence
approach under an American umbrella prevailed. Given the background of the
Korean War, this approach seemed realistic, though it did put back the efficient
unification of European forces until the next century. There were a number of
debates in the lower house about the value of the proposed EDC,[53] with some
members advocating that Britain join.[54] Britain did sign an agreement of co-
operation with the EDC regarding a common policy on military association
between UK forces and the EDC,[55] but this was as far as Britain was prepared to
go, an attitude that probably influenced the French Assembly decision of August
1954 not to go ahead with the EDC. Even in Britain, which had been sceptical
of joining the EDC, considerable parliamentary time was spent discussing what
was clearly becoming a doomed project.

Whether for political or military reasons, despite the demise of the EDC,
alternatives were sought. It was suggested in debates in the House in 1954 that
'an alternative solution' would be a 'looser and more flexible European defence
force', which 'would become an integral part of NATO'.[56] The Foreign Secretary,
Anthony Eden, endorsed this in October 1954, where he explained the birth of
the WEU as a 'simpler' organization, 'where the presence of the United Kingdom
might make up for some of the super-structure'.[57] He went on to state that 'in our

---

[49] *Hansard* HC vol 474, col 320, 20 April 1950 (Shinwell).
[50] *Hansard* HC vol 478, col 962, 12 Sept. 1950 (Attlee).
[51] Ibid., col 963 (Attlee).
[52] Ibid., col 984 (Churchill).
[53] *Hansard* HC vol 500, col 1453, 14 May 1952; vol 507, col 300, 6 Nov. 1952; vol 518, col 223, 21 July 1953; vol 520, col 11, 3 Nov. 1953; vol 522, col 579, 17 Dec. 1953.
[54] For example *Hansard* vol 510, cols 310–11, 28 Jan. 1953 (Wyatt, Harvey).
[55] *Hansard* HC vol 526, col 1141, 14 April 1954 (Eden).
[56] *Hansard* HC vol 529, col 456, 23 June 1954 (Boothby).
[57] *Hansard* HC vol 531, col 1038, 19 Oct. 1954 (Eden).

search for means to this end, it seemed that the Brussels Treaty, re-shaped and enlarged, could furnish the instrument we needed'.[58]

Whilst the failed EDC had received a vast amount of parliamentary time, its replacement the WEU was effectively announced to the House by the Conservative government as a *fait accompli*.[59] When challenged about the legal basis of the WEU which, it was asserted, conflicted with both articles 53 and 103 of the UN Charter, the government minister recognized the obligations of the Charter, but also recited the provisions of article 51 which permit the exercise of the right of collective self-defence, without any need for UN Security Council authority.[60] This exchange made it clear the UK's position that the WEU was a defensive pact, not a collective security organization empowered to take enforcement action.

Very little parliamentary debate on European security occurred between the advent of the WEU and Britain's entry into the Common Market in 1972. Indeed, even that momentous event was seen (quite rightly) as an issue of economic development, not of collective security, despite the premise underlying the Treaty of Rome. A debate on European security in December 1972 focused on the government's decision to participate in the Conference on Security and Co-operation in Europe (CSCE).[61] Although the Helsinki Final Act of December 1975 had a number of elements, including human rights and economic matters, the government made it clear that it saw its principal purpose as a forum 'to try to eliminate what is, in our view, the principal source of tension in Europe; the present—and growing—imbalance between the conventional forces of the NATO and Warsaw Pact countries in Europe'. The government also summarized the existing security architecture in Europe when the minister stated 'we believe in the need to maintain and foster the North Atlantic Alliance and to work for the gradual evolution of a more effective European contribution', and 'since the Treaty of Rome has no defence content, the enlargement of the Community is not relevant'.[62]

The CSCE was a traditional conference-type organization based on consent and co-operation between member states drawn from the Soviet bloc, Western Europe and North America. During the Cold War it provided a limited bridge between East and West, where the balance between the military alliances of NATO (and the WEU) and the Warsaw Pact secured an uneasy peace. At the end of the Cold War it underwent a limited transformation and in 1995 was renamed the Organization for Security and Co-operation in Europe (OSCE), which has greater powers of intervention in member states, but very limited military capability.

---

[58] Ibid.
[59] See further *Hansard* HC vol 531, col 1601, 25 Oct. 1954 (Eden).
[60] *Hansard* HC vol 542, cols 1005–6, 20 June 1955 (Zilliacus, Nutting). See further *Hansard* HC vol 543, cols 358–68, 28 June 1955 (Zilliacus, Turton).
[61] *Hansard* HC vol 847, cols 1798, 8 Dec. 1972.
[62] Ibid., cols 1882–3 (Royle). See further *Hansard* HC vol 895, col 1274, 15 July 1975.

8. Maastricht Debates and Beyond

As the momentous parliamentary debates of 1992 on the Maastricht Treaty approached, the Conservative government appeared relatively sanguine about the issue of defence and security within the European Community. In 1991 in response to a question on this matter, the Minister, Douglas Hogg, stated that discussions were underway within the framework of EPC, and that the government would not support any extension of EC competence into security and defence matters, the latter should be left to NATO and a strengthened WEU.[63] Further, Douglas Hurd, the Foreign Secretary, stated that 'NATO, including the presence of north American forces in Europe, remains the basis for our collective security', though there might be some strengthening of the European pillar by building up the WEU.[64] A slightly clearer picture was given by Douglas Hogg in May 1991 when he stated that 'as part of the process of political union we envisage intensified co-operation of national positions among the Twelve on a range of security issues. We believe that defence issues should continue to be dealt with in the Western European Union and NATO'.[65]

This bifurcation of defence and security matters was emphasized in a full debate in June 1991 on the progress of negotiations that would eventually lead to the Maastricht Treaty of 1992. Douglas Hurd conceded that there was a need for 'common institutions which are to some degree supranational', such as those governing 'the single market and its external manifestations in negotiations on world trade'. However, he declared that such 'logic does not apply in areas such as foreign and security policy' where it was no less European to have co-operation between member governments 'directly accountable to national Parliaments', rather than 'channelling all co-operation through the institutions of the Community'. Defence on the other hand 'should not be embraced by the European Community, which includes neutral Ireland and which is likely—I hope—to include other neutral countries during the 1990s'.[66] The government won support for its negotiating position by 312 votes to 158.[67]

The Conservative Prime Minister, John Major, introduced the final treaty to the House on 11 December 1991, the day after he had signed it at Maastricht:

The treaty creates a new framework for co-operation between member states in foreign and security policy and in the fight against international crime. That co-operation will take place on an intergovernmental basis outside the Treaty of Rome. That means that the Commission will not have the sole right of initiative and the European Court will have no jurisdiction. On defence, we have agreed a framework for co-operation in which

---

[63] *Hansard* HC vol 183, col 380w, 14 Jan. 1991 (Hogg).
[64] *Hansard* HC vol 185, cols 843–4, 13 Feb. 1991 (Hurd).
[65] *Hansard* HC vol 191, col 211w, 15 May 1991 (Hogg).
[66] *Hansard* HC vol 193, cols 1009–11, 26 June 1991 (Hurd).
[67] Ibid., col 1088.

the primacy of the Atlantic alliance has been confirmed and the role of the Western European Union has been enhanced.[68]

The government's justification for agreeing to the creation of the EU was that it only introduced traditional forms of inter-governmental co-operation in matters of foreign and security matters, in contrast to the supranational approach found in the more established EC pillar. This was put forward even more strenuously in the full debate that followed a week later, when the Prime Minister was concerned with convincing his own backbenchers that the creation of the EU was not a step too far towards a federal super-state:

> Had it not been for Britain's arguments, we would have had last week a treaty which brought foreign policy and interior and justice matters within the treaty of Rome. We would have had a community setting itself up as a rival defence organisation to NATO. The European Parliament would have had equal rights with the Governments of member states to decide on the policies and laws of the Community, and the Community's competence could have extended into virtually every area of our national life.[69]

The Prime Minister assured the House that 'we set the framework of a stronger and more coherent European foreign policy, in which our national independence of action is assured'.[70] Despite abundant criticism of the government from the opposition (mainly as regards the British opt outs on monetary union and the social chapter),[71] but, more importantly, from its own backbenchers, one of whom claimed to speak on behalf of the vast majority of the Conservative party who were 'fed up with the EEC, with what it is doing and what it is spending',[72] the government's decision to sign the treaty was endorsed in a vote on the European Communities (Amendment) Bill to implement it by 360 votes to 261.[73]

Debates surrounded later revisions of the Treaty of Rome, especially in 2008 concerning the Lisbon Treaty. Though Maastricht constituted the breakthrough for advocates of European security, the common foreign and security policy was something that seemed to enhance Europe's diplomatic and perhaps sanctioning capacity—in other words its competence to take non-forcible measures. There did not yet seem to be the real prospect of the deployment of forces under EU authority. Following the Treaty of Amsterdam of 1997, which further strengthened the second pillar, the government minister stated that the 'European Union does not take military action'.[74] Furthermore, the government emphasized that after the Treaty, though closer co-operation would be achieved between the EU and the WEU, 'the two organisations will remain separate until all Member

---

[68] *Hansard* HC vol 200, col 859, 11 Dec. 1991 (Major).
[69] *Hansard* HC vol 201, col 279, 18 Dec. 1991 (Major).
[70] Ibid., col 285 (Major).
[71] Ibid., col 286 (Kinnock). See also col 300 (Ashdown).
[72] Ibid., col 358 (Taylor).
[73] *Hansard* HC vol 208, col 593, 21 May 1992.
[74] *Hansard* HC vol 301, col 402w, 24 Nov. 1997 (Lloyd).

States...agree otherwise'.[75] British contributions to nascent European forces such as EUROFOR and Eurocorps were rejected by the government.[76]

It was not long though, following Labour's 1997 election victory, before talk had moved towards a firmer CFSP within the EU, and in a debate on the EU's defence policy in the House of Commons in 1998 the government minister spoke in terms of 'if Europe is to have a stronger voice in the world, European armed forces will need to be capable of supporting' the EU's policy. Further, he spoke of the 'need to put muscle behind Europe's foreign policy for those few hard cases when the normal instruments of foreign policy—trade, economic and political relations and diplomacy—are not enough'.[77] Indeed, at the St Malo Franco-British Summit on 4 December 1998, a Joint Declaration on European Defence was made by President Chirac and Prime Minister Blair, which stated that 'the Union must have the capacity for autonomous action, backed up by credible military forces, the means to use them, and a readiness to do so, in order to respond to international crises'. Though this was designed to create greater military co-operation within the Union, it was not designed to produce an integrated European army with EU command and control as the Prime Minister made clear in the House of Commons in May 1999. Furthermore, Tony Blair made it clear that 'the deployment of forces must remain a decision for national governments'.[78] In essence the government's policy amounted to treading a fine line between increasing co-operation on defence and security operations, which is acceptable; and integration, which appears to be a step too far. Following the Helsinki summit of EU leaders in December 1999, the government stated that:

At the Helsinki European Council, EU member states committed themselves to improving their military capabilities, including a specific headline goal of being able [by 2003] to assemble, deploy rapidly and sustain up to 50,000–60,000 troops for Petersberg Tasks, including peacekeeping. There is no intention to create a Standing European Peacekeeping Corps.[79]

With the WEU being largely subsumed into the EU by 2000,[80] and the Treaty of Nice of December 2000 further developing the second pillar, there clearly was greater momentum in defence co-operation though, with the perception that the public remained on the whole sceptical of the European project, the government was wary of integration. The government made it clear that the 50,000 troops would not constitute a 'European army', they would form a pool 'of potentially available national forces'. EU operations would occur only when NATO 'as a whole is not engaged', and that for the 'foreseeable future, such major operations

---

[75] *Hansard* HC vol 306, col 31w, 26 Jan. 1998 (Robertson).
[76] *Hansard* HC vol 307, col 161w, 24 Feb. 1998 (Reid).
[77] *Hansard* HC vol 319, col 304, 11 Nov. 1998 (Spellar).
[78] *Hansard* HC vol 332, col 12w, 24 May 1999 (Blair).
[79] *Hansard* HC vol 343, col 63w, 24 Jan. 2000 (Hoon).
[80] The government minister described the process as one of 'winding down' the WEU, rather than a merging of the WEU with the EU: *Hansard* HC vol 357, col 630, 27 Nov. 2000 (Hoon).

would draw on NATO assets and use NATO operational planning and command structures'.[81] On being pressed about the nature of the Rapid Reaction Force, the government minister was forced to reassert Labour's NATO credentials:

The situation is simple. NATO constitutes the cornerstone of our security. The United Kingdom is a leading member of NATO, and our forces make a key contribution to the alliance. Since the Attlee Labour Government played a key part in the foundation of the alliance in 1949, Britain and NATO have been indivisible. This Government are also wholly committed to NATO, and to European defence.[82]

The government dismissed arguments that the Nice Treaty's requirement of an independent European chain of command for the Rapid Reaction Force undermined NATO's supremacy.[83]

In a full debate on European Security and Defence Policy arising out of the Nice Treaty the government Minister, Keith Vaz, attempted to distinguish the circumstances in which European forces and NATO forces would act. He stated that the EU will carry out the Petersberg tasks 'humanitarian and rescue tasks, peace-keeping tasks and tasks of combat forces in crisis management, including peace-making', whereas 'war-fighting or collective defence... remain within NATO alone'. He reminded the opposition that the Petersberg tasks were agreed to by the previous Conservative government, 'so it is somewhat hypocritical to criticise the European Union for being ready to take on the same roles'.[84] He brushed away criticisms that the Rapid Reaction Force would take away capability from NATO: 'of course the force will draw on NATO assets, but will do so because NATO remains the cornerstone of our defence policy. There will not be any operations other than those in which NATO said that it will not act'.[85] He finished by declaring that: 'Nice was an important step towards realizing the goals of a NATO-friendly ESDP. It was a good result for NATO and a good result for Britain'.[86] Despite bruising criticisms from the opposition that there was nothing in the Nice Treaty that gave NATO first choice on any operation,[87]

---

[81] *Hansard* HC vol 357, col 311, 22 Nov. 2000 (Hoon). He later stated that up to 12,500 UK troops could be committed: vol 357, col 639w, 29 Nov. 2000 (Hoon). See also vol 360, col 349w, 8 Jan. 2001 (Spellar). The government reiterated this position on a number of occasions; Geoff Hoon, for instance stated on 10 Jan. 2001 that 'there is no such entity as a standing European Rapid Reaction Force. In the maximum scale operation envisaged at Helsinki—a corps-level deployment of up to 60,000 ground troops—the UK component could be around 12,500 strong. Maritime and air deployments of up to 18 warships and 72 combat aircraft could be made in addition. The appropriate scaling of medical staff and facilities to support such a deployment will be dependent on the operational circumstances at the time': vol 360, cols 543–4w, 10 Jan. 2001 (Hoon). This remains the government's position: see vol 450, col 1882w, 25 Oct. 2006 (Ingram), who repeated the above figures and stated that 'the commitment of national forces to an EU-led operation remains a sovereign decision for nations concerned'.
[82] *Hansard* HC vol 361, col 253w, 23 Jan. 2001 (Spellar).
[83] See for example *Hansard* HC vol 363, cols 700–1, 27 Feb. 2001 (Fabricant, Vaz).
[84] *Hansard* HC vol 365, col 139, 19 Mar. 2001 (Vaz).
[85] Ibid., col 144 (Vaz).   [86] Ibid., col 146 (Vaz).
[87] Ibid., col 157 (Howard).

the government's majority was such that it easily won a vote endorsing its policy on European security by 303 votes to 133.[88]

Inevitably after Maastricht the emphasis remained on NATO and the WEU providing concrete defence structures for Europe. Both organizations were also involved in the naval security operation in the Adriatic in the early 1990s enforcing UN and EC sanctions imposed against Serbia. As the government minister explained in the House of Commons: 'NATO and WEU naval forces are operating in the Adriatic to monitor and enforce compliance with the arms embargo against the whole of the former Yugoslavia and the trade sanctions against Serbia and Montenegro'.[89]

Nevertheless, the limitations of Maastricht were eroded at Nice in 2000, and as security co-operation increased, the EU moved towards mandating a number of EU operations, in Macedonia, the Democratic Republic of the Congo, Bosnia, and Chad. While the Bosnian conflict will be discussed in greater detail in the next chapter, it is worth briefly considering the role of Britain in the EU operation in Congo, which was rather cursorily considered by the House of Commons in June 2003.

With the UN peace operation in the Congo (MONUC) struggling to maintain order, especially in the Ituri Province centred around the town of Bunia, the EU decided on 5 June to send a 1,800 strong French-led force to that area, acting under a mandate from the UN Security Council adopted on 30 May. Although the operation came within the Petersberg tasks of the EU, the line between humanitarian or crisis management operations and war fighting is not as clear as the British government professed, as shown by the clashes between French troops and rival militias shortly after the EU force's deployment on 12 June. Having restored some calm, Operation Artemis was withdrawn on 1 September 2003.

The British contribution to this operation was limited to 85 personnel, mainly Royal Engineers to assist in improving Bunia airfield.[90] In the House the Minister reported that this was an EU-led operation undertaken without recourse to NATO assets, though NATO would be kept informed of the progress of the operation. France, as the lead nation, would provide the operation's headquarters, with officers from other participating nations including Britain.[91] In a further elaboration, the Minister stated that the forces involved would wear EU insignia and be under the political control and strategic direction of the EU Council of Ministers, exercised through the Political and Security Committee, consisting of representatives of member states. The force's success would be measured by the fulfilment of the Security Council's mandate in Resolution 1484, namely stabilizing Bunia and improving the humanitarian situation there, and securing the airport so that additional UN forces could land there.[92] On being asked whether it was wise to

---

[88] *Hansard* HC vol 365, col 458, 21 Mar. 2001.
[89] *Hansard* HC vol 216, col 239w, 16 Dec. 1992 (Hamilton).
[90] *Hansard* HC vol 407, col 702, 23 June 2003 (Ingram).
[91] *Hansard* HC vol 407, col 345w, 19 June 2003 (Ingram).
[92] *Hansard* HC vol 406, col 513w, 20 June 2003 (Ingram).

send British forces to 'a hugely dangerous theatre' without any combat elements, and only the 'French forces to defend them', the Minister responded by praising the French combat troops and stated that the British personnel were all trained in self-defence and the use of weapons. He stressed the limited time-scale of the operation, which should be terminated with the arrival of more UN troops.[93]

The success of Operation Artemis, and before that Operation Concordia in Macedonia, meant that by 2007, 654 British troops were on deployment in European Security and Defence Policy (ESDP) missions, but this was low compared to the number of British troops on NATO missions, which was 6,360.[94]

The failure of the EU Constitutional Treaty in 2005 and the subsequent signature of the modified version in the Lisbon Treaty in 2007, led to acrimonious debates in Parliament in March 2008 over the European Union Amendment Bill. On foreign policy aspects, the Foreign Secretary, David Miliband, was content to quote parliament's own Select Committee on European Scrutiny to the effect that 'the largely intergovernmental nature of the CFSP and ESDP will be maintained, with no significant departures from the arrangements which currently apply'. In so doing he dismissed the opposition's assertion that the New High Representative of the Union for Foreign Affairs and Security Policy would replace member states' voices in foreign affairs, and that further integration under the Lisbon Treaty would tear NATO apart.[95] The government won the day by 346 votes to 206.[96]

Though the debates raged about whether the Lisbon Treaty was the Constitution in disguise (an argument supported by the same European Scrutiny Select Committee report) and therefore, arguably, should have been the subject of a referendum as promised by the government, there was little of substance in the debate on the development of the ESDP. In particular, the expansion of the Petersberg tasks went largely unnoticed. New article 28B inserted by the Lisbon Treaty provides:

The tasks referred to . . . in the course of which the Union may use civilian and military means, shall include joint disarmament operations, humanitarian and rescue tasks, military advice and assistance tasks, conflict prevention and peace-keeping tasks, tasks of combat forces in crisis management, including peace-making and post-conflict stabilisation. All these tasks may contribute to the fight against terrorism, including by supporting third countries in combating terrorism in their countries.

Assuming the Lisbon Treaty enters into force, article 28B broadens the tasks of the Union in security matters. With the expansion of tasks will come the expansion of operations and the further development of the EU as a security organization.

---

[93] *Hansard* HC vol 407, col 703, 23 June 2003 (Ingram, Mercer).
[94] *Hansard* HC vol 455, col 1776w, 24 Jan. 2007 (Browne).
[95] *Hansard* HC vol 473, col 161, 11 Mar. 2008 (Milliband), quoting the 35th Report of the European Scrutiny Committee, Session 2006–7, 2 Oct. 2007 (HC 1014).
[96] *Hansard* HC vol 473, col 250, 11 Mar. 2008.

9. Conclusion

In the matter of military enforcement action, the UN Security Council still has constitutional authority on its side, by dint of the Charter and by reason of the peremptory rules of international law, but as with other constitutional systems it is dependent upon issues of legitimacy, authority and loyalty. If the UN Security Council cannot respect and uphold the fundamental principles of the Charter and of international law including principles of human rights law, then authority may pass elsewhere to regional organizations and to individually powerful states. While there may be confidence in the legitimacy of actions undertaken by the EU, this dissipates when considering action taken unilaterally or with one or two allies, as the invasion of Iraq in 2003 shows. Nevertheless, until a consensus is reached on a right of military intervention outside of the authority of the Security Council, then the emphasis must be upon making the Security Council work more effectively, including recognizing that it has a duty to act when faced with violations of human rights of the magnitude of genocide, crimes against humanity or large-scale commission of war crimes. Organizations like the EU need to build up their military capability, be better integrated, and be prepared to take effective military action at the behest of the Security Council when enforcement action is necessary, though there may be more independence for the EU in peace-keeping matters as the next chapter will show.

Progress for the EU though is slow, as some member states such as the UK show a reluctance to cede control in matters of military deployment. As a relatively effective military power Britain can operate independently of the EU, but this is both costly and has limitations when it comes to delivering significant military force in far flung corners of the globe. An effective European military force though is, at least in the short to medium term, dependent on Britain being committed to the project. Although there has been a significant warming to the idea in the last decade, there still remains a fair degree of scepticism over the ability of the EU institutions to achieve the necessary consensus to mandate military operations. Nevertheless, an encouraging development has been the creation in October 2008 of an EU-mandated naval operation to try and address the serious security concerns for international shipping caused by the actions of pirates off the coast of Somalia.

There have also been a number of occasions on which military operations mandated by international organizations have failed to deliver security to the country where they have been deployed. The failure of the UN in Bosnia will be considered in the next chapter, though the lessons learnt from this episode are applicable to all international organizations. It is to Bosnia that the book now turns.

6

What Peace? British Blue Helmets in Bosnia

1. Introduction

British troops were not often deployed as consensual peacekeepers during the Cold War. The main exception to this was the UN force in Cyprus in place since 1964. The end of the Cold War led to the lifting of the political factors that constrained the contributions of permanent members to UN forces and the development of peacekeeping, resulting in disastrous military operations in Somalia and Bosnia being undertaken under the rubric of UN peacekeeping but without the necessary conditions on the ground being present.

After considering the development and nature of UN peacekeeping, the decision to deploy British troops to Bosnia in 1994–5 is the focus of this chapter. The government's decisions to contribute to the UN peacekeeping force (the ineptly named UN Protection Force—UNPROFOR) and to the enforcement of the no-fly zone by a NATO operation are analysed in political and legal terms. The fact of there being UN authority and its effect on the decision to deploy British troops has to be considered alongside the absence of the legal and military conditions for peacekeeping. Was Parliament more willing to accept the decision to deploy British troops to Bosnia because UNPROFOR was seen as a UN-mandated consensual peacekeeping force? Was any attempt made in Parliament to address the issue of 'mission creep' as UNPROFOR's mandate was changed by the Security Council in an attempt to address the deteriorating situation?

The chapter then finishes with a consideration of British involvement in the NATO-led operation that replaced UNPROFOR after the conflict was brought to an end by the Dayton Accords in 1995. Did the new force (IFOR, then SFOR, and from 2004 EUFOR) represent a significant shift in British policy towards peacekeeping?

2. From Peacekeeping to Peace Operations

In modern UN parlance, the term used to describe deployments such as the EU force in Bosnia since 2004 is 'peace operation' (sometimes 'peace support operation'). The term emerged in the post-Cold War period, and was generally adopted after the UN-requested Brahimi Report of 2000, which proposed various reforms. It has come largely to replace or rather subsume the older and narrower concept of 'peacekeeping' as a key element of the UN's peace and security function. As a result of UN peacekeeping failures in places such as Bosnia in the mid-1990s, there has been a concerted move to change the conceptual and legal basis of modern peacekeeping.

Whereas peacekeeping forces are mainly military in composition, peace operations consist of a variety of professionals and experts, from soldiers, to police, relief workers, election monitors, human rights workers, development advisers and so on. According to the Henry L. Stimson Center 'peace operations comprise peacekeeping—the provision of temporary post-conflict security by internationally mandated forces—and peacebuilding—those efforts undertaken by the international community to help a war-torn society create a self-sustaining peace'.[1] This chapter will, in part, trace the change from peacekeeping to peace operations by considering both the UN's and the UK's experience in Bosnia.

Historically in practice the UN has concerned itself with defining and developing the concept of peacekeeping since the first full UN peacekeeping, or blue-helmeted, force in the Middle East emplaced after the Suez Crisis of 1956. Peacekeeping was defined by the UN at the end of the Cold War in 1991 as an 'operation involving military personnel, but without enforcement powers, undertaken by the United Nations to help maintain or restore international peace and security in areas of conflict. These operations are voluntary and are based on consent and co-operation'.[2]

Generally speaking peacekeeping operations consist of military contingents from troop contributing nations (TCNs) operating under UN command and control, specifically the Secretary General acting under delegated authority from the Security Council, exceptionally the General Assembly. This should be contrasted with the enforcement model that emerged out of chapter VII of the Charter, reviewed in chapter four, under which a coalition of the willing is authorized by the Security Council with command and control being vested in TCNs. In general terms military enforcement action is taken against the sovereignty of a state, while peacekeeping operations are undertaken with the consent and co-operation of the state or states in question. Peace operations share a common heritage with peacekeeping, indeed in the above definition peacekeeping is one of the two key elements of the term. However, the addition of the broader function of peacebuilding has necessitated the introduction of limited enforcement powers into

---

[1] <http://www.stimson.org/?SN=F220050602838> (accessed 26 Jan. 2009). It is also interesting to note that the Pearson Peacekeeping Centre now commonly uses the term 'peace operations' rather than peacekeeping operations <http://www.peaceoperations.org/> (accessed 26 Jan. 2009).

[2] *The Blue Helmets: A Review of United Nations Peacekeeping* (2nd edn, New York: United Nations, 1991). See also the International Court's advisory opinion in which it endorsed the development of peacekeeping: *Certain Expenses of the United Nations*, 1962 ICJ Rep. 151.

peace operations as discussed later in the chapter, a change shown in the marked difference between the security operation in Bosnia before the Dayton Accords of 1995 (namely UNPROFOR), and that in place after the Accords (namely the NATO-led IFOR and its successors).

3. Cold War Peacekeeping

Peacekeeping proved acceptable during the Cold War because it had limited objectives, normally assisting in the maintenance of a cease-fire and a separation of the belligerents, not by enforcement but by consent and co-operation. Hence peacekeeping was in 2003 stated by the UN General Assembly's Special Committee on Peacekeeping to be based on a trinity of virtues: consent, impartiality, and restrictions on the use of force.[3] While the latter clearly includes a peacekeeper using force in defence of his own life, his comrades and any person in his care, as well as his post, convoy, vehicle or rifle,[4] there has been a lack of clarity as to whether the force could also 'defend' its mandate, or civilians in its care.

UN Secretary General Dag Hammarskjöld recognized in 1956 that the wider the right of self-defence is drawn the more blurred the distinction between peacekeeping and enforcement action under chapter VII becomes.[5] Secretary General Waldheim's 1973 guideline on the use of force by peacekeeping missions, which stated that 'self-defence would include resistance to attempts by forceful means to prevent the force from discharging its duties under the mandate of the Security Council',[6] seemed to raise the prospect of a widely drawn mandate giving rise to enforcement action. However, during the Cold War, with the exception of the Congo operation in the 1960s, rules of engagement were drawn quite conservatively.[7]

A clear example of a consensual operation, restricted in its use of force, is the UN Force in Cyprus (UNFICYP). The initial deployment of UNFICYP in 1964 with its significant British contribution has been discussed in chapter three. Between 1964 and 1974 UNFICYP did not act as a buffer force between the Greek and Turkish communities, but acted in a gendarme-like role. The situation changed in 1974, with an invasion of Northern Cyprus by Turkey in July following a Greek-backed coup against President Makarios. Britain responded

---

[3] 'Report of the Special Committee on Peacekeeping', UN Doc. A/56/767, 28 March 2003, para 46.

[4] 'General Guidelines for Peace-Keeping Operations', UN Doc. UN/210/TC/CG95, 1995.

[5] Report of the Secretary General on UNEF I, UN Doc. A/3943 (1956), para 179.

[6] UN Doc. S/11052/Rev.1 (1973).

[7] M. Goulding, 'The Evolution of United Nations Peacekeeping' (1993) 69 International Affairs 451 at 455. Rules of engagement 'provide as clearly as possible the parameters within which armed military personnel assigned to a peacekeeping operation may use force': R. Zacklin, 'The Use of Force in Peacekeeping Operations', in N.M. Blokker and N. Schrijver (eds), *The Security Council and the Use of Force* (Leiden: Martinus Nijhoff, 2005) 100.

by sending an extra 600 troops to increase its contribution to the force to 1,350,[8] within an overall force increase from 2,400 to 4,328.[9] Though a significant increase, it was still a small, lightly armed force with limited rules of engagement. It was not there to enforce the cease-fire but to oversee it and by its physical presence deter breaches. UNFICYP was mandated to create a security zone between the Turkish forces in the north of the island and the Greek Cypriot forces in the south.[10] As one of the guaranteeing powers the British government was heavily involved in the negotiations that resulted in a cease-fire in 1974, and understandably debates in the Commons were dominated by the wider issues concerning the future of Cyprus, rather than the issue of British deployment. However, the conundrum created by classical peacekeeping was evident in the statement of the Labour Foreign Secretary James Callaghan when he said that 'the immediate aim had to be to remove the risk of war, but our abiding concern is the welfare of the people of Cyprus'.[11] Traditional peacekeeping can reduce the chances of war reoccurring but it cannot directly influence a long-term peace.

UNFICYP's presence helped in the entrenchment of the division of the island, with the *de facto* frontier known as the Green Line being under the watchful gaze of the blue-helmeted force. From 1974 UNFICYP represented the paradigmatic peacekeeping force, successful in keeping the parties apart but also establishing a barrier to peaceful solution. The Security Council has encouraged peacemaking through diplomacy in the guise of the Secretary General's good offices. There have been several attempts to broker agreements on the unification of Cyprus, most recently by UN Secretary General Kofi Annan in 2004. The UN plan was accepted in a referendum by the Turkish Cypriots but not by the Greek Cypriots and so failed. Though UNFICYP has helped to keep the peace on the island, it has also helped to perpetuate the division of the island and thus one of the most intractable international disputes remains unresolved.

4. Post-Cold War Peacekeeping

Post-Cold War peace operations, where peacekeeping was combined with peace-building under the principles of consent, impartiality, and the limited use of force, started with the UN operation in Namibia in 1989. In the early 1990s the UN rapidly developed a multi-dimensional peacekeeping and peacebuilding model, a number of examples of which were successful in achieving their more ambitious mandates, for example in Nicaragua, El Salvador, Cambodia, and Mozambique in the period 1989–95, though some struggled, most notably the

[8] *Hansard* HC vol 878, col 469, 30 July 1974 (Mason).
[9] *Hansard* HC vol 878, col 800, 31 July 1974 (Callaghan).
[10] SC Res. 355, 1 Aug. 1974.
[11] *Hansard* HC vol 878, col 798, 31 July 1974 (Callaghan).

operation in Angola (1988–97).[12] The model was centred upon a UN brokered peace agreement whereby the factions agreed to stop fighting and to disarm under the supervision of UN peacekeepers. A political process was also established that led to free and fair elections carried out under UN auspices.

The changing face of UN peacekeeping provoked an interesting debate in the House of Commons in February 1993, in which the Conservative government took the opportunity to scotch any arguments that the UK should give up its permanent seat in the Security Council, claiming (somewhat disingenuously) that the UK (and France) were contributing most out of the permanent members to UN peacekeeping. Given that historically there was an informal agreement to keep the P5 out of peacekeeping, this was not necessarily a decisive argument. The government though did welcome the Secretary General's *Agenda for Peace* of 1992, which represented an earlier post-Cold War effort to reform peacekeeping, and the UN successes in the operations mentioned above.[13] Much debate was centred upon the collapse of Yugoslavia, and the threat to regional and world order that this and other internecine conflicts represented. The Foreign Secretary, Douglas Hurd, warned that the 'international community should not lurch into enterprises the scope and duration of which have not been thought through'.[14] Arguably he should have taken his own advice before allowing British troops to be involved in the ill-fated UNPROFOR operation in Bosnia. Amidst those politicians who spoke about increasing world disorder, there were those who spoke more positively. Bearing in mind this was the period when liberals were proclaiming the victory of liberal ideology worldwide, most famously in Francis Fukuyama's *End of History*,[15] it was fittingly Sir David Steel of the Liberal Democrats who spoke in praise of emerging democracies such as Namibia:

… if one looks around the world today, or historically, it is difficult to find examples of mature parliamentary democracies, which have gone to war with one another. War is almost always created through some autocracy or other, so the development of genuine multi-party democracies as part of good government, as part of the new world order, should be attended to with far greater priority.[16]

Like Fukuyama, Sir David limited his democratic peace to the absence of conflict between democracies; he did not rule out war being waged against democracies by autocratic states, or *vice versa*.

The crucial problem with the development of peace operations from a practice and doctrinal basis in consensual and limited peacekeeping, is that while peace-keeping and peacebuilding can be perfectly compatible and complementary

---

[12] J.T. O'Neill and N. Rees, *United Nations Peacekeeping in the Post-Cold War Era* (Abingdon: Routledge, 2005) 139–68.

[13] *Hansard* HC vol 219, cols 773–85, 23 Feb. 1993 (Hurd).

[14] Ibid., 785.

[15] F. Fukuyama, *The End of History and the Last Man* (London: Penguin, 1992).

[16] *Hansard* HC vol 219, col 798, 23 Feb. 1993 (Steel).

when both are based on negotiated peaceful solutions with the consent and co-operation of all the parties, difficulties arise if the peacebuilding element is, or becomes, undertaken in an environment that is 'non-consensual' or at best 'semi-permissive',[17] for example through the actions of factions (commonly referred to as 'spoilers'), who would undermine the process. Spoilers have been defined as 'factions who see a peace agreement as inimical to their interests, power or ideology, [and] use violence to undermine or overthrow settlements'.[18]

The need for coercive enforcement action in these circumstances becomes difficult to avoid, especially given the need to prevent repetition of the failures of the UN forces in Rwanda in 1994 and in Bosnia in the period 1993–5. In such situations the traditional principles of peacekeeping cannot be fully upheld, though unless coercive action is taken against the sovereignty of a state, the military element of the peace operation would not normally become a full-scale enforcement action but would remain a peacekeeping operation with enforcement elements. Nevertheless, the desire to do something in the face of large-scale human rights abuse has led both to conceptual problems with redefining peacekeeping,[19] and serious practical problems in its implementation as evidenced by the failure of the operations in Somalia in 1993–5, as well as in Bosnia.[20] It is to the UN's difficulties in Bosnia in the early 1990s that the chapter now turns.

5. A Failure to Protect: UNPROFOR 1992–5

The Socialist Federal Republic of Yugoslavia (SFRY) started to implode in 1991 soon after the end of the Cold War. UNPROFOR, a force originally of 14,400 lightly armed peacekeepers was authorized by the Security Council in February 1992 to supervise a cease-fire between Serbia and Croatia.[21] The stationing of the Force's headquarters in the neighbouring republic of Bosnia quickly led to the UN being sucked into the deteriorating situation in that emerging country. Bosnia presented the international community with the most difficult of the Yugoslav wars indicated by a census in 1991 showing 44 per cent of its population as Muslim, 31 per cent Orthodox Serb, and 20 per cent Catholic Croatian.

As fighting and atrocities in Bosnia increased, the Security Council did try to supplement UNPROFOR's consensual, ineffective mandate by authorizing states or regional agencies to take 'all necessary measures to facilitate in coordination

---

[17] W. Hansen, O. Ramsbotham and T. Woodhouse, 'Hawks and Doves: Peacekeeping and Conflict Resolution' (Berghof Research Centre for Constructive Conflict Management, 2004) 6.

[18] High Level Panel Report 'A More Secure World: Our Shared Responsibility', UN Doc. A/59/565, 2 Dec. 2004, para 222.

[19] See Secretary General Boutros-Ghali, *Agenda for Peace*, 1992, paras 20–44; Boutros-Ghali, *Supplement to an Agenda for Peace*, 1995, para 35.

[20] O'Neill and Rees, *United Nations Peacekeeping*, 107–38.

[21] SC Res. 743, 21 Feb. 2002.

with the United Nations the delivery' of humanitarian aid.[22] Although 'necessary measures' is the phrase generally used by the Security Council to authorize enforcement action, and despite the fact that the authorization was adopted under chapter VII, little was done under this mandate, and humanitarian aid convoys under UNPROFOR protection generally relied on negotiation and consent, with the Bosnian Serbs proving the most intractable of the parties.

Michael Rose, the British general who took over command of UNPROFOR in January 1994, puts into perspective UNPROFOR's inadequacies in the face of continued fighting between the factions and the increasing number of atrocities committed in the main by the Bosnian Serbs. The peacekeepers of UNPROFOR 'were not there as imperialists to fight a war, nor defend a people or their territory. They came as peacekeepers whose purpose was to alleviate the suffering of all the peoples of the Balkans and to try, through peaceful means, to bring about an end of the war'. Despite the presence of the above-mentioned chapter VII authorizations, General Rose is adamant that 'peacekeeping was their mandate, and it is on this that they must be judged'. 'Although UNPROFOR used more force in Bosnia than had hitherto been used on any comparable mission, it never crossed the line into war-fighting and important principles regarding the permissible levels of force in peacekeeping were once again reaffirmed'. The simple fact is that there was no war-fighting will in the international community that could 'impose by armed force a just political settlement on the conflict in Bosnia'. Even the US, 'the militarily dominant partner in NATO, and the most vocal about the plight of Bosnia, also proved to be the most reluctant to deploy its own troops into the middle of the bloody civil war'.[23] The discrepancy between the wording of the Security Council's mandate and the reality and doctrines of peacekeeping is not uncommon, with many of the current crop of peace operations (including the joint UN/AU force in Darfur) having a chapter VII mandate to protect civilians but being incapable of performing this function.

More was achieved in Bosnia under Security Council resolutions authorizing the setting up of a no-fly zone over Bosnia, and safe havens consisting of Muslim enclaves in Serb held areas. Enforcement of these was also authorized by the Security Council,[24] but no such action was taken under these provisions until February 1994 when NATO threatened Serb gunners in the hills around Sarajevo, after they had killed sixty-eight civilians by lobbing mortar shells into the city;[25] and then shot down four Serb war planes violating the cease-fire. Other

---

[22] SC Res. 770, 13 Aug. 2002.

[23] M. Rose, *Fighting for Peace: Lessons from Bosnia* (London: Sphere, 1998) 4, 14, citing UN Secretary General Boutros Boutros-Ghali to the Security Council on 24 July 1994: 'UNPROFOR is deployed to work with the parties in a transparent and impartial mode; it is not a combat force and it is not equipped or deployed to take offensive action against any of the parties'.

[24] SC Res. 816, 31 March 1993; SC Res. 836, 4 June 1993.

[25] See *Hansard* HC vol 237, col 21, 7 Feb. 1994; vol 237, col 447, 10 Feb. 1994.

limited airstrikes were taken,[26] but it was not until August 1995, with other safe areas being threatened and overrun by the Bosnian Serbs, most infamously the massacre of nearly 8,000 unarmed Muslim men and boys by the Bosnian Serb Army under the noses of the Dutch UNPROFOR battalion at Srebrenica in July, that NATO launched multiple air strikes against the Bosnian Serbs. In addition, the Security Council authorized a NATO-led rapid reaction force to take more stringent measures on the ground to prevent further attacks on some of the safe areas.[27]

The change in emphasis from neutral peacekeeping by UNPROFOR to quasi-enforcement by NATO under UN authorization was a direct result of the parties' recalcitrance in respecting the cease-fire. To a certain extent it worked, but the Dayton Peace Accords of November 1995 were more a product of the changed military fortunes of the Bosnian Serbs, by far the most intransigent party, who not only suffered from NATO attacks but more importantly started to lose the war following the massive intervention of Croatian forces alongside Bosnian government troops. This, along with the Serb leadership of President Slobodan Milosevic distancing itself from the Bosnian Serb leadership of Radovan Karadzic, finally led to a peace agreement.

The Dayton Peace Accords on Bosnia signed by the leaders of Croatia, Serbia and Bosnia in November 1995 led to the UN Security Council authorizing the replacement of the UN Protection Force (UNPROFOR) with a NATO-led operation in the form of a 60,000 strong, heavily armed, implementation force (IFOR), whose task was to enforce the peace if the parties in Bosnia reneged on the Accords.[28]

6. The Nature of the Bosnian Conflict

According to Brendan Simms, the Conservative government of John Major, dominated on the issue of Bosnia by the Foreign Secretary Douglas Hurd and the Defence Secretary Malcolm Rifkind, was 'intellectually convinced' that a policy of non-intervention was the best one for Britain. Simms considers the government record through examining *Hansard* and other parliamentary documents and is coruscating in his demolition of it. According to Simms the government's policy was a pragmatic one, in which intervention could only ever be justified if it were in the British interest. As part of this, the government had a deep underlying 'hostility towards fragmentation in the international state system'. According to Simms, the government did not see the Bosnian conflict as being as a result of

---

[26] See also SC Res. 958, 19 Nov. 1994, which authorized NATO airstrikes against Serb air bases in Serb-held areas of Croatia in November 1994 discussed in *Hansard* HC vol 250, col 343, 21 Nov. 1994.

[27] SC Res. 998, 16 June 1995.

[28] SC Res. 1031, 15 Dec. 1995.

Serbian aggression against Bosnia, but a civil war in which all three parties were equally responsible —'a moral equivalence between the combatants'—a conflict in which they all committed atrocities.

But it was not enough to relativize and minimize the Bosnian war, it was also necessary to blur the distinction between aggressor and victim. It is, of course, true that the Bosnian government side committed atrocities, but these were essentially reactive and quantitatively and qualitatively distinct from the systematic campaign of ethnic cleansing waged by the Croatian and Bosnian Serbs.

Indeed, Simms is strongly of the opinion that Britain was instrumental in preventing any effective international action to help the Bosnian government, accusing Britain, in effect, of hiding behind the humanitarian aid effort which it argued would be jeopardized by any intervention on behalf of the Bosnian government.[29] With only a few dissenting voices in parliament, Simms accuses the establishment of failing to challenge the government's policy, though one Liberal Democrat inspired vote was held in November 1992 when a motion condemning government action as too little and too late was easily defeated.[30]

Although Simms is accurate in identifying the Bosnian Serbs as the main perpetrators of war crimes and crimes against humanity, the war in Bosnia was not a clear case of aggression by one state against another. When Yugoslavia itself was collapsing, the line between international wars amongst emerging states and an internal conflict covering the whole of Yugoslavia was blurred, but even when Bosnia was recognized as a state and admitted to the UN in May 1992,[31] the conflict was mainly between factions within Bosnia. Though the Serbian government of Slobodan Milosevic supported the Bosnian Serb faction led by Radovan Karadzic it was not necessarily sustained at such a level as to unequivocally legally attribute the actions of the Bosnian Serbs to the Serbian state.

This sort of reasoning is shown in the recent judgment of the International Court of Justice in the *Case Concerning the Application of the Convention on the Prevention and Punishment of the Crime of Genocide*.[32] The Court found it had jurisdiction in the case on the basis of article IX of the Genocide Convention 1948, which provides that 'disputes' between the contracting parties 'including those relating to the responsibility of a State for genocide', shall be submitted to the Court at the request of any of the parties to the dispute. Bosnia brought the case against Serbia for its actions during the Bosnian war on the basis of the consent of both parties located in article IX of the Genocide Convention. This meant that the Court could not consider other crimes allegedly committed by Serbia, or

[29] B. Simms, *Unfinest Hour: Britain and the Destruction of Bosnia* (London: Penguin, 2002) 2–48.
[30] Simms, *Unfinest Hour*, 274–5. *Hansard* HC vol 214, col 111, 16 Nov. 1992. The government won by 166 votes to 37.
[31] GA Res. 46/237, 22 May 1992.
[32] *Bosnia and Herzegovina v Serbia and Montenegro* 2007 ICJ Rep.

the Bosnian Serbs, during the conflict, it could only rule on the disputes between the parties covered by the Genocide Convention.[33]

On the issue of genocide the Court found that state parties had an obligation not to commit genocide, as well as to prevent its commission by individuals.[34] The Court was thus concerned with whether Serbia had breached the 1948 Convention, and it concluded on one of the main causes of the dispute that Serbia was not responsible for the acts of genocide that occurred in Bosnia, principally at Srebrenica in July 1995, since these were neither carried out by organs of the Serbian state, nor by individuals acting 'on the instructions of, or under the direction of' Serbia. The Court found that the Bosnian Serb leaders had a 'qualified, but real, margin of independence' from the Serbian leadership.[35] On this basis the acts of those who committed genocide at Srebrenica could not be attributed to Serbia under the rules of international law of state responsibility.[36] It did, however, find that though not liable for genocide itself, Serbia was responsible for failing to use its influence to prevent genocide being committed at Srebrenica since it 'must have been clear that there was a serious risk of genocide' there.[37] The Court found further that Serbia failed to comply with its obligation to punish genocide by not having arrested and transferred General Ratko Mladic, the Bosnian Serb military leader indicted for genocide at the ICTY and living in Serbia.[38]

Clearly the International Court separated in law the issue of individual criminal responsibility to be dealt with by an international penal tribunal such as the ICTY (established by the Security Council in 1993 to try suspected war criminals from the former Yugoslavia), from the responsibility of states under international law. The test it adopted for attribution of acts to a state is strict, and is one that has been criticized. Indeed, the ICTY itself had adopted a lower threshold in the *Tadic* case of 1999, where in effect it stated that for the purposes of classifying the conflict as internal or international within international humanitarian law the test did not have to be that of whether Serbia effectively controlled the Bosnian Serbs, but whether it was in overall control of them, which the Court found.[39] The disagreement between the Courts is perhaps a reflection of their different jurisdictions—the ICJ is concerned with issues of state responsibility, while the ICTY is concerned with individual criminal liability. However, the disagreement has been characterized by one leading jurist, Antonio Cassese (the President of the ICTY in the *Tadic* case), as being about the nature of the rules themselves. He has criticized the 'effective control' test adopted by the International Court

---

[33] '[The Court] has no power to rule on alleged breaches of other obligations under international law, not amounting to genocide, particularly those protecting human rights in armed conflict. This is so even if the alleged breaches are of obligations under peremptory norms, or of obligations which protect essential humanitarian values, and which may be owed *erga omnes*.', ibid., para 147.

[34] Ibid., paras 167–70.   [35] Ibid., para 394.

[36] Ibid., paras 395, 413, 415.

[37] Ibid., para 438.   [38] Ibid., paras 449–50.

[39] *Prosecutor v Tadic*, Appeals Chamber Judgment, 15 July 1999, Case No.IT-94-1-A, paras 117–20.

as not reflective of the nature of conflicts where non-state actors—be they armed groups, insurgents or terrorists—are rarely under the command and control of an outside state, but are under sufficient control to make that outside state liable for their actions in international law.[40] In the words of the *Tadic* judgment, not to impute responsibility to the state would enable those actors to escape 'international responsibility by having private individuals carry out tasks that may or should not be performed by state officials'.[41]

The end result of this debate is that we cannot say with any certainty whether Serbia was itself guilty of aggression against Bosnia, though the orthodoxy seems to suggest not. This orthodoxy though would mean that since Bosnia was not under direct attack by Serbia it had no right of self-defence, which would be an absurdity given the high level of support given by Serbia to the Bosnian Serbs. Furthermore, it also forgets the fact that at least in the early days of the Bosnian conflict, Bosnian Serb forces and those of the Yugoslav People's Army (dominated by Serbia) fought together in Bosnia.

There was a bitter debate in the UN about the continuation of the arms embargo—imposed by the Security Council against the whole of the former Yugoslavia in 1991[42]—against the new state of Bosnia which emerged in 1992. There were arguments that the embargo should be lifted to enable Bosnia to exercise its right of self-defence, not simply against aggression but against genocide. These arguments were supported by the UN General Assembly,[43] but the Security Council did not change its position. In fact, unlike the judgment of the International Court in 2007 on the issue of Serbia's involvement in genocide, the General Assembly in 1992 was without doubt that Serbia was guilty of acts of aggression against Bosnia and condemned Serbia (which still had remnants of the Yugoslav People's Army in Bosnia) and its surrogates (the Bosnia Serb army) for their acts of aggression and policy of ethnic cleansing. It urged the Security Council to lift the arms embargo against Bosnia to enable it to exercise its right of self-defence and to rectify the imbalance in weaponry between the government and the Bosnian Serbs, and to adopt a resolution authorizing member states in co-operation with the government of Bosnia 'to use all necessary means to uphold and restore the sovereignty, political independence, territorial integrity and unity' of Bosnia.[44] The fact that the Security Council did not follow this course of action must be, in part, due to the obfuscation of countries like Britain. While the United States voted for the General Assembly resolution, the other four permanent members of the Security Council—China, France, Russia, and the UK—abstained.

---

[40] A. Cassese, 'The *Nicaragua* and *Tadic* Tests Revisited in the Light of the ICJ Judgment on Genocide in Bosnia' (2007)18 EJIL 649 at 653–4, 663.

[41] *Prosecutor v Tadic*, 15 July 1999, IT-94-1-A, para 117.

[42] SC Res. 713, 25 Sept. 1991.

[43] GA Res. 46/242, 25 Aug. 1992, recognized that Bosnia as a sovereign state had the right of self-defence.

[44] GA Res. 47/121, 18 Dec. 1992, adopted by 102 votes to 0 with 57 abstentions.

As can be seen, international law in this area lacks clarity. While we can readily identify the aggressor in the case of classical inter-state conflicts, such as the Argentinian invasion of the Falklands in 1982 or Iraq's invasion of Kuwait in 1990, when it comes to the modern internecine war there is more difficulty, though in 1992 the majority of the international community clearly saw Serbia as the aggressor and the Bosnian government as the victim. There is evidence in the parliamentary debates that follow that the British government clearly ignored this and adopted a policy of non-intervention in the civil war, a policy which would only allow for a classical peacekeeping force based on consent, impartiality and the limited use of force in self-defence. The problem was that the situation on the ground where conflict raged and atrocities were being committed required something a great deal more coercive. In these circumstances UNPROFOR concentrated on the delivery of humanitarian aid to civilians, though it failed to protect them adequately as Srebrenica and other massacres testified—the end result of this failed policy was characterized by one commentator as 'the well-fed dead'.[45]

7. Britain and UNPROFOR

The British government (and indeed parliament) seemed reluctant to debate the issue of Yugoslavia even though a large country was disintegrating on the edge of Europe in an area that had been the cause or at least the focus of previous conflicts. As Simms notes the first full debate on Yugoslavia did not take place until 12 December 1991 and then was a very poorly attended affair held in the early hours of the morning. 'By then, of course, nearly one-third of Croatia had been occupied, hundreds of thousands of people, mainly Croats, expelled, and the Slavonian city of Vukovar had been levelled by Serb and "Yugoslav" artillery'.[46] Although UNPROFOR was deployed in February 1992, by July 1992 the British commitment amounted to a field ambulance team of nearly 300 men in Croatia. One MP expressed the view that though there was 'bound to be considerable support for ... humanitarian measures ..., such as the airlift and monitoring, but there is no support in the House or in the country for military intervention of a large scale, or of any kind, with the possible repercussions of getting bogged down in a civil war'.[47] The Foreign Secretary, Douglas Hurd, reassured the House that it was not 'right to send British troops to seek to settle by force any of these problems'.[48] The Labour opposition also showed a reluctance to intervene with Gerald Kaufman declaring that 'going in with force on the ground, without having

---

[45] T. Weiss, *Humanitarian Intervention: Ideas in Action* (Cambridge: Polity, 2007) 76.

[46] Simms, *Unfinest Hour*, 274.

[47] *Hansard* HC vol 210, col 978, 2 July 1992 (Winnick).

[48] Ibid., cols 979–80 (Hurd).

clear objectives, clear rules of engagement and a clear mandate from the United Nations Security Council, might do more harm than good to the people of the former Yugoslavia and would also place the lives of United Nations troops at risk. I do not see why that should be done, except in an inviolably good cause'.[49]

Considering that by June 1992 the conflict had spread to Bosnia and that the UN Security Council had upgraded the strength and mandate of UNPROFOR to enable it to secure the airport at Sarajevo as well as the delivery of humanitarian aid to the city,[50] the British establishment seemed to be deliberately burying its head in the sand as it headed for the summer recess of 1992. When parliament returned in September the government informed the House that it had offered 1800 British troops to UNPROFOR, while reassuring the House that 'Bosnia will not be a protectorate of the Community'.[51] The task the British troops were to undertake within UNPROFOR was a humanitarian one: 'the offer is for convoy protection only'. Further, the Foreign Secretary explained that both the 'Secretary General and the Security Council have agreed that in providing protective support to UNHCR organised convoys, the UNPROFOR troops concerned would follow normal peacekeeping rules of engagement. They would thus be authorised to use force in self-defence. In this context, self-defence is deemed to include situations in which our personnel are attacked by force to prevent UN troops from carrying out their mandate'.[52] It is noteworthy that the government restricted troops to self-defence, in traditional peacekeeping terms, while the Security Council's mandate in Resolution 770 was a wider one endorsing 'all necessary measures' in the delivery of humanitarian aid, thus permitting a far more coercive approach. Indeed, the Foreign Secretary referred to Resolution 776 which extended UNPROFOR's mandate,[53] but did not mention that this Resolution stated that this should be done in accordance with paragraph 2 of Resolution 770, which provided for enforcement action.[54] The Defence Secretary, Malcolm Rifkind, excluded the possibility of British troops using force to impose a safe corridor which 'would need a much greater deployment than is currently contemplated and it would imply a far more substantial and worrying military commitment than it would be appropriate to make now'.[55] The opposition, while agreeing that wide-scale force should not be used in Bosnia was critical of the government for not recalling parliament over the summer period to discuss the issue of deployment, arguing that since 1939 'the House has been recalled to discuss emergencies of crises of one kind or another and that eight of these occasions have involved foreign affairs'.[56]

[49] Ibid., col 989 (Kaufman).   [50] SC Res. 758, 8 June 1992.
[51] *Hansard* HC vol 212, col 120, 25 Sept. 1992 (Hurd).
[52] Ibid., col 125 (Hurd).   [53] Ibid., col 124 (Hurd).
[54] SC Res. 770, 13 Aug. 1992; SC Res. 776, 14 Sept. 1992.
[55] *Hansard* HC vol 212, col 184, 25 Sept. 1992 (Rifkind).
[56] Ibid., col 135 (Cunningham).

The government's approach until much later on in the Bosnian conflict seemed to be to interpret Security Council resolutions in a very limited way, in contrast to the techniques employed by the next (Labour) government in relation to the Kosovo and Iraq conflicts of 1999 and 2003 respectively, when resolutions that did not authorize the use of force were construed to mean the opposite. In addition, the House clearly understood the deployment to be part of a force with the character of a blue helmeted force, and not in any shape a coalition of the willing with enforcement powers. It is true that that Security Council endorsed enforcement measures in its mandates but it was guilty of not establishing a force to match its decisions. Executives at both national and international level failed to be clear in the tasks and functions of the operation, but above all failed to deploy an operation that would be able to reduce the level of violence in Bosnia, though it was largely successful in delivering humanitarian assistance.

Even with British UNPROFOR troop deployment up to 2400 by November 1992 the government minister, Douglas Hogg, did 'not believe that, by using any kind of military force...we would have stopped or could now stop the conflict'. Military action of the type used against Iraq was not appropriate: 'once the United Nations had used force in that way, it will disqualify itself from a range of other functions...notably the supply of humanitarian aid and the brokering role'. He also stressed that humanitarian convoys would not 'fight through obstacles' but had to negotiate safe passage.[57] Further British troop deployments were announced in January 1993 when Malcolm Rifkind told the House of Commons that the humanitarian operation 'has succeeded in its aims'. 'Our forces have been directly responsible for escorting some 146 convoys which have delivered 11,775 tonnes of aid. It is no exaggeration to say that there are many people in Bosnia today who owe their very survival to the presence of British and other United Nations forces'. However, the 'paramount concern' was for the safety of British troops who were increasingly under attack, hence the need for further troops to 'enhance the safety' of those already there.[58] British troops were not there to protect civilians from attack; their aim was to keep them alive through delivery of aid—though having the latter aim without having the former appears iniquitous and resulted in the killing of well-fed civilians. The reason given—that taking more coercive action would endanger the delivery of humanitarian aid—forgets that the coercive action required was not necessarily action designed to bring an end to the conflict, but rather the minimum necessary to protect civilians from attacks which were clearly in breach of all norms of humanitarian law. Such a mandate could have been carried out impartially if the force had protected civilians under attack whether the civilians, or indeed the attackers, were Muslim, Croat, or Serb.

---

[57] *Hansard* HC vol 214, cols 109–11, 16 Nov. 1992.
[58] *Hansard* HC vol 216, col 1057, 14 Jan. 1993.

The government's position was that 'British forces will not be used to intervene in the fighting between rival factions in the former Yugoslavia'. Furthermore, the British position remained 'that it is not appropriate to intervene in what is essentially a civil war',[59] which appears to have been difficult to sustain as Yugoslavia had broken into new states, and there was involvement of both Serbia and Croatia in Bosnia in support of factions there, but in any case it does not address the issue of why force was not used to protect civilians from attack by any of the factions. When the Liberal Democrat MP Menzies Campbell suggested that there might come a time when British troops could be deployed to protect the Muslim community in Bosnia from attack, this received little support in parliament.[60] Paddy Ashdown, the leader of the Liberal Democrats, argued for stronger military action and tried to counter the argument that it was not in Britain's interests to do so. He offered a moral justification that 'we have a moral duty to help those who are suffering'; a historical one that showed that 'appeasement' of the Serbs 'does not satisfy the appetite of aggressors'; a regional one that the Bosnian conflict would destabilize Europe; and an international one that 'if we do not stand up for the United Nations, its authority, and the basic standards of human rights and international law, then the UN will not be available to us when we need to rely on it in the years and months to come'.[61]

The government's attitude of moral equivalence towards the issue of responsibility for attacks on civilians was also used as a reason to remain uninvolved. For instance when fifty-six people were killed and seventy wounded in an artillery attack on Srebrenica in April 1993 (a predominantly Muslim town as later events in 1995 so tragically revealed), Malcolm Rifkind stated that the Bosnian Serbs 'appear to be responsible', though he qualified this by making it clear that they were not the only ones who had committed crimes.[62] Though NATO (including RAF aircraft and pilots) started in April 1993 to patrol the no-fly zones over Bosnia in accordance with Security Council Resolution 816,[63] there was no evidence offered that this would help Bosnian civilians.

The government could not as easily ignore the changes that occurred in UNPROFOR's mandate in mid-1993 as attacks by the Bosnian Serb forces against the Muslim population increased. The Security Council designated Srebrenica a safe area 'which should be free from armed attack or any other hostile act' in April 1993 after identifying a 'pattern of hostilities by Bosnian Serb paramilitary units against towns and villages in Eastern Bosnia'.[64] Further, in May 1993, the Security Council extended the safe areas to the other Muslim towns of Tuzla,

---

[59] Ibid., col 1058. See doubts cast on the idea that Bosnia was a civil war by Sir David Steel, vol 223, col 1170, 23 April 1993. See also statement by Clare Short that the Bosnians should be entitled to defend themselves necessitating the lifting of the arms embargo: vol 223, col 1180, 29 April 1993.

[60] Ibid., col 1060.

[61] *Hansard* HC vol 223, col 1192, 29 April 1993.

[62] *Hansard* HC vol 222, col 829, 14 April 1993.

[63] Ibid.   [64] SC Res. 819, 16 April 1993.

Zepa, Gorazde, Bihac as well as the capital Sarajevo under attack from Bosnian Serb forces, and UNPROFOR troops were deployed to these towns.[65] In June 1993 UNPROFOR was mandated to 'deter attacks against the safe areas', as well as to take the 'necessary measures, including the use of force, in reply to bombardments against the safe areas... or any armed incursion into them'. Member states were also authorized to use 'all necessary measures, through the use of air power, in and around the safe areas... to support UNPROFOR', in the protection of the safe areas.[66]

The British government recognized the new role of UNPROFOR and NATO air forces in the House of Commons,[67] though Prime Minister John Major made it clear that 'the Secretary General of the United Nations would have to approve air action by NATO on behalf of United Nations troops'.[68] This was the much criticized 'dual-key' that required the agreement of both the UN Secretary General's representative and the NATO commander before air power could be used. There appeared little that UNPROFOR or NATO could do to stop the safe area of Gorazde being attacked by the Bosnian Serbs from April 1994 onwards, the Defence Secretary falling back on the mantra that UNPROFOR was not a warfighting force, being in Bosnia for the purpose of humanitarian relief only.[69] The small contingent of British troops in Gorazde did help to deter some attacks but it was largely due to Bosnian resistance that the enclave held.[70] In November 1994 Bihac was attacked by the Bosnian Serbs with little consequence for the aggressors. UNPROFOR was a very limited operation but it is true to say, in the words of its commander, General Rose, that UNPROFOR 'far from being soft, had probably used more force than in any peacekeeping mission in the history of the UN',[71] but this was not enough to stop the slaughter at Srebrenica in July 1995.

A major escalation in the fighting in central Bosnia in Spring 1995 was discussed in several debates in the House, when one Labour MP, David Winnick asked, 'will the Foreign Secretary now tell the House whether it is the intention to make it perfectly clear to the Serbians that those safe areas are safe areas, and that military means will be used? Otherwise, the Serbs will take the point that they have always taken: if no action is taken against them, they will continue with their aggression'. The Foreign Secretary characterized the Bosnian Serb attacks as a brutal and disproportionate response to attacks on them by Bosnian government troops.[72] Although Prime Minister Major announced an increase in British troop deployment to Bosnia 'that does not mean that we are

---

[65] SC Res. 824, 6 May 1993.   [66] SC Res. 836, 4 June 1993.

[67] *Hansard* HC vol 226, col 183, 8 June 1983 (Hogg).

[68] *Hansard* HC vol 235, col 181, 12 Jan 1994 (Major). On the dual-key arrangements see vol 242, col 21, 25 April 1994 (Hurd).

[69] HC Deb. vol 241, col 642, 18 April 1994 (Rifkind).

[70] Simms, *Unfinest Hour*, 192. For discussion see *Hansard* HC vol 255, cols 525–30, 23 Feb. 1995 (Macdonald, Reid).

[71] Rose, *Fighting for Peace*, 210.

[72] *Hansard* HC vol 259, cols 330–31, 3 May 1995. See further vol 259, col 582, 9 May 1995.

taking sides in the conflict. The protection force remains neutral, and it remains impartial', though by the end of May Bosnian Serb forces had taken some British soldiers hostage, as NATO airstrikes against them had increased.[73] It seems odd that while making these statements, the UK was supporting a resolution in the Security Council which welcomed the establishment of a rapid reaction capacity to enable UNPROFOR to carry out its mandate, and deciding that the force be increased by up to an extra 12,500 troops. The resolution did, however, emphasize the continued impartiality of UNPROFOR.[74] It was ominous, though, that in the House of Commons, on 4 July 1995, Jon Owen Jones MP asked Malcolm Rifkind, Defence Secretary, whether he had read the latest report in the *Times* 'in which a United Nations spokesman was quoted as describing UNPROFOR troops in Sarajevo as "sitting ducks"?'. Mr. Rifkind did not agree,[75] yet on 6 July Bosnian Serb forces attacked Zepa and Srebrenica, the latter under the protection of 600 lightly armed Dutch UNPROFOR troops. The Dutch commander requested air support from NATO but did not receive such support until Dutch troops had been captured and threatened, which in turn led to the suspension of airstrikes. On 11 July Bosnian Serb forces entered Srebrenica and the massacre of nearly 8,000 unarmed men and boys occurred in the following five days.[76]

Though British troops were not deployed to Srebrenica, the events were closely discussed in parliament but before news of the massacre was known, with the Defence Secretary stating that while the UK, France and the Netherlands had contributed to the protection of the safe areas, other states had not, resulting in a significant shortfall of troops, and that the rapid reaction force was only just being assembled.[77] It was too late for the dead of Srebrenica, though when parliament reconvened in October, the Defence Secretary, Michael Portillo, could give the better news that a combination of NATO airstrikes and Bosnian Serb reverses would lead to a political solution to the conflict.[78] The Foreign Secretary, Malcolm Rifkind, welcomed the signing of the Dayton Accords in November 1995, which provided for a NATO implementation force (IFOR), to which the UK would contribute: 'Britain will play a central role in ensuring that the agreement in Dayton is translated into a peaceful future for all the people of the region'.[79] Mr Portillo announced that 13,000 British troops would partake in a NATO force of 60,000 and added:

Britain's contribution is formidable. It expresses our willingness to fulfil our obligations as a key member of NATO and our international role as a member of the permanent five

---

[73] *Hansard* HC vol 260, col 1004, 31 May 1995.
[74] SC Res. 998, 16 June 1995.
[75] *Hansard* HC vol 263, col 136, 4 July 1995.
[76] For full account see 'Report of the Secretary General Pursuant to GA Resolution 53/35 on the Fall of Srebrenica', UN Doc. A/54/549, 15 Nov. 1999.
[77] *Hansard* HC vol 363, cols 947, 954, 12 July 1995 (Rifkind).
[78] *Hansard* HC vol 264, col 45, 16 Oct. 1995.
[79] *Hansard* HC vol 267, cols 659–61, 22 Nov. 1995.

of the Security Council of the United Nations. It also indicates, in the clearest manner, the strength of our commitment to the security of Europe. Such responsibilities carry a cost which we are prepared to bear.[80]

Though the UN could not be trusted with the security of the new peace, it was praised by the Defence Secretary and the opposition: 'UNPROFOR has done much to contain the conflict, it has saved a lot of life, and it may take credit for its part in paving the way towards the peace agreement that we now have'.[81]

Such a positive assessment is out of line with most assessments of UNPROFOR. For example Michael Matheson, legal adviser in the US Department of State in the period, summarized the problems of a number of operations where rhetoric did not match deeds on the ground: 'on the whole, peacekeeping forces have had mixed success in carrying out' their responsibility to protect civilians, 'saving many civilian lives but also experiencing tragic failures where military strength, robust rules of engagement, or the political will to take the risk of serious fighting and casualties were lacking'.[82] Leading historian, Paul Kennedy, applies this specifically to UNPROFOR when he writes that 'four aspects of this sad tale deserve special note: the lack of unity among the great powers; the confusion about the mandates; the gap between operational aims and the resources provided; and the intermittent but powerful role of public opinion and domestic politics'.[83]

Mats Berdal takes the analysis further by first of all recognizing that the underlying problem with UNPROFOR was the disagreement and lack of political will in governments, not within the UN *per se*. He cites Sir David Hannay, British representative on the Security Council at the time, who explained that the reason why a more robust policy was not pursued in Bosnia 'was more due to the tensions between those member states with troops on the ground and those like the US without, than it was to any disembodied entity thought of as "the UN" pursuing a policy of excessive caution'. Berdal accurately explains why UNPROFOR did not use more force when it had a chapter VII mandate from the Council. UNPROFOR's original consensual and impartial mandate was never repealed in favour of a clear chapter VII one, instead enforcement elements were somehow added to this original mandate which neither made sense nor worked. Also, tellingly he writes that 'the fact is that by invoking chapter VII the Council was often just as concerned with conveying the impression of resolve as it was with taking meaningful action on the ground'. Britain in particular was amongst those who were 'unsupportive' of any real move towards enforcement, even as late as April and May 1995 when real pressure was mounting to take serious action. This was shown by the uncertainty surrounding the functions of the British and French

---

[80] *Hansard* HC vol 268, col 835, 12 Dec. 1995.

[81] Ibid., col 837 (Portillo).

[82] M.J. Matheson, *Council Unbound: The Growth of UN Decision Making on Conflict and Postconflict Issues after the Cold War* (Washington: The US Institute of Peace Press, 2006) 110.

[83] P. Kennedy, *The Parliament of Man: The Past, Present, and Future of the United Nations* (Toronto: HarperCollins, 2006) 98.

rapid reaction force sent in the summer of 1995.[84] In reality Dayton was made possible because of the military reverses of the Bosnian Serbs at the hands of the other factions assisted by the air superiority of NATO, rather than any contribution made by international troops on the ground. British politicians may have congratulated themselves on managing a successful outcome to the Bosnian conflict, but in reality the settlement of the conflict was due to events outside of their control. Indeed, arguably the policy of peacekeeping as opposed to war-fighting, unblinkingly pursued by the British government, prolonged the conflict and the suffering of the Bosnian people.

8. Stronger Peacekeeping

The desire to improve the creaking peacekeeping function whose credibility had suffered greatly in the mid-1990s, led the UN Secretary General Kofi Annan to establish a Panel on United Nations Peace Operations chaired by Lakhdar Brahimi. The aim was not simply to address the issue of how peacekeepers should approach human rights violations but went much wider to try in effect to address the tension between the traditional values of peacekeeping and the need for greater effectiveness of the UN in post-conflict situations.[85]

Although the Brahimi Report included conflict prevention and peacemaking within its concept of peace operation, the two core elements were those of peacekeeping and peacebuilding. First, 'peacekeeping', which has evolved from the traditional military model of observing cease-fires and forces separation best suited to inter-state conflicts, to 'incorporate a complex model of many elements, military and civilian, working together to build peace in the dangerous aftermath of civil wars'. Secondly, 'peacebuilding' consisting of 'activities undertaken on the far side of conflict to reassemble the foundations of peace and provide the tools for building on those foundations something that is more than just the absence of war'. It includes the reintegration of former combatants into civilian life, strengthening the rule of law (for example reforming and training the police and judiciary); improving respect for human rights; providing technical assistance for democratic development; and promoting conflict resolution and reconciliation techniques.[86]

From Brahimi onwards the military (peacekeeping) element of peace operations has three aims: avoiding any failure to protect civilians; ensuring that there are 'adequate self-defence mechanisms for peacekeeping forces and UN

[84] M. Berdal, 'Bosnia', in D. Malone (ed), *The UN Security Council: From the Cold War to the 21st Century* (Boulder: Lynne Rienner, 2004) 457–63.

[85] C. Gray, *International Law and the Use of Force* (2nd edn, Oxford: Oxford University Press, 2004) 238.

[86] Brahimi Report, 'Report of the Panel on United Nations Peace Operations', UN Doc. A/55/305-S/2000/809, paras 10–13.

staff', learning from Sierra Leone and East Timor in 1999 when UN staff were kidnapped and killed by mobs and militia; and finally preventing spoilers from undermining the peace process. Though Brahimi marked the turning point, the change to peacekeeping was also driven by the national defence academies of developed countries that had contributed to UN deployments in the 1990s, and who would 'no longer agree to send their military forces into conflict for which they were inadequately prepared and supported'.[87]

With the increasing involvement of more powerful states there came demands for more effective operations. The UK, learning from its difficulties in Bosnia, became a leading proponent of more effective 'peace support operations' (PSOs) that 'impartially makes use of diplomatic, civil and military means, normally in pursuit of United Nations Charter purposes and principles, to restore or maintain peace'. Such operations may include 'conflict prevention, peacemaking, peace enforcement, peacekeeping, peacebuilding and/or humanitarian' elements.[88] The military components of these are sometimes termed stabilization operations in recognition of the fact that they are the first component deployed to a semi-hostile environment to secure the peace before other elements of the PSO are sent. PSO doctrine has arguably been implicitly adopted by the EU in the development of its Petersberg tasks namely 'humanitarian and rescue tasks, peacekeeping tasks and tasks of combat forces in crisis management, including peacemaking',[89] and in its practice in the deployment of EUFOR, replacing the NATO-led Stabilization Force (SFOR) in Bosnia in 2004.

NATO has also adopted PSO doctrine defining such operations as 'multi-functional operations, conducted impartially, normally in support of an internationally recognized organization', and 'involving military forces and diplomatic and humanitarian agencies'. According to NATO such operations 'are designed to achieve a long-term political settlement or other specified conditions', and can include peacekeeping, peace enforcement as well as peacebuilding and humanitarian relief.[90]

It must not be assumed that PSO doctrine is universally accepted. The NATO version suggests that such operations would not necessarily require UN authorization even though they included elements of enforcement, while the British version suggests such operations might not be undertaken in pursuit of UN purposes and principles. Both doctrines suggest that regional organizations can act autonomously from the UN, though normally they would act in support of the UN and its principles.

In contrast to this more interventionist PSO doctrine the UN's Special Committee on Peacekeeping has reiterated that the traditional virtues of

---

[87] Hansen, Rambotham, and Woodhouse, 'Hawks and Doves', 7.

[88] UK Ministry of Defence, JWP 3.50, 2004: 7; A.J. Bellamy, P. Williams and S. Griffin, *Understanding Peacekeeping* (Cambridge: Polity, 2004) 165–85.

[89] Art 17(2) of the Treaty on European Union.

[90] NATO, AJP 3.4.1, 2001: para 202.

peacekeeping 'such as the consent of the parties, impartiality and the non-use of force' are essential to its success. This was preceded in the report by the Committee emphasizing respect for the principles of the UN Charter, especially sovereignty and non-intervention.[91] The failure by the Committee to develop the doctrine of peacekeeping to accurately reflect its role in peace operations is unsatisfactory, but may reflect the divisions within the UN with some states being unhappy about the increasingly interventionist nature of peace (support) operations.

In the period after 2000 complex peace operations have regularly been given certain chapter VII or enforcement powers to enable them to fulfil aspects of their mandates, tasks undertaken by the peacekeeping element, which is clearly a departure from traditional peacekeeping values,[92] though evidence from the force in Darfur suggest that there still remains that significant gap between the language of the mandate and the capability of the force. In fact from the turn of the twenty-first century it has become normal practice for a chapter VII mandate to be given to peace operations on the basis 'that even the most benign environment can turn sour when spoilers emerge to undermine a peace agreement and put civilians at risk'.[93]

Impartiality will also be justifiably impaired if peacekeepers are under a duty to protect civilians within their care, for they will sometimes have to use aggressive force to repel attacks on civilians as well as themselves. In such an environment the Brahimi Report recommended that peace operations be bigger and better equipped, so that they can deal with 'spoilers' and also protect civilians where necessary. The idea being that such forces would act as a credible deterrent in contrast to traditional peacekeeping forces, which were more symbolic and non-interventionist. Contributing states in such peace operations should be prepared to allow their troops to operate under robust rules of engagement and run the risk of casualties. While still supporting the peacekeeping principles of consent, impartiality and the use of force only in self-defence, the Report represented an attempt to draw the peacekeeping line nearer to chapter VII than chapter VI.[94] Impartiality became lack of partiality in the carrying out of the mandate, as opposed to the traditional approach that interpreted impartiality as neutrality and non-intervention. The latest UN peacekeeping doctrine of 2008, while still based on the traditional trinity of values, widened the third principle to allow for the tactical use of force to prevent the disruption of the political process, the protection of civilians, and to assist national authorities to maintain law and order.[95] The problem remains though that many TCNs still see peace

---

[91] Report of the Special Committee, 2003: paras 45 and 46. See also the Committee's 2007 report: UN Doc. A/61/19, 5 June 2007, paras 11 and 32.

[92] Zacklin, 'The Use of Force', 91.

[93] High Level Panel Report, para 213.

[94] Brahimi, paras 48–52.

[95] United Nations Peacekeeping Operations: Principles and Guidelines (The 'Capstone Doctrine') (UN Department of Peacekeeping Operations and Department of Field Support, 2008) 31–4.

operations in traditional peacekeeping terms and send under-equipped and limited contingents at least to UN operations, which continue to dominate the post-conflict landscape.

In 2006 the Security Council stated that peacekeeping and peacebuilding missions should, where appropriate, have a mandate that includes the 'protection of civilians, particularly those under imminent threat of physical danger, within their zones of operation' and stated its intention that such 'protection mandates' were to be implemented.[96] Certainly this is reflected in the more coercive mandates of recent UN peace operations. Arguments have been made that this reflects an emerging wider norm of a collective responsibility to protect in the event of genocide and other large scale killings, ethnic cleansing or serious violations of international humanitarian law which sovereign governments have proved powerless or unwilling to prevent.[97]

First introduced to the discussion by Boutros-Ghali in his *Agenda for Peace* of 1992,[98] peace enforcement has become more central to peace operations after Brahimi (although not clearly included in the definitions in that Report). Peace enforcement does not mean military victory over the enemy, so distinguishing it from pure enforcement action under chapter VII. Impartiality and consent are still the goals of any peace enforcement operation, though the former becomes the more important concept if factions indicate the withdrawal of their consent by attempting to undermine the peace. Furthermore, in such situations, according to the equivalent NATO peace support doctrine 'consent from the warring factions may be minimal and amount to nothing more than a phoney tolerance of the operation, whilst the rest of the population may be desperate for intervention and assistance'. According to NATO 'should the level of consent be uncertain, and the potential for opposition exist, it would be prudent to deploy a force capable of enforcing compliance and promoting consent from the outset'.[99]

Peace support operations must be 'sufficiently flexible, robust and combat ready', exemplified by the NATO-led force in Kosovo and the Australian-led force in East Timor, both deployed in 1999, and the role of British troops in support of the UN force in Sierra Leone in 2000. 'PSO doctrine recognises that the military's role, while robust, must also be a limited one: its objective is to create and safeguard the secure space within which humanitarian and civilian components can work to re-establish peace'.[100] In this regard they can be termed stabilization forces. Whereas pure chapter VII enforcement action attempts to impose a solution by force, a peace support operation is engaged in preventing violence that will undermine the participation of the parties and the population

---

[96] SC Res. 1674, 28 July 2006.

[97] High Level Panel Report, para 203; World Summit Outcome document in GA Res. 6/1, 24 Oct. 2005: para 139.

[98] *Agenda for Peace*, 1992, para 20.

[99] NATO, AJP 3.4.1., 2001, para 508.

[100] Hansen, Ramsbotham and Woodhouse, 'Hawks and Doves', 7.

as a whole in achieving peace. The aim of peace support operations is to achieve a political end-state, not victory over an enemy.[101]

In many ways, the stabilization forces in Bosnia from 1995, Kosovo from 1999, Afghanistan from 2001, the EU's Operation Artemis in the Democratic Republic of Congo in 2003, and ECOWAS in West Africa in the 1990s share structural characteristics of coalitions of the willing authorized by the Security Council under chapter VII to undertake enforcement action. Coalitions of the willing act under UN authority but they are not UN commanded and controlled operations in the peacekeeping/peace operation sense. The Australian-led force in East Timor fits this pattern as well, though this was an *ad hoc* force. Coalitions of the willing may fight a full-scale war as in Korea in 1950 and Iraq in 1991, but they can also be deployed to post-conflict situations where they have war fighting potential rather than just a peacekeeping function. It is interesting to note that, with the exception of the West African forces, regional peace support forces are undertaken by the 'global North', in contrast to peacekeeping operations (either traditional or as part of a peace operation) which are undertaken by the 'global South',[102] though the peacekeepers may be supported by separate enforcement elements drawn from the North. It is true to say though that those peace support operations from the North are far more effective in protecting civilians than peacekeeping operations from the South, even though they both have robust mandates.

9. Conclusion: Bosnia Post-Dayton

There is no doubt that the British contribution to the NATO-led force in Bosnia (IFOR, then SFOR and from 2004–7 EUFOR) has enabled peace to be kept in that country. The Defence Select Committee identified the force's crucial role in its reports, and the Chairman of the Defence Committee, Bruce George MP, reflected the new Labour government's desire to prevent any breakdown of the peace in Bosnia in June 1998 when he referred to the Prime Minister's 'ethical foreign policy', adding that 'I can think of nothing more ethical than preventing genocide'. He also agreed with the statement of one MP 'that the only reason why we can provide such excellent troops in their present shape is that they have retained a high-intensity war-fighting capability, which can then be flexed into other shapes, whereas if we had designed our troops around a peacekeeping or gendarmerie function, they would be nothing like as good at peacekeeping'. In agreeing Bruce George said that SFOR 'will buy time—more time to see how the other part of the equation works—the restoration of civil society in Bosnia, and

---

[101] NATO, AJP 3.4.1., 2001: para 204.
[102] J. Cockayne and D. Malone, 'United Nations Peace Operations: Then and Now' (2003) 9 *International Peacekeeping: The Yearbook of International Peace Operations* 1, at 13.

democratisation, with social and economic regeneration', which will 'certainly need time'.[103]

While there can be little doubt that such a stabilization force does provide more security in such a situation than a peacekeeping force, it is not necessarily any more effective in promoting a self-sustaining peace. Once the military and civilian props provided by NATO, the EU, OSCE, and UN are removed, there is still the danger that Bosnia could again self-destruct. Indeed it has been argued by commentators that the whole peace (state) building process is inimical to the successful achievement of self-determination by the Bosnian people.

The reality of such an approach is that although it appears impartial at ground level, at an ideological level it is informed by the political ideas of dominant states. Roland Paris has argued that 'most international organisations engaged in peace-building have internalised the broadly liberal political and economic values of the wealthy and powerful industrialised democracies', and have in effect 'trans-planted' those values (elections, civil and political rights and market reforms) into weak countries in which peace operations have been located. This process he argued amounts to the 'globalisation of the very idea of what a state should look like and how it should act'.[104]

David Chandler goes further by questioning the compatibility of such an imposition with its long-term effectiveness.

The experience of international democratisation has demonstrated that it is not pos-sible to impose a common bond on the people of Bosnia merely by administrative fiat. As long as the Bosnian people have little relationship to decision-making processes, it is unlikely that any broader sense of common interest will emerge. Although it is easy to argue that division and segmentation is not a way forward for the Bosnia people, external attempts to overcome this division appear only to have institutionalised these insecurities. The extended mandates of the international implementation of the Dayton settlement, which have undermined all the main parties, have not created a political basis for a unitary Bosnia, except in so far as it is one artificially imposed by the international community.[105]

International intervention has done little to 'resolve the political divides in Bosnia'; the Bosnian people still vote for the 'dominant nationalist parties'. Chandler con-cludes that 'the one solution that has not been advocated by the international community and those that want to regulate Bosnian society, or educate Bosnian people about democracy and co-operation, is that of letting the Bosnian people begin to work out their own way forward' through negotiation.[106] However, it

---

[103] *Hansard* HC vol 314, cols 301–3, 17 June 1998 (George, Brazier). See also First Report of the Defence Select Committee 1997–8 on Peace Support Operations in Bosnia, 3 Dec. 1997 (HC 403) and the Government Response, 4 Feb. 1998 (HC 535).

[104] R. Paris, 'International Peacekeeping and the "Mission Civilisatrice"' (2002) 28 Review of International Studies 637, at 638–9.

[105] D. Chandler, *Bosnia: Faking Democracy after Dayton* (2nd edn, London: Pluto, 2000) 197.

[106] Ibid., 198.

is the fear of a return to conflict (and maybe guilt at not ending it earlier) that inhibits the international community, preventing it from loosening the bonds in which they have wrapped Bosnia. As the Defence Select Committee said in 1997: 'considerations of altruism and national self-interest lead to the same conclusion in respect of our involvement in the former Yugoslavia. The price of peace would be far outweighed by the costs of a resumption of war'.[107] There are positive signs, not least the scaling down of the peace support operation, with the EU force in Bosnia, taking over from SFOR in 2004 being only 7,000 strong, though its mandate remains a robust one.[108] Britain initially contributed 1,000 troops to EUFOR,[109] those being withdrawn in 2007 as the security situation improved. In the thirteen years of British military involvement in Bosnia, fifty-five personnel lost their lives.[110] Despite the improvement in security and the end of 'the international community's governor-like role in Bosnia in 2007',[111] the government is right to recognize that 'nationalist sentiments among all three constituent peoples in' Bosnia 'continue to obstruct the reform process'.[112]

The lessons of Bosnia are both that peacekeeping is an inadequate response to a continuing civil war, but also that peacebuilding requires the consent and co-operation of the leaders and people of the country. In supporting a consensual model of peacekeeping in the shape of UNPROFOR during the conflict, and a paternalist administrative model for state building after Dayton, Britain seems to have moved from a policy of non-intervention in the conflict stage under a Conservative government to intervention in the post-conflict phase largely under a Labour government, when it might have been more effective if it had supported coercive intervention to stop the fighting, and consensual peace-building to help construct the country.

---

[107] HC 403, para 79.

[108] SC Res. 1575, 22 Nov. 2004.

[109] *Hansard* HL vol 424, col 199w, 16 Sept. 2004 (Symons). HC vol 425, col 596w, 19 Oct. 2004 (Ingram).

[110] *Hansard* HC vol 457, col 1084, 1 March 2007 (Ingram).

[111] Ibid., col 1084 (Fox).

[112] *Hansard* HC vol 435, col 1577w, 29 June 2005 (Alexander). See also vol 464, col 246w, 8 Oct. 2007 (Miliband).

7

Defending the Nation: the Falklands

1. Introduction

Despite the growing institutionalization and internationalization of military operations, the classical unilateral military action must not be forgotten. The invasion of the Falklands/Malvinas islands by Argentina in 1982 led to a huge British military operation to recapture them. Despite being based on the inherent right of a sovereign state to defend itself from attack, the operation attracted considerable debate both domestically and internationally. This chapter explores the political and legal dynamics that fuelled that debate, and considers whether the Falklands did represent a post-Second World War highpoint of electoral and political support for a military operation, as is commonly assumed. Did parliament play any critical role, either in the decision to send the task force or in the conduct of the war? Was the fact that there was a clear international legal basis for the operation in the face of external aggression a factor in determining the level of electoral and political support?

2. The Modern Right of Self-Defence

One of the most sacred trusts placed in the government of any state is to defend that country from its enemies. The classical jurist Emmerich de Vattel declared in 1758 that 'self-defence against an unjust attack is not only a right which every Nation has, but it is a duty, and one of its most sacred duties'.[1] Even ultra-conservative proponents of a 'minimal state', in which governmental functions are severely limited, see the *raison d'etre* of the government as one of protection of the citizens in the territory of the state.[2]

Something of the history of the concept of self-defence was recounted in chapter two, and it is not intended to repeat in full the evolution of what has become the main exception to the ban on force in the post-1945 world order.

---

[1] Vattel, *The Law of Nations or the Principles of Natural Law*, Book III, III, 35 (3 Classics of International Law ed, C.G. Fenwick trans, 1916) 246.
[2] R. Nozick, *Anarchy, State and Utopia* (Oxford: Basil Blackwell, 1974) 15–17, 113.

However, it is necessary to put the development of the concept of self-defence in context. It was pointed out in chapter two that before there emerged a regulation of the use of force in international law with the League of Nations Covenant of 1919, the doctrine of self-defence was just one of many justifications put forward by states when using military force against another state. It cannot be said that the concept had any precise juridical content because it was contained within the much wider doctrines of self-preservation and self-help, which were recognized in the period leading up to the First World War.

While there can be no doubt that self-defence was a factual condition arising whenever a state was under attack by another state, it must be the case that the doctrine of self-defence only began to take shape as a legal concept after 1919 when the regulation of the use of force began in earnest. This casts some doubt on the relevance of state practice prior to that, such as the oft-quoted *Caroline* incident of 1837, considered in chapter two. Arguably the modern law of self-defence could be said to have finally emerged once there was a clear prohibition on the use of force, and that only occurred with the UN Charter in 1945. Given that the right of self-defence is a response to an unlawful attack against a person or state, in other words the attacker has breached their legal duty not to attack,[3] self-defence as a precisely defined legal right will be dependent on there being a clear prohibition on using force unilaterally in the international legal order. As Yoram Dinstein, in his modern classic, makes clear: 'the thesis of self-defence as a legitimate recourse to force by Utopia is inextricably linked to the antithesis of the unlawful use of force by Arcadia (its opponent)'.[4]

The qualified prohibition on the use of force in the League's Covenant of 1919 was improved if not perfected by the Pact of Paris of 1928, which outlawed war as an instrument of national policy. Self-defence was not mentioned in the text of the Pact. However, US Secretary of State Kellogg, one of the authors of the treaty, responded to French fears over not including the right of self-defence by making clear that:

There is nothing in the American draft of an anti-war treaty which restricts or impairs in any way the right of self-defence. That right is inherent in any sovereign state and is implicit in every treaty. Every nation is free at all times and regardless of treaty provisions to defend its territory from attack or invasion and it alone is competent to decide whether circumstances require recourse to war in self-defence.[5]

This statement attempts a juridical definition of self-defence. It is important to note the use of the phrases 'attack' and 'invasion', signifying core elements of the right, which are not out of line with the post-1945 international legal order.

---

[3] D. Rodin, *War and Self-Defense* (Oxford: Clarendon Press, 2002) 29.
[4] Y. Dinstein, *War, Aggression and Self-Defence* (4th edn, Cambridge: Cambridge University Press, 2005) 178.
[5] J.T. Shotwell, *War as an Instrument of National Policy* (New York: Harcourt, Brace and Co, 1929) appendix vi.

Although such a statement should not be taken in isolation, it seemed to have been accepted in the pre-War period by Germany, Britain and Japan.[6] However, the concept of self-defence remained unclear in this period, in particular the element of auto-interpretation, which was prominent in the statement by Kellogg. Japan, for instance, relied in part on this to justify its invasion of Manchuria in 1931 as an act of self-defence. What is clear is that for a right of self-defence to exist it must be capable of evaluation independently of any subjective interpretation of the situation by a particular state. If this was unclear before 1945, it has been clear since that date; while the state acting in self-defence exercises the right at its discretion it does so at its own risk since its actions will be examined by various international actors (states, organizations, possibly the International Court) to see if they comply with the conditions for the exercise of the right. The necessity of defensive action in the face of an attack signifies that although there must be some latitude given to the defending state, 'the standard of action remains an objective not a subjective one'.[7]

A certain amount of controversy surrounds the embodiment of the right of self-defence in the UN Charter, in particular, it is often stated that article 51 does not contain the customary right of self-defence which is, it is argued, much wider.[8] Bearing in mind Kellogg's restriction of the right to attack and invasion, article 51 does not seem to be reflecting any narrower right,[9] at least in restricting the trigger mechanism to an 'armed attack'. An attack must be a prelude to an invasion and includes bombardment (by artillery, missiles . . .) as well as incursion by troops and armour. All are covered by the concept of 'armed attack'. Writers in favour of a wider right point to the reference in article 51 to the 'inherent' right of self-defence as somehow incorporating 'wider' customary law, but a more convincing interpretation is put forward by the International Court in the *Nicaragua* case to the effect that article 51 was intended to *preserve* the already existing right of self-defence.[10]

The fact that article 51 was inserted at a late stage, and that there was no similar provision in the Dumbarton Oaks proposals of 1944 that were a precursor to the Charter, are inconclusive arguments for limiting the impact of article 51. The provision was inserted at a late stage in 1945 to preserve the freedom of action by regional organizations to act in collective self-defence. Article 51 was in part

[6] D.W. Bowett, *Self-Defence in International Law* (Manchester: Manchester University Press, 1958) 133.

[7] Rodin, *War and Self-Defense*, 42.

[8] Bowett, *Self-Defence in International Law*, 187–92; M.S. McDougal and F.P. Feliciano, *Law and Minimum World Public Order* (New Haven: Yale University Press, 1961) 232–41; J. Stone, *Aggression and World Order* (London: Stevens, 1958) 44; C.H.M. Waldock, 'The Regulation of the Use of Force by Individual States in International Law' (1952) 81 Recueil des Cours 455; B. Asrat, *Prohibition of Force under the UN Charter* (Stockholm: Iustus, 1991) 107–8. See also Judge Schwebel's dissenting opinion in the *Case Concerning Military and Paramilitary Activities in Nicaragua* 1986 ICJ Rep. 14 at 347.

[9] J.P. Cot and A. Pellet (eds), *La Charte des Nations Unies* (Paris: Economica, 1985) 770–1.

[10] 1986 ICJ Rep. 94.

intended to allow collective action in self-defence without prior approval of the Security Council,[11] but in deciding to allow this the delegates then had to incorporate the right of self-defence into the Charter. The words chosen to embody the right and subsequently objected to by some writers, particularly the phrase 'if an armed attack occurs', were not the subject of any particular challenge during the negotiations at San Francisco.[12] Overall, Ian Brownlie appears to be correct when he states that 'the terms in which the right of self-defence is defined in article 51 are much closer to customary law as existed in 1945 than is commonly admitted'.[13] Indeed, the development of the law since the UN Charter shows that article 51 embodies customary international law,[14] although as the International Court pointed out in the *Nicaragua* case, article 51 does not contain all the elements of the right of self-defence, such as proportionality and necessity.[15] It does, however, contain the key element, namely the act that entitles a state to act in self-defence, which must be an armed attack.

3. Defensive Action against Threats

It follows from this analysis that there is no right of self-defence in response to acts which though seemingly aggressive do not amount to armed attacks, such as threats of force, or minor border transgressions, or support for rebels by arming them for instance.[16] In relation to the Cuban Missile Crisis of 1962 Myres McDougal tried to justify the American quarantine of the island by arguing that it was a legitimate defensive response to the threat of force represented by the Cuban acquisition of missiles from the Soviet Union.[17] Although threats of force are prohibited by article 2(4) of the Charter, they do not give rise to the right of self-defence, as the right is restricted to 'armed attacks' in article 51. The debate then becomes one of whether a 'wider' customary right recognizes that self-defence can be exercised in response to a threat.

The *Caroline* incident certainly suggests that defensive force can be used in response to an attack that is imminent though not yet fully materialized. Remember, the phrase used in the diplomatic exchange was that the state

---

[11] Though article 51 states that the right of self-defence only exists until the Security Council has taken measures necessary to restore peace.

[12] R.B. Russell and J.E. Muther, *A History of the United Nations Charter* (Washington: Brookings Institute, 1958) 699–706; UNCIO Vol 12, 687.

[13] I. Brownlie, *International Law and the Use of Force by States* (Oxford: Oxford University Press, 1963) 274.

[14] H. Kelsen, *The Law of the United Nations* (London: Stevens, 1951) 797–8; J.L. Kunz, 'Individual and Collective Self-Defense in Article 51 of the Charter of the United Nations' (1947) 41 AJIL 872 at 877–8.

[15] *Nicaragua* case, 1986 ICJ Rep. 14 at 94.

[16] Ibid., 101–3, 118–27.

[17] M.S. McDougal, 'The Soviet-Cuban Quarantine and Self-Defense' (1963) 57 AJIL 597 at 600.

exercising the right of self-defence had to 'show a necessity of self-defence, instant, overwhelming, leaving no choice of means, and no moment for deliberation'. There was no evidence of an imminent attack coming from Cuba against the United States in 1962, if anything Cuba could make a stronger case that it was in danger of being attacked by the United States, given the attempted CIA-backed Bay of Pigs invasion of the previous year. This usefully shows the flaw in the anticipatory self-defence scenario. When two states are facing each other, and are involved in a spiralling arms race (India and Pakistan would be a modern example), both are under threat from the other and both could make arguments that they are entitled to strike first if the law allowed a degree of anticipation.

The possession of nuclear weapons and other weapons of mass destruction, which can be launched from great distances, is often pointed to in support of the argument that states must be allowed to launch first-strikes in the face of imminent attacks, otherwise they would be easy targets.[18] Such an argument would seem to be in contradiction with the strict wording of article 51, which requires that an 'armed attack *occurs*'. Nevertheless, to interpret article 51 to mean that a state must wait for the missiles to cross its frontiers before it can respond would appear to be condemning the state, a victim of an aggression, to destruction in whole or in part.

The International Court of Justice, when asked about the legality of the use of nuclear weapons in 1996 by the UN General Assembly, was of the opinion that nuclear weapons were subject to the same rules as found in the UN Charter, which suggests that they could be used in self-defence against an armed attack, though their use would normally violate the rules of international humanitarian law because of their indiscriminate nature. The Court did not deal with the issue of an anticipatory strike against a state threatening to use nuclear weapons, though by sticking to the wording of the Charter, including article 51, the tenor of the opinion seems to be against this. The Court did confuse the matter saying, by dint of the casting vote of the President of the Court, that it was unclear whether the 'threat or use of nuclear weapons would be lawful or unlawful in an extreme circumstance of self-defence, in which the very survival of the State would be at stake'.[19] While very unsatisfactory, in the sense that it leaves a lacuna, the reality is that once a state is using nuclear weapons, or using force against nuclear weapons, the nuances of international law have probably ceased to be relevant. However, for a Court to endorse this seems to be an admission that international law has little relevance in influencing the decisions of governments to use such apocalyptic weapons.

Nevertheless, it would be an unfair law that restricted a victim state's right of self-defence to waiting for the attack to hit its territory. But to strike first without being under attack would turn the state from being the victim to being the

---

[18] See for example Waldock, 'Use of Force', 498.
[19] *Legality of the Threat or Use of Nuclear Weapons*, 1996 ICJ Rep. 226 at 266.

aggressor. In attempting to solve this paradox, the word 'occurs' in the phrase an 'armed attack occurs' can be interpreted to mean that an armed attack has been launched, either when the missiles leave their launch pads but have not yet crossed the frontiers of the victim state, or even earlier when the victim state has clearly detected that the firing sequence has been initiated—to put it more bluntly, when the button has been pressed. The danger with the latter is that the state preparing to attack could arguably be said to have a 'locus poententiae'[20] (a brief period) in which it could cancel the firing sequence.

However, it can safely be said that the armed attack has occurred once the aggressor state has clearly committed itself to the attack, a commitment which is not shown by mere preparations for war, but is present in the launch of the missiles or perhaps earlier when the launching sequence has been irrevocably started. In January 1991, during the Gulf Crisis, Iraq launched many SCUD missiles against Israel, which was not a party to the more general conflict that was occurring. In the exercise of its right of self-defence Israel tried to shoot down the SCUD missiles using US-supplied Patriot missiles. The evidence is that these attempted interceptions took place over Israeli territory, but it would be difficult to deny Israel the right to shoot them down before they crossed the Israeli frontier if they were clearly on route to targets in Israel. Indeed, given that the missiles passed over a third state's territory on the way to Israel, it could be argued strongly that Israel had the right, although it might not have had the technical ability, to knock the missiles out as they were being launched in Iraq.

This allows for what Dinstein calls an 'interceptive' right of self-defence. He gives the hypothetical example of the United States using force against the Japanese fleet on its way to Pearl Harbor in 1941, thus preventing a devastating attack from materializing. Having identified this, Dinstein then tends to interpret it too widely, stating that Israel was exercising such an interceptive right in 1967 to open the Six Day War against Egypt, Jordan and Syria by attacking military airfields in all three countries.[21] After initially stating that Egypt had attacked first,[22] Israel then argued that an attack was imminent, pointing to the Egyptian ejection of the UN peacekeeping force (UNEF I) that had been in place between Israel and Egypt since 1956, and the build up of Egyptian forces along the frontier. In fact the evidence of an imminent attack was not conclusive,[23] and although it can be argued that Israel should have been allowed to take military action first if it reasonably believed an attack had been launched, there was actually little evidence of the attack being launched or put in motion, only a collection of circumstantial evidence indicating that an attack might have been launched. Israel's action, most obviously its strikes on Jordan and Syria, but also its attack

---

[20] Brownlie, *International Law and the Use of Force by States*, 259.
[21] Dinstein, *War, Aggression and Self-Defence*, 187–92.
[22] SC 1347th mtg, 5 June 1967.
[23] A. Shapira, 'The Six Day War and the Right of Self-Defence' (1971) 6 Israeli Law Review 65 at 76.

on Egypt, were not interceptive but anticipatory, and there is limited evidence, at least until the events of 11 September 2001, that international law accepts the right of anticipatory self-defence. We will return to the issue of self-defence after 9/11 in the next chapter.

The argument, that to deny a state the right to take anticipatory action would leave it as an easy target seems to ignore the fact that, if there is a danger of an attack, a state can and should prepare for it and indeed it can invite its allies to assist in preparations. The despatch of American and British troops to Saudi Arabia in August 1990 was not undertaken on the basis that these troops would take pre-emptive action in the face of a potential attack by Iraq against Saudi Arabia, but on the basis that they would adopt a defensive posture in case the Iraqis decided to try to add Saudi Arabia to its conquest of Kuwait earlier in the month.[24]

An earlier example of such a 'precautionary' deployment in the same region occurred in 1961 when 7,000 British troops were deployed to Kuwait, which shortly after its independence from Britain was faced with an apparent Iraqi troop build-up on the frontier, causing the threat of attack by Iraq to subside. Mark Curtis argues that the Iraqi threat may well have been fabricated or at least over-exaggerated by the British government so that 'intervention was intended to secure both the Kuwaiti emir's firm reliance on Britain for protection and favoured treatment for the huge economic stake in the country'.[25] Even post-Suez, the British government was intent on exercising some level of control over the Middle East, shown by its intervention in Kuwait in 1961 in the face of an alleged threat, and in Jordan three years earlier when 2,000 troops were deployed at the request of King Hussein in the face of an alleged attempted coup.[26] Still, despite the dubious grounds of intervention, the 1961 lesson in precautionary deployment should have been applied again in July 1990 in the face of imminent attack on Kuwait by Iraq.

If the right of anticipatory self-defence became established then, because of its inherent subjectivity and flexibility, it allows states to justify acts that are clearly self-help as acts of self-defence. Israel, perhaps perceiving that its arguments of anticipatory self-defence in 1967 were not overwhelmingly condemned, sought to rely on the same doctrine in 1981 when it bombed a nuclear reactor in Iraq. Israel alleged that the reactor was designed to produce material for nuclear weapons eventually to be used against Israel, and that although the reactor would not be able to produce the material for the weapons in the near future, the Israelis had decided to knock it out before it became 'hot' so that its destruction would not cause widespread damage.[27]

---

[24] UN Doc. S/21492 (1990).

[25] M. Curtis, *The Ambiguities of Power: British Foreign Policy Since 1945* (London: Zed Books, 1995) 102–3.

[26] Ibid.   [27] SC 2288th mtg, 19 June 1981.

The Israeli argument appears to be flawed even within the doctrine of anticipatory self-defence itself, in that there was no imminent armed attack from Iraq. It was only after the Gulf War of 1991 that the Security Council ruled that Iraq should give up its nuclear programme, at least as far as it was intended to produce nuclear weapons.[28] The fact that the Israeli strike against Iraq in 1981 was not justified in self-defence and was a breach of article 2(4) itself, was clearly stated when even its staunchest supporter on the Security Council (the United States) voted for a Security Council resolution, which 'strongly condemn[ed] the military attack by Israel in clear violation of the Charter of the United Nations and the norms of international conduct'.[29]

Similar arguments were put forward by Israel after it had bombed the PLO headquarters in Tunisia on 1 October 1985. The Security Council, with the United States abstaining, vigorously condemned 'the act of armed aggression perpetrated by Israel against Tunisian territory' in violation of international law.[30] On this occasion Israel did extend its argument, relying not only on the prediction that future terrorist operations were likely to be planned at the headquarters, but also arguing that the fact that many past attacks had been planned there should be taken into account.[31] This argument is based on the theory developed by Israel that when a state is subject to many relatively small attacks it is entitled to defend itself by launching large-scale operations to wipe out the sources of these attacks and should not be restricted to merely responding to each attack individually.[32]

Israel invaded Lebanon in 1978, 1982 and 2006, and undertook several more limited military actions against armed bands in southern Lebanon on this basis, for example in April 1996, in order to destroy Palestinian bases and more recently Hezbollah bases, and to establish a security zone in southern Lebanon to protect Israel from rocket attacks and terrorist strikes. In justifying its actions, Israel stated that it is under constant attack from terrorists and therefore can exercise its right to self-defence even if it is not in direct response to an individual armed attack.

The International Court of Justice took the opportunity to comment on this cumulative approach to self-defence in 2003 in a case brought by Iran against the United States for armed actions against Iranian oil platforms in the Gulf during the tanker war of the 1980s (a by-product of the Iran-Iraq war of that period). The Court rejected the US arguments that it struck at the oil platforms in self-defence as they were the source of attacks against US flagged tankers, and in so doing it did not accept the American use of an 'accumulation of events' argument—that a series of small attacks against it could be justifiably reacted to by one major response. Interestingly the Court thought that 'even taken cumulatively . . . these

---

[28] SC Res. 687, 3 April 1991. [29] SC Res. 487, 19 June 1981.
[30] SC Res. 573, 4 Oct. 1985. [31] SC 2615th mtg, 4 Oct. 1985.
[32] Y.Z. Blum, 'State Responses to Acts of Terrorism' (1976) 19 GYBIL 223 at 233.

incidents do not seem to the Court to constitute an armed attack on the United States, of the kind ... qualified as a "most grave" form of the use of force', thus dismissing the argument not on the basis that a cumulative approach would always fail, but that in the case before it the series of incidents did not amount to a sufficiently serious use of force as to equate to an armed attack.[33] Whether this is the position of states after 9/11 is considered in the next chapter, especially in the light of the reaction to Israel's most recent invasion of Lebanon in 2006, which was provoked by the capture of two Israeli soldiers by Hezbollah.

4. Limitations on the Right of Self-Defence

The basic core of the right of individual self-defence is that the response to an armed attack must be necessary and proportionate. A third requirement, that of immediacy, was more prominent before the attacks of 11 September 2001, but since then the dominant requirements seem to have shifted to those of necessity and proportionality, reflected in the International Court's judgment in the *Oil Platforms* case of 2003, when, in rejecting the US argument of self-defence, the Court took the opportunity to clarify the elements of the right:

> Therefore, in order to establish that it was legally justified in attacking the Iranian platforms in exercise of the right of individual self-defence, the United States has to show that attacks have been made upon it for which Iran was responsible; and that those attacks were of such a nature as to be qualified as 'armed attacks' within the meaning of that expression in Article 51 ... and as understood in customary law on the use of force ... The United States must also show that its actions were necessary and proportional to the armed attack made on it, and that the platforms were a legitimate military target open to attack in the exercise of self-defence.[34]

Christine Gray groups the requirements together and states that 'necessity and proportionality mean that self-defence must not be retaliatory or punitive; the aim should be to halt and repel an attack'.[35] Dinstein still identifies 'immediacy' as a separate requirement to 'necessity' and 'proportionality', with the proviso that 'a State under attack cannot be expected to shift gear from peace to war instantaneously'.[36] David Rodin approaches the matter somewhat differently. He identifies 'three intrinsic limitations to the right' of self-defence—'necessity, imminence, and proportionality'—with imminence being a 'component and corollary of the requirement of necessity'. While necessity 'refers to indispensability

---

[33] *Oil Platforms (Islamic Republic of Iran v United States of America)*, 2003 ICJ Rep. 161 at 191–2; citing its judgment in the *Nicaragua* case, 1986 ICJ Rep. 14 at 101.

[34] Ibid., 186–7.

[35] C. Gray, *International Law and the Use of Force* (2nd edn, Oxford: Oxford University Press, 2004) 106.

[36] Dinstein, *War, Aggression and Self-Defence*, 212.

and unavoidability rather than inevitability',[37] 'imminence' means (in the words of George Fletcher):

A pre-emptive strike against a feared aggressor is illegal use of force used too soon; and retaliation against a successful aggressor is illegal use of force used too late. Legitimate self-defence must be neither too soon or too late.[38]

Rodin goes on to say that 'if necessity and imminence require a particular relationship between the defensive act (the content of the right) and the aggressive or attacking act, proportionality requires us to balance the harmful effects of the defensive action against the good to be balanced'. He makes the point that proportionality does not require that the means of force deployed in self-defence must somehow balance the aggressive force used—so for instance an attack by missile strikes against military targets requires a response by counter-strike using similar weapons; rather 'the proportionality that is required is between the harm inflicted and the good to be preserved', so that if all the defending state has available in response to a missile attack is bombardment from naval vessels against military targets then the use of force is proportionate.[39]

   Rodin though is sceptical about whether the moral basis underpinning the right of personal self-defence is to be found at the international level. On the individual level the innocent victim is faced by a wrongful aggressor, while at the international level, the victim is often far from innocent since there is likely to be a whole history of bad relations between the two states in question. In this regard he makes a challenging point in relation to the Falklands War of 1982, to which we will return in this chapter:

Britain's war for the Falklands/Malvinas was undeniably a defensive one, but in a deeper sense we cannot but be troubled by the question of whether Britain had the right to be there in the first place.[40]

A similar difficulty exists over the Arab-Israeli wars where the history of hostility since the creation of the state of Israel in 1948 makes deeper judgements as to who is the aggressor and who the defender difficult. To take an example, on 6 October 1973 Egypt and Syria launched a co-ordinated surprise attack against Israel. In the ensuing Yom Kippur War the Arab armies were eventually repulsed by Israel, but it is the justifications given for the initial attack that are of the greatest interest. The Syrian argument that Israeli had initiated the immediate hostilities was clearly spurious.[41] The more challenging argument was put forward by Egypt, whose UN representative stated, 'Egypt and Syria are defending

---

[37] Rodin, *War and Self-Defense*, 40–1.
[38] G. Fletcher, *Basic Concepts of Criminal Law* (Oxford: Oxford University Press, 1998) 133 cited in Rodin, *War and Self-Defense*, 41.
[39] Rodin, *War and Self-Defense*, 41–2.
[40] Ibid., 190.   [41] UN Doc. S/11009 (1973).

themselves... The Arab people have been the victim of aggression since 1967, not the aggressors'.[42]

Given that Israel had launched their attack in 1967 arguably unlawfully then the Arab states, the victims of that aggression, were *prima facie* entitled to the right of self-defence. Their actions appeared proportionate in that they were primarily aimed at recovering the territories occupied by Israel, the only problem was that of immediacy or imminence—a problem that appears to render the Arab surprise attack of 1973 unlawful, although one could view the use of force by the Arab states as a legitimate use of force to rid their countries of an *occupying* aggressor, whose use of force did not end in 1967 but continued as long as the occupation continued. This argument seemed to persuade some members of the Security Council at the time.[43]

However, to permit such a development may lead to the acceptance of a state's right to try to recover territory lost hundreds of years ago. In 1961 India invaded the Portuguese enclave of Goa stating that this was a response to a conquest that had occurred 450 years ago. India added that it had only just responded because for 430 years it had itself been the subject of colonial domination.[44] This argument is difficult to sustain in the face of the commonly cited doctrine of inter-temporal law, as stated by arbitrator Max Huber in the *Island of Palmas Case*,[45] concerning a territorial dispute between the United States and the Netherlands. This case established, at least for the purposes of international law, that title to territory has to be judged by the law governing relations between states at the time. Thus the Portuguese seizure of Goa at a time when title to territory by conquest was lawful signified that it did have title in 1961, so that India was unjustified in using force on the grounds of self-defence. This approach would suggest that the British did have title to the Falklands in 1982 at the time of the Argentinian invasion. However, though the doctrine of inter-temporal law appears to be a central component of the international legal order and it does provide some degree of certainty in international relations, it seems to be a doctrine shaped by former colonial powers for their benefit. Interestingly, though, the Goan situation can be distinguished from the Yom Kippur War of 1973, in that Israel had illegally occupied the Arab territories in 1967 after the right to acquire territory by conquest had been lost—in other words Israel lacked and continues to lack a title to the territories.

The moral basis of the personal right of self-defence is not easily transferable to the international plane where there are numerous actors involved in a government's decisions to go to war, and in this sense Rodin's thesis constitutes a serious challenge to the legitimacy of self-defence in international law. Rodin does admit though that his sceptical thesis is more difficult to sustain when faced with

---

[42] SC 1745th mtg, 11 Oct. 1973.

[43] SC 1744th mtg, 10 Oct. 1973 (USSR, Yugoslavia, France, Indonesia, India, Sudan); SC 1745th mtg, 11 Oct. 1973 (Nigeria, Guinea, Peru).

[44] SC 987th mtg, 1961.   [45] (1928) 2 RIAA 829.

aggressive regimes 'as repugnant as Nazi Germany or Stalinist Russia'. He states further that 'by locating the conditions which could potentially justify military action, we can identify those forms of military action which are, if not perfectly justified, then closer to being just than others'.[46]

Despite his doubts about the legitimacy of the right of self-defence by a state, Rodin's analysis of the limitations upon the right at a conceptual level do, for this author at least, amount to a clear conception of when the right is being exercised justly, whether at the level of individual self-defence or national defence. The requirements of necessity and imminence signify that a state is only entitled to legitimately rely on the right in the face of an armed attack. In such a situation it has no choice but to act, as the attack is about to hit or has just hit the territory or fleets of the defending state. If the state strikes too early in response to what appears to be a threat, or if it strikes too late in response to an attack that has already past, then it is not legitimately exercising its right of self-defence (despite what it might claim), but is claiming some form of preventive right or retaliatory right, both of which lack a moral basis though they have been practised by states. The Bush administration's claim to be able to take preventive action in the face of terrorist threats after 9/11 will be considered in the next chapter.

5. Modern Reprisals

In chapter two the doctrine of retaliatory or punitive reprisals was considered. Though it was accepted as lawful subject to certain limitations prior to 1945, the post-War consensus was that reprisals were no longer acceptable. This was made clear in a consensus resolution, the Declaration on Friendly Relations, adopted by the General Assembly in 1970, which stated that 'States have a duty to refrain from acts of reprisal involving the use of force'.[47] Only self-defence was a right reserved for states.

The doctrine of reprisals is distinguished from self-defence in that the latter is limited to a response to an attack, a response that is aimed solely at countering that particular attack. The doctrine of reprisals allows a state to respond at its leisure, delaying while a target is chosen, a target which need only be related to the original attack in a general way. Reprisals are punitive in nature, an aspect which carries with it an element of deterrence. Fine distinctions are sometimes drawn between deterrence and punishment in order to make a case for legitimizing reprisals, by arguing that if they are intended to deter rather that punish then they are more acceptable as defensive rather than punitive reprisals.[48] However, although states may put emphasis on the deterrent or overall defensive value of

---

[46] Rodin, *War and Self-Defense*, 198–9.
[47] GA Res. 2625, 24 Oct. 1970.
[48] J. Stone, *Legal Control of International Conflicts* (London: Stevens, 1959) 289.

reprisals, their inherently punitive nature is inescapable. Indeed, when states claim that their acts which clearly are reprisals are defensive, they are not trying to justify reprisals as such, instead they are attempting to legitimize their acts as self-defence. It is worth noting that if we accept the argument of deterrence put forward by states and writers, it becomes difficult to distinguish reprisals from acts of anticipatory self-defence, another doctrine that departs from the essence of self-defence. All this illustrates the fact that any movement away from a well defined and legitimate doctrine of self-defence, will mean a move towards a rejuvenated doctrine of self-help.

A recent example of what appeared to be a reprisal, involving the use of American airbases in Britain, was the US air strikes on targets in the Libyan cities of Tripoli and Benghazi on 15 April 1986. The targets were a compound that included the Libyan leader's home, military installations and alleged training sites for terrorists. Over one hundred civilians were killed in the raids. Ten days earlier a bomb explosion in a Berlin discotheque had killed a US soldier and injured about 200 civilians. The United States alleged that Libya was involved. President Reagan referred to this bombing in his speech in which he tried to justify the US bombings. If he had stopped there he would have been propounding a pure doctrine of reprisals. However, his argument then moved towards a very wide doctrine of anticipatory self-defence when he stated that the mission was justified under article 51 of the UN Charter, adding that 'this pre-emptive action . . . will not only diminish Colonel Kadhafi's capacity to export terror, it will provide him with reasons and incentives to change his criminal behaviour'.[49] In the Security Council, the US ambassador stated that 'in the exercise of self-defence . . . United States military forces executed a series of carefully planned airstrikes against terrorist related targets in Libya . . . This necessary and proportionate action was designed to disrupt Libya's ability to carry out terrorist acts and to deter future terrorist acts by Libya'.[50]

Using the language of self-defence does not convert an unlawful act of punishment into a lawful act of self-defence. There was no element of imminence driving the American action—it was not an action aimed at repelling an attack. However, the United States did receive a degree of support due in large part to the distaste for the Libyan regime to be found in many states. In the Security Council a draft resolution condemning the 'armed attack' by the United States was defeated by nine votes in favour to five against, with one abstention.[51] However, two of the votes against can be explained by the lack of balance in the resolution in that there was no condemnation of the acts of terrorism that provoked the US action.[52] In its annual session the General Assembly adopted a resolution similar

[49] *Keesing's Record of World Events*, 1986, 34457.
[50] SC 2674th mtg, 1986.
[51] UN Doc. S/18016/Rev.1 (1986). Those voting against were the US, UK, France, Denmark, and Australia.
[52] SC 2682nd mtg, 1986 (Denmark and Australia).

in content to the defeated draft, but it was only adopted by seventy-nine votes in favour to twenty-eight against with thirty-three abstentions.[53] The majority of states found no justification for the US raid and so the incident cannot be said to have changed the law in any way. Indeed, it is possible that if the resolution had been a balanced one condemning both the acts that led to the reprisal, as well as the reprisal itself, then the resolution would have been more widely supported.

6. The Falklands War

The issue of whether the war to recover the Falklands in 1982 was a paradigmatic case of self-defence has already been raised. This was not an attack on mainland UK along the lines of the aerial bombardment and threatened German invasion of 1940. These are islands in the South Atlantic 300 miles from the coast of Argentina that Britain has occupied since 1833. Spain, the former colonial power, had withdrawn in 1811, and although the newly independent Argentina had undertaken acts of administration over the islands in the 1820s up to 1833, the British position was that these islands were lawfully acquired in 1833 and effectively occupied thereafter. This position was stated by the government after the War in a statement made before the Foreign Affairs Select Committee:

Britain's title is derived from early settlement, reinforced by formal claims in the name of the Crown and completed by open, continuous, effective and peaceful possession, occupation and administration of the islands since 1833 (save for 10 weeks of forcible Argentine occupation in 1982). The exercise of sovereignty by the United Kingdom over the Falklands Islands has, furthermore, consistently been shown to accord with the wishes of the islanders through their democratically elected representatives.[54]

However, the British case is not as strong in law as it is in fact. In essence the government's case is an international version of the old adage that 'possession is nine-tenths of the law'. While the UK has enjoyed largely uninterrupted possession since 1833, to acquire title lawfully the islands must either have been *terra nullius* (land belonging to no-one) in 1833, or their occupation must have been acquiesced to by the state having title to territory before 1833, or finally it must be established that the UK took the islands by dint of conquest in 1833. The problem for the British government is that it cannot clearly rely on any one of these, so the result is that it falls back on an argument of effective occupation in combination with the wishes of the islanders. It cannot prove that the islands were truly *terra nullius* in 1833, or that Argentina had acquiesced since Argentina irregularly protested against British occupation from 1833 onwards. Nor can Britain prove it had the necessary intention or indeed used force to conquer the territory

[53] GA Res. 41/38, 20 Nov. 1986.
[54] Fifth Report of the Foreign Affairs Committee of the House of Commons, 1983–4, Vol 1 (HC 268-I); Misc.1 (1985), Cmnd. 9447, para 3.

in 1833. On the other hand it is difficult for Argentina to establish that it clearly succeeded to the Spanish title, and that it effectively objected to British occupation. In the words of the Foreign Affairs Select Committee overall 'the historical and legal evidence demonstrates such areas of uncertainty that we are unable to reach a categorical conclusion on the legal validity of the historical claims of either country'.[55]

In the modern era the British government consistently refers to the wishes of the 2,000 or so inhabitants as the determining factor in justifying its continued possession of the Islands. In 1986, ninety-four per cent of the inhabitants of the Falklands voted to retain their association with the UK. Politically this is clearly something that cannot easily be ignored, but it is not absolutely clear that legally speaking the islanders have a right of self-determination. Self-determination emerged in the 1960s as a limited rule of international law 'by which the political future of a colonial or similar non-independent territory should be determined in accordance with the wishes of its inhabitants, within the limits of the principle of *uti possidetis*'.[56] The latter principle is the restrictive element and confines expressions of self-determination to territorial boundaries on decolonization of the territory. From the Argentine perspective, on Spanish decolonization the islands were within the boundaries of the newly emerging state of Argentina, and although it was not able to fully exercise sovereignty over them, self-determination cannot subsequently be applied to a small part of the population within those boundaries. On the other hand Britain could claim that it had colonized the islands from 1833 and that the Falklanders have this right, but in so doing they are admitting that the Falklands is a colonial or similar territory that still exists in a post-colonial age. Furthermore, the UN Special Committee on Decolonization has taken the view that the wishes of the population should not be paramount in the case of the Falklands (and it adopts the same approach as regards Gibraltar) because it is an imported colonial population. The Committee and the General Assembly have invited the UK and Argentina to negotiate the future of the islands 'taking due account of the interests' of the population.[57]

Certainly before the war in 1982, as Walter Little points out, British governments had been keen to seek a negotiated solution 'in which the Argentine claims for sovereignty would be met and the desire for the islanders to retain a British way of life safeguarded'. Both sides were considering 'a formal transfer of sovereignty with a lease-back of the territory to Britain for a long period'. The main blocks to this were parliamentary opposition to such a deal and the growing pressure in

---

[55] Ibid., para 22.

[56] D.J. Harris, *Cases and Materials on International Law* (6th edn, London: Sweet and Maxwell, 2004) 112. See GA Res. 1514 Declaration on the Granting of Independence to Colonial Territories and Peoples, 14 Dec. 1960.

[57] Special Committee Res. A/AC.109/2003/24 (2003). See earlier GA Res. 2065, 16 Dec. 1965.

Argentina for a military solution.[58] Little accurately summarizes the political and legal context that existed at the outset of the conflict:

It was clear that neither nation's basic survival was at stake and, though each government enjoyed a momentary boost in its public standing, neither was particularly popular at the time and neither wished to have to confess to its citizens its miscalculation about the other's intentions. Furthermore, though each side made great play about the inflexibility of the other, neither wanted to be branded an aggressor in the eyes of third parties. Thus Argentina stressed not only its legal claims but also the 'peaceful' nature of the islands' seizure and the 'disproportionate' nature of the British response. Britain, on rather more solid legal grounds, cited the self-defence provision of Article 51 of the UN Charter.[59]

Furthermore, because both sides accepted that the issue was not about survival, the means deployed should be limited and proportionate so that fighting was confined to the islands and the surrounding area. In this context, the sinking of the Argentinian ship the *General Belgrano*, outside the British imposed exclusion zone, became a major issue 'precisely because it seemed to breach' the principle of proportionality and, with it, 'Mrs Thatcher's moral armour'.[60]

Popular perception that Britain was caught completely by surprise by the Argentinian invasion on 2 April 1982 is too simplistic. Although the Franks Report, published after the conflict in January 1983, exonerated the triumphant government of Margaret Thatcher, stating that 'the invasion of the Falklands on 2 April could not have been foreseen';[61] in fact the British government saw that Argentina was moving towards conflict, but its intelligence let it down as to the timing of the invasion. In early 1982 'British intelligence was clearly indicating

[58] W. Little, 'Anglo-Argentine Relations and the Management of the Falklands Question', in P. Byrd (ed), *British Foreign Policy under Thatcher* (Oxford: Philip Allan, 1988) 137. See the contrasting answers by the newly elected Conservative government in the House of Commons in 1979 *Hansard* HC vol 967, col 296w, 25 May 1979 (Sir Ian Gilmour stating that the Argentine government was 'left...in no doubt' as to British sovereignty over the Falklands), while in June 1979 in vol 969, col 153w, 26 June 1979 (Nicholas Ridley stating that sovereignty was one of the issues to be discussed with the Argentine government). See further Nicholas Ridley's report to the House on negotiations with Argentina held in New York in 1980: vol 984, cols 1476–8, 14 May 1980; and also his discussions with the Falklanders where he raised the lease-back option: vol 995, cols 128–34, 2 Dec. 1980. A full debate on the future of the Falklands was held later in the month when a number of members expressed concern about the lease-back proposal: vol 996, cols 647–52, 18 Dec. 1980, at col 649 when John Farr made it clear that the idea had 'upset' many members and was 'totally unacceptable'. It was later reported to the House that the Falklanders did not like the idea either: vol 997, col 248–9, 21 Jan. 1981 (Gilmour). On talks held at the UN in February 1982 see vol 19, col 263, 3 March 1982 (Luce), where the Minister took a stronger line with Argentina. Aggressive statements in the Argentine press were pointed to by one member who asked 'will he assure us that all necessary steps are in hand to ensure the protection of the islands against unexpected attack?' (col 264, Avery).

[59] Little, 'Anglo-Argentine Relations', 138.   [60] Ibid.

[61] Franks Report: 'Falkland Islands Review' Report of a Committee of Privy Counsellors, 18 Jan. 1983, Cmnd 8787, paras 266 and 339. The Committee of Privy Councillors chaired by Lord Franks was established by the government to 'review the way in which the responsibilities of Government in relation to the Falklands Islands...were discharged in the period leading up to the Argentine invasion...': *Hansard* HC vol 27, col 51w, 6 July 1982 (Thatcher).

a breathing space of months, if not a year'.[62] However, the arrival of Argentinian scrap metal merchants on South Georgia in March 1982 (lampooned in the British press as a 'comic opera'),[63] and protests in Buenos Aires against the military junta of General Galtieri (fulfilling the prediction in the Argentine press that 'the only thing that can save this government is war'),[64] led to escalation with the British government ordering three submarines to the islands in late March.

In the period immediately before the invasion there is evidence that the Royal Navy was preparing for a task force to be despatched, something agreed to by the Prime Minister and her senior ministers meeting in something like a pre-war informal cabinet.[65] Though questions were raised in the House of Commons there was no ministerial admission that submarines had been dispatched or of any other planned military deployment.[66] While this might be defended on the basis that secrecy was essential so as not to escalate the crisis, it could be argued that a clear statement of Britain's intent to fight for the islands might have deterred Argentina from invading. Hastings and Jenkins comment that 'it is perhaps no more than a constitutional curiosity that at this stage an expedition had been approved by neither the British cabinet nor the British Parliament. Nor indeed had the Argentinians yet invaded the Falklands'.[67] Given that the vast majority of MPs were averse to negotiating the future of the Falklands, many in fact speaking about the need to prepare for the defence of the islands, the decision to send a task force was unlikely to be undone by a rebellious House of Commons. Nevertheless, for a decision that sent the forces of a democratic country to war to escape scrutiny or approval by political decision-making bodies shows serious weaknesses in the democratic process when it comes to military deployment.

Overcoming limited military resistance by the small British force present on the Falklands, the Argentinian occupation of the islands started on 2 April. Bizarrely, problems in communications meant that the government minister spoke in the House on 2 April of a 'real expectation that an Argentine attack against the Falklands will take place very soon'.[68] This provided an opportunity for the other parties to express their support for the defence of the Islands if this should prove necessary, but they also took the opportunity to criticize the government for its misjudgment of the situation.[69] Criticism increased in the afternoon of the 2 April as government ministers were still unable to confirm the invasion had taken place.[70] Although 'the full British cabinet played a minor role in the Falklands war' it did meet on 2 April to agree on the dispatch of the task force, though 'no cabinet minister believed for a minute that the outcome of their decision would be

---

[62] M. Hastings and S. Jenkins, *The Battle for the Falklands* (London: Book Club Associates, 1982) 57.
  [63] Ibid.   [64] Ibid., 65.
  [65] Ibid., 65–9.   [66] Ibid., 64.
  [67] Ibid., 71.
  [68] *Hansard* HC vol 21, col 571, 2 April 1982 (Atkins).
  [69] Ibid., cols 571–2 (Silkin and Owen).
  [70] *Hansard* HC vol 21, col 619, 2 April 1982 (Pym).

open war'. The time it would take the task force to get to the Falklands was widely seen as the period in which diplomacy would produce a solution. So the cabinet agreed to the force but not to war; furthermore it agreed because 'the government could not face Parliament the following day without a task force'.[71]

A full debate in the House of Commons occurred on 3 April after the decision to dispatch the task force had been made, but it represented an opportunity for MPs to rally round the flag. Prime Minster Margaret Thatcher called on the House to condemn 'this totally unprovoked aggression by the Government of Argentina against British territory', which 'has not a shred of justification and not a scrap of legality'. She further declared that it was the 'Government's objective to see that the islands are freed from occupation and are returned to British administration at the earliest possible moment'. Mrs Thatcher announced the government's decision to send a 'large task force', but stressed that 'I cannot foretell what orders the task force will receive as it proceeds', expressing hope that diplomatic efforts would meet with success.[72] The Leader of the Opposition, Michael Foot, expressed his support for the Falklanders and declared that Argentine aggression should not be allowed to succeed. He also accused the government of betraying the islanders,[73] and though this was vigorously denied by the Conservatives, several ministerial resignations (most particularly Lord Carrington, the Foreign Secretary) followed. His successor, Francis Pym re-opened the debate on 7 April informing the House that the task force was on its way and that it constituted a 'formidable demonstration of our strength and strength of will'.[74]

The international legal basis of the British response was clearly stated to be self-defence under the UN Charter. The Foreign Secretary asked the House to declare its full support 'for those who are now embarked in defence of British territory and to protect the rights which we and the Falkland islanders hold equally dear'.[75] No vote was taken though the lengthy debate showed the House's resolve to recover the islands. Political control though was in the hands of a War Cabinet (technically a sub-committee of the Cabinet's Overseas Development Committee), initially consisting of a core of the Prime Minister, the Home Secretary (William Whitelaw), the Foreign Secretary (Francis Pym) and John Nott who had been persuaded not to resign as Defence Secretary at the time of the invasion, as well as senior civil servants and the Chief of the Defence Staff. Cecil Parkinson, the Chairman of the Conservative Party, soon joined this group, which often consulted the Attorney General (Sir Michael Havers) and the Foreign Office Legal Adviser, Sir Ian Sinclair, on matters of international law.[76]

---

[71] Hastings and Jenkins, *Battle for the Falklands*, 77.
[72] *Hansard* HC vol 21, cols 633–8, 3 April 1982 (Thatcher).
[73] Ibid., col 640 (Foot).
[74] The task force was dispatched on 6 April and eventually consisted of two aircraft carriers, sixteen frigates and destroyers, plus support ships: Hastings and Jenkins, *Battle for the Falklands*, 95.
[75] *Hansard* HC vol 21, col 960–2, 7 April 1982 (Pym).
[76] Hastings and Jenkins, *Battle for the Falklands,* 81–2.

With the task force at least seven weeks away from the Falklands, diplomacy dominated, led first by the American Secretary of State Alexander Haig and then the UN Secretary General Javier Perez de Cuellar, who both tried to broker a deal that would involve military withdrawal by both sides, followed by an interim administration and then some form of long term-settlement.[77] However, the path towards war was becoming clearer, with Britain securing by dint of massive diplomatic persuasion Security Council Resolution 502 demanding Argentinian withdrawal after determining that there had been a breach of the peace in the region of the Falkland Islands,[78] as well as persuading her European partners to impose non-military measures against Argentina by means of a binding regulation.[79] Sir Anthony Parsons, the UK representative on the Security Council expressed British 'condemnation of this wanton act of armed force—it is a blatant violation of the United Nations Charter and of international law'.[80] EC Foreign Ministers condemned Argentina's 'armed intervention' and appealed to it to withdraw.[81]

The British Cabinet announced a 200 mile exclusion zone around the Falklands, and the War Cabinet's response to Haig's overtures 'left no room for doubt. The nation would return to the negotiating table when Argentina honoured Resolution 502'.[82] The War Cabinet also gave the navy broad rules of engagement when meeting enemy ships.[83] Although Mrs Thatcher told the Commons in mid-April that 'our strategy has been based on a combination of diplomatic, military and economic pressures',[84] a military solution was looking the most likely, and most MPs seemed to support the strategy that the task force represented a real threat of force unless Argentina withdrew.

The Argentine position was made clear by Admiral Anaya whose view was that 'the British had no stomach for a fight; that democracies could not sustain casualties; and that the task force would simply break down in the South Atlantic winter'.[85] It looked like the threat of force by Britain would have to be carried out, but since it was based on the sovereign right of self-defence, parliament was clear that it had right on its side. The government made it clear that Resolution 502 did not affect Britain's right of self-defence,[86] a view generally supported by parliament and the wider international community. The Attorney General had also advised the War Cabinet that action taken in self-defence should be restricted to

[77] Ibid., 107.
[78] SC Res. 502, 3 April 1982 by 10 votes to 1 (Panama) and 4 abstentions (China, Poland, Spain, USSR).
[79] EC Regulation 877/82, OJ L102/1.
[80] SC 2346th mtg, 2 April 1982.
[81] Bulletin of the European Communities, 4–1982, 7.
[82] Hastings and Jenkins, *Battle for the Falklands*, 107.   [83] Ibid., 137.
[84] *Hansard* HC vol 21, col 1146, 14 April 1982 (Thatcher).
[85] Hastings and Jenkins, *Battle for the Falklands*, 111.
[86] *Hansard* HC vol 22, col 982, 29 April 1982 (Thatcher).

the islands, since any attack on mainland Argentina would be disproportion-ate.[87] When the Prime Minister announced to the House on 26 April that British forces had retaken South Georgia,[88] the scene was set for the real battle for the Falklands.

The move towards full armed conflict was put beyond any shadow of doubt by the War Cabinet's authorization for one of the submarines, *Conqueror*, to sink the Argentinian cruiser the *General Belgrano*, 35 miles outside the exclusion zone on 2 May,[89] with the loss of over 350 lives. The Prime Minister defended this action in the Commons by stating that the *Belgrano* 'posed a very obvious threat to the men in our task force'.[90] While this showed Britain's intent, and represented a serious blow to Argentina's naval capability, it was seen as a significant escalation that led to further bloody clashes between the two opposing forces, most imme-diately the loss of the British destroyer *HMS Sheffield* hit by an Exocet missile on 4 May, with the loss of over thirty lives.[91] The success of Argentinian air attacks on the task force meant that it was very difficult for the British to mount a success-ful amphibious landing. Despite this the War Cabinet decided on 8 May to send the landing force from Ascension island.[92] The plan for the landing, codenamed 'Operation Sutton', was outlined by the chiefs of staff to the War Cabinet and then the Cabinet on 18 May. The government received support from the House of Commons for increased military pressure,[93] by overwhelmingly rejecting a motion put forward by one of the war's biggest critics, Tam Dalyell, by 296 votes to 33. After six Commons debates the country was ready for war. The government position was clearly expressed by the Foreign Secretary, Francis Pym, who told the House of Commons that 'the world knows that the international rule of law would be dangerously undermined if Argentine aggression were allowed to stand'.[94]

From the point of landing at San Carlos Water on 21 May, the battle to recover the Falklands was not an easy one. The British forces did not have air superiority, or superior equipment, and although the Royal Navy controlled the seas around the Falklands it was severely hampered by attacks from the Argentinian air-force. Indeed, in the fierce battles that took place after the landings (21–25 May), three British naval ships were lost—the *Ardent*, the *Antelope* (both frigates), the destroyer *Coventry*, as well as the merchant navy ship the *Atlantic Conveyor*, and a number of other ships were damaged, with significant loss of life and injury. The House of Commons was kept informed on military progress and losses by the Defence Secretary, John Nott.[95] On the Falklands, the British landing forces

[87] Hastings and Jenkins, *Battle for the Falklands*, 162.
[88] *Hansard* HC vol 22, col 395, 26 April 1982 (Thatcher).
[89] Hastings and Jenkins, *Battle for the Falklands*, 148–9.
[90] *Hansard* HC vol 23, col 16, 4 May 1982 (Thatcher).
[91] See statement by Defence Secretary ibid., col 120 (Nott).
[92] Hastings and Jenkins, *Battle for the Falklands*, 169.
[93] *Hansard* HC vol 24, col 546, 20 May 1982 (Healey).
[94] *Hansard* HC vol 23, col 953, 13 May 1982 (Pym).
[95] *Hansard* HC vol 24, col 648, 24 May 1982 (Nott); vol 24, col 921, 25 May 1982 (Nott).

initially were bystanders as the crews of the ships fought for survival as well as trying to protect the beachhead.[96]

The land campaign started with the capture of the Argentinian base at Goose Green on 29 May, driven out of a desire to secure a 'tangible victory' after the naval losses. The War Cabinet was shocked by the loss of so many ships,[97] and despite assurances to the House that the commanders on the ground must be left to decide when to move,[98] the decision came from London.[99] Of little strategic value, Goose Green was a 'politicians' battle', and a hard won one, with seventeen paratroopers killed and thirty-five wounded.[100] 'The Argentinians had been given a devastating demonstration of Britain's absolute will to achieve victory at whatever cost in blood and treasure'.[101] 'Parliament departed for the Whitsun recess temporarily sated with success'.[102] However, the War Cabinet had realized that further quick victories were unlikely, and left planning and timing for the assault on Port Stanley to the military. Political and public opinion had moved away from any negotiated settlement, the press quoting one British soldier: 'if they're worth fighting for, they must be worth keeping'.[103]

The British had to fight their way to Port Stanley, the capital, and suffered a major loss when the landing ship *Sir Galahad* was sunk on 8 June with the death of fifty-one Welsh Guards;[104] but within three days of the tragedy, the British had embarked on the final battle for the Falklands, taking the mountains surrounding the capital one by one in fierce fighting. With Argentine soldiers (mainly conscripts) finally fleeing back to the capital, their commander General Menendez decided not to put up further resistance, and on 14 June he surrendered to the British military commander, Major General Moore. The surrender was announced to the House of Commons on the 14 June when Prime Minister Thatcher reported that the Argentines were 'flying white flags over Port Stanley'.[105] The victory was welcomed by the Leader of the Opposition, Michael Foot.[106] On 15 June the Prime Minister declared that 'our purpose is that the Falkland Islands should never again be the victim of unprovoked aggression'.[107]

---

[96] Hastings and Jenkins, *Battle for the Falklands*, 205, 210.

[97] Ibid., 254.

[98] *Hansard* HC vol 24, col 648, 24 May 1982 (Nott).

[99] See also the debates in the UN around SC Res. 505, 26 May 1982 that called upon the parties to co-operate to end the hostilities. The government simply saw this as reiterating Resolution 502: *Hansard* HC vol 24, col 1049, 27 May 1982 (Thatcher). A draft resolution calling for a cease-fire on 4 June was vetoed by the UK.

[100] Hastings and Jenkins, *Battle for the Falklands*, 231, 251.

[101] Ibid., 253.   [102] Ibid., 256.

[103] Ibid., 260–1.

[104] See statement of Defence Secretary: *Hansard* HC vol 25, col 399, 10 June 1982 (Nott).

[105] *Hansard* HC vol 25, col 700, 14 June 1982 (Thatcher).

[106] Ibid.

[107] *Hansard* HC vol 25, col 730, 15 June 1982 (Thatcher).

The conflict had cost the lives of 255 British and 655 Argentinian personnel. The British lost six ships with a further ten badly damaged; nine aircraft were also lost. The cost to the British taxpayer for the loss of ships and planes was put at £900 million and the campaign at £700 million.[108] Billions of pounds have since been spent on making sure that the Falklands are properly defended, despite international opinion swinging away from Britain very quickly after the conflict had ended. On 4 November 1982 the UN General Assembly adopted a resolution which expressed an awareness 'that the maintenance of colonial situations is incompatible with the United Nations ideal of universal peace', and requested the governments of Argentina and Britain 'to resume negotiations in order to find as soon as possible a peaceful solution to the sovereignty dispute relating to the question of the Falkland Islands (Malvinas)'.[109] With international community support ebbing away, 'the Falklands had become a costly fortress'.[110]

The abovementioned Franks Committee exonerated the government from any blame for the invasion itself. The Prime Minister welcomed this in the House in January 1983,[111] and although there was some discussion of the campaign itself, Mrs Thatcher summarized this as representing 'total agreement that the campaign was brilliantly conducted and bravely fought'.[112] Earlier the Defence Secretary announced a white paper assessing defence lessons from the conflict.[113] This was debated in the House of Commons on 14 December 1982, and concerned military lessons learned, having regard to what the Defence Secretary called the 'unique' nature of the campaign to recover the Islands.[114] There was also an updated report on the economy of the Falkland Islands produced by Lord Shackleton discussed by the House of Commons in December 1982.[115] But apart from the lingering doubts over the decision to sink the *Belgrano*,[116] there was limited criticism of the campaign, and little questioning of its necessity or legality.[117]

Though the Prime Minister dismissed Tam Dalyell's suggestion that a full inquiry into the Falklands conflict was necessary 'taking into account the precedent of the inquiry into the Crimean war',[118] the sinking of the *Belgrano* was

[108] Hastings and Jenkins, *Battle for the Falklands*, 316–7. *Hansard* HC vol 26, col 19w, 21 June 1982 (Baker).

[109] GA Res. 37/9, 4 Nov. 1982 by 90 votes to 12 with 52 abstentions.

[110] Hastings and Jenkins, *Battle for the Falklands*, 327.

[111] *Hansard* HC vol 35, col 174, 18 Jan. 1983 (Thatcher). For full debate see vol 35, col 789, 25 Jan. 1983.

[112] *Hansard* HC vol 35, col 984, 26 Jan. 1982 (Thatcher).

[113] *Hansard* HC vol 28, col 910, 27 July 1982 (Nott).

[114] *Hansard* HC vol 34, cols 128–30, 14 Dec. 1982 (Nott). See full debate vol 34, col 845, 21 Dec. 1982. For report see 'The Falklands Campaign: The Lessons', 14 Dec. 1982, Cmnd. 8758.

[115] *Hansard* HC vol 33, col 851, 8 Dec. 1982 (Pym). See full debate vol 34, col 974, 22 Dec. 1982.

[116] See for example *Hansard* HC vol 49, col 897, 30 Nov. 1983 (Dalyell).

[117] Third Report from the Defence Committee, 1982–3, 12 Aug. 1983 (HC 154) contained a discussion about the future defence of the Islands.

[118] *Hansard* HC vol 42, col 110w, 5 May 1983 (Dalyell).

discussed by the Foreign Affairs Committee in 1984. The Ministry of Defence gave evidence that naval rules of engagement had been changed to allow the attack on the *Belgrano* when it was outside the exclusion zone, but also stating that the UK was acting in self-defence under article 51 of the Charter which gave it the right to deal with any threat to British forces.[119] However, the issue refused to go away and it was not until February 1985 that the government finally drew a line under the incident by securing a vote by 351 votes to 0, which resolved that 'the sinking of the *General Belgrano* was a necessary and legitimate action in the Falklands Campaign; and agrees that the protection of our Armed Forces must be the prime consideration in determining how far matters involving national security and the conduct of military operations information can be disclosed'. An opposition amendment that would have found that Ministers had 'betrayed their responsibility to Parliament' by seeking to conceal information on the incident from the House of Commons was defeated by 350 votes to 202.[120] Despite difficulties over the sinking of the *Belgrano,* the right of self-defence (and the self-determination of the islanders) provided a rock-solid justification for the government, parliament and the electorate, which remained consistently behind the deployment and operation, even when losses were considerable.

7. Conclusion

The battle for the Falklands showed that legally and politically little had changed since 1945 in terms of decisions to go to war. Dominated by the Prime Minister, the War Cabinet and military chiefs, parliament was simply there to be kept informed and to be relied upon to give the enemy a clear indication of the British resolve to re-capture the islands. Though title to the islands was not as clear as the government made out, the right of self-defence and the protection of the Falklanders provided a strong legal case to convince parliament, the public and the wider international community. While arguably the requirements of necessity and imminence had passed once the Islands had been occupied by Argentina, and further the British government could either have rescued the islanders or more realistically successfully negotiated with Argentina for their repatriation to Britain, there was never any real doubt about the legality of Britain's action. Though the British response took several weeks to reach the Islands, it could not

---

[119] Third Report of the Foreign Affairs Committee 1984–5, 'Events Surrounding the Weekend of 1–2 May 1982, (HC 11); HC Paper 261-I, 16 July 1984, 154. See further L. Freeman, *The Official History of the Falklands Campaign: Volume II War and Diplomacy* (London: Routledge, 2005) chs 6, 21, 49.

[120] *Hansard* HC vol 73, cols 732–836, 18 Feb. 1985. Much of the debate concerned the leak of information in 1984 to Tam Dalyell MP by Clive Ponting, a senior civil servant at the Ministry of Defence. Ponting was acquitted in 1985 after being prosecuted for breaching the Official Secrets Act of 1911.

be classified as retaliatory given that the nexus between the attack by Argentina and the British response was not broken. Such delays show the inherent weakness in the right of self-defence at the international level, where instead of instinctive action to ensure self-preservation that characterizes the right at the level of individual self-defence, we have a slow and cumbersome response as thousands of troops and vast amounts of equipment are deployed.

Nevertheless, even with a less than certain legal title, international law in the UN-era provides that territorial disputes must be settled by peaceful means, so that Argentina's capture of the Islands did indeed give rise to the right of self-defence. But with the Islands back in British hands, the issue of sovereignty was once again back on the international community's agenda, though regrettably not something countenanced by parliament. Though willing to fight to uphold the principles of international law, Britain is unwilling to discuss the issue of sovereignty as part of its international obligation to settle disputes by peaceful means.

8

Helping a Friend in Afghanistan

1. Introduction

The end of the Cold War represented a fundamental change in the political shape of the world, leaving a single superpower. The events of 11 September 2001 (iconically known as 9/11) represented another sea-change, in that the sole remaining superpower found itself under attack not from other powerful states but from non-state actors. The world watched in horror as airliners hijacked by members of al-Qaeda hit the Pentagon in Washington and World Trade Center in New York, bringing the twin towers crashing down, killing nearly 3,000 citizens.

The war on terrorism, starting in earnest with the military action in Afghanistan in October 2001, involved British troops acting alongside the United States against al-Qaeda and the Taliban on the basis of the right of self-defence, the same right that was invoked in the Falklands War. Was the British reliance on the right of self-defence controversial either domestically or internationally? Was the fact that the action seemed to have approval from the Security Council as well as NATO important? While the initial operation (Operation Enduring Freedom) was based upon article 51 of the UN Charter preserving the right of self-defence, once the Taliban had been removed and al-Qaeda routed, Britain led a Security Council authorized security presence in and around Kabul providing stability while a nascent Afghan government tried to assert authority over the country. Concern was expressed in parliament at 'mission creep' as the functions of the NATO force (ISAF) changed, and British troops faced a resurgent Taliban in Helmand province from 2006 onwards.

2. Pre-Emptive Self-Defence

In the period after the coalition's victory against Iraq in 1991, the US and the UK, sometimes with other states, have placed incredible pressure on the legal framework governing the use of force contained in the UN Charter in a concerted effort to widen both exceptions to the ban on the threat or use of force in article 2(4), namely the right of self-defence contained in article 51, and military action taken under the authority of the Security Council derived from article 42.

While Operation Desert Storm conducted by a coalition of states against Iraq in 1991, under US command but with Security Council authority, was generally viewed as lawful, initially as an action in self-defence and then once Resolution 678 of November 1990 was secured as action under UN authority, the military action taken against Iraq commencing on 20 March 2003 was much more controversial. While the UK argued that it was justified under Security Council resolutions, the US always reserved the right to take action against Iraq in self-defence. The claim of self-defence in relation to Iraq in 2003 was wider than the claim made after 9/11, when the US and its allies argued that the terrorist attack against it justified a response in self-defence directed at al-Qaeda in Afghanistan along with the Taliban regime there. While discussion of Iraq will be left to chapter ten, the focus of this chapter will be on Afghanistan, which itself was by no means a straightforward application of the right of self-defence.

Before discussing the response to 9/11, we need to remind ourselves of the law relating to self-defence as outlined in the last chapter. Self-defence under the UN Charter has to be in response to an armed attack against a state. While some latitude may be given as to when an armed attack has started, there must be both imminence of attack and necessity of defence before a response is lawful. To strike too early is pre-emptive, while to strike too late is retaliatory and a reprisal.

In the aftermath of 9/11 the US attempted to shift the law to allow for pre-emptive strikes. The Bush Doctrine, or more formally 'The National Security Strategy of the United States of America', promulgated on 17 September 2002[1] represented the latest in a long line of US Presidential doctrines going back to the Monroe Doctrine of 1823. Specifically on the issue of using force, and in response to the events of 9/11, the Bush Doctrine focused on the recent and continuing threat posed by 'terrorist organizations of global reach and any terrorist or state sponsor of terrorism which attempts to gain or use weapons of mass destruction (WMD) or their precursors'. This meant that the US was committed to 'identifying and destroying the threat before it reaches' US borders, acting alone if necessary, 'to exercise our right of self-defense by acting preemptively against such terrorists, to prevent them from doing harm against our people and our country'. Further, the US was prepared 'to stop rogue states and their terrorist clients before they are able to threaten or use weapons of mass destruction against the United States and [its] allies and friends'. This sort of pre-emptive strike was viewed by the US as an adaptation of the doctrine of anticipatory self-defence, allowing nations 'to defend themselves against forces that present an imminent danger of attack'. The adaptation signifies that the emphasis is no longer on the imminence of the attack but the magnitude of the threat. 'The greater the threat, the greater is the risk of inaction—and the more compelling the case for taking

---

[1] 'The National Security Strategy of the United States of America', Sept. 2002, available at <http://georgewbush-whitehouse.archives.gov/nsc/nss/2002/index.html> (accessed 23 Feb. 2009).

anticipatory action to defend ourselves, even if uncertainty remains as to the time and place of the enemy's attack'. Deterrence, it is claimed, cannot be relied upon as the mechanism for securing peace; positive action is 'the only path to peace and security'.[2]

Unlike the previous post-1945 Presidential doctrines that juxtaposed a statement of political intent against an acceptance of the narrower strictures of international law, the Bush Doctrine not only constituted a statement of political intent, it also constituted an exposition of the conditions under which the US viewed the use of force as acceptable under international law. Between the end of the Second World War and the announcement of the Bush Doctrine it was common for the political statement of the incumbent President on issues of power to be balanced by more legal statements of US representatives, for example in the Security Council. Consider, for example, the statement by President Johnson in 1965 that 'the American nation cannot permit the establishment of another Communist dictatorship in the Western hemisphere', given as a justification for the US intervention in the Dominican Republic.[3] Contrast this with the statements of the US representative in the Security Council who argued that the legal basis for the intervention was to be found in the doctrine of protection of nationals and in the involvement of the OAS.[4]

International lawyers would concede that article 2(4) was not always adhered to during the Cold War since despite the legal protestations of the US and the USSR both direct hemispheric and indirect extra-hemispheric interventions regularly occurred that were clearly breaches of that norm. However, article 2(4) survived for, to paraphrase the words of the International Court of Justice in the *Nicaragua* case, all the relevant actors—the victim states and the intervening states—appealed to the rule and its exceptions, and the general attitude of the rest of the world was one of condemnation for breach of the rule.[5] Law did not prevent superpower interventions but it did appear to be relevant in assessing that conduct. Debates and controversy centred around the applicability of the rules governing the use of force but the presence of the legal rules and principles signified that the 'controversy [was] normative not [simply] empirical'.[6]

It is not the aim of this book to argue for the uncritical application of a strict interpretation of articles 2(4) and 51 of the UN Charter in the shape of a straightforward application of the formal rules embodied in the Charter to factual circumstances. This would ignore the dynamic built into both treaty law and customary law in the shape of (subsequent) practice which, if combined with an

---

    [2] 'National Security Strategy', v, 6, 14, 15, 30.
    [3] (1965) 52 US Dept of State Bulletin 745.
    [4] SC 1196th mtg, 1965.
    [5] *Case Concerning Military and Paramilitary Activities in and Against Nicaragua*, 1986 ICJ Rep. 14 at 98.
    [6] M. Koskenniemi, 'The Place of Law in Collective Security' (1996) 17 Michigan J Intl L 455 at 469, 490.

acceptance of the legality of that practice (*opinio juris*), may modify the treaty rules or create new customary law. States using force, or proposing to use force, normally attempt to justify their actions either as actually coming within the treaty framework, or they try and stretch that framework, or they claim a customary basis for their action, or sometimes they admit that their actions are exceptional and not precedential. Law is either confirmed or re-shaped by these claims and the responses of other states and actors to them. In effect, the legal rules claimed to be applicable in any given conflict or dispute are put into the international spotlight and either survive intact or are modified.

This analysis focuses on the attempts by states, including the UK who was centrally involved alongside its ally the US in both Afghanistan and Iraq, to stretch the treaty exceptions to the ban on the use of force and, in the case of self-defence, to recognize or create wider customary rules. However, we must not be too ready to assume that the law has changed when we are faced with behaviour that appears to disregard laws even if that behaviour is claimed to be reflective of a new law. While it is true that in issues of high politics exemplified by the decision to threaten or use force in international relations, politics may (always) be in the ascendancy, laws, particularly fundamental ones, are not easily swept aside by the rise and fall of political tides.

The Bush Doctrine presents us with a new controversy because it is not predicated on the separation or indeed the dismissal of the relevance of law to the issue of 'ultimate power',[7] it is an attempt to bring power and law together, to reshape international law. In effect this would take us back to the Monroe Doctrine which seemed to achieve acceptance in international law as exemplified by its preservation in the Covenant of the League of Nations.[8] The Monroe Doctrine of 1823 was of course adopted against the background of a virtually unregulated right to use force in international relations, a situation in which self-defence, as discussed in the *Caroline* incident of 1837, was simply one of many justifications for the use of force. The League of Nations' Covenant may have been an attempt to restrict a state's sovereign right to go to war, but it was flawed in many ways, including the acceptance of the Monroe doctrine and other similar 'regional understandings', which was a reference to the so-called British Monroe Doctrine.[9]

In the post-Cold War era it is once more the combination of the US and UK seeking to gain acceptance of their understandings of the international order. However, in contrast to the Monroe Doctrine, which was adopted against a background of lawlessness, the Bush Doctrine of 2002 is adopted against the background of a post-1945 order based on a ban on the use of force in article

---

[7] See statement of Dean Acheson on the Cuban Missile Crisis of 1962: 'law simply does not deal with...questions of ultimate power' (1961–3) 14 ASIL Proc. 14–15.

[8] Art 21 of the Covenant of the League of Nations, 1919.

[9] L. Lloyd, *Peace through Law: Britain and the International Court in the 1920s* (London: Boydell, 1997) 126–30.

2(4), a norm that is generally accepted as *jus cogens*,[10] and allowing of only two exceptions. The exceptions permitted in the Charter are actions in individual or collective self-defence in response to an 'armed attack' embodied in article 51, or military enforcement actions undertaken with Security Council authority under chapters VII and VIII of the UN Charter.

The Bush Doctrine represents the highpoint of a concerted effort by the US to both undermine and change this order. It is aimed at widening the right of self-defence as embodied in the Charter, or perhaps more accurately in recognizing a wider customary right of self-defence than the treaty right embodied in the Charter since it harks back to though it greatly widens the doctrine of anticipatory self-defence embodied in the *Caroline* incident of 1837. But this is only one part of a three-pronged assault on the order contained in the UN Charter. The other two prongs consist of first an effort to widen the circumstances in which it is deemed that the Security Council has sanctioned military action, and secondly the resurrection of other customary rights to use force, principally the doctrine of humanitarian intervention, reviewed in the next chapter.[11] The Bush Doctrine and the most recent post-Cold War military actions against Yugoslavia (as regards Kosovo) in 1999, Afghanistan in 2001 and Iraq in 2003 together seem to represent an assault on the order regulating the use of force contained in the UN Charter.

3. An Era of Anglo-American Military Expeditions

It is essential at this stage to put the Afghan conflict within the context of the growing use of military force by the US and the UK in the late twentieth century and into the new millennium. Since the end of the Gulf Conflict in 1991 there have been many instances of military action against Iraq, taken in the main by the US and the UK, culminating in the threat of overwhelming force if Iraq did not comply with Resolution 1441 of 8 November 2002, and the subsequent use of force against Iraq commencing on 20 March 2003 (reviewed in chapter ten). In between March and June 1999, NATO states, primarily the US with UK support, undertook the concerted bombing of the Federal Republic of Yugoslavia (FRY) in order to prevent crimes against humanity being committed by FRY (Serbian) forces against the ethnic Albanian majority in Kosovo (reviewed in chapter nine). In between October and December 2001 (although military action has continued thereafter) the United States with some British support and the significant involvement of the Afghan Northern Alliance undertook military

---

[10] See for example B. Simma, 'NATO, the UN and the Use of Force: Legal Aspects' (1999) 10 EJIL 14.

[11] M. Byers, 'The Shifting Foundations of International Law: A Decade of Forceful Measures Against Iraq' (2002) 13 EJIL 21 at 22.

action against the Taliban regime and their al-Qaeda allies in Afghanistan in response to the attacks on the United States of 11 September 2001. All of these military actions are problematic when considering the rules governing the use of force in the UN Charter. None were clearly authorized by the Security Council and none were clearly responses in self-defence, at least in Charter terms, though Operation Enduring Freedom against Afghanistan comes closest.[12] However, before concluding that they constituted violations of article 2(4) as illegal uses of force it is essential to evaluate the legal justifications put forward by those states using force and the responses of other states to those claims.

In all three military actions the states using force have put forward a three-pronged argument: that the action was justified under Security Council resolutions; as an act of self-defence; and as justifiable humanitarian intervention, but with varying degrees of emphasis. Violations of Security Council resolutions by Iraq were a constant refrain by those states threatening or using force against that country since April 1991. This has been the main justification though on occasions there have been references to the rights of humanitarian intervention and self-defence. Indeed, the latter seemed to increase in importance in the shape of pre-emptive self-defence enunciated in the Bush Doctrine as that country sought in 2002–3 to justify carrying out its latest threat to use force against Iraq. The justification for the use of force against the FRY was again breach of Security Council resolutions, though the impression was more that it was a clear expression of the right of humanitarian intervention. Self-defence played a minor role, though it has been invoked both by politicians[13] and in the literature.[14] In the case of Afghanistan, the facts led to an almost exclusive reliance on the right of self-defence with some reference to Security Council resolutions. Reference to humanitarian intervention in this case tended to take the form of criticism of the users of force for not invoking it as a basis of the action given the oppressive denial of human rights to at least half of the population (the women) of Afghanistan.

When considering the above military actions, there does seem to be significant practice by some states that lends credence to the idea that force can be taken in support of Security Council resolutions; especially (and probably only) those that have made a crucial finding of a threat to or breach of the peace under article 39 of the UN Charter, though they do not contain an express 'authorization' to take 'necessary measures' (the Security Council's euphemism for military action). It is interesting that in the three main conflicts examined reliance on this ground

---

[12] See J.I. Charney, 'The Use of Force Against Terrorism and International Law' (2001) 95 AJIL 835 at 835, questioning the claim of self-defence. But see T.M. Franck, 'Terrorism and the Right of Self-Defense' (2001) 95 AJIL 839 at 840; and A. Randelzhofer, in B. Simma (ed), *The Charter of the United Nations* (2nd edn, Oxford: Oxford University Press, 2002) 802, supporting the claim of self-defence.

[13] See President Clinton's speech on Kosovo of 25 Mar. 1999, *New York Times*, 25 Mar. 1999, A15.

[14] P.T. Egan, 'The Kosovo Intervention and Collective Self-Defence' (2001) 8(3) International Peacekeeping 39–58.

was strongest in two (Kosovo and Iraq), suggesting a preference for uses of force that can be justified under the UN collective security umbrella rather than customary rights that are exercised unilaterally. Indeed, in Afghanistan much is made of the fact that the Security Council apparently endorsed the exercise of the right of self-defence.[15] The greater legitimacy that UN authority brings has created tremendous pressures within the Security Council and on its resolutions.[16] Interestingly though neither of the resolutions adopted in the aftermath of 9/11 was clear-cut on the issue, with the primary purpose of 1368 being condemnation of the attack, while 1373 was concerned with the adoption of non-forcible measures by states against terrorist organizations. Although both resolutions affirmed the right of self-defence, neither determined that the terrorist atrocities of 11 September constituted an 'armed attack' or indeed a 'breach of the peace' or an 'act of aggression', preferring instead to find a 'threat to the peace'. In the past the Security Council has been clear on when it believes that member states have the right of self-defence. For example in response to the invasion of Kuwait by Iraq in 1990 the Council affirmed the 'inherent right of individual or collective self-defence, in response to the armed attack by Iraq against Kuwait, in accordance with Article 51 of the UN Charter'.[17]

Afghanistan, Iraq and the Bush Doctrine all exert pressure on the law of self-defence to allow for more flexibility in responding to terrorist attacks as well as threats from terrorism and weapons of mass destruction. Often a vengeful motive provoking a response to a terrorist attack is combined with a desire to prevent future attacks from occurring. Operation Enduring Freedom against Afghanistan was in part a response to the attacks of 9/11 and in part an anticipatory action based on the continuing threat of terrorist attacks emanating from that country. Some writers have analysed Enduring Freedom as purely anticipatory, while others have seen it as solely reactive to a specific armed attack.

Mary Ellen O'Connell argues that Operation Enduring Freedom against Afghanistan was justified under a narrow doctrine of anticipatory self-defence, where a 'state need not wait to suffer the actual blow before defending itself, so long as it is certain that the blow is coming'. Citing terrorist strikes against the US going back to 1993 (World Trade Center), the 1998 embassy bombings in Africa, the attack on the *USS Cole* in 2000, and continuing with the attacks on 11 September 2001, O'Connell states that there was plenty of evidence of further imminent attacks on the US and the UK justifying anticipatory self-defence against al-Qaeda and their supporters (including the Taliban) in Afghanistan.

---

[15] SC Res. 1368, 12 Sept. 2001; SC Res. 1373, 28 Sept. 2001. See E.P.J. Myjer and N.D. White, 'The Twin Towers Attack: An Unlimited Right to Self-Defence' (2002) 7 JCSL 5 at 9–11. But see M. Byers, 'Terrorism, the Use of Force and International Law After 11 September' (2002) 51 ICLQ at 401–403, 409: NATO and the OAS both categorized the terrorist atrocities of 11 September as an 'armed attack'.

[16] C. Gray, 'From Unity to Polarization: International Law and the Use of Force Against Iraq' (2002) 13 EJIL 1 at 8.

[17] SC Res. 661, 6 Aug. 1990.

However, she then argues that there has been no acceptance of a wider right of pre-emptive self-defence as embodied in the Bush Doctrine. In other words no state 'has the right to use force to prevent possible, as distinct from actual, armed attacks'.[18] The universal rejection of the legality of Israel's 1981 strike against the Iraqi nuclear reactor at Osirik is clear evidence of this.[19] Proponents of the doctrine of pre-emptive strikes rely primarily on the word 'inherent' in article 51 to suggest the preservation of a much wider right than that contained in the Charter, one that pre-existed in customary law. Ironically though the *Caroline* doctrine which is said to be the basis of the customary right can only really be read as justifying a very narrow doctrine of anticipatory self-defence, since the threat of attack has to be 'instant, overwhelming, and leaving no choice of means, and no moment for deliberation'.[20] Indeed, '[e]ven if earlier custom allowed preemptive self-defense, arguing that it persisted after 1945 for UN members requires privileging the word "inherent" over the plain terms of article 2(4) and the words "armed attack" in article 51. Indeed, it requires privileging one word over the whole purpose and structure of the UN Charter'.[21] Furthermore, O'Connell rightly points out that pre-emptive self-defence is 'not a right that the United States wants others to have'. It can 'hardly wish to see an anarchic regime in which every state is entitled to initiate the use of force against its adversaries in preemptive self-defense'.[22] To claim that the US has this right but not other states,[23] not only goes against the whole nature of sovereign equality (at least in lawmaking) but simply will not work.[24] If the Bush Doctrine constitutes an offer to the rest of the world to agree to a wholly new view of self-defence that is inconsistent with previous understandings of the law, then it is problematic to assume that even if there is acceptance, it is acceptance to the effect that only the US has this right.

In contrast to O'Connell who argues that Operation Enduring Freedom was an acceptable extension of the right of self-defence to include anticipatory though not pre-emptive action, Michael Byers argues that it amounted to an acceptance of the Schultz Doctrine of 1986, namely the right to attack terrorists on the territory of other states as a response to terrorist attacks such as the 1986 Berlin bombing, or the response to 9/11. This is narrower than the Bush Doctrine which is not dependent upon there having been a previous attack.[25] Both Byers and O'Connell agree however that although it is an extension of

[18] M.E. O'Connell, 'The Myth of Preemptive Self-Defense' (August 2000) ASIL Task Force Papers, 3, 8, 10.

[19] See SC Res. 487, 19 June 1981.

[20] 29 British and Foreign State Papers 1137–8; 30 British and Foreign State Papers 195–6.

[21] O'Connell, 'The Myth', 13.

[22] O'Connell, 'The Myth', 15–16. O' Connell also points to the fact that pre-emptive strikes are very unlikely to be proportionate responses, 19.

[23] See Byers 'The Shifting Foundations'.

[24] O'Connell, 'The Myth', 19.

[25] M. Byers, 'Self-Defence or Pre-emptive Actions? The Law and Politics of Normative Change' (2003) 16 Ethics and International Affairs 52.

the right of self-defence the Afghan precedent is much narrower than the Bush Doctrine of pre-emptive strikes. There certainly seems to have been an uncritical reaction by states to Operation Enduring Freedom in Afghanistan, but the question remains whether this amounted to an endorsement of the Schultz Doctrine that was rejected fifteen years earlier. While the *prima facie* case for the legality of responses like Operation Enduring Freedom looks promising, the signs are that the Bush Doctrine has received a negative reception, not least from most European states.[26] The Australian Prime Minister warned of Australian pre-emptive action against terrorists in the wake of the Bali bombings of 12 October 2002, though he more straightforwardly appealed for a change in international law governing self-defence to allow for such action to lawfully occur. It is worth noting that the claim to pre-emptive action was rejected by the states in the region.[27] Thus there appears to have been no acceptance of the Bush Doctrine. There is evidence that the majority of states are resistant to such a large-scale extension of the right of self-defence that allows a state to take military action based solely upon its perception of a threat.

We must also be wary of simply accepting the legality of military actions based on the precedent of Operation Enduring Freedom. This was not a straightforward application of article 51, or of the customary rules of immediacy and proportionality. In essence the armed attack of 11 September 2001 had ceased by the time the United States came to respond on 7 October. That there were good reasons for this delay is clear enough, but there no longer remained an aggression that had to be remedied as with the invasion of the Falkland Islands by Argentina in 1982. In essence then what was being claimed in the operation in Afghanistan was a wider right of self-defence, a right to respond to terrorist attacks within a reasonable period of time in the territory of other states where the government has harboured or possibly supported terrorists, the aim being to prevent future such attacks occurring. The Bush Doctrine goes even further since it does not require the occurrence of an armed attack; military force can be triggered by the perception of a threat.

Nevertheless, if Operation Enduring Freedom has been accepted as a precedent for a wider right of self-defence, then there may not be such a great leap between it and the Bush Doctrine.[28] Operation Enduring Freedom was only in part a response for the attack of 9/11. Its purpose was not simply to respond to those terrorists behind the attacks of 9/11, but it was an attempt to try and remove terrorists and their supporters from Afghanistan, which would probably be a source of a future attack. The imminence of such a future attack would determine whether the action was anticipatory in the sense of the *Caroline* incident, or

---

[26] *Keesing's Record of World Events* (2002) 144832.
[27] *The Canberra Times*, 2 Dec. 2002.
[28] See C. Greenwood, 'International Law and the Pre-Emptive Use of Force: Afghanistan, Al-Qaida and Iraq' (2003) 4 San Diego Intl L J 7 at 15–16, 37.

a pre-emptive strike in the sense of the Bush Doctrine.[29] There has been debate on whether a further attack from Afghanistan was imminent, but that appears to have been of little importance in state practice that seems to have accepted the legality of Operation Enduring Freedom.

In this light an acceptance of Operation Enduring Freedom could amount to a recognition that the Israeli practice of reprisals, and the American retaliations against Libya in 1986 (in response to the Berlin bombing), Iraq in 1993 (in response to the attempted assassination of Bush Senior), and Sudan and Afghanistan in 1998 (in response to the embassy bombings), now constitute a line of practice that has finally been accepted as lawful with the uncritical reaction to the use of force in Afghanistan. While most of those responses were linked to past terrorist acts, the link was sometimes tenuous, and on other occasions (Libya and Sudan for instance) was shown not to exist.[30] As with the response to 9/11 these military actions were both punitive in response to an attack and anticipatory or pre-emptive (sometimes called preventive) to prevent future attacks. Their general disproportionality can only be explained by the existence of an anticipatory or pre-emptive element. Operation Enduring Freedom was a disproportionate response to the attacks of 9/11 against the US but may be viewed as proportionate if the purpose is also seen as anticipatory or pre-emptive (depending on the imminence of the threat).

By their nature anticipatory strikes, and more so pre-emptive strikes, aim to eliminate not only perceived threats but also all possible sources of future threats and therefore tend to be overwhelming. Thus Enduring Freedom and those retaliatory acts that have gone before are not far removed from the Bush Doctrine, since even under that Doctrine there must be some evidence of terrorist activities or weapons of mass destruction. In fact the US itself linked its actions taken in self-defence against Afghanistan starting on 7 October 2001 with a wider and continuing right to defend itself against other threats. In a letter to the Security Council, the US stated 'we may find that our self-defense requires further actions with respect to other organizations and states'.[31] Thus Operation Enduring Freedom and the claimed right to take pre-emptive strikes are not seen as separate events by the US but as part of a defensive war against terrorism.[32]

The dangers of anticipatory, and more significantly pre-emptive, self-defence are clear but international lawyers may have to accept them if they become part of state practice. Kirgis states that customary international law is not static: 'it may be modified over time by new assertions of rights, if other states acquiesce

---

[29] Myjer and White, 'The Twin Towers Attack', 6–9; but see M.E. O'Connell, 'Evidence of Terror' (2002) 7 JCSL 19–36. See letter to the SC of 7 Sept. 2001, UN Doc. S/2002/946 in which the US explained its action in self-defence as a response to the 'attacks on 11 September and the ongoing threat to the United States and its nationals posed by the Al-Qaeda organization'.

[30] Similarly, the pre-emptive strike against Iraq in 2003 appears to have been based on a misperception of the threat from weapons of mass destruction. See chapter ten.

[31] UN Doc. S/2001/946, 7 Oct. 2001.

[32] W.M. Reisman, 'In Defence of World Public Order' (2001) 95 AJIL 833.

in those assertions'.[33] Further, Byers claims that 'current evidence suggests that the customary process is in fact changing...weakening those aspects of the law that disfavour the powerful while maintaining and strengthening those aspects, such as the rules concerning acquiescence, that operate in their favour'.[34] While acquiescence does play a role in the formation of customary international law, one must not assume it. As Byers states, little publicity was given to the rejection of humanitarian intervention by the Non Aligned states in 2000 but their statement was a clear rejection of attempts to reinvent the doctrine in the Kosovo episode.[35]

Is it the case in this area governing the use of force that custom can be formed by assertions of new rights that are acquiesced to by other states? Two question marks can be raised in the context of claimed new rights to use force in international relations. First: what if the assertions of new rights appear to violate a norm of *jus cogens*? Second: what if the silence of the majority is not indicative of assent to the proposed change? Gaining acquiescence by the use of pressure is an issue in the case of the war against terrorism following 11 September. There has not been a clear instance of collective rejection of the application of self-defence in Operation Enduring Freedom. It seems that in the absence of clear protestations, powerful states can properly take the opportunity to claim that there is acquiescence to and therefore acceptance of the asserted right to self-defence.[36] However, we must be careful in analysing the quality of that acceptance. We need to ask and answer the question of why would less developed and weak states accept the dismantling of the collective security structure that at least provides them with rules that purport to protect their vulnerability? In seeking an answer we must take account of the pressure being exerted on them not to criticize military action being taken against terrorist organizations or rogue states by powerful states. President Bush sounded a warning against such criticism on 6 November 2001, when he stated that those nations not 'for' the United States were 'against us'.[37] While acquiescence can be viewed as acceptance, one must be careful not to assume this. As Ian Brownlie says: 'the real problem is to determine the value of abstention from protest by a substantial number of states in face of a practice followed by some others. Silence may denote either tacit agreement or a simple lack of interest in the issue'.[38] Clearly the latter does not constitute acceptance, and if this is the case, acceptance cannot be presumed when the silence is a result of fear of the potential political and economic consequences of protest.

[33] F.L. Kirgis, 'Pre-emptive Action to Forestall Terrorism' (June 2002) ASIL Insights.

[34] Byers, 'Shifting Foundations', 36.

[35] Declaration of the Group of 77 South Summit, Havana, Cuba, 10–14 April 2000 <http://www.g77.org/summit/Declaration_G77Summit.htm> para 54 (accessed 23 Feb. 2009).

[36] Byers, 'Terrorism After 11 September', 412.

[37] BBC News, 'Bush Urges Anti-Terror Allies to Act', 6 Nov. 2001, <http://news.bbc.co.uk/2/hi/world/europe/1642130.stm> (accessed 26 Jan. 2009).

[38] I. Brownlie, *Principles of Public International Law* (6th edn, Oxford: Oxford University Press, 2003) 7–8.

Retaliatory/anticipatory and pre-emptive strikes are all uses of force *prima facie* contrary to article 2(4). Although they may constitute attempts to widen the exceptions to that rule found in chapter VII of the UN Charter, this does not by itself absolve them of their violative character. When practice is apparently violative of a peremptory norm, it is not enough to have acquiescence in the face of a breach in order to establish a new or extended right. It is argued that there needs to be more positive acceptance of the claim, positive proof that states have accepted the modification of the peremptory norm, proof in other words of *opinio juris*. Arguments about acquiescence seem to assume the emergence of new rights in a legal vacuum, but that is not the case. Brownlie puts this clearly when he states that 'the major distinguishing feature of such [peremptory] rules is their relative indelibility. They are rules of customary law which cannot be set aside by treaty or acquiescence but only by the formation of a subsequent customary rule to contrary effect'.[39]

4. Britain in Afghanistan: Helping a Friend in Collective Self-Defence

From the perspective of British troops in Afghanistan they seem to be in a similar position to their colleagues in Iraq—fighting extremist Muslim terrorists and insurgents to achieve security and stability in a country so that it can be built. However, they are arguably in a stronger position, not necessarily militarily but in terms of legality and legitimacy and this arguably also affects the sustainability of the operation. This is not to say that there are no problems with the legality and legitimacy of military operation in Afghanistan, it is merely that compared to Iraq there are more positives in this regard.

The events of 9/11 provoked the invasion of Afghanistan on 7 October 2001. Al-Qaeda was responsible for the attacks and that terrorist group had bases in Afghanistan. Moreover, they had a close relationship with the unrecognized but effective government of Afghanistan—the Taliban. The US and the UK claimed that their military actions in Afghanistan against al-Qaeda and the Taliban were legitimate exercises of the right of self-defence.[40] This was endorsed by the EU, NATO and significantly, though not unequivocally, the Security Council.[41] Thus the action seemed to be in accordance with international law. However, the action in Afghanistan was not a straightforward application of the right of individual or collective self-defence in a number of ways. As has been pointed out in effect it appears to be an attempted development of the right of self-defence

---

[39] Ibid., 488.
[40] See UN Docs. S/2001/946 and S/2001/947, 7 Oct. 2001.
[41] SC Res. 1368, 12 Sept. 2001.

to allow states to respond to terrorist attacks, in particular to take action against states harbouring terrorists.[42]

First, there was no on-going armed attack against the US.[43] The attacks were over, unless the vision of 9/11 as part of a wider war on terror is accepted. If the invasion of Afghanistan was a response to the armed attack of 9/11 it appeared more punitive than defensive—more akin to a reprisal. Secondly, if the invasion of Afghanistan was anticipatory self-defence, in other words it was designed to stop more imminent attacks, then this is more akin to the *Caroline* doctrine than the UN Charter rules which formally require the occurrence of an armed attack. Thirdly, self-defence should be both necessary, in other words leaving no choice, and proportionate. On the latter, although 9/11 was stated to be the equivalent of the Japanese attack on Pearl Harbor that brought the US into the Second World War thus justifying a war against the whole country from which the attack could be said to have originated,[44] it can be argued that this is overstating the case and that strikes against the terrorist bases would have been a more proportionate response. Fourthly, the response seemed to make the Taliban equally responsible with al-Qaeda for the 9/11 attacks—by harbouring terrorists and not giving them up. But according to 'the test generally accepted by states' 'the use of force by individuals constituted an armed attack only when there has been a sending by . . . a State of armed bands, groups, irregulars or mercenaries which carry out acts of armed force against another State of such gravity as to amount to an act of aggression', thus justifying self-defence by the attacked state and its allies against the sending state.[45] The Taliban government did not send al-Qaeda terrorists to launch the attacks on 9/11.

Despite question marks about the targeting of the Taliban and the overall proportionality of the response, world opinion seemed either to endorse the view that the action against Afghanistan which resulted in the overthrow of the government and the rout of al-Qaeda from its strongholds, was justifiable self-defence, or was silent on that matter. Though not straightforward it seemed to be accepted as a lawful application of the right of self-defence.

Acceptance of this wider right by some world leaders was due to it being a just war prosecuted in response to the atrocious targeting of thousands of innocent civilians. In the aftermath of 9/11 the British Prime Minister Tony Blair

---

[42] S. Ratner, 'Ius ad Bellum and Ius in Bello after September 11' (2002) 96 AJIL 906.

[43] This is not to say that an attack by a terrorist group cannot be an 'armed attack' within the meaning of article 51 of the UN Charter. But see the International Court's advisory opinion in *Legal Consequences of the Construction of a Wall in the Occupied Palestinian Territories*, 2004 ICJ Rep. 136, where the Court stated: 'Article 51 thus recognizes the existence of an inherent right of self-defence in the case of an armed attack by one State against another State. However, Israel does not claim that the attacks against it are imputable to a foreign state' (para 138).

[44] Y. Dinstein, *War, Aggression and Self-Defence* (4th edn, Cambridge: Cambridge University Press, 2005) 241.

[45] C. Gray, *International Law and the Use of Force* (2nd edn, Oxford: Oxford University Press, 2004) 165, summarizing the GA's 1974 Definition of Aggression, art 3(g) as utilized in the *Nicaragua* case, 1986 ICJ Rep. 14 at para 195.

stated that 'the world should stand together against this outrage'.[46] Further, 'our beliefs are opposite to theirs. We believe in reason, democracy and tolerance. These beliefs are the foundation of our civilised world. They are enduring, they have served us well, and as history has shown, we have been prepared to fight when necessary, to defend them'.[47] It is noticeable how a much wider notion of defence—defence to protect beliefs is being used here—although reference is also made to the invocation of the defensive right by NATO. Such moral outrage was matched by Iain Duncan Smith, the Leader of the Opposition, who stated that politicians on both sides of the House were 'guardians of a set of values that are underpinned by...democracy and the rule of law' and were united 'to defend civilised values against those who seek to bring them down by violence'. He congratulated NATO's Secretary General, Lord Robertson, for invoking article 5 of the Treaty on the basis that 'an attack on one is an attack on all'.[48]

On 4 October the Prime Minister was able to relate to the House the evidence gathered to determine who was responsible:

Our findings have been shared and co-ordinated with those of our allies and they are clear. They are: first, that it was Osama bin Laden and the al-Qaeda, the terrorist network which he heads, that planned and carried out the atrocities on 11 September; secondly, that Osama bin Laden and the al-Qaeda were able to commit these atrocities because of their close alliance with the Taliban regime in Afghanistan, which allows them to operate with impunity in pursuing their terrorist activity.

...

In the face of this evidence, our immediate objectives are clear. We must bring bin-Laden and other al-Qaeda leaders to justice and eliminate the terrorist threat that they pose, and we must ensure that Afghanistan ceases to harbour and sustain international terrorism. If the Taliban regime will not comply with that objective, we must bring about a change in that regime to ensure that Afghanistan's links to international terrorism are broken.[49]

The Foreign Secretary, Jack Straw, made it clear that the government was acting 'entirely within the framework of international law', namely article 51 of the UN Charter which permits states to act individually or collectively in self-defence when they come under armed attack. He also answered questions about the proportionality of the response by saying that 'action must be proportionate, but we must bear in mind the proportion of the attack against the United States and the proportion of the threat still posed by the al-Qaeda organisation'. When asked whether direct authority from the Security Council should be sought Jack Straw indicated there was no need and placed reliance on the decision of NATO to invoke article 5 and the fact that 'all 19 NATO allies have accepted the evidence of bin Laden's and al-Qaeda's guilt'.[50] In a later statement before the Foreign Affairs

---

[46] *Hansard* HC vol 372, col 605, 14 Sept. 2001.
[47] Ibid., col 606.   [48] Ibid., col 607.
[49] *Hansard* HC vol 372, col 673, 4 Oct. 2001.
[50] Ibid., cols 690–2.

Committee, the Foreign Secretary avoided answering a question on whether a right of pre-emption exists, by stating that 'if country X receives very good information that country Y or terrorist group Z is about to attack it, and takes action in self-defence to stop that attack, it is acting consistently with Article 51 of the UN Charter but the exact circumstances are going to vary'.[51] The other political parties agreed that there was no need for any express Council authorization to use force, and also that self-defence was both a reaction to 9/11 and a necessary action to prevent further uses of force by al-Qaeda.[52]

Thus the legal and moral ground was cleared for military action. Also, through two lengthy debates on the matter in the House of Commons between 9/11 and the launch of the military response, overwhelming political support in the House was established, though not by means of a formal vote. The Prime Minister returned to moral rhetoric in a statement to the House announcing the start of hostilities on 8 October when predominantly American forces launched bombing and missile strikes against military and terrorist targets in Afghanistan:

So this military action we are undertaking is not for a just cause alone, though this cause is just. It is to protect our country, our people, our economy, our way of life.

. . . .

If attacked, we will respond. We will defend ourselves.

. . . .

We will see this struggle through to the end and to the victory that would mark the victory not of revenge but of justice over the evil of terrorism.[53]

The fact that the British contribution to this initial phase of military action was limited, consisting of the firing of cruise missiles from Royal Navy submarines and reconnaissance and refuelling RAF sorties in support of the United States,[54] does not diminish the significance of the wider support—both political and legal—that this represented. In these statements the Prime Minister envisages a much wider vision of defence. An atrocious attack on the United States is portrayed as an attack on the civilized world, and the response is a just one aimed at protecting our way of life against an ongoing evil. Though of course this mixture

---

[51] (2001) UKMIL, item 16/45, oral evidence to the Foreign Affairs Committee on 5 Dec. 2001. See further statements by the Foreign Secretary before the Foreign Affairs Committee during 2002 relating the doctrine of pre-emption to the doctrine propounded in the *Caroline* case: (2002) UKMIL, items 16/8–16/11. The government also responded to a Defence Committee report by stating that it might need 'ultimately to act to destroy active terrorist cells with military action': (2002) UKMIL item 16/19, HC 667, 5 March 2002. The Attorney General stated before the House of Lords that the 'right of self-defence under international law includes the right to use force where an armed attack is imminent' (*Hansard* HL vol 660, cols 369–72, 21 April 2004).

[52] See for example *Hansard* HC vol 372, col 704, 4 Oct. 2001 (Menzies-Campbell).

[53] *Hansard* HC vol 372, col 814, 8 Oct. 2001.

[54] *Hansard* HC vol 372, col 1131, 16 Oct. 2001 (Hoon). Other countries providing direct military support were Australia, Belgium, Canada, Denmark, France, Germany, Italy, Jordan, South Korea, the Netherlands, New Zealand, Portugal, Romania, Singapore, Spain, Turkey and Ukraine: vol 373, col 621, 29 Oct. 2001 (Hoon).

of political and moral rhetoric is not clear evidence of *opinio juris*, it could be said to provide the political platform on which legal arguments of a wider right of defence have been put forward and apparently accepted. The Prime Minister answered in the affirmative when he was asked again to reaffirm the legal base of the action and that the Law Officers' advice was that the 'action was in line with the provisions of the' UN Charter.[55] The Defence Secretary, Geoff Hoon, was pushed on the question whether the UK had formally notified the Security Council of its action in self-defence as required by article 51 of the UN Charter.[56] He answered by saying that 'this is a coalition operation and I have no doubt that for technical legal purposes, we are covered by the notification that the United States has given, but I will certainly investigate whether that legal advice is right and whether we need to make a formal notification ourselves as a country'.[57]

It is clear from the legal statements in the House that article 51 was seen as the basis of the military operation against Afghanistan, though the understanding of the right of self-defence is broader than the orthodox interpretation given to that provision.

While the just war arguments over Kosovo produced a conclusion that the action was illegal but moral, the just war arguments over Afghanistan seemed to help create a widened notion of self-defence and thus both a lawful and just war. The question remains whether this widened right would be acceptable on future occasions without the moral outrage that followed the attacks of 9/11. For some states, however, acceptance of the wider right may have been more a question of unwillingness to criticize in the face of the 'for us or against us' rhetoric of President George W Bush.[58] If that were the case it would be difficult to accept that there was a true consensus about the modification of fundamental rules of the international community governing the use of force.

While the action in Afghanistan might be stronger than that in Iraq in terms of legality and legitimacy, it is by no means a cast iron case. If we add in the problems already identified about the proportionality of the response and the incorrect imputation of responsibility to the Taliban as well as al-Qaeda, this again might be a case where the moral outrage of the atrocity allowed a military response to be mounted that would not normally have been acceptable to the international community. The fact that this was no ordinary defence of the UK or US is shown by the continued military operations in Afghanistan giving rise to a seemingly endless exercise of the right of self-defence. The reality is that this was an intervention to try to eliminate terrorism and a regime that supported

---

[55] Ibid., col 821 (Llwyd and Dalyell).

[56] Ibid., col 832 (Salmond).

[57] Ibid. See further col 851 (Short) who confirmed that the UK representative at the UN had informed the Security Council.

[58] N.D. White, 'The Will and Authority of the Security Council after Iraq ' (2004) 17 LJIL 645 at 664.

terrorists, but as one MP warned: 'history suggests that Afghanistan is a place where countries get in easy and get out bloody'.[59]

It might have been a shorter military campaign, and arguably a more proportionate one had the government taken the advice of another MP, Robert Marshall-Andrews, who accepted that the 'United States and the international community have legitimacy to enter Afghanistan, if necessary by force—certainly by force—in order to arrest and apprehend Osama bin Laden', but questioned whether the bombing campaign was a means of achieving it.[60] In a later debate the same MP pressed for the establishment of an international court to try bin Laden, but was rebuffed by the Foreign Secretary on the grounds that the Statute establishing the International Criminal Court of 1998 was not yet in force, besides which the Court's jurisdiction when it came into force was prospective. On this basis Jack Straw stated that 'no such tribunal exists, or is likely to exist to try bin Laden. The sooner ... the few members that share his view, accept that we are not seeking to evade the clear choice that lies before us, the better'.[61] As Mr Marshall-Andrews later pointed out, the Foreign Secretary had deliberately misunderstood his point,[62] which was that an *ad hoc* international tribunal could be set up as at Nuremberg, or more recently for the Former Yugoslavia or Rwanda, but the Foreign Secretary's dissembling was indicative of the decision by the two allies to adopt a military solution to 9/11 rather than one based on criminal justice.

In mid-November 2001, with the Taliban regime collapsing, the Prime Minister reported that British forces were involved in the airstrikes against Taliban and al-Qaeda forces, and ground forces had supported the Northern Alliance troops who had undertaken most of the fighting. He also stated that several thousand British troops were ready to be deployed, to provide some stability in the period between the end of the conflict and the reconstruction phase.[63] Although the remnants of al-Qaeda were to prove elusive, necessitating continuing action in 'self-defence', the British involvement was to become far more concentrated on the reconstruction of Afghanistan, necessitating a Security Council mandate.

5. The Battle for Helmand

In mid-December 2001 the Foreign Secretary, Jack Straw, informed the House of the 'astonishing success' of the agreement whereby all non-Taliban Afghan factions 'sat down together in Bonn and thrashed out an agreement which puts Afghanistan back on the path to peace', the first step being the creation of an

[59] *Hansard* HC vol 372, col 852, 8 Oct. 2001 (Salmond).
[60] Ibid., col 834 (Marshall-Andrews).
[61] *Hansard* HC vol 372, cols 1055–6, 16 Oct. 2001.
[62] Ibid., col 1079.
[63] *Hansard* HC vol 374, col 862, 14 Nov. 2001.

interim Afghan authority. He went on to say that 'the House can be proud of this country's role in the liberation of the Afghan people', suggesting the war aims had become much wider, though there was still the need to remove the remnants of the Taliban and al-Qaeda with fighting continuing in the Tora Bora mountains. He further pointed to the necessity of a security force around Kabul to secure the foothold of the Interim Afghan Authority. Jack Straw expressed Britain's willingness to play a lead role in the security force.[64] The opposition expressed concern that such a force was being put together without the House being 'told fully what is intended':

What would be the limits to the time and extent of any involvement? What would be the remit of any such engagement? In the past, we have expressed reservations about being involved in what has been described as 'nation building', especially as we have been protagonists in the campaign so far.[65]

The Defence Secretary did not give any specific answers to these prescient questions, but stressed the need to 'convince every Afghan to have confidence in [the interim] authority and in the Bonn Agreement'.[66] He later explained that the longer-term aim of Operation Enduring Freedom included securing 'the reintegration of Afghanistan as a responsible member of the international community and to end its self-imposed isolation', which was 'vital if we are to ensure that the link between Afghanistan and international terrorism is broken'.[67] While US forces continued to exercise the right of self-defence to try and defeat the remnants of al-Qaeda and the Taliban, the Security Council endorsed the creation of ISAF to provide security to the capital.[68] Legally this put the basis of ISAF under the other exception to the ban on the use of force—military enforcement action under UN Security Council authority—thereby making it distinct from action taken in self-defence to the attacks of 9/11 and the continuing threat from al-Qaeda.

The history of ISAF's involvement in Afghanistan shows all the hallmarks of the mission creep that the opposition was so concerned about, despite the government's assurance that Britain was taking on leadership of the force 'for a limited period of three months'. The initial British contingent consisted of 1,800 troops, about a third of the force.[69] The Prime Minister also reassured the House by saying 'I know that there has been some speculation that we would be sending thousands upon thousands of troops—we are not—or that they would be there for a very long time—they will not be'.[70] The UK-led UN authorized security

[64] *Hansard* HC vol 376, cols 848–9, 12 Dec. 2001.

[65] Ibid., cols 852–3 (Ancram).

[66] *Hansard* HC vol 376, cols 89–92, 12 Dec. 2001 (Hoon).

[67] *Hansard* HC vol 377, col 688, 10 Jan. 2002 (Hoon).

[68] SC Res. 1386, 20 Dec. 2001.

[69] *Hansard* HC vol 377, cols 304–5, 19 Dec. 2001 (Hoon); vol 378, col 51w, 14 Jan. 2002 (Hoon).

[70] *Hansard* HC vol 377, col 287, 19 Dec. 2001 (Blair).

force was established in and around Kabul to provide security to enable elections and further reconstruction. Turkey took over command of ISAF in June 2002, though Britain still contributed a reduced contingent of 400 to the force, but increased its contribution (at one point to 1,700 troops) to the continuing US-led efforts against the Taliban and al-Qaeda.[71]

NATO in fact provides the bulk of contributing nations to ISAF and in April 2003 (a month after the invasion of Iraq) NATO agreed to take over command of ISAF, which it did in August 2003. In October the Security Council authorized the expansion of security to be provided by ISAF beyond Kabul.[72] Very little was said in parliament about the expanded role for ISAF, even though the UK still contributed to the force.[73] ISAF deployment in stages one and two in the Northern and Western Provinces was achieved by September 2005.

Stage three in the less secure Southern provinces (including Helmand and Kandahar) was agreed in December 2005, and ISAF took over from US troops and military/civilian Provincial Reconstruction Teams in July 2006 (this technique was adopted and adjusted by ISAF). The Defence Secretary, John Reid, announced the deployment of a 3,300 strong British force as part of ISAF in the lawless Helmand province on 26 January 2006, bringing British troops in Afghanistan to over 5,000. In explanation he stated that 'all of this has but one aim—a secure, stable, prosperous and democratic Afghanistan, free from terrorism and terrorist domination'.[74] On 27 February 2006 John Reid, made clear the link between the actions of ISAF and 9/11.

We are in Afghanistan under a UN mandate with the support of the world community...to help the democratically elected government of Afghanistan extend their democratic authority and build their own security forces, and to assist them in their economic development. That is precisely why we go to the south.... It is more dangerous and difficult than the first two stages...but...we are there to prevent Afghanistan from being used as a training ground, a planning area and a launch platform for terrorist acts such as the one we saw in New York – the worst terrorist act in history.[75]

The Defence Secretary made it clear that the ISAF deployment was separate from the continuing action against al-Qaeda. 'Our troops are not there to seek out and destroy the terrorists, that is being done under Operation Enduring Freedom by an American-led multinational coalition'.[76] But the continuing link to 9/11 is crucial, for although the legal basis for ISAF is different from that of the initial US/UK operation in Afghanistan, ISAF's presence builds on the

---

[71] *Hansard* HC vol 384, col 649, 29 April 2002 (Hoon); vol 387, col 409, 20 June 2002 (Hoon).

[72] SC Res. 1510, 13 Oct. 2003.

[73] *Hansard* HC vol 411, col 588w, 22 Oct. 2003 (Ingram), who simply reported an increase in the UK-led Provincial Reconstruction Team pursuant to SC Resolution 1510.

[74] *Hansard* HC vol 441, cols 1531–3, 26 Jan. 2006.

[75] *Hansard* HC vol 443, cols 2–3, 27 Feb. 2006.

[76] Ibid., col 12.

initial operation. One member of the House urged the Defence Secretary to 'halt the dispatch of small contingents of our forces to south Afghanistan to undertake incompatible tasks that could not be successfully performed even by 100,000 troops…remember that in the 1980s the Russians sent 300,000 troops into Afghanistan, but that, several years later, they fled the country, leaving 10,000 dead behind'.[77] During a short debate, John Reid defended the government's decision in saying:

There is a difference on two grounds between this intervention and all previous ones. First, we are there at the behest and with the authority of the world community in the United Nations. Secondly, we are there at the invitation of the democratically elected Afghanistan Government.[78]

In overthrowing the Taliban in the first operation, Western troops now faced them as opponents in the state-building phase, making such a job extremely difficult to achieve.[79] Stage four in relation to the Eastern provinces commenced in October 2006 when NATO took over from US forces there.

The overall aim of the NATO-led ISAF operation is to achieve security in the whole of Afghanistan, which will allow for the reconstruction of the state and the strengthening of democracy. As the Defence Secretary, Des Browne, stated in June 2006: 'the ISAF mission…is to help the Afghan Government to create a secure environment in which their authority can be extended across the entire country and reconstruction of the country can be taken forward'. He suggested the British troop contribution would increase in response to a statement by an MP that 'that objective will not be secured with only 6,000 troops in the southern part of Afghanistan'.[80] Des Browne announced an increase in British troops deployed to Helmand in response to the increasing violence there in July 2006—from 3,600 to 4,500.[81] He also announced that thirty-six countries contributed a total of 10,000 troops to ISAF.[82] A further increase in overall force levels in Afghanistan to 7,700 was announced in February 2007. The Defence Secretary managed to justify these increases while at the same time claiming progress was being made in facing down 'the Taliban in their own back yard, delivering security and bringing the reach of the Afghan Government to places that have hardly seen it before'.[83]

In increasingly fierce fighting forty-eight British military personnel lost their lives in Afghanistan between 7 October 2001 and 30 April 2007.[84] This figure increased to 102 by mid-June 2008 as battles against the Taliban intensified.[85]

---

[77] Ibid., cols 3–4 (Tapsell).   [78] Ibid., col 4.
[79] S. Lamb, 'Britain told: do peace deal with Taliban', *The Sunday Times*, 26 Nov. 2006, 21.
[80] *Hansard* HC vol 448, col 11, 26 June 2006 (Mackay).
[81] *Hansard* HC vol 448, col 1134, 10 July 2006.
[82] *Hansard* HC vol 449, col 762w, 24 July 2006.
[83] *Hansard* HC vol 457, col 619–20, 26 Feb. 2007 (Browne).
[84] *Hansard* HC vol 460, col 215w, 9 May 2007 (Browne).
[85] *Hansard* HC vol 477, col 676, 16 June 2008 (Browne).

On 12 December 2007, the new Prime Minister, Gordon Brown, made it clear 'at the outset that as part of a coalition we are winning the battle against the Taliban insurgency. We are isolating and eliminating the leadership of the Taliban; we are not negotiating with them'.[86] The British contribution to ISAF was increased to over 8,000 by Spring 2009.[87]

6. Conclusion

Rules governing the use of force in the UN Charter, and its subsequent interpretations in General Assembly resolutions and in the International Court, are premised on the need to prevent an escalation of conflict. Escalation will lead to further chaos and more devastating destruction. That is why both the threat and use of force are prohibited by article 2(4); that is why self-defence is only permitted in response to certain breaches of article 2(4); that is why the International Court and the Assembly have made it clear that article 2(4) should be interpreted to mean that force cannot be used against any of the sovereign rights of a state;[88] and that is why the Court in the *Nicaragua* case did not permit the American arguments of counter-intervention even though they were offered as arguments of collective self-defence.[89] Individual interpretations of the Charter and of Security Council resolutions, the occasional inconsistent resurrection of the right of humanitarian intervention, and ever-widening claims to a right to take preemptive military action will lead to an escalation of violence. To accept these claims and interpretations as lawful would remove the brakes on escalation. The world will descend into a remorseless and endless cycle of violence with blows followed by even more devastating counter-blows. Tom Farer anticipated this when commenting on the developing Bush Doctrine and the gradual victory of the unilateralists:

Signalling their triumph would be preemptive and punitive acts or threats of force increasingly unrelated to the specific events of 9/11 and an endorsement of the unrestrained use of violence by client regimes themselves acting in the name of counterterrorism. Battered by these initiatives and the intense opposition they would induce, the basic force-regulating provisions of the UN Charter, the frame of international relations for the past half century, would break along with the restraints on the use of terror by states against their own populations...

Once the frame of order is broken, we can reasonably anticipate increasingly norm-less violence, pitiless blows followed by monstrous retaliation in a descending spiral of hardly

---

[86] *Hansard* HC vol 468, col 303, 12 Dec. 2007.
[87] *Hansard* HC vol 477, col 676, 16 June 2008 (Browne).
[88] *Corfu Channel* case, 1949 ICJ Rep. 4; GA Resolution on Non-Intervention, Res. 2131, 21 Dec. 1965.
[89] *Nicaragua* case, 1986 ICJ Rep. 14 at 119.

imaginable depths. The Israeli experience could well prove a microcosmic anticipation of the global system's future . . . [90]

Around the turn of the twenty-first century we are seeing liberal democratic countries willing to use force in circumstances that are not readily reconcilable with the rules contained in the UN Charter. This does not simply represent a continuation of the Cold War approach of the superpowers which tended to disingenuously state that they were operating within the bounds of international law, while at the same time putting power above the law. Rather it represents a concerted attempt by these countries to expand the recognized exceptions as well as to establish additional exceptions to the ban on the use of force. British governments though have something of a track record of attempting to develop the law in this area. On occasions its approach is viewed as a breach of international law as in the Corfu Channel incident in 1946 and ten years later in the disastrous Suez campaign, on others it is seen as a development of the law as with the idea that the Security Council can authorize volunteer states to undertake military action under its authority, as shown by the Korean War and the Beira Patrol.

However, the lessons of history drawn from earlier British practice show that there are a number of significant hurdles that have to be overcome to develop a legal doctrine that is not simply a clear application of the rules contained in the UN Charter. The first is legal and found in the nature of the rules themselves. As peremptory rules or *jus cogens* these rules reflect the basic values of the international system as created in 1945. The rule prohibiting the use of force has been fought for by leaders, politicians, states and many other interest groups and individuals over the centuries. Its embodiment in the UN Charter represented the climax of that struggle and it is something that will not be given up easily. For a start world opinion must come behind any attempted change to the rules.

Public opinion also constitutes a political obstacle to the legitimacy of military operations that have a controversial pedigree. British governments will struggle, as happened in the Suez Crisis of 1956, to maintain a military campaign unless it has support within parliament and within the country. While the government of the day might be able to win support in parliament in the short-term, the longer-term consequences for its credibility and its electability will be serious if it continues to prosecute an unpopular war. Admittedly there is no direct correlation between the illegality of a war and its unpopularity, but it is apparent that while politicians and the public will generally support a war that is in defence of the nation, or in furtherance of clearly stated universal values, wars that fall short of these requirements will usually be unpopular.

Thus while the Security Council endorsed the occupation of Iraq after an illegal invasion in 2003, the Council authorized ISAF after an invasion which generally had more support in the international community, even though it

[90] T.J. Farer, 'Beyond the Charter Frame: Unilateralism or Condominium?' (2002) 96 AJIL 359 at 364.

seemed to go further than the concept of self-defence as previously understood. The greater level of legitimacy achieved in the military actions in Afghanistan, by a combination of seemingly accepted arguments of an expanded right of self-defence and widespread moral outrage following the attacks of 9/11, may mean that the commitment from Western democracies to the military deployment is more sustainable and therefore likely to be more successful than that in Iraq, where grave doubts about the initial invasion have undermined the legitimacy of the subsequent actions (despite Security Council authorization), as well as under-mining domestic support for the conflict in both Britain and the United States.

While its troops may face similar problems in Iraq and Afghanistan, Britain may be able to sustain its commitment in Afghanistan in the longer term because of the continuing belief in the legal and moral bases for the initial action. The initial military action in Afghanistan was not without its legal problems though they seemed to be swept away. In the longer term it may be that the dispropor-tionate nature of the response, directed at the Taliban government as well as the terrorists, will serve to undermine the legitimacy of the current state-building enterprise. From being a war launched to deal with the threat from al-Qaeda, it is now a war mainly fought against the supporters of the former effective govern-ment of Afghanistan. Arguably one of the problems lies with the initial response to 9/11, which although taking the form of defensive action against al-Qaeda, was also directed more widely than appeared necessary by including the Taliban. While defensive action is still being undertaken against al-Qaeda in pockets of resistance, the main military action now focuses on Security Council author-ized enforcement action being undertaken by ISAF throughout Afghanistan. By treating the Taliban as the enemy in 2001, British troops are now facing the prob-lem of providing security and helping reconstruction in the face of continuing Taliban hostility. Though in practical military terms in might not have been pos-sible to distinguish the Taliban from al-Qaeda in 2001, there can be no doubt that this has made the job of British troops in 2008–9 extremely difficult to achieve.

9

Bombing in the Name of Humanity:
the RAF over Kosovo

1. Introduction

In addition to trying to develop the law of self-defence after 11 September 2001, the British government has also been at the forefront of attempting to develop a controversial justification for the use of force, namely humanitarian intervention. This is not limited to the Labour governments in power since 1997, but was unveiled by the Conservative administration as an argument for the intervention in northern Iraq in 1991 following the repression of the Kurds. The arguments though were brought to a head in the Spring of 1999 when, faced with the brutal repression of the ethnic Albanian population in the Serbian province of Kosovo, NATO planes bombed Serbian targets between 24 March 1999 and 10 June 1999. The debates in parliament were intense over the Kosovo intervention. The level of discussion over the international legal basis of the operation both within the House of Commons and the country was unprecedented. The greater reliance on seeking Parliamentary support could be due to the lack of a clear international legal basis for the British decision to contribute air power to the operation (even though it was a NATO operation), but could also be due to the proposed mode of protecting human rights—by bombing from a safe height.

2. A Controversial Doctrine

Uninvited military interventions to protect widespread violations of the right to life has a doubtful pedigree in international law even before 1945, mainly because the intervening state has more often than not abused the doctrine to remove problematic governments and to install friendly ones. With the advent of a firm rule prohibiting the use of force in the UN Charter of 1945, one that has attained the status of *jus cogens*, allowing of only two exceptions—self-defence and Security Council authorized military action—the doctrine seemed to have even less chance of establishing itself in the new international legal order.

This might seem harsh when mass killings often by agents of the state have not abated in the twentieth and twenty-first centuries. The atrocities in Rwanda, the Congo, and the Darfur region of Sudan all occurring around the millennium show that genocide and crimes against humanity are being committed with appalling regularity (particularly in Africa), and the international community has done little to prevent them. Although it is perfectly feasible that the Security Council could authorize a military intervention to prevent further loss of life, its track record is poor. It pulled out the UN peacekeepers in Rwanda in 1994 in the face of the genocide being committed there, and it bizarrely authorized France (a supporter of Hutu regimes in the past) to undertake a limited military intervention, which had no affect on the genocide of nearly a million Tutsis and moderate Hutus.[1] In the Democratic Republic of the Congo it is estimated that somewhere between two and four million people have lost their lives in conflicts that have raged in that country since the end of the 1990s, although a robust Security Council authorized peace operation now keeps an uneasy peace there.[2] In Darfur at least a quarter of a million civilians have been killed by government forces and the Janjaweed militia since 2003, though an African Union/UN peace operation with a mandate to protect civilians has finally been agreed to by the government of Sudan[3]—the very perpetrators of the crimes being committed against the people of Darfur.

In these horrific circumstances, one might legitimately ask how it could possibly be illegal for a state or group of states, acting without Security Council authority, to intervene to protect human life. This question becomes even more challenging to the orthodoxy when the violation of the right to life attains the level of crimes against humanity (acts of murder and extermination 'committed as part of a widespread or systematic attack directed against any civilian population, with knowledge of attack'),[4] or genocide (similar acts 'committed with intent to destroy in whole or in part, a national, ethnical, racial or religious group'),[5] the prohibitions on both of which are recognized as *jus cogens*.

During the Cold War there was little evidence that states accepted the legality of humanitarian intervention within the post-1945 legal order.

Sadly, there have been several modern instances of a state killing or attempting to kill large numbers of particular groups within its own frontiers, actions which have on occasions led to military intervention. On other occasions, no state has been prepared to intervene militarily, even when it was clear that a large number of citizens were being massacred. In May 1967, Biafra declared its independence from Nigeria. In the ensuing civil war many thousands of the Ibo tribe, which inhabited Biafra, died, due in part to the brutality with which the insurrection

---

[1] SC Res. 929, 22 June 1994.   [2] SC Res. 1565, 1 Oct. 2004.
[3] SC Res. 1769, 31 July 2007.
[4] Art 7, Rome Statute of the International Criminal Court 1998.
[5] Art 6, Rome Statute of the International Criminal Court 1998, reproducing the definition in art II of the Convention on the Prevention and Punishment of the Crime of Genocide 1948.

was put down—brutality directed at the whole of the Ibo tribe not just the combatants. However, whilst only five African states were prepared to recognize Biafra, none were prepared to intervene to protect the Ibos, preferring instead to leave attempts to solve the crisis to the Organisation of African Unity (the predecessor of the AU) which had a clear policy against secession.[6]

A leading Biafran women's activist, Mrs Oyibo Adinamadu, travelled to London to lobby the Labour government for assistance for the Biafran cause. The government refused to meet her. Indeed, Britain was a key arms supplier to Nigeria enabling the government to suppress the rebellion. The reason for British inaction given by the Foreign Secretary, Michael Stewart, was that cutting all connections with the Nigerian government in protest at the suppression would encourage 'in Africa the principle of tribal secession—with all the misery that could bring to Africa in the future'.[7]

In other instances of mass killings there have been military responses, but neither the intervening state, nor other states, have sought to justify the action solely as a humanitarian intervention, thus reflecting the fact that there is little *opinio juris* amongst states for such a right. The Pakistani army's brutal repression of the rebellion in East Pakistan in 1971, which resulted in Indian military intervention and the eventual emergence of the independent state of Bangladesh, is cited as an instance of humanitarian intervention by supporters of the doctrine.[8] However, India, in the Security Council chamber relied on the clear exception to the ban on force, namely self-defence in response to alleged Pakistani aggression.[9] Although India had not been attacked, it is quite significant that it relied primarily on the recognized exception to article 2(4). However, there are also points at which India seemed to be referring to the more controversial right, most particularly Prime Minister Gandhi who spoke of 'the annihilation of an entire people whose only crime was to vote for democracy', though she also referred to Pakistan's 'unprovoked aggression'.[10]

In other instances of state practice, though the target state had clearly been guilty of horrendous atrocities against its own people, the state using force did not rely on the doctrine of humanitarian intervention. In Kampuchea (Cambodia), the Khmer Rouge took power in 1975 and under the direction of Pol Pot it embarked upon a policy which directly led to the death of three million people. In December 1978, Vietnam invaded Kampuchea, overthrew the Pol Pot regime

---

[6] M. Reisman and M.S. McDougal, 'Humanitarian Intervention to Protect the Ibos', in R. Lillich (ed), *Humanitarian Intervention and the United Nations* (Charlottesville: University Press of Virginia, 1973) 167 at 194.

[7] B. Philips, 'Biafra: Thirty Years On' <http://news.bbc.co.uk/1/hi/world/africa/596712.stm>, report 13 Jan. 2000 (accessed 26 Jan. 2009).

[8] F.R. Teson, *Humanitarian Intervention: An Inquiry into Law and Morality* (3rd edn, New York: Transnational, 2005) 179.

[9] SC 1606th mtg, 1971.

[10] *Keesing's Record of World Events* (1972), 25053. See further J. Musson, 'Britain and the Recognition of Bangladesh in 1972' (2008) 19 Diplomacy and Statecraft 125.

and established a Vietnamese-backed regime. On this occasion the intervening state sought to deny that it had ever intervened at all, claiming that the events in Kampuchea were purely internal.[11]

Britain joined the majority of UN member states at the UN in calling for 'the immediate withdrawal of all foreign forces from Kampuchea'. It also called upon states 'to refrain from all acts or threats of aggression and all forms of interference in the internal affairs of States in South-East Asia'.[12] In the Security Council Sir Anthony Parsons, the British delegate, clearly portrayed Kampuchea as the victim in declaring that it was 'a small member state which has been invaded by a powerful neighbour in violation of article 2(4) of the Charter. It is imperative for all of us to uphold the principle of the inadmissibility of the threat or use of force against the territorial integrity or political independence of any state; otherwise the aggressor will take comfort'.[13] In the House of Commons, Sir Ian Gilmour, the Lord Privy Seal, put the government's view: 'I do not condone the Vietnamese invasion. The Vietnamese invaded not as liberators, but as occupiers, in flagrant violation of the Charter of the United Nations'.[14]

In the same period the Tanzanian army, accompanied by a number of Ugandan rebels, entered Uganda and eventually overthrew the brutal dictatorship of Idi Amin in April 1979. The Tanzanian government claimed that this was an act of self-defence following the Ugandan annexation of some disputed territory in October 1978. The Tanzanian response was clearly not a proportionate one and so cannot be justified as self-defence. The British view of the international legality of this and other earlier interventions can be found in a document produced in July 1984 by the Foreign Office.[15]

The two most discussed instances of alleged humanitarian intervention since 1945 are the Indian invasion of Bangladesh in 1971 and Tanzania's humanitarian invasion of Uganda in 1979. But, although both did result in unquestionable benefits for, respectively, the peoples of East Bengal and Uganda, India and Tanzania were reluctant to use humanitarian aims to justify their invasion of a neighbour's territory. Both preferred to quote the right to self-defence under Article 51. And in each case the self-interest of the invading state was clearly involved. In fact, the best that can be made in support of humanitarian intervention is that it cannot be said to be unambiguously illegal.

Of course if the UN authorizes intervention for humanitarian purposes then the action has a clear legal basis—the authorization of the American-led UNITAF into Somalia in 1992 is a clear example.[16] On other occasions, though there is a UN resolution condemning the repression there has been no clear authority.

---

[11] SC 2180th mtg, 1979.
[12] GA Res. 34/22, 14 Nov. 1979, adopted by 91 votes to 21 with 29 abstentions.
[13] SC mtg, 13 Nov. 1979 in (1975–2001) UKMIL Part Sixteen. item 6.
[14] *Hansard* HC vol 975, col 719, 6 Dec. 1979.
[15] Foreign Policy Document No 148, 'Is Intervention Ever Justified?', paras 21–2 in (1975–2001) UKMIL Part Sixteen.I. item 70.
[16] SC Res. 794, 3 Dec. 1992.

In these instances Britain has relied on a combination of the resolution and humanitarian necessity.

In April 1991 after Iraq's defeat in Kuwait led to a failed attempt to oust Saddam's regime, the Security Council adopted a resolution categorizing Iraq's repression of the Kurds as an action which threatened international peace and security.[17] The Resolution did not authorize military measures, but Western states at least appeared to think that the resolution justified them sending up to 20,000 troops to occupy a large part of northern Iraq to prevent further repression and to protect the distribution of humanitarian aid. Although unauthorized by the UN, the intervention in Northern Iraq, which was followed up by the imposition by the US, UK and France of no-fly zones over northern Iraq starting on 6 April 1991 (to protect the Kurds), and southern Iraq starting on 26 August 1992 (to protect the Shias), did not appear to be full-blown humanitarian intervention. It did not seek to overthrow the brutal regime of Saddam Hussein; indeed, it appeared to be an action somewhere between the well-accepted right of states to provide humanitarian aid and the generally unacceptable right of humanitarian intervention. Given that very few states objected to the operation, it may be that such a limited right might have been acceptable in the future.

However, there were mixed messages coming from the British government and its officials. The Foreign Secretary spoke on BBC radio in answer to questions about the legality of the military measures taken to protect vulnerable people inside Iraq, specifically the no-fly zone of August 1992. First he stated that 'we operate under international law. Not every action that a British Government or an American Government or a French Government takes has to be underwritten by a specific provision in a UN resolution provided that we comply with international law'. In relying on general international law he did not claim an unfettered right of intervention to protect human rights but stated that 'international law recognizes extreme humanitarian need' when acting 'in support of' Resolution 688.[18] Legal opinion from the Foreign Office though suggested that this was simply an application of the customary right of humanitarian intervention given that Resolution 688 did not mandate the actions taken.[19]

3. Kosovo—the Crystallization of a Customary Right?

There was undoubtedly a situation of extreme violence in Kosovo in 1998–9, symbolized by the brutal massacre of over forty ethnic Albanians by Serbian forces in the Kosovo village of Racak on 15 January 1999. Such killings took

---

[17] SC Res. 688, 5 April 1991.
[18] (1975–2001) UKMIL Part Sixteen.IV. item 10.
[19] Oral evidence given by Mr Anthony Aust, Legal Counsellor, FCO, to the Foreign Affairs Committee, 2 Dec. 1992 in (1975–2001) UKMIL Part Sixteen.IV. item 15.

place within a vicious war between the Serbian forces and the Kosovo Liberation Army (KLA) in which civilians were targeted on both sides, though the Serbian attacks were more atrocious and may well have amounted to crimes against humanity (President Milosevic of Serbia was indicted for crimes against humanity in Kosovo by the ICTY, though he died in March 2006 before a conviction could be secured).

It is clear that the levels of violence and suppression in Kosovo in the thirteen-month period leading up to the NATO bombing constituted a threat to the peace. Indeed, the Security Council made that determination prior to the bombing.[20] There is little doubt that this determination potentially removed the restriction on UN intervention in the internal affairs of a state.[21] UN sanctioned military intervention, though, normally requires the express authority of the Security Council. The issue is whether states can take 'humanitarian' military action 'in support' of resolutions which make determinations of a threat to the peace, breach of the peace or act of aggression, even though there is no express authorization to do so.

The interventions in northern Iraq in 1991 and Kosovo in 1999 appear to be context-breaking actions, aimed at creating a new right to take military action in support of Security Council resolutions. Did they succeed? Are the Iraq and Kosovo operations further lawful developments of the *jus ad bellum* or are they so inconsistent as to be incompatible with the UN Charter? Treaty regimes can be developed quite radically but there are limits to this development (this applies to the NATO treaty as well). Furthermore, for subsequent practice to modify a treaty it must be widely supported by the members. Is the fact that the then nineteen members of NATO supported the action in Kosovo sufficient by itself, not only to modify the NATO treaty (which in article 5 clearly establishes a defence pact) but also the requirements of the UN Charter? This section will consider whether the inability of the Security Council to authorize military action was a justification for NATO taking action. The lack of alternatives debated before the UN, apart from the stark choice between bombing or inaction, needs to be considered, as does the possibility of seeking a mandate from the General Assembly.

As with the other isolated instances in international practice, it is possible to look at the interventions in Northern Iraq and Kosovo and pick out from the morass of legal justifications certain statements by some states and, assuming acceptance by the international community, present this as evidence of *opinio juris* for a right of humanitarian intervention. However, as with earlier interventions, recent attempts to resurrect the doctrine have been combined with other justifications which attempt to base the actions on norms acceptable to the international community. In 1991 the UK, in justifying its part in the intervention

---

[20] See for example SC Res. 1199, 23 Sept. 1998.
[21] Art 2(7) of the UN Charter.

in Northern Iraq, at one point invoked the doctrine of humanitarian intervention, while at another it purported to place the action within the context of Resolution 688,[22] thereby trying to give the action some sort of UN sanction, knowing that Security Council authorized operations are, alongside self-defence, the universally recognized exceptions to the ban on the use of force.

In 1999, the UK was seen, perhaps above all other NATO states, as the chief advocate of humanitarian intervention to justify the actions of the RAF, but it failed overall to invoke it in its pure form. When announcing the launch of NATO airstrikes to the House of Commons on 24 March, 1999, Deputy Prime Minister John Prescott stated that the action was supported by all nineteen members of NATO, and was 'intended to support the political aims of the international community' set out in Council Resolutions 1199 and 1203, both of which had been breached by the FRY. The action was further 'justified as an exceptional measure to prevent an overwhelming humanitarian catastrophe'.[23] The danger in accepting this sort of layered argument as a justification for unilateral or multilateral humanitarian intervention is that it ignores the reasons why India in 1971 and the UK in 1991 and again in 1999 did not rely on the doctrine as sole justification. Instead, they tried to invoke recognized exceptions to article 2(4) despite knowing full well that the operations did not fit the requirements of the exceptions—there was no armed attack against India in 1971, and there was no express authority from the Security Council to use force against Iraq or Serbia.

Although the approach taken by the intervening states in Iraq and Kosovo weakens the doctrine of humanitarian intervention, at least in its pure form, probably beyond repair, it still leaves the question of whether military intervention taken in support of or in the spirit of Security Council resolutions is a new and accepted concept in international law. In the absence of a clear mandate from the Security Council, the intervening states have invoked the argument that they are acting on behalf of the 'international community'. The Security Council resolutions represent the will of the international community and the states are enforcing that will. The 'international community' seems to be the concept underpinning the recent actions in Iraq in 1991 and Kosovo in 1999. The increased recognition of this notion, much derided in the past by powerful states,[24] is necessitated when military intervention is taken to uphold fundamental norms of the international community prohibiting crimes against humanity which were being committed in northern Iraq and Kosovo.

---

[22] See further the statements by the UK Prime Minister John Major and UK Foreign Secretary Douglas Hurd in M. Weller (ed), *Iraq and Kuwait: The Hostilities and their Aftermath* (Cambridge: Cambridge University Press, 1993) 149, 723–4.

[23] *Hansard*, HC vol 308, col 484, 24 March 1999.

[24] J.M. Grieco, 'Anarchy and the Limits of Cooperation: A Realist Critique of the Newest Liberal Internationalism' (1988) 42 International Organization 485.

The British Foreign Secretary, Robin Cook, seemed to realize that it was pointless trying to find or imply authority from specific resolutions, and instead the argument had to be based on the will of the international community, when he was pushed before the Foreign Affairs Select Committee of the House of Commons in April 1999 to justify the apparent contravention of the prohibition on the use of force. He stated that 'the legal basis for our action is that the international community [of] states do have the right to use force in the case of overwhelming humanitarian necessity'.[25]

It is easy to invoke the 'international community' to legitimate a military intervention, but who or what is the 'international community'? The dangers of simply basing it on international laws—no matter how fundamental—are clear, for there is a huge leap from recognizing that there are laws prohibiting crimes against humanity, and imbuing states with the right unilaterally or in combination with their allies to enforce those norms. Such a system of law will rapidly descend into self-help, whereby the name of the 'international community' is simply invoked at the discretion of powerful states as a cloak for their military interventions and to further their hegemony. However, in the cases of Iraq in 1991 and Kosovo in 1999 some of the discretion was removed in that there were Security Council resolutions recognizing the gravity of the human rights abuses in those countries. Does this not give a certain objectivity lacking in the old doctrines based on self-help such as humanitarian intervention? Discretion, though, remains for this new form of intervention is only claimed as a legal right not a duty, though it is often cloaked in the rhetoric of moral obligations. Furthermore it is somewhat disingenuous to claim that the international community's will is embodied in a Security Council resolution when that organ has the capacity to expressly authorize military action to enforce its will. The determination of a threat to the peace is not the same as a mandate to take military action to combat the threat. Again the argument fails to recognize the gap between statements of law and their enforcement.

In the case of Kosovo, the subsequent authorization by the Security Council of NATO-led KFOR to secure the post-conflict stage in Kosovo[26] cannot be seen as retrospective endorsement of the NATO bombings. First, Russia and China made this particularly clear when the mandating resolution for KFOR was adopted.[27] Second, the Security Council as a political organ concerned with the maintenance or restoration of peace and security will quite often have to 'build upon facts or situations based on, or involving illegalities'.[28] This does not signify an acceptance of their legality, though it might undermine the legitimacy of an inconsistent Council. What it does mean is that NATO stepped outside the parameters of the UN Charter when it suited the organization, and then it

---

[25] Foreign Affairs Committee, Minutes of Evidence, 14 April 1999, para 152 (HC 188-ii).
[26] SC Res. 1244, 10 June 1999.   [27] SC 4011st mtg, 10 June 1999.
[28] B. Simma, 'NATO, the UN and the Use of Force: Legal Aspects' (1999) 10 EJIL 1 at 11.

stepped back in again when it, or rather the G8, had produced a suitable formula for ending the bombing which satisfied Russia and was agreed to by Serbia.

Although binding chapter VII resolutions were breached by Serbia this was not a sufficient justification for what Nico Krisch has labelled the 'unilateral enforcement of the collective will'.[29] The lack of consensus in the Security Council that a simple chapter VII resolution condemning and demanding certain action can give rise to military action by willing states if the resolutions are ignored is telling. Indeed, all that will happen if Western states continue to utilize resolutions in this way, is that there will be no agreement on any type of chapter VII resolution in the future in case certain states take it upon themselves to undertake military action to enforce them.

The collective security system has been stretched and pulled by the practice of mainly Western states and as a result is quite generous to them, but they still need to seek and gain a Security Council mandate. The desire of Western states to base their military actions on Security Council resolutions is significant though, for it seems to undermine the argument that the NATO bombardment of the FRY and the intervention in northern Iraq are strong evidence of a re-emergence of a unilateral right to humanitarian intervention.[30] After examining the claims of NATO states both before international and national fora and in pleadings before the International Court in May 1999,[31] Krisch concludes that despite the odd (and inconsistent) statements by the US and the UK which seemed to favour unilateral humanitarian intervention, both those states and the remainder of NATO members tried to justify their action on the basis of the collective authority of the UN rather than on the right of humanitarian intervention. 'Thus, a purely unilateral humanitarian intervention seems even more difficult after the case of Kosovo than before'.[32] It seems that by trying to force the military actions under the UN umbrella, NATO states have probably done more damage to the already precarious doctrine of humanitarian intervention, as well as breaching, and therefore undermining, the constitutional parameters of the UN collective security system they helped to create. The failure of the Security Council to condemn the NATO action when member states rejected a Russian draft on 26 March 1999 by twelve votes to three,[33] cannot be seen as an authorization of the bombing, nor an endorsement of it, since a major concern for many states voting against the

---

[29] N. Krisch, 'Unilateral Enforcement of the Collective Will: Kosovo, Iraq, and the Security Council' (1999) 3 MPYBUNL 59.

[30] But see A. Cassese, 'Ex Inuria Ius Oritur: Are We Moving Towards International Legitimation of Forcible Humanitarian Countermeasures in the World Community?' (1999) 10 EJIL 23.

[31] See *Case Concerning Legality of the Use of Force (Yugoslavia v United Kingdom)* Request [by the FRY] for Provisional Measures, 1999 ICJ Rep. 826. The Court refused to grant the request, although it did express its concern both at the loss of life in Kosovo, and 'with the use of force in Yugoslavia' which 'under the present circumstances raises very serious issues of international law' (paras 15–16).

[32] Krisch, 'Unilateral Enforcement', 93. See his analysis of NATO claims at 81–6.

[33] UN Doc. S/1999/328.

resolution was its lack of balance in that it failed also to condemn the brutality of the repressive measures taken by the FRY.[34] Above all, lack of condemnation by the Security Council cannot be seen as an authorization to use force.

It must not be forgotten that in the case of Kosovo there was an authorization from an international organization, NATO. Do nineteen democracies acting in concert represent the international community? Can such an organization be in breach of international law? The fact that NATO is composed of democracies does not by itself suggest that it is the fulcrum of the international community, although there has been a significant trend in the international community towards democratic government. In fact in taking decisions to go to war, whether under international authority or not, many of the constitutional checks and balances present in liberal democracies for most forms of governmental decision-making in NATO states, are not applicable. This is certainly the case in the UK where the power to take such decisions rests within the executive. The only real democratic control on such military actions is public opinion, and the exercise of democratic accountability at the next election. In essence then, NATO has no greater claim to represent the international community than would any other organization of a similar size.

The legality and legitimacy of NATO action is also undermined when a consideration of its own Treaty is undertaken. Although it has claimed the right to take 'non Article 5' operations,[35] in other words not only military action in self-defence, these cannot simply be those determined by NATO alone. NATO can only operate within the framework of international law, in particular the UN Charter which has supremacy over any other international treaty when there are conflicting obligations.[36] Although NATO members, by consensus, can re-interpret their own treaty to allow them to take non-defensive military operations, they cannot somehow contract out of the UN system,[37] to set themselves up, in effect, as a competitor to the UN. It was thus incorrect for the US under Secretary of State, Strobe Talbott, to state that 'we must be careful not to subordinate NATO to any other international body',[38] for the whole international security system is based on a hierarchy with the UN at the apex.

The House of Commons Defence Select Committee was similarly in error in March 1999 when it announced that 'insistence on a UN Security Council mandate for such ... operations would be unnecessary as well as covertly giving Russia a veto over Alliance action. All 19 Allies act in accordance with the principles of international law and we are secure in our assertion that the necessity of unanimous agreement for any action will ensure its legality'.[39] To allow smaller

---

[34] See SC 3989th mtg, 26 March 1999. Krisch, 'Unilateral Enforcement', 84–5.

[35] Resolution on 'Recasting Euro-Atlantic Security', adopted by North Atlantic Assembly, NATO Doc. AR 295 SA (1998).

[36] Art 103 of the UN Charter.   [37] In particular arts 42 and 53 of the UN Charter.

[38] Cited in Simma, 'NATO, the UN' at 15.

[39] House of Commons Defence Select Committee in its Third Report 1998–9, 13 April 1999, para 176 (HC 39).

groups of states forming alliances or organizations the right of 'self-authorization' to take enforcement action would be to let the genie out of the lamp,[40] and would lead to competing claims to intervention.

It is worth noting that the US and UK assert the primacy of the UN Charter over other conflicting treaty regimes when it suits. The essence of the two states' arguments in the *Lockerbie* cases in the 1990s was that the obligations imposed on Libya by the Security Council prevailed by virtue of the UN Charter over Libya's rights and duties contained in the 1971 Montreal Convention for the Suppression of Unlawful Acts against the Safety of Civil Aviation.[41] It is inconsistent for these two states to argue the supremacy of the UN Charter in the case of Libya, and yet dismiss it in the case of the NATO intervention in Kosovo.

It is because the UN represents the vast majority of the world's states that it has the only legitimate claim to be acting on behalf of the international community. Indeed, given its broad membership and broad purposes, practically it is the only organization that can claim to be the international community. When states set it up in 1945 it was imbued with exceptional powers that no state or other organization could possess, unless they received authority from the UN. It was because the UN represented 'the vast majority of the Members of the international community' at the time[42] and now more so that it has the powers of the international community. Within the UN, it is the General Assembly that is reflective of the political will of the organization. 'The special value of the General Assembly is its universality, its capacity to be a forum in which the voice of every member state can be heard'.[43]

Certainly after the bombing campaign was over and KFOR was established under Security Council authority, NATO members seemed to recognize, if not the illegality of their bombing campaign, certainly the dangerous precedent that it set. Kosovo seemed re-packaged as a unique situation forced upon NATO by exceptional conditions that somehow set it apart from later catastrophes that year in East Timor and Chechnya. In the general debate of the General Assembly in October 1999, the representative of Belgium, for instance, hoped that resorting to force without the approval of the Security Council would not constitute a precedent, while expressing concern about a return to the law of the jungle.[44] Germany stated that state sovereignty would remain the guiding principle in international relations.[45] President Bill Clinton portrayed the Kosovo situation not as a triumph for NATO but somehow as a triumph for the United Nations.[46] Even Russia suggested that lessons had been learned from the crisis and that

---

[40] Simma, 'NATO, the UN', 20.
[41] *Cases Concerning Questions of Interpretation and Application of the Montreal Convention Arising From the Aerial Incident at Lockerbie (Libya v UK), (Libya v US)* 1992 ICJ Rep. 3 and 114 (Provisional Measures Judgments); (1998) 37 ILM 587 (Preliminary Objections Judgments).
[42] *Reparation for Injuries Suffered in the Service of the United Nations* 1949 ICJ Rep. 174, 185.
[43] *Report of the Commission on Global Governance* (Oxford: Oxford University Press, 1995) 242.
[44] GA 14th plen. mtg, 25 Sept. 1999.   [45] GA 27th plen. mtg, 6 Oct. 1999.
[46] GA 6th plen. mtg, 21 Sept. 1999.

it would be prepared to develop a legal framework for enforcement actions 'of the international community' in the case of humanitarian emergencies in the future.[47] These statements show that, without prejudicing the positions of states on the legality of the operation, Kosovo was being labelled as an exceptional action without any legal precedence. Nevertheless, the Netherlands warned the Council that its repeated inaction would push the organization towards the margins as a custodian of the peace, and it called on the Assembly to demand that the veto power be exercised with maximum restraint.[48]

4. The General Assembly: an Alternative Source of Authority?

The statement by the Dutch representative in the General Assembly debates in its 54th session in Autumn 1999 shows the dilemma that NATO states have over whether the Security Council has exclusive competence over military enforcement action, or whether the Assembly has a role. The Dutch suggested that the Assembly should act as a mechanism of accountability to ensure that the veto was not misused in similar situations in the future. They did not go so far as to say that the Assembly itself could, if the Security Council was deadlocked, authorize or recommend such action. However, there are strong arguments that the General Assembly has residual enforcement powers in exceptional cases, and indeed it should have been the fall-back forum for seeking authority to undertake the bombing of the FRY. The argument by NATO that it had no choice but to undertake the bombing without an authorization from an organ which truly represents the international community is thus revealed to be incorrect. Indeed, if any forum can legitimately claim to represent or indeed embody the international community, then it has to be the General Assembly of the UN. The General Assembly not only has subsidiary competence in the field of collective security, it has primary competence in issues of human rights.[49] Claims to intervene in Kosovo to protect human rights would thus have all the attributes necessary for the Assembly to grant authority, though only if it was convinced by a two-thirds majority of NATO's case.[50]

Debates over the competence of the General Assembly to recommend military measures to be taken when the Security Council has failed to exercise its primary responsibility for collective security, tend to be clouded by question marks

---

[47] GA Fourth Committee debate, 12th mtg, 20 Oct. 1999. But see China GA 35th plen. mtg, 20 Oct. 1999.

[48] UN Press Release GA/9607 (1999).

[49] N.D. White, *Keeping the Peace: The United Nations and the Maintenance of International Peace and Security* (2nd edn, Manchester: Manchester University Press, 1997) 169–72.

[50] Abstentions do not count as votes, so the required number of votes in favour of military action may not be as high as thought: see F.L. Kirgis, *International Organizations in their Legal Setting* (2nd edn, St Paul Minn.: West Publishing, 1993) 213.

over the legality of the Uniting for Peace Resolution adopted by the General Assembly in 1950.[51] The immediate reason for the adoption of the Resolution was the return, in August 1950, of the Soviet Union to the Security Council, leading to the discontinuation of the Council as the body dealing with Korea. In fact the Assembly had adopted an 'enforcement' resolution on Korea after the Soviets had returned to the Security Council but before the Uniting for Peace Resolution was adopted.[52]

However, the reasons for Uniting for Peace went beyond Korea, in that the Western influenced majority in the General Assembly at the time was also of the view that the frequent casting of the Soviet veto during the period 1946–50 was an abuse of that right, and that the ideal of Great Power unity at San Francisco was no longer attainable. The Western states wanted an alternative form of collective security, based not on permanent member agreement in the Security Council, but on the basis of the will of the majority in the Assembly. Such a concept of collective security, whilst opening up the potential for economic and military actions against transgressors, also had the potential, in theory, for allowing the General Assembly to authorize military action against one of the permanent members. A more likely scenario would be for the Assembly to authorize military action that would affect the interests of a permanent member. It may be because this system of collective security was potentially dangerous that the resolution restricted the Assembly's power to recommend military measures to the most flagrant violations of international peace, namely breaches of the peace or acts of aggression, and did not expressly permit the Assembly to take such measures as a response to threats to the peace.

The Soviet Union objected strongly to the Resolution; in particular it argued that it violated the Charter requirement that coercive power was granted solely to the Security Council.[53] In 1962, the International Court in the *Expenses* case stated that 'action', which is the preserve of the Security Council,[54] refers to coercive action but it failed to state whether this excluded the Assembly from recommending coercive measures. At some points the Court suggested that 'action' is restricted to mandatory, coercive action 'ordered' by the Security Council. In other words the Assembly did not appear to be barred from recommending enforcement action as part of its significant responsibility for the maintenance of peace as recognized by the Court.[55] Furthermore, despite the wording of the Uniting for Peace Resolution, there appears to be no cogent argument against allowing the Assembly to recommend military measures to combat threats to the peace.[56]

---

[51] GA Res. 377, 3 Nov. 1950. [52] GA Res. 376, 7 Oct. 1950.
[53] GA 301st plen. mtg, 1950.
[54] Art 11(2) of the UN Charter.
[55] *Certain Expenses of the United Nations* 1962 ICJ Rep. 151, 162–5.
[56] S.D. Bailey and S. Daws, *The Procedure of the UN Security Council* (3rd edn, Oxford: Clarendon Press, 1998) 296.

However, when looking at the issue from the perspective of the ban on the use of armed force, a rule of *jus cogens* from which no derogation is allowed, doubts may be cast on the legality of the Uniting for Peace Resolution and the power of the Assembly to recommend military measures. The exceptions to article 2(4) are explicitly stated in the UN Charter to include only action in self-defence under article 51 of the UN Charter and military action authorized by the Security Council under articles 42 or 53. To state that the General Assembly can authorize military action arguably creates a third exception, which would appear to be contrary to the *jus cogens* in article 2(4). However, the Security Council is authorizing military action on behalf of the UN and so the exceptions to the ban on force are those undertaken in legitimate self-defence and those authorized by the UN. The question of which organ within the UN authorizes them is an internal issue and does not effect the legitimacy of UN action *vis-à-vis* a transgressing state.[57] The internal issue can be resolved in favour of both organs having the ability to authorize military action, given that the Assembly effectively has all those recommendatory powers possessed by the Council,[58] albeit at a supplementary level of competence.

The Uniting for Peace Resolution, whereby the Assembly can be activated in the face of a deadlocked Security Council by a procedural vote in the Council that is not subject to the veto, has been used in the past to gain UN authority for innovative military actions. In the face of a military intervention by two permanent members in the Suez crisis of 1956 and, more relevantly, in the face of a threat to the peace in the Congo in 1960 which was in a state of collapse, the Security Council, unable to take substantive action itself due to the veto, transferred the matter to the Assembly.[59] The Assembly duly became the organ of authority in the case of UNEF, a traditional peacekeeping force, and temporarily in the case of ONUC, which acted in a more muscular fashion. Although it may be argued that these two operations were more 'peacekeeping' than 'enforcement', and thus are not direct precedents for seeking an enforcement mandate for an intervention in Kosovo, the Congo operation came very close to enforcement.[60] In addition, the General Assembly had, even before the adoption of the Uniting for Peace Resolution, become involved in the Korean enforcement operation. In fact the Assembly made a substantial contribution to UN action in Korea in 1950 by passing a resolution which allowed the UN force to continue its operations to establish 'a unified, independent and democratic government of Korea' after the Security Council had been deadlocked by the return of the Soviet representative.[61] This resolution was seen as endorsing General MacArthur's crossing of the 38th parallel and so can be classified as authorizing enforcement action. The British Foreign Secretary, Ernest Bevin, who was instrumental in the

---

[57] *Expenses* case, 168.   [58] Arts 10 and 14 of the UN Charter.
[59] SC Res. 119, 31 Oct. 1956 (UK and France voted against); SC Res.157, 17 Sept. 1960 (USSR voted against).
[60] But see *Expenses* case, 177.   [61] GA Res. 376, 7 Oct. 1950.

resolution, saw it as essential to have the authority of the UN for the intervention in North Korea.[62]

It is somewhat ironic that a procedure advocated by Western states in 1950 was conveniently forgotten in the case of the Kosovo crisis in 1999. The cumbersome nature of convening an emergency special session of the Assembly is no real excuse given that NATO first threatened to use force without express authority in October 1998. The matter could have been put forward before the Assembly during its 53rd annual session. Indeed, the Assembly did consider the situation of human rights in Kosovo and adopted a resolution on 9 December 1999 that was very critical of the violations of human rights and international humanitarian law by the FRY, and was supportive of the demands made by the Security Council.[63] Although adopted against a background of a reduction in the oppressive actions carried out by the FRY forces in Kosovo, this still represented an opportunity for NATO to seek authority for its airstrikes.

It may be argued that in the Kosovo crisis, as with Iraq in 1991, the Security Council was failing to take the necessary military action to combat breaches of Security Council resolutions, and in the face of situations that clearly constituted threats to the peace. In these circumstances it was breaching the trust put in it by member states when they established the United Nations. Assuming that the Security Council was being blocked by an illegitimate threat of the veto in a situation that clearly warranted Security Council authorized military action, it is still not legally permissible for states to take it upon themselves, whether in the forum of another organization or not, to enforce those resolutions. Such a contention presumes that states had these powers before they 'collectivized' them in the Security Council, which is very doubtful. It also ignores the fact that legally speaking they must be expressly returned or granted to them by the UN. Furthermore, when the UN Charter speaks of the Security Council having 'primary responsibility' to maintain or restore international peace and security, it is recognizing that the General Assembly, not states or organizations acting outside the UN, has significant secondary responsibility in the field of peace and security, which may be invoked when the Security Council is unable to act. Indeed, when combined with its undoubted competence in matters of human rights and its legitimate claim to represent the international community, the General Assembly was the natural alternative when the Security Council was deemed to have failed to take adequate action in the face of repression by the FRY. The need for the authority of the UN is made graphically clear by Jules Lobel and Michael Ratner who argue that 'warfare is of limited utility as a means

---

[62] See A. Farrar-Hockley, *The British Part in the Korean War: Volume 1: A Distant Obligation* (London: HMSO, 1990) 209.

[63] GA Res. 53/164, 9 Dec. 1998. Adopted by 122-3-34. Russia voted against the resolution and China abstained. The Russian vote against was explained in the GA Third Committee debate on the draft on the basis that the resolution did not sufficiently respect the territorial integrity of the FRY: UN Press Release GA/SHC/3511, 18 Nov. 1998.

of solving complex, long-standing, underlying problems; that a world order that allows individual or coalitions of nations to deploy offensive military might for what they deem are worthy causes amounts to anarchy—these perils require that force be only used as a last resort as determined by a world body'.[64]

Although Lobel and Ratner see the Security Council as that world body, it is argued above that the world body is the UN, which acts normally via the Security Council, but exceptionally via the General Assembly. If the Security Council were unable to act because of legitimate concerns that the situation does not require it to exercise its primary responsibility to authorize military action, then it would be unconstitutional for the Assembly to have exercised its competence. However, if there is a genuine threat the peace, breach of the peace or act of aggression so dangerous and overwhelming that it requires a military response then the Assembly is entitled, indeed obliged, to act. In the Kosovo crisis, the Security Council had determined there to be a threat to the peace, and there was strong evidence of massive repression and crimes against humanity. However, instead of pushing the matter before the Security Council to see if Russia or China would actually veto a resolution authorizing the bombing, it was simply assumed that it would be the case. This appears to be a correct assumption, although it may be because Russia in particular wanted to negotiate a less volatile and more humane military intervention than bombing. Furthermore, to have put a resolution before the Council and have it vetoed would then have freed NATO states to put forward a procedural resolution before the Council transferring the matter to the General Assembly, where a vote on the proposed NATO action should have been held. Assuming that such a request for authority would have won both a procedural vote in the Security Council and a substantive vote in the General Assembly, NATO then would have had a sound legal basis upon which to launch its air strikes.

Why NATO did not follow this course remains a matter of conjecture since, at least on the surface, it does not appear to have been on the agenda. Three reasons may have been pertinent. First of all a fear that the method of military action being put forward (bombing) would not be acceptable to two-thirds of the membership. Bombing in the name of humanity may be a cause for concern for the international community. The main reason why this was the only option on the table for NATO was 'a desire, understandable in itself, to minimize NATO casualties'.[65] Secondly, securing UN authority would have created an expectation, though not a legal obligation, that NATO would launch military action thereby restricting NATO's freedom of choice. Thirdly, a fear that the use of the General Assembly to sanction military action would set a dangerous precedent and could be used against NATO states in the future. This ignores the fact that

---

[64] J. Lobel and M. Ratner, 'Bypassing the Security Council: Ambiguous Authorizations to Use Force, Cease-Fires and the Iraqi Inspection Regime' (1999) 93 AJIL 124 at 153.

[65] H. McCoubrey, 'Kosovo, NATO and International Law' (1999) 14 International Relations 34 at 38.

the precedents for securing Assembly authority are already there, they have simply been conveniently forgotten; it also ignores the fact that bombing without any UN authority is an even more dangerous precedent.

5. Regional Autonomy?

Despite the Assembly having supplementary powers, the UN system is still dominated by the Security Council, a body often criticized for the legitimacy of its decision-making processes.[66] Can the authority of the UN be undermined by the undoubted selectivity and lack of representation in Security Council decision-making? Furthermore, does this signify that the failure to take military enforcement measures by the Council allows states or regional bodies to take action in its stead—as occurred in the case of NATO's military enforcement action to bring an end to the repression in Kosovo in 1999? There seem to be some implications of this type of approach in the 1999 Security Protocol of ECOWAS,[67] the 2000 Constituent Treaty of the AU,[68] and the EU's Security Strategy of 2003.[69] Claims to take military action in these documents can be interpreted very widely indeed, and yet they are subject to much more muted criticism when compared to the US claims to use force in a wide range of situations in the National Security Strategy or Bush Doctrine of 2002. It seems that they have greater legitimacy because they were adopted by regional organizations representing the collective view of groups of states.

Could it not also be argued that either the European Council of twenty-seven countries or the NATO Council of twenty-six states acting by consensus is more representative than the UN Security Council of fifteen? In answer it must be pointed out that the European Council represents European states

---

[66] See N. Tsagourias, 'The Shifting Laws on the Use of Force and the Trivialization of the UN Collective Security System: The Need to Reconstitute It' (2003) XXXIV NYBIL 55.

[67] See arts 3(a), 22(c) and 25(c). Art 22(c) provides for 'humanitarian intervention in support of humanitarian disaster'.

[68] Art 4(h) provides for 'the right of the Union to intervene in a Member State pursuant to a decision of the Assembly in respect of grave circumstances, namely: war crimes, genocide and crimes against humanity'. However, it is worth noting that in the 2002 Protocol Relating to the Establishment of the Peace and Security Council of the African Union, there are provisions that show greater deference to the UN Charter rules. Art 17(1) provides that 'in the fulfilment of its mandate in the promotion and maintenance of peace, security and stability in Africa, the Peace and Security Council shall cooperate closely with the United Nations Security Council, which has primary responsibility for the maintenance of international peace and security...'. Art 17(2) further states that 'where necessary, recourse will be made to the United Nations...to provide the necessary financial, logistical and military support for the African Union's activities in the promotion and maintenance of peace, security and stability in Africa, in keeping with the provisions of Chapter VIII of the UN Charter on the role of Regional Organizations in the maintenance of international peace and security'.

[69] 12 Dec. 2003. At 7 the Strategy states that 'we should be ready to act before a crisis occurs', tackling such threats not 'by purely military means'.

only, while the Security Council, for all its defects, represents the international community.[70] At the UN's founding constitutional moment in 1945, it was the international community as a whole creating something unique, that only the international community (all states acting together in another constitutional moment) could subsequently take away. The founders also established fundamental universal rules such as the non-use of force, which can only remain valid if they are ultimately regulated by universal organizations. This signifies that only the UN can authorize any derogation from the prohibition of the use of force beyond a state's inherent right of individual or collective self-defence. Regional self-authorization would be subject to too much abuse. Indeed, the likelihood of competing regional police forces would be great. Consequently, instead of having universal rules governing the use of force, there would emerge potentially conflicting regional rules.

Nevertheless, the universal organization is in need of significant improvement. The problem of legitimacy in the Security Council signifies the need for either a more representative and accountable Council exercising its primary responsibility for peace and security in a proactive consistent manner, or a re-invigoration of the subsidiary powers of the General Assembly. However, weaknesses in the universal organization do not signify that regional organizations can step in to fill the gaps, at least in matters of military enforcement. The international community created a universal organization to police universal rules, something not possessed by individual states, or even non-universal organizations. Only the international community as a whole could take this away. Until that happens, we are stuck with the Security Council, currently with its in-built selectivity, and a very limited Assembly with subsidiary powers to recommend enforcement measures that can be exercised in exceptional circumstances.

But if the UN High Level Panel's recommendations of late 2004 are adopted there should emerge a more representative, more accountable, Security Council concerned with upholding fundamental rules of international law. The most significant of the Panel's recommendations would remove some of the most delegitimating selectivity by endorsing:

the emerging norm that there is a collective, international responsibility to protect, exercisable by the Security Council authorising military intervention as a last resort, in the event of genocide and other large-scale killing, ethnic cleansing or serious violations of humanitarian law which sovereign Governments have proved powerless or unwilling to prevent.[71]

---

[70] Art 24(1) of the UN Charter.

[71] From Report of the High-level Panel on Threats, Challenges and Change (UN, 2004), 'A More Secure World: Our Shared Responsibility', recommendation 55, see also 56, 73–81. See further the Report of the Secretary General, 'In Larger Freedom: Towards Security, Development and Human Rights for All' (UN, 2005), para 125 of which states: 'As to genocide, ethnic cleansing and other such crimes against humanity, are they also not threats to international peace and security, against which humanity should be able to look to the Security Council for protection?'. See also para 126.

Unfortunately, the inability of the Security Council to deal with the crimes against humanity being committed in the Darfur region of Sudan[72] from 2003 onwards is evidence of the continued failure of the Council to take action in all cases of serious violations of international law. The smokescreen sent up by its reference of the matter to the International Criminal Court in March 2005,[73] and the inadequacy of the AU force and its replacement AU/UN force, should not distract from the fact that the Council has failed to prevent the crimes against humanity being committed. An investigation ordered by the UN's Human Rights Council in 2007 strongly argued that the responsibility to protect was applicable.[74]

The version of the responsibility to protect adopted by world leaders at the UN's World Summit in September 2005 shows, by its wording, that selectivity and discretion will still be preserved for the Security Council even in cases of gross human rights violations. Member states declared 'we are prepared to take collective action, in a timely and decisive manner, through the Security Council, in accordance with the UN Charter, including Chapter VII, on a case by case basis in co-operation with relevant regional organizations as appropriate, should peaceful means be inadequate and national authorities manifestly fail to protect their populations from genocide, war crimes, ethnic cleansing and crimes against humanity'.[75] Thus by locking up the rules on the use of force on the matter of enforcing fundamental rules of international law in the Security Council, the drafters created an inherently selective and weak system. To unlock those rules in favour of regional organizations, however, may prove to be more disastrous. The better course is for a reformed and legitimate Council to emerge out of the current pressure for change,[76] while rediscovering the Assembly's subsidiary competence.

6. Britain and the Bombing Campaign

As early as March 1998 Prime Minister Tony Blair gave warning of future British involvement in Kosovo when telling the House that the Foreign Secretary was being dispatched to speak to President Milosevic:

That shows again the importance of the role that Britain can play, not merely in Bosnia but in the whole region in stabilising it, bringing peace and attempting to prevent conflict growing. I have no doubt that if there is a substantial conflict [in Kosovo] it will have an impact on us and on the whole of Europe as well as on that part of the world.[77]

---

[72] That this level of abuse has occurred is determined by a commission set up by the Council itself. See report of the International Commission of Inquiry on Violations of International Humanitarian Law and Human Rights Law in Darfur (UN Doc. S/2005/60).

[73] SC Res. 1593, 31 March 2005.   [74] UN Doc. A/HRC/4/80, 9 March 2007, para 67.

[75] GA Res. 60/1, 24 Oct. 2005.

[76] See Report of the Secretary General, 'In Larger Freedom', paras 167–170.

[77] *Hansard* HC vol 307, col 1055, 4 March 1998.

The Foreign Secretary, Robin Cook, reported to the House on his mission to Belgrade which was undertaken against the background of Serbian security operations around Dreniza where fifty-one people where killed. 'It is simply not credible that all those killed were terrorists', given that less than half the corpses were men of military age—most were women and children.

I made it clear that I [visited Belgrade] not just on behalf of Britain, but as the presidency of the European Union. I regret to tell the House that President Milosevic sought to present the events in Kosovo as a legitimate police response to terrorism. Britain's record against terrorism is firm and resolute. We strongly condemn the use of violence for political objectives, including the terrorism of the self-styled Kosovo Liberation Army. Terrorism, however, cannot be used as a pretext for the indiscriminate use of force against a civilian population.

The Foreign Secretary then outlined the approach of the six-nation Contact Group (UK, US, Russia, France, Germany and Italy), which was based primarily on sanctions, monitoring and accountability to the ICTY for war crimes. Use of military force, though raised in the ensuing discussion in the House was not at this stage an option,[78] a position that seemed to be supported by Ministerial answers to the Foreign Affairs Committee in March 1998.[79] The possibility of NATO involvement soon started to enter into House of Commons' debates though as the situation quickly worsened.[80]

The incremental involvement of NATO in Kosovo, first through threats of force and then on 23 March 1999 by the use of force, meant that there was a significant opportunity for parliamentary involvement, though there was no full debate and vote before the bombing campaign began. On 13 October 1998 the NATO Council authorized activation orders for airstrikes aimed at coercing the regime in Belgrade to withdraw forces from Kosovo, and to comply with Security Council Resolution 1199. In the House of Commons the Foreign Secretary, Robin Cook, made a statement regarding this on 19 October, declaring that the commitment of President Milosevic to withdraw would not have been secured 'if the diplomatic efforts backed by the contact group had not also been backed by the credible threat of military action by NATO'.[81] There was very little debate in the House, with the opposition expressing reserved support for the government's policy.

Interestingly, the government first spelled out its legal justifications for its threats of force on 16 November 1998 in the House of Lords. The government Minister, Baroness Symons, stated although there was 'no general doctrine of humanitarian necessity in international law' there were cases where limited uses of force were justifiable 'in support of purposes laid down by the Security

---

[78] *Hansard* HC vol 308, cols 317–8, 10 March 1998.
[79] Foreign Affairs Committee, Minutes of Evidence, 19 March 1998 (Lloyd) (HC 649-i).
[80] *Hansard* HC vol 311, cols 460–1, 20 April 1998 (Menzies-Campbell, Cook).
[81] *Hansard* HC vol 317, col 953, 19 Oct. 1999.

Council but without the Council's express authorisation when that was the only means to avert an overwhelming humanitarian catastrophe'.[82] The Foreign and Commonwealth Office reinforced this argument in its statement on the legal authority of proposed military action given in evidence before the Foreign Affairs Select Committee on 26 January 1999 namely that 'there may also be cases of overwhelming humanitarian necessity where, in the light of all the circumstances, a limited use of force is justifiable as the only way to avert a humanitarian catastrophe'.[83]

With parliamentary support for the threat of force seemingly there, in many ways it was easier to carry that support forward for the use of force, particularly after the House's attention was drawn to the killings at Racak and Rugovo in January 1999, both in violation of the ceasefire agreement brokered by US envoy Richard Holbrooke in October 1998.[84] On 24 February 1999, the Foreign Secretary reported on the parlous state of the negotiations conducted at Rambouillet in France, which gave both sides until 15 March to conclude an agreement. In so doing he stated that the NATO threat of force remained in place and that use of force would become a reality if there were major violations of the cease-fire by Belgrade, and 'to secure compliance from Belgrade' in the negotiations.[85] There were limited criticisms in the lower house directed at the lack of Security Council authorization, and the government's overriding desire to maintain the credibility of NATO. The effectiveness of the proposed use of force—bombing—was also called into question.[86]

On 23 March 1999 with the Belgrade talks brokered by US envoy, Richard Holbrooke, failing, Prime Minister Tony Blair announced that 'Britain stands ready with its NATO allies to take military action' with 'a minimum objective to curb continued Serbian repression in Kosovo in order to avert a humanitarian disaster'. At this stage he received the 'Opposition's wholehearted support for the British forces who might have to take part in the NATO action' from the Leader of the Opposition, William Hague. Both party leaders agreed that the cause of the problem was President Milosevic. The Prime Minister expressed his satisfaction at this support saying that 'it is important that we in this House take a united view'. When pressed about the possibility of deploying ground forces, the Prime Minister expressed the 'clear objective to curb Milosevic's ability, through his military capability, to engage in . . . repression. That is our objective, and we shall carry on until it is fulfilled'.[87] Criticism of the proposed bombing came from isolated members of the Conservative party, the left of the Labour

---

[82] *Hansard* HL vol 594, cols 139–40w, 16 Nov 1998. This was oft-repeated in the upper house for example vol 600, cols 436–7, 29 April 1999 (Symons).

[83] Foreign Affairs Committee, Kosovo, Minutes of Evidence, 26 Jan. 1999, 1 (HC 188-i).

[84] *Hansard* HC vol 323, col 565, 18 Jan. 1999 (Cook); vol 324, col 597, 1 Feb. 1999 (Cook).

[85] *Hansard* HC vol 326, cols 409–12, 24 Feb. 1999 (Cook).

[86] Ibid., cols 409–12 (Benn and Daylell).

[87] *Hansard* HC vol 328, cols 161–6, 23 March 1999.

party, and the Scottish nationalists, and took different forms, principally that the bombing would be a violation of Yugoslav sovereignty and a breach of international law, though others cast doubt on the likelihood of bombing being successful by itself.[88]

Tony Benn, MP for Chesterfield, questioned the legal basis of the proposed military action, lacking as it did any express authority from the United Nations. He also criticized the government for not allowing a proper debate in parliament: 'to treat the House as though it were just an audience for "Newsnight" on so grave a matter is simply below the standard that we are entitled to expect'. Tony Blair responded by saying that his statement to the House 'where I can be questioned, not the least by my right hon. friend' was hardly an interview on the television. He also pointed out that the Serbs had violated two key resolutions of the Security Council (1199 and 1203), which had demanded an end to the repression and a withdrawal of Serbian forces. 'The plain fact of the matter is that we have to act now to avert the humanitarian disaster', and so a full debate would come later.[89]

The launch of airstrikes was announced to the House on 24 March 1999 by the Deputy Prime Minister John Prescott. The lack of express UN authority for the operation did not seem to present a problem for the bulk of the House. As previously stated Prescott declared that the NATO action was supported by all nineteen members of NATO and supported 'the political aims of the international community', set out in Council Resolutions 1199 and 1203, both of which had been breached by Milosevic. The action was 'justified as an exceptional measure to prevent an overwhelming humanitarian catastrophe'. Furthermore he warned the members of the Yugoslav army and other forces 'who may be in receipt of orders to repress the Albanians in Kosovo' that individual responsibility will ensue if they breach international law, with possible prosecution by the ICTY.[90]

The statement shows the UK placing reliance for its own actions on a controversial legal proposition permitting humanitarian intervention in support of Security Council resolutions, while at the same time fully supporting the enforcement of established norms of international humanitarian law against Serbian forces. The presence of Security Council resolutions which clearly indicated that the situation was a threat to the peace, and the consensus in NATO on the use of force, were the two international institutional pillars on which the government built this new form of intervention. This was sufficient to give the action legitimacy. The opposition again gave its 'full support' to the action.[91] Political unity was shown by a visit to British forces involved in the Kosovo campaign on 29 March 1999 by the Defence Secretary (George Robertson), the Shadow Defence Secretary, and the Defence Spokesman for the Liberal Democrats.[92]

---

[88] Ibid., cols 167–9 (Tapsell, Benn, Salmond).   [89] Ibid., cols 168–9.
[90] *Hansard* HC vol 328, col 484, 24 March 1999.   [91] Ibid., col 486 (Lilley).
[92] *Hansard* HC vol 328, col 1204, 31 March 1999 (Robertson).

Individual members of the Commons criticized, *inter alia*: the lack of clear legal authority for the launch of the bombing raids, the lack of express approval by the House of Commons, the anger caused in Russia, the lack of action against the KLA, the counter-productive nature of bombing, and later the extent of the atrocities being committed in Kosovo.[93] However, in general contributions of MPs took the form of statements supporting the action and the RAF pilots, although some were concerned about the lack of a long-term strategy. The overall view was expressed by Labour member, Bruce George, who asked 'the doubters what consolation it would be to a Kosovan running away from being killed to be able to say that the British Government did not act, but were upholding a precise, legalistic definition of international law? We can be proud of what we are doing'.[94] During the debate the Deputy Prime Minister rightly claimed that 'there is solidarity for our purpose and unity in support of our service people'.[95]

In the debate on the following day (25 March), the Foreign Secretary Robin Cook, when pressed again on the legality of the bombing stated more generally that 'we are acting on the legal principle that the action is justified to halt a humanitarian catastrophe'.[96] This led to a critical statement by the Shadow Foreign Secretary, Michael Howard, which while expressing support for the service people engaged in the action, pointed out that 'one of the requirements of a just war is that the suffering that is an inevitable consequence of military action should be less than the suffering that the action prevents'. The remainder of the debate focused on the legal issue, and was characterized by lack of agreement as to whether the action was justified by Security Council resolutions or under a wider doctrine of humanitarian intervention, or a combination of both. The question of whether there was a duty to intervene was also raised, in which case it was argued there were numerous other just causes around the globe. The answer the government gave was that this was a humanitarian catastrophe in Europe, which affected British and NATO interests.[97] There was insufficient dissent in the House to allow for a vote on the matter, despite Tony Benn pressing for one.[98]

A second full debate following the commencement of the bombings was held on 19 April and although there was some discussion of holding a substantive vote on the issue, those in favour had insufficient support to force any kind

---

[93] *Hansard* HC vol 328, cols 487–92, 24 March 1999 (Benn, Hogg, Daylell, Galloway, Smyth); vol 328, col 574, 25 March 1999 (Clark).
[94] *Hansard* HC vol 328, col 489, 24 March 1999 (George).
[95] Ibid., col 493 (Prescott).
[96] *Hansard* HC vol 328, col 541, 25 March 1999. See also statement by Defence Minister George Robertson (col 617). See further the statement by Robin Cook before the Foreign Affairs Select Committee, 14 April 1999, para 154 (HC 188-ii).
[97] *Hansard* HC vol 328, cols 542–51, 25 March 1999 (Howard, Campbell, Gill, Anderson).
[98] Ibid., col 619.

of vote.[99] The foreign affairs spokesman for the Liberal Democrats, Menzies-Campbell, made a forceful statement in support of Tony Benn:

If we are to ask our young men, and increasingly our young women, to risk their lives in the furtherance of political objectives, surely they ought to know that they have the endorsement of the House of Commons.... The right hon. Member of Chesterfield (Mr. Benn) has, of course, a long history of endeavouring to reform the prerogative power, and I have some sympathy with that point of view. It seems to me that, at a time when we are engaged in remarkable constitutional reforms in relation to Scotland and Wales, the adoption of the European convention on human rights into our domestic law ... there is time for a proper examination of that issue.[100]

These initial debates reveal the importance of two factors for the government in taking its decision to bomb Serbia as part of a NATO operation. First that the action is taken, or is at least represented as being taken, on behalf of the 'international community'. This concept has been much criticized in international legal and political theory relying as it does on a Grotian rationalist conception of the world.[101] However, its revitalization by the British government was necessitated by its reliance on a form of humanitarian intervention, taken 'in support of' UN resolutions. The unanimity of NATO, shown at the organization's 50th summit held in Washington in April 1999,[102] was combined with the edicts of the Security Council, and later the G8,[103] to give the action the necessary communitarian pedigree. Reliance is also placed on the fact that the Security Council did not condemn NATO's bombing;[104] indeed, it was argued that the vast majority of States on the Council (with the main exceptions of China and Russia) supported it.[105] The lack of a clear legal basis in the NATO treaty does not appear to have been any cause for concern at the time, presumably on the grounds that if one state has the right of humanitarian intervention, then even more so will nineteen countries acting through a military alliance.

Although the government attempted to portray the action as having a cast-iron legal basis, the reality is that the bombings were a challenge to the orthodox view that the UN Charter does not allow for humanitarian intervention without

---

[99] *Hansard* HC vol 329, col 668, 19 April 1999.   [100] Ibid., col 590.

[101] See H. Bull, 'The Importance of Grotius in the Study of International Relations', in H. Bull, B. Kingsbury and A. Roberts (eds), *Hugo Grotius and International Relations* (Oxford: Clarendon, 1992) 71–2.

[102] *Hansard* HC vol 330, col 21, 26 April 1999 (Blair).

[103] G8 support was relied on at a later stage, see *Hansard* HC vol 331, col 885, 18 May 1999 (Cook). On 6 May 1999 the G8 laid down the general principles upon which a political solution to the Kosovo crisis would be based. This brought Russia on board but it did not persuade Russia (or China) that NATO's bombings were lawful. See Security Council meeting at which resolution 1244 was adopted authorizing KFOR: SC 4011st mtg, 10 June 1999, 7 (Russia), 8–9 (China).

[104] See SC 6659th mtg, 26 March 1999 when a Russian draft resolution (UN Doc. S/1999/328) demanding a cessation of the use of force against the FRY was defeated, with only China, Russia and Namibia voting for it.

[105] *Hansard* HC vol 328, col 615, 25 March 1999 (Robertson); vol 329, col 579, 19 April 1999 (Cook).

the express authority of the Security Council. A precedent for this new form of humanitarian intervention could have been drawn from the western intervention in northern Iraq in 1991, taken in support of, but not authorized by Security Council Resolution 688. This was indeed mentioned by the former Conservative Defence Minister, Tom King, during the Kosovo debates.[106]

The second factor relied upon by the government was that the action, at least initially, had the apparent overwhelming support of the House of Commons, though this was not put to a vote, despite attempts by dissenters. There was a much greater effort on this occasion to inform the House and to ensure it was behind the action. There was dissent on the legal basis, and criticism of the strategy (increasingly in the latter case from the opposition),[107] but the government managed to carry sufficient support in the House for the duration of the war. However, the unforeseen length of the bombing campaign did cause some problems for the government in maintaining this support. When parliamentary support began to falter, the government relied more heavily on claiming that public opinion was on its side,[108] as well as support from the Kosovan Albanians themselves,[109] whose suffering seemed to be exacerbated by the NATO action, although this alleged effect of the bombing was vehemently denied by the government.[110] Thus although the UK's contribution to the war was conducted and led by the executive, it was only able to maintain its grip on the action while it had a large measure of parliamentary support. The government's claims as to the amount of degradation being caused to the Yugoslav army were clearly important in keeping the House on its side. For instance, the Defence Secretary made claims in the House on 22 May 1999 that twelve Yugoslav tanks were destroyed, and on 25 May a further five tanks were destroyed, as part of a 'very effective air campaign'.[111] During the air campaign the RAF flew 1,008 sorties, and delivered 1,618 strikes (overall NATO figures were 10,484 sorties and 38,004 strikes). The RAF sustained no losses.[112] The evidence of the impact of NATO airstrikes on Serbian forces suggests that the government's claims about the level of destruction were exaggerated, although they may have been honestly made.[113] Nevertheless, the bombing campaign did persuade President Milosevic to withdraw his forces from Kosovo.

---

[106] *Hansard* HC vol 328, col 553, 25 March 1999.

[107] *Hansard* HC vol 329, cols 21–3, 13 April 1999 (Hague, Ashdown); vol 329, col 583, 19 April 1999 (Howard); vol 330, col 24, 26 April 1999 (Hague); vol 331, col 891, 18 May 1999 (Howard).

[108] See Foreign Affairs Select Committee, 14 April 1999, para 158 (Cook) (HC188-ii). See also the Labour Chairman of the Commons Defence Select Committee, Bruce George in P. Wintour, 'Onslaught on Belgrade May Avert Split', *The Observer*, 4 April 1999, 20.

[109] *Hansard* HC vol 328, col 1204, 31 March 1999 (Robertson).

[110] Ibid., col 1212 (Robertson). See also the Foreign Secretary before the Foreign Affairs Select Committee, 14 April 1999, para 106 (HC188-ii).

[111] *Hansard* HC vol 332, col 255, 26 May 1999 (Robertson).

[112] <http://www.britains-smallwars.com/Kosovo/RAF.html> (accessed 26 Jan. 2009).

[113] S. Castle, 'Doubts still linger over NATO's war evidence', *The Independent*, 17 Sept. 1999, 16.

7. Democratic Accountability

In terms of democratic accountability, the House of Commons certainly was not simply a rubber stamp for the executive's actions over Kosovo. Indeed, it seemed to be informed in a way not seen before in times of war. It debated the issue regularly during the bombing and questioned the Prime Minister, Foreign Secretary and Defence Secretary fairly closely.[114] Furthermore, the government was not only held accountable before the House, but also before the Foreign Affairs Select Committee of the House, which for example on 14 April 1999 questioned the Secretary of State for Foreign Affairs very closely on NATO errors, legality, lack of preparation for the influx of refugees, and the lack of preparation for a ground force which might be necessary if the bombing failed. On being questioned about the wisdom of stating that a ground force was not on the agenda, the Foreign Minister replied that he operated 'in a democratic environment in an alliance with 19 democratic states', which meant that no unilateral statement on the use of a ground force was possible,[115] though it turns out that the British government was at the fore of secretly planning a ground campaign.[116] The Chairman of the Select Committee claimed, with some justification, that the questioning of the Foreign Secretary had 'been a most helpful exercise in democratic accountability at a critical time'.[117] Nevertheless, despite the frequent public debates on the matter there is some truth in the criticism that parliament was being treated as some kind of 'press conference', in which MPs could ask questions but could not alter the course of the war, nor influence government strategy.[118]

The schisms that were beginning to open in parliament were closed when the Yugoslav authorities agreed to withdraw and accept NATO's conditions early in June 1999 after eleven weeks of NATO bombing. The Prime Minister's report to the House on these developments and the imminent embodiment of the peace plan in a Security Council resolution,[119] including KFOR operating under chapter VII of the Charter, was welcomed by the opposition which supported the continued bombing until the verified withdrawal of Serb forces.[120] In a sense the debate then started over again, revolving around the role of British troops in KFOR. In essence the debates on the post-conflict stage initially took a similar course in the House, though the impression was that with Security Council approval given on this occasion, dissent was muted. The clear international legal basis of KFOR seemed to have reduced the critical attitude that the House

---

[114] By 18 May 1999 there had been three full day debates on the NATO military action, and five statements to the House: *Hansard* HC vol 331, col 965, 18 May 1999 (Robertson).

[115] Foreign Affairs Select Committee, 14 April 1999, para 146 (HC 188-ii).

[116] P. Wintour and P. Beaumont, 'How Nato Planned to Invade', *The Observer*, 18 July 1999, 1.

[117] Foreign Affairs Select Committee, 14 April 1999, para 168 (HC 188-ii).

[118] *Hansard* HC vol 329, col 579, 19 April 1999 (Benn).

[119] SC Res. 1244, 10 June 1999.   [120] *Hansard* HC vol 332, cols 464–6, 8 June 1999.

adopted towards the bombing by NATO. The initial debates seemed to be more as to the effects of the Resolution 1244, the logistics of the operation, the role of the Russian contingent, the disarming of the KLA, and the security of British military personnel, rather than the legitimacy of the operation.[121] However, in the longer term, debate ensued in the lower house as to the 'precedential' nature of the initial bombings of Kosovo.[122]

Further detailed scrutiny of the UK's role in the Kosovo crisis ensued before the House of Commons Select Committees on International Development, Defence and Foreign Affairs. Of particular interest to the current project are the reports of the latter two.[123] The Defence Committee's report was largely on lessons learned from the conflict, though it did criticize the threat and then the use of force by NATO as being more about its credibility as an effective military organization than about military necessity, a criticism further compounded by the Alliance's policy of bombing, the purpose of which was unclear in that it started as a means of preventing ethnic cleansing (for which the Committee thought it unsuitable) and then ended as a means of coercing Milosevic into compliance.[124]

The Foreign Affairs Committee produced a very full report on 7 June 2000 after seeking evidence from a number of witnesses, including leading inter-national lawyers. The report may be seen as a necessary democratic balance to the use of prerogative powers by the executive.[125] However, the longer-term impact of this report seems limited. It was even noticeable that coming over a year after the initiation of the bombing campaign, it did not catch the attention of the pub-lic, or more importantly the media, with only the isolated article realizing its sig-nificance.[126] As the report itself concluded as regards the problems facing the international community in dealing with the aftermath of the conflict: '[t]his is a formidable challenge which deserves the full support of the international community. We are concerned that the attention span of the international com-munity is short'.[127] The same could be said of the vagaries of public concern, which was intensely focused on Kosovo in the lead up to and during the bombing cam-paign, but quickly moved on to other matters when Serbia withdrew its forces.

Interestingly, the Foreign Affairs Committee report contradicts some of the positions taken by the government during the bombings, positions that had the support of parliament at the time. The report ranged from the period before

---

[121] See debates on 9 June 1999, 14 June 1999, 17 June 1999.

[122] See for example *Hansard* HC vol 340, col 372, 22 Nov. 1999 (Maples).

[123] See International Development Committee, Third Report, *Kosovo: The Humanitarian Crisis*, 11 May 1999 (HC 422).

[124] Defence Committee Fourteenth Report on the Lessons of Kosovo (HC 347-I), 23 Oct. 2000, paras 31, 42, 45, 60, 70, 72 (HC 347-I). See government's response, 24 Jan. 2001 (HC 178).

[125] *Hansard* HC vol 333, col 594, 17 June 1999 (Maples).

[126] I. Hilton, 'NATO's Shame', *The Guardian*, 8 June 2000, 23.

[127] HC Foreign Affairs Select Committee, Fourth Report 1999–2000, 7 June 2000, para 320 (HC 28-I).

the conflict to the post-conflict situation and contained many critical findings. Concentrating here on its review of the legality of *Operation Allied Force*, the Committee noted that while the government was confidently asserting the certainty of the international legal basis, the Committee's view was that the operation was contrary to the UN Charter having received no UN authorization, neither from the Security Council nor had any recommendation been sought from the Assembly. Furthermore, it concluded that 'at the very least, the doctrine of humanitarian intervention has a tenuous basis in current customary international law, and that this renders NATO action legally questionable'. This serious criticism was balanced by the finding that in the face of the threat of Russian and Chinese vetoes 'the NATO allies did all that they could to make the military intervention in Kosovo as compliant with the tenets of international law as possible'. However, given the other statements made in the Committee's report it is clear that NATO did not go far enough in this regard, reflected in the conclusion that 'NATO's military action, if of dubious legality in the current state of international law was justified on moral grounds'. The Committee thus advocated that the UK argue for and support new principles to be adopted by the UN governing humanitarian intervention.[128]

The Committee's report was clearly very different from the position adopted and supported by the vast majority of MP's during Operation Allied Force, bearing in mind that Select Committees are drawn from the membership of the House of Commons. The absence of strict party political control over the Select Committee may have a great deal to do with this divergence in opinion. While welcoming a more critical appraisal of the government's actions, it seems to be a weakness in the UK's system of accountability that this critique comes too late to affect the military operation in question, though its affects may be felt in the future. The government simply responded by reasserting its confidence in the legality of its actions.[129] By the time the Foreign Affairs Select Committee adopted its report in June 2000, the UK had already committed troops to combat threats to the peace in East Timor and Sierra Leone, leaving the report consigned to history.

In addition to questioning the government's failure to put its case before the UN General Assembly, the Foreign Affairs Committee was also critical of the lack of democratic decision-making before parliament, where although there were plenty of discussions on Kosovo, there was no clear vote in favour of the action. The Foreign Affairs Select Committee report of 2000 did not purport to recommend a change in the prerogative powers of the executive to deploy troops. It did recommend however that the government 'should take a substantive motion in the House of Commons at the earliest opportunity after the commitment of troops to armed conflict allowing the House to express its view, and allowing Members

---

[128] Ibid., paras 124–44.
[129] (1975–2001) UKMIL Part Sixteen.IV. item 80. See also item 83 (statement by Robin Cook, Foreign Secretary on 7 June 2000). See also his response to the Fourth Report (Cm 4825, Aug. 2000).

to table amendments'. The requirement that the government should win the vote over contrary proposals in the lower house would give 'extra democratic legitimacy to military action'.[130] The report thus recognizes the need for proper parliamentary approval of such action, even if it had received authority from an international organization. In the case of Kosovo, where there is no clear authority, and the legal basis is arguable, there is an even greater need to have this clear expression of support. Such a requirement may also encourage a more critical attitude by parliament towards the government's actions, rather than the supine attitude present in most debates on military deployment. The report fell short though of requiring that positive parliamentary approval be given prior to the government's decision to deploy. It did, however, start a reform debate in parliament, which will be reviewed in chapter eleven.

8. Conclusion: the Future of Humanitarian Intervention

Despite the uncertain *opinio juris* in favour of a doctrine of humanitarian intervention in the build-up to and during the Kosovo crisis, the British government alone seemed to persist in its view that such intervention was justified in certain circumstances. Indeed, to its credit it tried to convince others of the merits of its approach. In 1999, after the Kosovo bombings and the withdrawal of Serb forces, the UK submitted to the UN Secretary General a 'framework to guide intervention by the international community'. In a speech to the American Bar Association on 19 July 2000, the Foreign Secretary Robin Cook outlined six of the principles upon which intervention should be based. First, intervention should be reduced by more effective conflict prevention; second, armed force should only be used as a last resort; third, 'the immediate responsibility for halting violence rests with the state in which it occurs'; fourth:

When faced with an overwhelming humanitarian catastrophe, which a government has shown it is unwilling or unable to prevent or is actively promoting, the international community should intervene. Intervention in internal affairs is a sensitive issue. So there must be convincing evidence of extreme humanitarian distress on a large scale, requiring urgent relief. It must be objectively clear that there is no practicable alternative to the use of force to save lives.

Fifth, 'any use of force should be proportionate to achieving the humanitarian purpose and carried out in accordance with international law'; and sixth 'any use of force should be collective'. The latter signifies that the authority of the Security Council should be secured 'whenever possible', but if not then action by regional bodies such as NATO was sufficiently collective.[131]

---

[130] Foreign Affairs Select Committee Fourth Report, 7 June 2000, paras 165–6 (HC 28-I).
[131] (1975–2001) UKMIL Part Sixteen.IV. item 82 (see also item 90).

The movement away from there being a right to intervene towards the argument that there is a responsibility or a duty to protect vulnerable populations has become part of the UN debate. However, the World Summit outcome document of 2005 was based on there being a responsibility to protect based firmly on the Security Council, not on other organizations. Herein is the key difference between the British approach and the consensus in the UN as a whole. The reality though is that humanitarian action is discretionary, whether under Security Council authority or under another collective guise. This is shown by the answer given by Robin Cook's successor (Jack Straw) on 25 June 2002 in response to a question about the parlous state of the citizens of Zimbabwe under the brutal regime of Robert Mugabe:

If only it were possible simply by wishing for an international coalition to end the damage Mugabe is doing, it would be done. If it were possible to do 'what happened in Kosovo' ... it would be done. However, it is irresponsible to cite that example as a criticism of the Government and the international community and neither to rule it out nor rule it in. Everyone knows that the suggestion that we embark on a bombing campaign, as we had to do in Kosovo for 78 days, comes from fantasy land, and it would be deceiving the people of Zimbabwe to pretend otherwise.[132]

Furthermore, the government's claim that it has gained support for its doctrine,[133] is contradicted by Foreign Office statements that there has been a lack of support for the UK's guidelines, illustrative of the 'reluctance on the part of much of the international community to accept change in the abstract'.[134]

Nevertheless, the government has expressed support, at least in abstract, for the emerging doctrine of the 'responsibility to protect' (known as R2P). For example in 2005, in the House of Lords the government was asked whether it was committed to the emerging R2P norm. In response the minister stated that it welcomed the recommendations of the UN's High Level Panel of 2004 which were similar to the government's proposals of 1999.[135] Whether this created any sort of legally binding commitment to intervene on the part of the British government was made clear by a minister's statement before the House of Commons in 2007 that responsibility to protect remains a 'political commitment rather than a legal obligation, but it is in the UK's interests to make sure that this commitment holds'.[136]

The very idea, consistently advocated by the British government as part of its support for humanitarian intervention/R2P, namely that humanitarian intervention should be limited to protecting the endangered civilians, is also

---

[132] *Hansard* HC vol 387, col 813, 25 June 2002 in (2002) UKMIL Part Sixteen: II.B.2., item 16/48.

[133] See for example *Hansard* HC vol 419. cols 1234–6, 26 March 2004.

[134] Foreign Affairs Committee Seventh Report, Foreign Policy Aspects of the War Against Terrorism, 5 July 2004 (HC 441-ii).

[135] *Hansard* HL vol 670, col 56w, 7 March 2005.

[136] *Hansard* HC vol 461, col 254w, 4 June 2007 (McCartney).

undermined by the fact that NATO's intervention in Kosovo produced a chain of events that resulted in Kosovo's controversial declaration of independence from Serbia on 17 February 2008 thereby changing the very nature and make-up of the country being intervened in, and also leading to calls for independence for other putative micro-states, including the breakaway regions in Georgia. Security Council Resolution 1244 adopted in 1999 after the withdrawal of Serb forces, clearly reaffirmed the 'commitment of all Member States to the sovereignty and territorial integrity of the Federal Republic of Yugoslavia', as well as calling for 'substantial autonomy and meaningful self-administration for Kosovo'. The Resolution authorized an international civil presence (UNMIK) to promote the 'establishment, pending a final settlement, of substantial autonomy and self-government in Kosovo'.[137] It seems impossible to read this resolution as allowing for a unilateral declaration of independence by Kosovo as a form of 'settlement', in the absence of any enabling Security Council resolution, which was not forthcoming.

For the Foreign Secretary, David Miliband, in explaining the UK's recognition of the new state of Kosovo, to argue that Resolution 1244 does not preclude independence,[138] would seem to be another example of the British government reading a UN resolution in the face of its clear meaning—a technique that had already been used unconvincingly in the arguments put forward to justify the invasion of Iraq in 2003. Despite the huge controversy that this provoked, it seems the British government cannot resist the temptation to place reliance on unsupported interpretations, and furthermore to display immense hubris in claiming their correctness.

---

[137] SC Res. 1244, 10 June 1999.
[138] Interview on Radio 4 Today Programme, 19 Feb. 2008. See his more cautious answer to the House of Commons: *Hansard* HC vol 472, col 21w, 19 Feb. 2008. By the end of September 2008, 46 countries had recognized Kosovo as an independent state: *Guardian Weekly*, 26 Sept. 2008, 4.

10

The Road to Basra

1. Introduction

The involvement of British service personnel in the invasion of Iraq in 2003 took place against a background of division both domestically and internationally. The legal basis, revolving principally around the meaning of Security Council resolutions, was hotly disputed and has led to continuing political ramifications as the British and American military presence in Iraq continues. At the domestic level the role of legal advice in the process of executive decision-making and its presentation to parliament became particularly apparent. Moreover, the whole process of executive decision-making, at both the international and domestic levels requires reconsideration in the light of both Kosovo and Iraq. The inability of the Security Council to achieve consensus on how to tackle either crisis, calls into question its continued role as the fulcrum of collective security. At the domestic level the executive appeared to be effective in sending troops without clear UN authority, and although parliament seemed to play an increased role there are still questions as to whether it was an adequate democratic counterweight to the executive. The desperate search, especially by the British government, for a second UN resolution early in 2003, and the inability to stop the growing momentum towards war in March are realities that are often hidden in international legal literature by the dry arguments of whether the war was justified by existing UN resolutions. This chapter opens out the legal and political debate to discern both the legality and legitimacy of the military operation to topple Saddam, and the subsequent occupation and attempted rebuilding of Iraq.

2. The Security Council: More Than a Meeting Place

The legal fog surrounding the 2003 Anglo-American invasion of Iraq arises out of a disagreement about the nature of the Security Council and its decision-making competence. On the one hand the Security Council can be seen simply as a collection of states, no different from the Concert of Europe in the nineteenth century or the G7/8 of more modern times. In these fora governments simply agree or disagree on strategy or policy and any decision is just an amalgamation of the views or wills of those governments. On the other hand, the Security Council can be viewed 'as a corporate entity, displaying an emergent will and purpose that can be identified with it as a collective organ . . .'.[1]

Britain has generally adopted a pragmatic approach to the Security Council, seeing it as an instrument of governance when necessary, for example when adopting wide ranging anti-terrorism measures after 9/11,[2] at other times as a useful vehicle for encouraging settlement, for example when it sponsored Resolution 242 after the Six Day War of 1967, a resolution which is still viewed as the basis for settlement of the Israeli/Palestinian conflict.[3] On other occasions a resolution is viewed as being a compromise incorporating the views of member states while reserving the competence of the Council as a whole. Thus, from the British perspective Resolution 678 of 1990 which authorized 'necessary measures' against Iraq was sufficiently flexible to permit fairly wide interpretation by those acting under it, such as Britain, but did not prevent the Council from imposing its own judgment.[4] The difficulty caused by this view will be seen in this chapter as the British government argued that the authority granted by Resolution 678 of 1990 still applied in March 2003 to justify the invasion of Iraq.

With the odd historical aberration such as the Korean War in the 1950s the Cold War prevented the Security Council from developing a separate will through executive action. This though did not prevent the Council from functioning. As Inis Claude noted, the requirement of consensus among the five permanent members of the Council (P5) meant that the Council was intended to perform both an executive and a diplomatic function. 'The Council was designed to serve as an instrument of action whenever a unanimous vote of the great powers revealed the existence of a consensus, and a forum for negotiation whenever the use of the veto revealed the absence of a consensus'.[5] In other words there can be said to be two Councils: a corporate one, especially when adopting decisions under chapter VII; and a traditional conference one, when acting as a forum for negotiations that may be productive but do not lead to a Security Council decision.

Organizations without separate will (known in international law as legal personality)—the G8 for instance—can be said to have a separate existence but not separate will at least in a legal sense. True, the G8's communiqués reflect the collective view of eight states but, without separate will, such communiqués do not have legal status as G8 decisions *per se*. Without separate will the G8 has

---

[1] I. Claude, 'The Security Council', in E. Luard (ed), *The Evolution of International Organizations* (London: Thames and Hudson, 1966) 68 at 88.

[2] SC Res. 1373, 28 Sept. 2001.

[3] G. Perry, 'Security Council Resolution 242: The Withdrawal Clause' (1977) 31 Middle East Journal 413.

[4] F. Berman, 'The Authorization Model: Resolution 678 and Its Effects', in D.M. Malone (ed), *The UN Security Council: From the Cold War to the 21st Century* (London: Lynne Rienner, 2004) 153 at 158.

[5] Claude, 'The Security Council', 83.

no law-making power. Regular G8 meetings indicate its separate existence, but states have not transferred any of their will to the G8, or given it the elements that would enable it to develop a will of its own. Thus 'for an international entity to be regarded as existing separately from its Member States, the entity must have a decision making organ that is able to produce a "corporate" will, as opposed to a mere "aggregate" of the wills of the Member States'.[6] Nevertheless, the impact of certain fora lacking formal personality should not be underestimated. As Niels Blokker notes 'G8 consensus was crucial in the spring of 1999 to 'solve' the Kosovo crisis'.[7]

Contrast the output of the G8 with a decision of the Security Council adopted in accordance with its voting rules.[8] Such a decision is a reflection of the will of the Security Council not the combined view or even combined wills of the members of that body. The separate personality of the UN, recognized as early as 1949 by the International Court,[9] establishes the autonomy of the organization as a whole, though in the case of the Security Council there is a concentration of will, enabling it, for example, to take mandatory decisions imposing non-military measures binding on the whole membership,[10] a power it has utilized significantly since the end of the Cold War. As well as powers expressly granted by the UN Charter, there are those said to be granted implicitly, although the reality is that they have been developed in practice, and often with controversy, by the Council itself. The competence to legislate to create international criminal tribunals for Rwanda and the former Yugoslavia in the 1990s or to legislate to combat terrorism as it has done after 9/11, for instance, can hardly be said to have been the intention of the founding states, in reality they are a creation of the Security Council itself, a product of its separate will.

That the Council has significant separate will was evident in 1945. Indeed, what occurred then was a collective action of states imbuing the Security Council with unique powers that individual states did not possess thereafter. Even if states had a collective police power before 1945, at that point they embodied it for better or for worse (though the intention was to improve the ambiguous and selective nature of collective interventions) in the Security Council.[11] It would be accurate to state that the parameters, even existence, of such a collective power before the advent of the UN Charter was legally highly doubtful. It was by establishing the UN that the vast majority of states decided to create

---

[6] R.A. Wessel, 'Revisiting the International Legal Status of the EU' (2000) 5 EFAR 507 at 517.
[7] N.M. Blokker, 'Proliferation of International Organizations: An Exploratory Introduction', in N.M. Blokker and H.G. Schermers (eds), *Proliferation of International Organizations: Legal Issues* (The Hague: Kluwer, 2001) 1 at 6.
[8] Art 27 of the UN Charter.
[9] *Reparation for Injuries Suffered in the Service of the United Nations* 1949 ICJ Rep. 174 at 179.
[10] Arts 25 and 41 of the UN Charter.
[11] I. Brownlie, *International Law and the Use of Force by States* (Oxford: Oxford University Press, 1963) 332–3; D. Sarooshi, *The United Nations and the Development of Collective Security* (Oxford: Oxford University Press, 1999) 26–32.

a body with novel competence. Thus the adoption of the UN Charter in 1945 was a defining moment, not in the sense of codifying an already existing legal regime, though one was arguably emerging during the course of the Second World War with the idea of the United Nations,[12] but in the sense of creating a new world order with the Charter assuming the position as the foundational constitutional document. Thereafter the UN possessed powers which states did not, and arguably never did, possess. The decision to impose economic sanctions or authorize military action to deal with threats to the peace as well as acts of aggression belongs to the Security Council, though subsidiary responsibility arguably falls to the General Assembly. Even some modern-day advocates of anticipatory self-defence accept that while the Security Council can take action against threats that are not imminent, states cannot, thus recognizing the uniqueness of the Council.[13]

Once the Cold War ended and the Security Council started taking copious amounts of action expressing its 'corporate will' there was potentially more danger to the UN Charter scheme than when the Council was deadlocked. Powerful states have realized the potential of the Security Council given the huge range of its powers and the limited forms of accountability for their exercise. In general terms of legality and legitimacy Security Council approval is the key powerful states seek to unlock coercive non-defensive action. All those doubts that remain about whether a state can undertake humanitarian intervention, or anticipatory action, are swept away if the Security Council authorizes it as a response to a threat to the peace. Whatever the weaknesses of the Council, recent conflicts in Kosovo and Iraq, even Afghanistan, show the unique authority of that organ in collective security matters, as the states using force attempted to justify their actions as coming under Security Council resolutions. If powerful states manage to persuade the Council to adopt resolutions tackling threats to or breaches of the peace within the meaning and purposes of the Charter as developed by practice then the international community generally accepts the legitimacy of such actions and will support the Council. Witness the support for the coalition in the Gulf Conflict of 1991.[14]

But the Security Council is a political body; this is not only reflected in its chequered history in the realm of collective security, but also by its make-up and the wide discretion given to it in the UN Charter. In such a body it is inevitable that a member or group of members wanting it to act in a certain way must persuade the remaining members to its way of thinking. While the United States with British support won the argument in the case of Resolution 678 which

---

[12] See 'Declaration by the United Nations', 1 Jan. 1942. For text see R.B. Russell and J.M. Muther, *A History of the United Nations Charter* (Washington: Brookings, 1958) appendix C.

[13] C. Greenwood, 'International Law and the Pre-Emptive Use of Force: Afghanistan, Al-Qaida, and Iraq' (2003) 4 San Diego Intl L J 7 at 36.

[14] P. -M. Dupuy, 'The Constitutional Dimension of the Charter of the United Nations Revisited' (1997) 1 MPYBUNL 20.

authorized necessary measures against Iraq in 1991, they lost it as regards gaining Security Council authority to invade Iraq in March 2003.

3. The Security Council and the Invasion of Iraq

Consensus amongst the five permanent members (P5) is clearly crucial for the effectiveness of the Council. Each with a veto power, a permanent member can block a decision of the Council by casting a negative vote. But also each permanent member will look to the Council to endorse a course of action it wants legalized and legitimated. Britain and the US will often combine, sometimes with France, to push for a decision, while Russia and China are cast as the sceptics that have to be convinced by dint of diplomacy and persuasion. While the US and the UK (and to a lesser extent France) are liberal interventionists, Russia and China are seen as non-interventionists, though the reality is these are only positions taken when it protects each state's own interests. So, for example, Russia is prepared to intervene in its own backyard (shown recently by its intervention in Georgia in September 2008), just as the United States historically has.

But powerful states do not always get what they want from the Council. In such conditions there has been a trend towards powerful states interpreting previously adopted Council decisions in ways that breach the understanding underlying the resolution. In these cases other member states while not necessarily accepting the interpretations given to the decision will view the Council warily since it appears that action is being taken in its name. This must affect the authority of the Council. If it appears that resolutions can be pulled this way and that, or can be resurrected after a number of years, or can be enforced even though there is no provision in them for coercion, then the wider UN membership will rightly view resolutions with a great deal of scepticism. If such a trend continues then member states will no longer respect the authority of the Council. Its unique position in the international system as the primary body for collective security will be undermined. The point is that it is not the effectiveness or not of the Security Council that calls into question the Charter scheme, but the authority the Council has when it takes action and the effect on its authority when action is taken under its name. If it takes action that the majority do not accept as clearly within its powers then its authority is diminished; and if action is being taken under its name that the majority do not accept as legitimate then its authority is being abused and diminished. The latter in particular threatens the Charter scheme for collective security as it has led to states threatening or using force in the name of the UN, thus eroding the prohibition on the threat and the use of force.

However, the Iraq crisis of 2003 does seem to suggest that the majority of the Council and member states are not prepared to acquiesce in unilateral interpretations of Council resolutions. In one sense the failure of the Security Council in its diplomatic function to solve the Iraq crisis in early 2003 did not undermine the authority of the Security Council. This was because the Council had agreed on the executive action to be taken in the shape of a lengthier inspection process, and it was the American and British rupture of this consensus that was not accepted by the membership. The Americans and British pointed to Security Council decisions that could sustain a legal case for the use of force, but their cleverly constructed legal arguments did not hold sway for they ignored the clear political and legal consensus in the Council and in the wider membership. Bearing in mind that the Security Council acts on behalf of the whole membership in collective security matters,[15] in effect the US and the UK were ignoring the will of the UN.

In a legal sense the invasion of Iraq in 2003 was the culmination of a decade of pressure and bullying tactics by the US and the UK directed at changing the legal framework governing the use of force contained in the UN Charter in a concerted effort to widen both exceptions to the ban on the threat or use of force in article 2(4), namely the right of self-defence contained in article 51, and military action taken under the authority of the Security Council derived from article 42. After the adoption of Resolution 1441 on 8 November 2002, the US and the UK brought the above mentioned pressures to bear by making claims that the resolution was sufficient when read alongside earlier resolutions stretching back to 1990 to justify the use of force against Iraq even though it did not contain clear authorizing language. Furthermore, the US claimed that even if the resolution did not authorize force, and in the absence of a further clearer resolution, it still had the right to use force in self-defence against the threat posed by Iraq. According to these views the use of force against Iraq was justified under either or both exceptions to the ban on the use of force, despite the fact that Resolution 1441 did not authorize measures necessary against Iraq (the accepted mode of delegation under article 42) and the fact there had been no armed attack against the US by Iraq within the meaning of article 51.

The desire to bring actions under the authority of the UN reflects an acceptance of this as a mechanism for lawfully using force, but it also inevitably results in spurious claims by some states to be acting under UN authority. It is also telling that despite the invocation of the Bush Doctrine of pre-emptive self-defence in September 2002,[16] the US was persuaded at least temporarily not to invade Iraq on the basis of a claim to self-defence but on the basis of a Security Council resolution. The negotiation of Resolution 1441 took many weeks, and even then the result was not a clear authorization to use force. Nevertheless, the fact that the United States in the build-up to conflict was prepared to proceed on the basis of a not completely satisfactory resolution was telling. It showed doubts about the

---

[15] Art 24(1) of the UN Charter.
[16] 'The National Security Strategy of the United States of America', September 2002, available at <http://www.whitehouse.gov/nsc/nss.pdf> (accessed 26 Jan. 2009).

Bush Doctrine's claim to the existence of a wide right of pre-emptive defence. The pressure put on the US by the UK, its chief ally, to go to the Security Council is reflective of the lack of belief in pre-emptive self-defence within the UK government as well.

Despite the lack of clear authority in Resolution 1441 the UK in particular subsequently interpreted it to justify the use of force against Iraq. Wide interpretations of Security Council resolutions may be acceptable if the interpretation reflects the views of the Security Council as a body. In the context of an organ such as the Security Council the 'interpretive task is to ascertain what the text means to the parties collectively rather than to each individually'.[17] Subsequent practice can be relied on to re-interpret a resolution when it reflects a shared understanding.[18] Such practice has to be checked against the limitations contained in the Charter and must be undertaken in fulfilment of the purposes of the UN.[19] Subject to these limitations, if the Council members agree that a resolution's wording amounts to an authority to use force then that is what it means. If they disagree and some view it as granting such authority while others do not, this does not signify that it grants authority, at least in attributing meaning to the Security Council as a whole.

Interpreting a resolution of a body like the Security Council requires careful consideration of the text and the discussions that led up to it.[20] To interpret the words of a resolution in a way that is directly contrary to the consensus (which may be an agreement to disagree) underlying the resolution would undermine the Council as a forum for achieving compromise. Military action undertaken with Security Council authority is only permitted when there is agreement in accordance with the voting rules that such action is being authorized. Agreement to the effect that the Council is authorizing the use of force has been achieved in the past by a formula that combines the phrase 'necessary measures' with an 'authorization' to use them.[21] However, there is no need to stick to this formula if all the members especially the P5 agree that a threat of 'serious consequences' in the face of a 'material breach' as found in Resolution 1441 signifies the authorization of necessary measures or the use of force. But clearly there was no such

---

[17] See I. Johnstone, 'Treaty Interpretation: The Authority of Interpretative Communities' (1991) 12 Michigan J Intl L at 381.

[18] S. Rosenne, *Developments in the Law of Treaties* (Cambridge: Cambridge University Press, 1989) 244.

[19] *Certain Expenses of the United Nations* 1962 ICJ Rep. 151, 167–8.

[20] *Legal Consequences for States of the Continued Presence of South Africa in Namibia (South West Africa) Notwithstanding Security Council Resolution 276 (1970)* 1971 ICJ Rep. 16 at 53. See further M.C. Wood, 'The Interpretation of Security Council Resolutions' (1998) 2 MPYBUNL 73 at 74–5, 79, 95.

[21] See generally N.M. Blokker, 'Is the Authorization Authorized? Powers and Practice of the UN Security Council to Authorize the Use of Force by "Coalitions of the Able and Willing"' (2000) 11 EJIL 541–68.

consensus.[22] As Johnstone correctly observes '[i]n any communicative enterprise, the participants tend to operate according to a set of conventions, practices and shared understandings'.[23] The shared understanding of 1441 was that it did not amount to an authority to use force against Iraq.

John Negroponte, the US representative at the crucial meeting when Resolution 1441 was adopted, clearly accepted that the resolution did not contain any 'hidden triggers' and no 'automaticity' with 'respect to the use of force'. He added that 'further Iraqi breach, reported to the Security Council by UNMOVIC, the IAEA, or Member State' will lead to the matter returning to the Council. This shows an acceptance of the interpretation of the Resolution shared by virtually all the other members of the Council. The UK representative, Sir Jeremy Greenstock, made a statement on this point that was virtually the same as his American counterpart, except that he concluded that when the matter was returned to the Council, 'we would expect the Council to then meet its responsibilities'. Other members spoke about the lack of the automatic right to use force in the resolution (Mexico, Russia, Bulgaria, Syria, Cameroon, China), labelled the 'two stage approach' by the French representative; and the clear assurances about the lack of basis in the resolution for the use of force (Ireland, Columbia); while Norway referred to the Council's responsibility recognized in the resolution to secure international peace. Singapore, Guinea and Mauritius made statements that cannot be said to favour one interpretation over another. The sense of the meeting is best summed up by the representative of Ireland, Richard Ryan, when he thanked the sponsors of the Resolution (the US and UK) for their assurances that the purpose of the 'resolution was to achieve disarmament through inspections, and not to establish the basis for the use of force'.

Thus the resolution did not authorize the use of force. This is made clear by the US representative, John Negroponte, when he stated 'if the Security Council fails to act decisively in the event of further Iraqi violations, this resolution does not constrain any Member State from acting to defend itself against the threat posed by Iraq or to enforce relevant United Nations resolutions to protect world peace and security'. By this statement the US is making it clear that despite the lack of authority in the Resolution itself, the United States claims the right to defend itself against threats as outlined in the Bush Doctrine, as well as the right to enforce UN resolutions. The latter seems superfluous but follows from practice in Kosovo and against Iraq where the American argument has not been so much as to interpret the relevant Security Council resolutions as authorizing the use of force, but more the claim to be able to enforce Security Council resolutions that have been breached.

---

[22] C. Gray, 'From Unity to Polarization: International Law and the Use of Force Against Iraq' (2002) 13 EJIL 1 at 9.

[23] I. Johnstone, 'Security Council Deliberations: The Power of Better Argument' (2003) 14 EJIL 437 at 456.

The consensus at the meeting at which Resolution 1441 was adopted was that it did not authorize the use of force if Iraq was in material breach of its disarmament provisions. Indeed, the US and the UK assured the other members in the meeting that no 'automaticity' or 'hidden triggers' were contained in the resolution,[24] but then outside the meeting repeatedly stated that there was no legal need for another resolution on the basis that Resolution 1441 was sufficient by itself. Prime Minister Tony Blair warned Saddam, 'defy the UN's will and we will disarm you by force. Be in no doubt whatever about that', while President George Bush declared that the 'outcome of this crisis is already determined. The full disarmament of weapons of mass destruction will occur. The only question for the Iraqi regime is to decide how. His cooperation must be unconditional or he will face the severest consequences'.[25]

Clearly the US and the UK were speaking to different audiences in making these contradictory statements. Subsequently though both the US and the UK consistently engaged in unilateral interpretations of 1441 as permitting them to use force against Iraq. This is based on the fact that the Resolution not only invoked the concept of 'material breach' at several points but also stated that Iraq failed to take the final opportunity to comply with its disarmament obligations granted in the resolution, and thus must face the 'serious consequences' warned of. This argument built on the previous justifications put forward by the US and the UK for using force against Iraq to enforce its disarmament obligations since 1991 (for example in January 1993 and December 1998). Indeed, they could argue that the adoption of Resolution 1441 signified that the Security Council endorsed their position that 'material breach' of the disarmament provisions of Security Council Resolutions, from 687 of 3 April 1991 to 1441 of 2002,[26] suspends the operation of the cease-fire Resolution 687, thus allowing states to use force under the open-ended provisions of Resolution 678 of 29 November 1990. However, it is clear from the debates preceding the adoption of Resolution 1441 that it was not the intention of the Council to endorse that argument, and that any response to a material breach of the Resolution would come from the Security Council not individual member states, in other words that the 'serious consequences' were to be determined by the Council. Apparently the final version of Resolution 1441 left out the words of the original US and UK draft authorizing member states 'to use all necessary means to restore international peace and security in the area', reinforcing the underlying consensus in the Council against force.[27]

Further it is also clear from the meeting at which 1441 was adopted as well as the history of Security Council diplomacy that a combination of 'material breach' and 'serious consequences' in the resolution is not understood by the

---

[24] SC 4644th mtg, 8 Nov. 2002.   [25] *The Independent*, 9 Nov. 2002, 1 and 5.
[26] See for example prior to the 1998 airstrikes: *The Times*, 19 Feb. 1998.
[27] See N. Grief, 'The Iraq Hearing' <http://bbc.co.uk/radio4/today/reports/archive/international/iraq_hearing.shtml> (accessed 12 Feb. 2009).

Security Council to include the use of armed force,[28] though that may be the subsequent interpretation put on the phrase by the US and UK. 'Serious consequences' and 'material breach' were clearly put in the resolution by the US and the UK to enable them to make these arguments as was the recollection of previous resolutions including Resolution 678, but the non-acceptance of this position by the rest of the Council signified that the use of force had not been authorized by the Security Council as a reflection of its will. In reality, in the absence of a further mandating resolution, the US and UK relied on a combination of alleged Security Council authority and the Bush Doctrine of pre-emptive self-defence as justifications to use force against Iraq. It is true that Resolution 1441 came closer to the US and UK position than previous resolutions dealing with Iraqi breach of Resolution 687,[29] but it did not meet the agreed requirements that for states to take military action under the auspices of chapter VII there must be a clear and unambiguous mandate in the form of an authorization to use force.[30] All other arguments—unilateral interpretations and claims to a right of enforcement—fall short, for the simple fact is that if the Council wants to authorize the use of force it will do so using clearly accepted language. It has not done so in the case of Iraq since the end of the conflict in 1991.[31]

While maintaining the position subsequently adopted outside the Council that force was legally justified against Iraq without a further Council resolution, in January and February 2003 the UK in particular moved towards the position that a further resolution was politically desirable, though an 'unreasonable veto' (by France, Russia, or China) in the Prime Minister's words would not deter the UK from using force.[32] Even then, the resolution being mooted in early February by the UK still did not envisage a clear authorization to use force, because in the absence of evidence of Iraqi armaments this was thought by the UK to be unachievable though it contained a further determination of a 'material breach'. British officials insisted that this would constitute authority to use force.[33] The contradiction in this argument is manifest, unless the members of the Security Council indicated that they had changed their minds and that such language did indeed signify authorization to use force.

There was unconvincing evidence of WMD in Iraq in the period leading up to the invasion, apparent from the critical but not damning reports from the Heads of the UN Monitoring, Verification and Inspection Commission

---

[28] But see F.L. Kirgis, 'Security Council Resolution 1441 on Iraq's Final Opportunity to Comply with Disarmament Obligations' (Nov. 2002) ASIL Insights.

[29] See for example SC Res. 1154, 2 Mar. 1998; 1194, 9 Sept. 1998; 1205, 5 Nov. 1998.

[30] J. Lobel and M. Ratner, 'Bypassing the Security Council: Ambiguous Authorization to Use Force, Cease-Fires and the Iraqi Inspection Regime' (1999) 93 AJIL 124.

[31] T.M. Franck, 'What Happens Now? The United Nations after Iraq' (2003) 97 AJIL 607 at 610–14.

[32] A. Grice, 'Defiant Blair says UN has no veto on war', *The Independent*, 14 Jan. 2003, 1.

[33] D. Usborne, J. Lichfiled, P. Waugh and A. Penketh, 'Tony Blair, A Man with his Hands Full', *The Independent*, 8 Feb. 2003, 1.

(UNMOVIC) (Dr Hans Blix) and the IAEA (Dr Mohamed ElBaradei) of 27 January, 14 February,[34] 28 February, and 7 March 2003.[35] In his report to the Security Council of 27 January, Dr Blix concluded that there were serious gaps in knowledge about Iraq's chemical and bacteriological weapons programmes, and that Iraq was not fully cooperating with the inspectors. He noted that UNMOVIC's capability had increased over a short period of time, inferring that more time was needed. Dr ElBaradei concluded by saying that 'we have to date found no evidence that Iraq has revived its nuclear weapons programme since the elimination of the programme in 1990', but that a more definite conclusion could be provided in the next few months if the inspection process had been allowed to continue.[36] In his report of 28 February Dr Blix was critical of Iraq, stating that it should show greater credible evidence of disarmament. On 28 February, Iraq started destroying missiles that exceeded the 150 km permitted range. UNMOVIC's Chairman Dr Blix stated this was a 'very significant piece of real disarmament'.[37] Before the Security Council Dr Blix made it clear that he thought the disarmament process was working by famously describing the destruction of missiles: 'we are not watching the breaking of toothpicks. Lethal weapons are being destroyed'. In addition, the evidence presented by US Secretary of State, Colin Powell, to the Security Council on 5 February was limited and failed to persuade most members of the Council to change their view that the use of force was not yet justified. On 14 February, Colin Powell declared that it was not UNMOVIC's job to produce evidence of Iraqi breach rather it was the responsibility of Iraq to disarm, which it clearly had not done. According to the US this was a further 'material breach' and a failure by Iraq to take the final opportunity afforded to them in Resolution 1441 and should have led to the 'serious consequences' called for in that Resolution.[38]

The UK made it clear that it would support the US military action even without a further resolution. On 17 February, the UK Foreign Secretary, Jack Straw, stated that 'in terms of mandate resolution 1441 gives us the authority we need, but in terms of political desirability we have always said that we would prefer a second resolution'.[39] Further, on 21 February he stated that 'diplomatic parlance is notoriously ambiguous, but in this case the terminology had one meaning: disarmament by force'.[40]

On 24 February the US and the UK introduced a draft second resolution into the Council, though they made it clear that it was for discussion and would not be voted on until after further reports from the weapons inspectors.

---

[34] SC 4708th mtg, 14 Feb. 2003.   [35] SC 4714th mtg, 7 March 2003.

[36] SC 4692nd mtg, 27 Jan. 2003, 8, 12.

[37] UN Doc. S/2003/232; *UN News Centre*, 28 Feb. 2003.

[38] SC 4708th mtg, 14 Feb. 2003, 21.

[39] S. Castle, 'France set to block second UN resolution against Iraq', *The Independent*, 18 Feb. 2003, 1.

[40] *The Independent*, 22 Feb. 2003, 4.

Legally it seemed to add little to 1441. There was no explicit authorization to use necessary measures. After invoking chapter VII, the initial draft had one operative paragraph where it 'decides that Iraq has failed to take the final opportunity afforded to it in Resolution 1441'. The preamble recalled 1441's reference to 'material breach' and its warning of 'serious consequences'. In effect it found that Iraq had breached that Resolution by 'noting that Iraq has submitted a declaration...containing false statements and omissions and has failed to comply with, and to cooperate fully in the implementation of' Resolution 1441.[41] In last ditch attempts to make this draft acceptable and thus to avoid the threatened vetoes of Russia and France as well as other probable negative votes, the UK amended the draft to provide for a further short deadline for Iraqi compliance of 17 March, and finally to list the various actions Iraq must undertake to demonstrate compliance.[42] This did not persuade Russia and France who insisted that the inspection process was working and should therefore be given several months to work through.[43] Furthermore, they were probably concerned that the second resolution had become of such symbolic significance for world opinion that its adoption would be seen as giving a green light for war despite the fact that it was not viewed as so doing by the Council as a whole. More importantly for the US and the UK a second resolution would have served domestic purposes particularly in the UK where the public was much more willing to support the use of force if a second resolution could have been adopted.

The failed efforts to obtain a second iconic resolution in the Council meant that when full-scale conflict was engaged in Iraq on 20 March, American rhetoric had moved towards claiming that the legal basis was self-defence, by reiterating its reliance on pre-emptive action. When debates were going against the draft on 7 March 2003 President Bush stated that 'we don't really need the United Nations' approval to act...When it comes to our security, we do not need anyone's permission'.[44] Further, on 18 March he outlined the nature of the threat. 'The danger is clear. Using chemical, biological or, one day, nuclear weapons obtained with the help of Iraq, the terrorists could fulfil their stated ambitions and kill thousands or hundreds of thousands of innocent people in our country or any other'.[45]

However, in its letter to the Council reporting its initiation of hostilities against Iraq, the US relied on Security Council resolutions.[46] The UK preferred to argue solely on the basis that the war was legally justified on the basis of existing Security Council resolutions. In a parliamentary written answer on 17 March 2003, the

---

[41] <http://news.bbc.co.uk/1/hi/world/europe/2795747.stm> (accessed 12 Feb. 2009).
[42] UN Doc. S/2003/215, 7 March 2003.
[43] See D. Usborne, 'On the Brink of War', *The Independent*, 8 March 2003, 1.
[44] R. Cornwell, 'The Quiet Man', *The Independent,* 8 March 2003, 3.
[45] <http://news.bbc.co.uk/1/hi/world/middle_east/2858965.stm> (accessed 26 Jan. 2009).
[46] UN Doc. S/2003/351, 21 March 2003. See further W.H. Taft and T.F. Buchwald, 'Pre-emption, Iraq and International Law' (2003) 97 AJIL 557.

Attorney General Lord Goldsmith stated that the basis for force was Resolution 678 of 1990 containing the original authority to use force, which was reactivated in the light of material breach of Resolution 687 of 1991 and all subsequent disarmament resolutions up to and including Resolution 1441. He concluded that 'all that resolution 1441 requires is reporting to and discussion by the Security Council of Iraq's failures, but not an express further decision to authorise force',[47] since there was original authority in 678. The weakness of this argument has been demonstrated by the fact that it had not been accepted by other members of the Council shown above, but also by the fact that the authority of Resolution 678 of 1990 does not extend beyond Resolution 687 of 1991, which declared in its final paragraph that the Council decided to 'remain seized of the matter and to take such further steps as may be required for the implementation of this resolution and to secure peace and security to the area'. The delegation of power to take military action that occurred in Resolution 678 was effectively revoked by Resolution 687, including the authority in 678 to restore 'international peace and security to the area'.[48] For the Attorney General to state that 'material breach of resolution 687 revives the authority to use force under resolution 678', which is the crucial step in his reasoning back to 678, has no basis in those resolutions and thus no basis in law. Ultimately, it represented an unconvincing attempt to unlock Resolution 678, which was the only resolution in which the Council authorized 'necessary measures' against Iraq.

It is interesting to see that in the year after the invasion of Iraq, with the occupation by the US and the UK continuing, attention was turned in both the US and the UK to the issue of whether there was convincing evidence prior to the invasion that Iraq posed a sufficient threat to those countries. The main issue in the UK was the suspect evidence presented to parliament at various points, by Prime Minister Blair in particular, before the outbreak of hostilities on 20 March 2003 to the effect that Iraq could deploy WMD under an hour of the order being given.[49] Though the political discourse in these countries seemed to be turning to debate self-defence, it must be remembered that the arguments that the US and the UK were enforcing/applying Council resolutions on disarmament in the end relied on WMD being found in Iraq. Hence the issue of whether Iraq had WMD at the time of the conflict was germane to both the self-defence argument (where their presence can be evaluated in terms of the threat posed by them), and to the enforcement/application of Council resolutions (where their presence would be a violation of those resolutions). The Iraq Survey Group sent by the US into Iraq after the overthrow of Saddam to find evidence of WMD failed to find any in its report of 30 September 2004. After it became clear in 2004 that Iraq had no WMD, Tony Blair was adamant

---

[47] <http://news.bbc.co.uk/1/hi/uk_politics/2857347.stm> (accessed 26 Jan. 2009). Also found in (2003) 52 ICLQ 819.
[48] SC Res. 678, 29 Nov. 1990.
[49] A. McSmith, 'The 45-minute case collapses', *The Independent*, 8 Feb. 2004, 1.

that the war was still justified, saying in a speech that 'everyone thought he [Saddam] had them. That was the basis of Resolution 1441'.[50] But as has been seen Resolution 1441 did not provide a basis for the war; in fact it provided the basis for an enhanced inspections regime that was meant to find out if Saddam had continued to breach Security Council resolutions on WMD.

The critical reaction of many states and other actors to the decision of the US and the UK to use force without Security Council authority is of course significant in evaluating the legality of that action, as well as the legitimacy of their interpretations of Security Council resolutions. On 10 March, before the outbreak of war, the Secretary General, Kofi Annan, was clearly of the opinion that it would be unlawful when he warned that 'if the US and others were to go outside the Council and take military action it would not be in conformity with the Charter'.[51] Criticisms of the impending war and warnings of illegality were voiced by the majority of members of the Council when meeting on the eve of the war.[52] After full scale force was unleashed by the US and UK on 20 March 2003, there were immediate statements condemning it as a violation of international law by China, Russia, France, Iran, Pakistan, India, Indonesia, and Malaysia, while support was given by Australia, the Philippines, Japan, and South Korea.[53]

The Security Council debates on Iraq and the reactions of states to the unauthorized use of force of 20 March 2003 show that to argue that a new purposive interpretative rule has been accepted that allows individual states to unilaterally interpret and enforce Security Council Resolutions and even the UN Charter, does not reflect the consensus of the international community.[54] The fact that the same minority of states that seek to justify the above interventions argue for the emergence of a new rule of interpretation is sufficient to show that such arguments are self-serving and are not accepted by the majority of states. In reality a Security Council resolution is not to be pulled this way and that over many years, it is a document of an executive body charged with taking action within its competence to fulfil the purposes of the UN Charter. As a piece of subsequent practice adopted under the auspices of a treaty, each resolution exists primarily as a reflection of the will of the Security Council.[55]

---

[50] (2004) UKMIL Part Sixteen.II. B.I item 16/14.

[51] UN News Service, 10 March 2003 available at <http://www.un.org/apps/news/story. asp?NewsID=6399&Cr=iraq&Cr1=inspect&Kw1=Secretary&Kw2=General&Kw3=> (accessed 12 Feb. 2009).

[52] SC 4721st mtg, 19 March 2003. Statements by Germany, France, Russia, Syria, Pakistan, Mexico, Chile, Angola, China. See also open meeting of the Security Council SC 4717th mtg, 12 March 2003, when fifty-one states spoke.

[53] <http://news.bbc.co.uk/1/hi/world/middle_east/2867027.stm> (accessed 26 Jan. 2009). Thirty-four countries contributed militarily to the 1991 campaign, while four countries contributed to the 2003 campaign (US—200,000; UK—45,000; Australia—200; Poland—200).

[54] But see M. Byers, 'The Shifting Foundations of International Law: A Decade of Forceful Measures against Iraq' (2002) 13 EJIL 21 at 27.

[55] Wood, 'Interpretation', at 77, 95. See also H. Thirlway, 'The Law and Procedure of the International Court of Justice' (1996) 67 BYBIL 29.

4. Political Debate over the Legality of the Invasion

In the British government's intelligence dossier of September 2002 on Iraq's weapons of mass destruction the case for war is made.[56] In the introduction to the document, the Prime Minister, Tony Blair, explained that the report was the work of the Joint Intelligence Committee (JIC), which is the 'heart of the British intelligence machinery' made up of the heads of the UK's intelligence agencies (MI5, MI6 and Government Communications Headquarters (GCHQ)), the Chief of Defence Intelligence, and senior officials from key Government departments. 'For over 60 years the JIC has provided regular assessments to successive Prime Ministers and senior colleagues on a wide range of foreign policy and international security issues'. The Prime Minister then explained why the report had been made public:

[The JIC's] work, like the material it analyses, is largely secret. It is unprecedented for the Government to publish this kind of document. But in the light of the debate on Weapons of Mass Destruction (WMD), I wanted to share with the British public the reasons why I believe this issue to be a current and serious threat to the UK national interest.

The Prime Minister also took the opportunity in introducing the document to set the context and provide his view of the evidence.

In recent months, I have become increasingly alarmed by the evidence from inside Iraq that despite sanctions, despite the damage done to his capability in the past, despite the UN Security Council Resolutions expressly outlawing it, and despite his denials, Saddam Hussein is continuing to develop WMD, and with them the ability to inflict real damage upon the region, and the stability of the world.

What I believe the assessed intelligence has established beyond doubt is that Saddam has continued to produce chemical and biological weapons, and he continues in his efforts to develop nuclear weapons, and that he has been able to extend the range of his ballistic missile programme. I also believe that, as stated in the document, Saddam will do his utmost to try to conceal his weapons from UN inspectors.

I am in no doubt that the threat is serious and current, that he has made progress on WMD, and that he has to be stopped.

Saddam has used chemical weapons, not only against an enemy state, but against his own people. Intelligence reports make clear that he sees the building up of his WMD capability, and the belief overseas that he would use these weapons, as vital to his strategic interests, and in particular his goal of regional domination. And the document discloses that his military planning allows for some of the WMD to be ready within 45 minutes of an order to use them.[57]

The report largely supports the Prime Minister's assertions, though on the 45 minute deployment issue the executive summary states that Iraq has 'military

---

[56] *Iraq's Weapons of Mass Destruction: The Assessment of the British Government* (HMSO, 24 Sept. 2002).
[57] Ibid., 2–4.

plans for the use of chemical and biological weapons, including against its Shia population. Some of the weapons are deployable within 45 minutes of an order to use them',[58] which suggests a limited range for these weapons. However, in the bulk of the report the JIC states in successive bullet points that 'Iraq possesses extended-range versions of the SCUD ballistic missile in breach of UNSCR 687 which are capable of reaching Cyprus, Eastern Turkey, Tehran and Israel'; then that Iraq's military planning specifically foresees the use of chemical and biological weapons; and then that Iraq's military forces 'are able to use chemical and biological weapons, with command, control and logistical arrangements in place. The Iraqi military are able to deploy these weapons within 45 minutes of a decision to do so'.[59] This tends to suggest that these weapons were deliverable by missile to other countries including UK bases in Cyprus. As well as judging that the intelligence revealed that Iraq had 'continued to produce chemical and biological weapons' and had 'military plans for the use of chemical and biological weapons' (some of which were deployable within 45 minutes of an order to use them); the dossier stated that the Iraqi regime had 'tried covertly to acquire technology and materials which could be used in the production of nuclear weapons' (including seeking 'significant quantities of uranium from Africa').[60]

The Prime Minister introduced the dossier to the House of Commons on the day of its publication, 24 September 2002. Tony Blair explained to the House why Saddam had not let the weapons inspectors back in since 1998, when they were withdrawn prior to an Anglo-American air and missile strike on Iraq:

The dossier that we publish gives the answer. The reason is that his chemical, biological and nuclear programme is not a historic left over from 1998. The inspectors are not needed to clean up the old remains. His weapons of mass destruction programme is active, detailed and growing. The policy of containment is not working. The weapons of mass destruction programme is not shut down; it is up and running now.[61]

The intelligence, he stated, 'is extensive, detailed and authoritative'. 'It concludes that Iraq has chemical and biological weapons, that Saddam has continued to produce them, that he has existing and active military plans for the use of chemical and biological weapons, which could be activated within 45 minutes, including against his own Shia population, and that he is actively trying to acquire nuclear weapons capability'.[62] This justified, according to the Prime Minister, the use of force if necessary; 'not that we take military action come what may, but that the case for ensuring Iraqi disarmament, as the UN itself has stipulated, is overwhelming'.[63] His speech also revealed that the British government had gone far beyond just anticipating the return of inspectors to Iraq:

We have no quarrel with the Iraqi people. Indeed, liberated from Saddam, they could make Iraq prosperous and a force for good in the middle east. So the ending of this

---

[58] Ibid., 5.   [59] Ibid., 17.   [60] Ibid., 5–6.
[61] *Hansard* HC vol 390, col 3, 24 Sept. 2002.   [62] Ibid.
[63] Ibid., col 5.

regime would be the cause of regret for no one other than Saddam. But our purpose is disarmament. No one wants military force…Disarmament of all weapons of mass destruction is the demand. One way or another it must be acceded to.[64]

The opposition leader, Iain Duncan Smith, agreed with the evidence presented and the conclusions drawn saying 'the only question remaining is whether Saddam has the motive to strike against Britain, and I believe that it is fair to assume that he has', given Britain's military actions against it in the past. He also reminded the House that 'there are more than 3,000 British service men and women in Cyprus, 200 in Turkey, 300 in Saudi Arabia and 400 in Kuwait, all of whom are in range of the missiles that Saddam possesses today', those missiles being capable of 'carrying the various warheads that he needs'.[65] Criticism did come from the leader of the Liberal Democrats, Charles Kennedy, who demanded an opportunity for the 'House to vote on any proposal involving the possible use of British forces', warned against any unilateral approach, and the idea of regime change in Iraq 'if Saddam's regime falls, what kind of government system is envisaged as a replacement?'.[66] When pushed further about whether the UK would take unilateral action with the United States, the Prime Minister did not answer in clear terms, but spoke of action being taken in the 'event of the UN's will not being complied with', and further 'if we cannot get the UN resolution—I believe that we can—we have to find a way of dealing with this'.[67]

This discussion led to Tam Dalyell, Labour MP for Linlithgow, proposing that a motion be adopted 'that this House declines to support a war against Iraq using the royal prerogative unless it has been authorised by both the United Nations Security Council and a motion carried by this House'.[68] Jack Straw, the Foreign Secretary, deflected such criticisms by telling the House that a new resolution, 'setting out the case for a tough and intrusive weapons inspection regime' was being discussed by the P5 in New York.[69] Criticism still followed, for example from Alan Simpson, Labour MP for Nottingham South, who stated that 'if the world is being asked to move away from a doctrine of containment and deterrence and towards a doctrine of pre-emptive strikes, regime change, attacks and displacements of potential enemies or unsympathetic regimes, the implications for the planet are enormous'.[70]

In a House of Commons debate in October 2002 Glenda Jackson Labour MP for Hampstead and Highgate asked of the Defence Minister 'on the issue of a strike against Saddam Hussein, it would seem that the international community has reduced to two sovereign states, namely the United Kingdom and the

---

[64] Ibid., col 6.   [65] Ibid., col 8.   [66] Ibid., col 11.
[67] Ibid., cols 15, 20.
[68] Ibid., col 24. See also the questions raised in vol 391, col 683, 29 Oct. 2002 (Dalyell), where he made the point that President Bush had obtained authority to use force against Iraq from Congress, while the British government had not done so. See further vol 397, col 173, 8 Jan. 2003 requesting a substantive vote before any more troops were committed.
[69] Ibid., col 34.   [70] Ibid., col 81.

United States. Is he saying that this now constitutes the international community and that we will engage against Iraq if the rest of what I understood to be the international community stays where it is, firmly saying no to a pre-emptive strike?'. In response Geoff Hoon referred to efforts being made to obtain a new Security Council resolution.[71] As negotiations on what was to become Resolution 1441 proceeded, Menzies Campbell, Foreign Affairs spokesman for the Liberal Democrats, asked the Foreign Secretary to 'assure the House that any resolution supported by the United Kingdom will not bestow on any member of the Security Council an automatic right to take military action if that state alone considers Iraq to be in breach of its obligations? Will he also give the House an assurance that if military action is considered necessary as a last resort, it is for the Security Council as a whole to make that decision? Will he resist any attempt to put any military action on a hair trigger to be pulled by any state that so chooses?' Jack Straw's response was somewhat equivocal stating that there was no suggestion that the 'resolutions should permit a hair trigger', but he went on to say that 'we reserve the right to take military action against Saddam Hussein's defiance of international law, but within international law, if the United Nations fails to meet its clear responsibilities'.[72]

On the eve of the adoption of Resolution 1441, Jack Straw went through the draft in the House, but was not clear on the issue of when military force would be used. He pointed to history to 'tell us that if diplomacy is to succeed it must be combined with the credible threat of force', which led to the prospect of Saddam readmitting the inspectors. He then said ominously that the 'choice for Saddam Hussein is to comply with the UN or face the serious consequences' indicated at the end of the Resolution. He followed this up by saying that while 'we would prefer to stay with the UN Security Council route', 'we reserve the right, within our obligations under international law', which is based on the 'UN Charter, Security Council resolutions and customary international law', 'to take military action if we deem that necessary, outwith a specific Security Council resolution being passed in the future', but he did indicate that there would be the opportunity to have a substantive vote in the House.[73]

Thus at the point of the adoption of Resolution 1441, the government was not convinced that, by itself, it was sufficient to warrant the use of force, and hinted at a legal basis that was not derived from Security Council authority, but on wider customary international law. This was certainly different to the legal argument that the government ultimately relied upon to invade Iraq in March 2003. The debate about the meaning of 1441 rumbled on in the House of Commons through the winter of 2002–3. In one debate Alan Simpson MP stated that 'a large number of members of NATO and the international community regard

[71] *Hansard* HC vol 390, col 496, 17 Oct. 2002.
[72] *Hansard* HC vol 392, cols 126–7, 5 Nov. 2002.
[73] *Hansard* HC vol 392, cols 433–4, 443, 7 Nov. 2002.

UN Resolution 1441 as carrying no specific mandate for a war against Iraq', and then asked the Prime Minister to 'give the House an assurance that before he commits any troops or supports such a war, he will seek, first, a specific mandate for a war through the UN, and secondly, a specific vote in advance from the House of Commons?'. Tony Blair answered that the Resolution was 'predicated on the basis that if there is a breach, there is an agreement to act'.[74] At this juncture Jack Straw introduced a substantive motion that the House 'supports UNSCR 1441 as unanimously adopted by the UN Security Council; agrees that the Government of Iraq must comply fully with all provisions of the Resolution; and agrees that, if it fails to do so, the Security Council should meet in order to consider the situation and the need for full compliance'.[75] The motion deliberately left unsaid the next step after consideration by the Security Council. There was considerable disquiet in the House of Commons over this omission and whether this meant that a further resolution was required or not; nevertheless a proposed amendment to the motion was defeated by 452 votes to 85, with the main question being agreed to.[76]

Debates were held in the Commons on the progress being made by the weapons inspectors of UNMOVIC and the IAEA. During these the government also kept the House updated about the 'contingency preparations' being made to keep open military options, while stressing its 'preference' for a second Security Council resolution in the event of Iraqi non-compliance.[77] On 20 January 2003, the Secretary of State for Defence announced that the government had 'reached a view on composition and deployment of a land force package to provide military capabilities for potential operations against Iraq', consisting of 26,000 troops plus equipment. In further stating that 'we will now begin to deploy the combat equipment and personnel of the formations comprising the land force package',[78] Mr Hoon was making it clear that force was going to be used whether a second resolution was secured or not, though he added that any final decision to use force had not been made yet. While noting that this deployment amounted to a quarter of the British Army, the opposition spokesman left no doubt about its support for deployment.[79] When questioned on the legal basis of any use of force, Mr Hoon reminded the House (inaccurately) 'that the UN Charter does allow for self-defence, and pre-emptive action is no more than modern jargon to deal with the ancient right of self-defence'.[80]

The government built its case for war in January and February 2003 by referring to material breaches by virtue of the Iraqi regime failing to co-operate with the inspectors. On 3 February 2003, Prime Minister Blair declared that 'should Dr. Blix continue to report Iraqi non-compliance, a second resolution should be passed confirming such a breach'. Further he stated that if Saddam 'rejects

---

[74] *Hansard* HC vol 395, col 43, 25 Nov. 2002.   [75] Ibid., col 47.
[76] Ibid., col. 128.   [77] *Hansard* HC vol 397, col 24, 7 Jan. 2003 (Hoon).
[78] *Hansard* HC vol 398, col 34, 20 Jan. 2003.
[79] Ibid., col 35.   [80] Ibid., col 39.

the peaceful route, he must be disarmed by force'.[81] The opposition agreed, Iain Duncan Smith saying of a second resolution, 'although it is not a prerequisite for future action, it is highly desirable'.[82] With the chances of a second resolution slipping away from its grasp, the government resorted to a reinterpretation of Resolution 1441. When asked about the ambiguity in the resolution and whether 'serious consequences' 'could only mean disarmament by force?', the Foreign Secretary Jack Straw stated (inaccurately) that 'in diplomatic speak the choice was between "all necessary means" and "serious consequences", and that 'everybody in the diplomatic community knows that "serious consequences" means the use of force'.[83] Government support though was slipping shown by a House of Commons vote on 26 February, held on a substantive government motion effectively giving Iraq one last chance to comply. The government won the vote by 434 votes to 124, after defeating an amendment by 393 votes to 199.[84]

It became clear to the government and to the House of Commons on 17 March that no second resolution on Iraq was going to be adopted by the Security Council. Jack Straw made the point that no country in the Security Council 'has claimed that Iraq is in full compliance with the obligations placed upon it', but he blamed France for putting a 'Security Council consensus beyond reach', given that President Chirac had made it clear that France would veto any proposed second resolution.[85] Dissent amongst some senior Labour politicians was shown by the resignation of the Leader of the House of Commons, Robin Cook on 17 March 2003. In his resignation speech the former Foreign Secretary distinguished the case for war over Kosovo (when he was in office) and that made for war against Iraq, and further undermined the government's claim that Saddam was a threat:

The legal basis for our action in Kosovo was the need to respond to an urgent and compelling humanitarian crisis. Our difficulty in getting support this time is that neither the international community nor the British public is persuaded that there is an urgent and compelling reason for this military action in Iraq... We cannot base our military strategy on the assumption that Saddam is weak and at the same time justify preemptive action on the claim that he is a threat.... Iraq probably has no weapons of mass destruction in the commonly understood sense of the term... Nor is our credibility helped by the appearance that our partners in Washington are less interested in disarmament than they are in regime change in Iraq.... It has been a favourite theme of commentators that this House no longer occupies a central role in British politics. Nothing could better demonstrate that they are wrong than for this House to stop the commitment of troops in a war that has neither international agreement nor domestic support. I intend to join those tomorrow night who will vote against military action now.[86]

---

[81] *Hansard* HC vol 399, cols 22–3, 3 Feb. 2003.   [82] Ibid., col 23.

[83] *Hansard* HC vol 399, col 1072, 13 Feb. 2002.

[84] *Hansard* HC vol 400, cols 265–363, 26 Feb. 2003.

[85] *Hansard* HC vol 401, col 703, 17 March 2003.

[86] Ibid., col 726.

The government-promised substantive vote on the war occurred the next day following a lengthy debate. The government's motion, introduced by the Prime Minister, was a lengthy one but in essence recognized that Iraq's weapons of mass destruction and long range missiles, as well as its continuing non-compliance with Security Council resolutions (including material breach of 1441), were a threat to international peace and security; that Iraq had failed to take the last opportunity given to it by Resolution 1441; this meant, following the Attorney General's advice published on the previous day that the 'authority to use force under Resolution 678 has revived'; so that the House 'believes that the United Kingdom must uphold the authority of the United Nations as set out in Resolution 1441 and many Resolutions preceding it, and therefore supports the decision of Her Majesty's Government that the United Kingdom should use all means necessary to ensure the disarmament of Iraq's weapons of mass destruction'. The motion also asked the House to 'endorse an appropriate post-conflict administration for Iraq, leading to a representative Government which upholds human rights and the rule of law for all Iraqis'.[87] Thus the House was clear that the government intended to use force for regime change and not just to remove the threat of Iraq's weapons of mass destruction. The Prime Minister's speech was premised on the fact that 'the only persuasive power' to which Saddam 'responds is 250,000 allied troops on his doorstep',[88] but the logic of relying on the threat of force (itself unlawful under international law) is that force will have to be used if the threat does not work. It is for this reason that the UN Charter prohibits both the threat and use of force. Once the US and UK had deployed troops and threatened force against Iraq if it did not comply then inevitably, if there was any remaining doubt about Iraq's compliance, force must be used.

The opposition leader supported the government's motion while Charles Kennedy, the leader of the Liberal Democrats, remained 'unpersuaded as to the case at this time for war', and questioned 'whether British forces should be sent into a war without a further UN mandate having been achieved', pointing out the reassurances given in the Security Council by the US and UK at the time of the adoption of Resolution 1441 that there was no automatic right to use force; while giving 'full moral support to our forces', who had no part 'in the civilian political decision in relation to what they are being asked to do, but they must carry out that task in all our names'. He also pointed to 'the huge public anxiety in Britain', with many people not 'persuaded that the case for war has been adequately made at this point'.[89] Having survived a Liberal Democrat inspired proposed amendment to the motion by 319 votes to 217 the government won support for its motion by 412 votes to 149.[90]

---

[87] *Hansard* HC vol 401, col 760, 18 March 2003.   [88] Ibid., col 764.
[89] Ibid., cols 782–7.   [90] Ibid., cols 906–11.

5. Post-Invasion Political Debate and Inquiry

Along with the failure to discover any evidence of chemical or biological weapons after the invasion in March 2003, it was also shown that Iraq had no nuclear weapons programme and had not tried to acquire uranium from Africa. The Hutton Report discussed below found that there was no proof that the September 2002 dossier on Iraq's weapons had been changed before it was published at the request of the Prime Minister or those working for him, so the conclusion must be that the intelligence was seriously flawed. In reality Iraq did not represent a threat to the UK; the government, along with its ally, had lost patience with Saddam and hence had invaded a weak country. The realization that this was the case led to parliament being more critical of the invasion after the fact than before it, especially with regards to the 45 minute claim made by the government back in September 2002 and upon which the momentum towards war was built. Parliament's attention was thus still on the decision to invade when it should have been concerned with addressing the disintegrating situation in Iraq.

The Foreign Affairs Committee of the House of Commons produced a report on the decision to go to war in July 2003, several months after the invasion.[91] The Committee introduced its report by stating that 'unlike previous conflicts, the war in Iraq took place only after a substantive vote in parliament, a development which we welcome'.[92] However, given that the government had claimed that the prime objective of the military campaign was to 'rid Iraq of its weapons of mass destruction', it was important to assess the evidence presented by the government that Iraq still had WMD despite the inspection process put in place by Security Council Resolution 687 adopted in 1991. The question was then whether Parliament had been misled by the government in presenting the case for war based on an assessment of Iraq's WMD.[93]

After the invasion and with no WMD yet to be found in Iraq,[94] the Foreign Affairs Committee concluded that 'it was too soon to tell whether the Government's assertions on Iraq's chemical and biological weapons will be borne out. However, we have no doubt that the threat posed to United Kingdom forces was genuinely perceived as a real and present danger and that the steps taken to protect' British troops from attack by chemical and biological weapons 'were justified by the information available at the time'.[95] However, it also concluded that the '45 minutes claim did not warrant the prominence given to it in the [September 2002] dossier, because it was based on intelligence from a single, uncorroborated source'.[96] The Committee also tellingly pointed to the fact that

---

[91] Foreign Affairs Committee: *The Decision to go to War in Iraq, 9th Report of Session 2002–3*, 7 July 2003 (HC 813-I).

[92] Ibid., para 1. [93] Ibid., paras 3–4.

[94] Ibid., para 170. [95] Ibid., para 41.

[96] Ibid., para 70.

the US had made no such claim.[97] The Committee had not received a satisfactory answer to the questions: 'why the 45 minute claim was highlighted by the Prime Minister when he presented the dossier to the House, and why was it given such prominence in the dossier itself, being mentioned no fewer than four times, including in the Prime Minister's foreword and in the executive summary'.[98] It further concluded that 'continuing disquiet and unease about the claims made in the September dossier are unlikely to be dispelled unless more evidence of Iraq's weapons of mass destruction comes to light'.[99] The Committee was also dismissive of the later dossier of what the Prime Minister had called 'further intelligence' on Iraqi concealment published on 3 February 2003 (known as the 'dodgy dossier'), parts of which were plagiarized from an article published in 2002 in the *Middle East Review of International Affairs*, which undermined the credibility of the government's case for war.[100] The Committee concluded that the Prime Minister had misrepresented the status of the February dossier by stating it constituted 'further intelligence', although he had done this inadvertently.[101]

In the government's response to the Report of the Foreign Affairs Committee, the Foreign Secretary, Jack Straw, refuted most of the critical findings of the Committee, and left the issue of the 45 minute claim to Lord Hutton's Report, which was finally published in January 2004.[102]

The government set the terms of Lord Hutton's inquiry narrowly. It was not an inquest into the reasons given for invading Iraq, but one into the circumstances surrounding the death of Dr David Kelly.[103]

Dr Kelly was a weapons expert with considerable experience in Iraq who was named as the possible source of a BBC story of 29 May 2003 on the government's September 2002 dossier, in which BBC reporter Andrew Gilligan stated that the government knew the claim that Iraq could launch WMD in 45 minutes was wrong.[104] Cruelly exposed and having been subject to close questioning before the Foreign Affairs Committee on 15 July, Dr Kelly committed suicide on 17 July 2003.[105]

Though great expectations were had of the Report, in particular that it would consider the justifications for going to war, Lord Hutton (a retired Law Lord) was not prepared to go beyond the narrow terms given to him by the government. The

---

[97] Ibid., para 63.   [98] Ibid., para 69.
[99] Ibid., para 107.   [100] Ibid., para 138.
[101] Ibid., para 137.
[102] *Response of the Sec of State for Foreign Affairs to the 9th Report of FAC: the Decision to go to War in Iraq* (Cm 6062, Nov. 2003). See also his statement to the House of Commons where he attempted to reconcile the statements about the lack of 'automaticity' in 1441 with the actions of the UK and US in invading Iraq, since all the resolution required was for the Security Council to meet again to consider the issue: *Hansard* HC vol 418, cols 1411–13, 9 March 2004 (Straw).
[103] Lord Hutton's report, *Report of the Inquiry into the Circumstances Surrounding the Death of Dr. David Kelly*, 28 Jan. 2004 (HC 247).
[104] Ibid., para 32.   [105] Ibid., paras 14 and 467.

terms of reference were that Lord Hutton was 'urgently to conduct an investigation into the circumstances surrounding the death of Dr. Kelly'. According to Lord Hutton:

In my opinion these terms of reference required me to consider the circumstances preceding and leading up to the death of Dr Kelly insofar as (1) they might have an effect on his state of mind and influenced his actions preceding and leading up to his death or (2) they might have influenced the actions of others which affected Dr Kelly preceding and leading up to his death. There has been a great deal of controversy and debate whether the intelligence in relation to weapons of mass destruction set out in the dossier published by the Government on 24 September 2002 was of sufficient strength and reliability to justify the Government in deciding that Iraq under Saddam Hussein posed such a threat to the safety and interests of the United Kingdom that military action should be taken against that country. This controversy and debate has continued because of the failure, up to the time of the writing of this report, to find weapons of mass destruction in Iraq. I gave careful consideration to the view expressed by a number of public figures and commentators that my terms of reference required or, at least, entitled me to consider this issue. However I concluded that a question of such wide import, which would involve the consideration of a wide range of evidence, is not one which falls within my terms of reference.[106]

Lord Hutton did however consider aspects of the 45 minute claim since it was alleged that Dr Kelly was the source of Andrew Gilligan's story in which he stated that the government probably knew the 45 minute claim put in the September dossier was false, even before it was published.[107] After looking at the intelligence upon which this claim was made Lord Hutton concluded that 'whether or not at some time in the future the report on which the 45 minutes claim was based is shown to be unreliable, the allegation reported on 29 May 2003 that the government probably knew that the 45 minute claim was wrong before the government decided to put it into the dossier was unfounded'.[108] However, while not in the conclusions of his report, Lord Hutton did refer to the evidence which strongly suggested that intelligence pointed to Iraqi battlefield chemical and biological weapons being deployable at 45 minutes notice, not strategic longer range weapons which might be used against British targets beyond an Iraqi battlefield. While most of the evidence presented to the Inquiry in this regard indicated that the dossier should have made it clear that the 45 minute claim related to battlefield weapons only,[109] Lord Hutton refused to make this part of his conclusion by declaring that a 'consideration of this issue does not fall within my terms of reference relating to the circumstances surrounding the death of Dr. Kelly'.[110]

Lord Hutton did concede in his conclusions though that the Prime Minister's desire was to 'have a dossier which, whilst consistent with the available intelligence, was as strong' as possible 'in relation to the threat posed by Saddam

---

[106] Ibid., para 9. [107] Ibid.
[108] Ibid., para 467. [109] Ibid., paras 221–7.
[110] Ibid., para 9.

Hussein's WMD', and this may have 'subconsciously influenced' John Scarlett (Chair of the JIC) 'to make the wording of the dossier somewhat stronger than it would have been if it had been contained in a normal JIC assessment', though still consistent with the intelligence available. This meant that Andrew Gilligan's allegations on the 29 May were unfounded. Lord Hutton also found that the information given by Dr Kelly to Andrew Gilligan did not support the latter's allegation that the government knew that the 45 minute claim was false.[111] The blame was thus placed on the BBC, leading not only to Andrew Gilligan's resignation, but also that of the BBC's Director General Greg Dyke.

The government was largely exonerated of responsibility for Dr Kelly's death by the Hutton report, and only mildly criticized for its presentation of the evidence against Iraq. The Hutton Report was debated in the House of Commons on the day of its release (28 January 2004). The Prime Minister felt completely vindicated by the report, which refuted allegations against him that he lied 'over the intelligence that formed part of the Government's case in respect of Iraq and weapons of mass destruction'.[112] Despite the fact that the opposition leader, Michael Howard, asked the government to establish an independent inquiry into the wider questions of whether weapons of mass destruction existed and what 'the Government told the country in the run-up to the war', issues which were beyond the remit of Lord Hutton,[113] the government ordered no such inquiry.

However, the Hutton Report was not the end of the government's difficulties over the invasion of Iraq, as there were still many doubts about the intelligence on WMD as well as the legal basis of the invasion. A report into the former issued by Lord Butler, a former senior civil servant, concluded that the intelligence behind the September 2002 dossier on Iraqi production of WMD was 'seriously flawed'; and that the 45 minute claim was 'unsubstantiated'.[114] Despite this the Prime Minister defended his decision to go to war on the basis that he relied on the intelligence given to him by the JIC, but he also stated 'it was absolutely clear that he [Saddam] had every intention of carrying on developing those weapons, that he was procuring materials to do so'.[115]

On the issue of the legal basis, political pressure finally led to the release of the full advice given by the Attorney General on the legality of the war with Iraq on 28 April 2005.[116] The document was marked 'secret' and dated 7 March

---

[111] Ibid., para 467.

[112] *Hansard* HC vol 417, col 338, 28 Jan. 2004.

[113] Ibid., col 443. See further vol 417, cols 767–83, 4 Feb. 2004, where the Prime Minister defended himself from accusations about misleading on the 45 minute claim, especially in the foreword to the September 2002 dossier.

[114] Lord Butler's report: Review of Intelligence on Weapons of Mass Destruction: Report of a Committee of Privy Counsellors, 14 July 2004 (HC 898), para 436. Para 511 concludes that the 'JIC should not have included the 45 minute [claim] in its assessment and in the Government's dossier without stating what it believed it referred to' ie battlefield weapons (see also para 507).

[115] *Hansard* HC vol 424, col 200, 20 July 2004.

[116] Full text of the advice about the legality of the war with Iraq given by the Attorney General, Lord Goldsmith, to Prime Minister Blair, on 7 March 2003, released on 28 April 2005

2003 and was obviously not intended for general release. It contains much more nuanced advice than released to MPs later on 17 March 2003 immediately prior to the invasion which was a very definite statement about the legality of the invasion.[117] As regards the earlier (full) version of the advice, the Attorney had been asked about the legality of military action against Iraq without a further resolution of the Security Council. The Attorney General had discussed the background to Resolution 1441 with Sir Jeremy Greenstock, the UK representative on the Security Council, and had heard the views of the US, who were co-sponsors of the Resolution. Sir Jeremy's advice contains some insights into the negotiations leading up to 1441. The Attorney outlined the possible legal basis for any use of force. First, the use of force in self-defence in the face of an 'actual or imminent threat of an armed attack', which was inapplicable in the case of Iraq as the Attorney General rejected the doctrine of pre-emption put forward by the US. Secondly, the use of force to avert overwhelming humanitarian catastrophe (as argued during the Kosovo campaign), which again was not applicable in the case of Iraq. The final possibility was the use of force authorized by the Security Council and taken under chapter VII of the UN Charter.

In considering whether Resolution 1441 constituted an authorization to use force, the Attorney made it clear that he rejected the views of most academic commentators 'who assert that nothing less than an explicit authorisation to use force in a Security Council resolution will be sufficient'. He supported the revival argument namely that a material breach of Resolution 687 could revive the authorization to use force granted in November 1990 in Resolution 678. On this basis the Attorney opined that Resolution 1441 did not immediately revive Resolution 678, but gave Iraq a final opportunity to comply by co-operating with the enhanced inspection regime established by Resolution 1441. The issue then was whether Iraq co-operated and, if not, what was the next step before 678 was revived—the matter returning to the Council for discussions that did not produce a conclusion, or discussions that needed to produce an authorizing resolution. It is really only at this point that his opinion differs from the one presented to parliament later in March 2003, but the difference is crucial. Instead of stating that there was clearly only a need for the issue to return to the Council before the terms of Resolution 1441 revived the authorization to use force in Resolution 678 as he stated before parliament, the Attorney was much more nuanced, concluding that

---

<http://www.guardian.co.uk/politics/2005/apr/28/election2005.uk3> (accessed 12 Feb. 2009). See also earlier debate in House of Commons at *Hansard* HC vol 432, cols 1003–12, 24 March 2005 (Straw).

[117] For some explanation of the change in advice between that given to the Prime Minister on 7 March 2003 and that released to Parliament on 17 March, see statement to the House of Lords by Lord Goldsmith (*Hansard* HL vol 682, col 71w, 5 June 2006) referring to a disclosure document, annex 6 of which referred to the legality of military action in Iraq, para 16 of which stated that in this period 'the Attorney had reached the clear conclusion that the better view was that there was a lawful basis for the use of force without a second resolution': <http://www.attorneygeneral.gov.uk/sub_disclosure_log_2006.html> in (2006) UKMIL Part Sixteen: II.B.I item 16/18.

only a 'reasonable case' could be made out for such a position, and 'if the matter ever came before a court' it 'may well' conclude that Resolution 1441 did require 'a further Council decision in order to revive the authorisation in resolution 678'. Even the reasonably arguable case that Resolution 1441 'alone has revived the authorisation to use force . . . will only be sustainable if there are strong factual grounds for concluding that Iraq has failed to take the final opportunity'.

Lord Goldsmith also warned that 'it must be recognised that on previous occasions when military action was taken on the basis of a reasonably arguable case, the degree of public and Parliamentary scrutiny of the legal issue was nothing like as great as today'. It may well be because of this fear of accountability for launching a war whose legality was only reasonably arguable, that the Attorney General's full advice was not released until 2005 when the issue was forced (ironically) during the middle of an election campaign. Although the Labour administration of Tony Blair was damaged by Iraq and the revelation that the legal basis on which it had taken action was flawed, it was still re-elected in May 2005, though with a reduced majority.

6. The Security Council and Post-Invasion Iraq

Though the invasion was successful, with Baghdad falling on 9 April 2003, and President Bush declaring the end of major combat hostilities on 1 May 2003, the post-conflict stage quickly became the post-invasion stage, with a brutal conflict developing between occupying forces and insurgents (Saddam supporters, Sunni and Shia militias, and later al-Qaeda members), as well as between the different armed groups in Iraq. The capture of Saddam in December 2003 did little to reduce the level of violence. The bloody battles of Fallujah between the US forces and Iraqi insurgents in both the spring and winter of 2004 were an alarming symbol of the despair into which the country had descended.

The dominant desire in the international community for the UN to play the leading role in post-conflict Iraq reflects the unique authority and legitimacy of the UN, developed by its practice in Kosovo and East Timor. The Security Council's endorsement of a post-conflict coalition of the willing in Iraq in Resolution 1483 adopted on 22 May 2003 was a positive development in the sense that it at least shows recognition of the legitimacy that such authority confers especially by those states previously questioning the relevance of the Council. It was a less appealing development given that the role of the UN in the post-conflict stage was much reduced, though Afghanistan also manifested a downplaying of the UN's role in post-conflict administration. Any chance of a UN administration of Iraq was removed when the UN headquarters were destroyed by a bomb on 19 August 2003, with significant loss of life including that of Sergio Vieira de Mello, the Special Representative of the UN Secretary General.

Resolution 1483 did make it clear that the US and UK must act consistently with the Charter and other principles of international law in post-invasion Iraq, though its terms seem to be deliberately ambiguous. Resolution 1483 was adopted under chapter VII in response to the continuing threat to international peace and security caused by the situation in Iraq. It recognized the 'specific authorities, responsibilities, and obligations under applicable international laws' of the US and the UK as 'occupying powers under unified command' called 'the Authority'.[118] It further called upon 'the Authority, consistent with the Charter of the United Nations and other relevant international law, to promote the welfare of the Iraqi people through the effective administration of the territory, including in particular working towards the restoration of conditions of security and stability and the creation of conditions in which the Iraqi people can freely determine their own political future'.[119] The resolution and subsequent resolutions, especially Resolution 1546 of 8 June 2004, indicate that the process by which the Iraqi people should realize their internal right of self-determination was by free and fair elections.

From May 2003 to June 2004 Iraq was subject to a Security Council endorsed military occupation in which US and UK military forces strove to retain order and security in Iraq against a growing tide of violence. The Solicitor-General in the UK stated to the House of Commons that Resolution 1483 'together with the relevant provisions of humanitarian law' on occupation governed UK and US conduct.[120] The Coalition Provisional Authority (CPA) was headed by President Bush's envoy, L. Paul Bremer III, while the UK was initially represented by Major General Tim Cross. On 16 May Bremer announced the CPA's first regulation which declared that the CPA would exercise 'powers of government temporarily in order to provide for the effective administration of Iraq', and stated that the CPA was 'vested with all executive, legislative and judicial authority necessary to achieve its objectives to be exercised under UN Security Council resolutions...and the laws and usages of war'.[121]

On 13 July 2003 the CPA appointed an advisory Iraqi Governing Council (IGC) consisting of representatives of the various ethnic and religious groups, though it contained no members of the former ruling Baath party as a reflection of the CPA's policy of de-Baathification of Iraq (which was based on the de-Nazification of post-Second World War Germany). The Security Council saw the IGC as embodying the sovereignty of the Iraqi people during 'the

---

[118] On the effect of the Resolution on the law of occupation, see D. Scheffer, 'Beyond Occupation Law' (2003) 97 AJIL 842.

[119] See statement by the Foreign Secretary Jack Straw to the House of Commons: *Hansard* HC vol 411, col 8, 14 Oct. 2003 ('the multinational force needs to be authorised by the United Nations').

[120] *Hansard* HC vol 409, col 206w, 15 July 2003.

[121] A. Carcano, 'End of Occupation in 2004? The Status of the Multinational Force in Iraq after the Transfer of Sovereignty to the Interim Iraqi Government' (2006) 11 JCSL 41 at 45.

transitional period'.[122] With the guidance of the CPA, the IGC adopted the 'Law of Administration for the State of Iraq for the Transitional Period', as the interim constitution of Iraq, on 8 March 2004.[123] On 28 May 2004, Dr Ayad Allawi, formerly an Iraqi exile, was named Interim Prime Minister of Iraq, and an interim (unelected) government emerged by the end of June. The Security Council fixed a timetable for establishing a constitutionally elected government of Iraq, and established that the legal basis of the US-led multinational force was to be at the invitation of the interim government reflected in letters of invitation and acceptance from Dr Allawi and Secretary of State Powell annexed to the Resolution.[124] As Jack Straw, the British Foreign Secretary said, after the occupation ended 'the relationship will be, as it were, between two sovereign governments',[125] and as the Defence Secretary said it was 'no longer simply a question of the Americans deciding and doing, but a matter for the Iraqi Interim Government'.[126] Elections were held on 30 January 2005 in which sixty per cent of the Iraqi population voted for the election of a national assembly. This assembly drafted a new constitution which was ratified in a referendum on 15 October 2005. This in turn led to elections held under the new constitution on 15 December 2005, which produced an elected coalition government under the leadership of Prime Minister Nouri al-Maliki.

While the insurgency continued unabated in 2004–7, the legal components for a new Iraq had been put in place. The international legal base of the US and Security Council's actions were problematic, especially the wide-ranging powers exercised by the CPA when the law of occupation calls for minimal change;[127] and the ability of the interim government to 'invite' in the US/UK forces seemed doubtful, given that it was neither democratic nor effective.[128] Nonetheless, the end result was an elected government, whose forces in 2008 were slowly taking on the burden of security from the invited British and American forces. Though British troop numbers were down to 4,100 by July 2008,[129] there were still over 140,000 American troops in the country. Anything up to three quarters of a

---

[122] SC Res. 1511, 16 Oct. 2004.   [123] Carcano, 'End of Occupation?', 44.

[124] SC Res. 1546, 8 June 2004.

[125] Foreign Affairs Committee Seventh Report, Foreign Affairs Aspects of the War against Terrorism, Oral Evidence, 30 March 2004, qu.103 (HC 441-II).

[126] *Hansard* HC vol 425, col 632, 18 Oct. 2004 (Hoon).

[127] The Foreign Office's view was that the law of occupation had been lawfully altered by SC Res. 1483, allowing the occupiers to carry out more extensive reforms to Iraq than otherwise would have been permitted: Foreign Affairs Committee Tenth Report, *Foreign Policy Aspects of the War Against Terrorism, Written Evidence*, Memorandum from the Foreign Office, 13 and 22 May 2003, para 28 (HC 405).

[128] A government minister stated that 'the multinational force is in Iraq with the agreement of the Iraqi Government, who may terminate their presence at any time or request their continued presence. The UK therefore will continue to provide troops for as long as the Iraqi Government wants us to remain. We have no desire to stay a moment longer than necessary, but we will not leave the job before it is done': *Hansard* HC vol 434, col 162, 18 May 2005 (Alexander).

[129] See statement by Prime Minister Gordon Brown to the House of Commons: *Hansard* HC vol 479, col 660, 22 July 2008.

million Iraqis have died in the conflict between May 2003 and September 2008, with 4,300 coalition soldiers losing their lives, 4,000 of them being American, 175 being British. Other troop-contributing countries sustaining significant loss of life were Italy, Poland, Ukraine, Bulgaria, and Spain.

7. Conclusion

Far from witnessing new rules of interpretation we are witnessing breaches of international law by powerful democratic liberal states. Following the maxim that is applicable to international law that old law has to be broken in order to make new law these breaches also constitute a very concerted attempt to change the legal order governing the use of force in international relations. While some flexibility is necessary for developing a legal order that is capable of dealing with terrorist violence as well as upholding human rights, we must be careful not to remove the legal brakes on the use of force in international relations. If accepted, purposive and unilateral interpretations of Security Council resolutions will lead to the collapse of the legal order contained in the UN Charter.

While the Security Council seems to have survived the decision of the US and UK of 20 March 2003 to use force against Iraq outside of the UN framework, the danger is that the unwillingness of powerful states to put their coercive power in the hands of the Council except on their terms, will contribute not only to a weaker collective security system, but also more fundamentally to an erosion of the rules governing the use of force that are the foundation of such a system. Although the immediate result of this military action seems to be that a genuine collective security system is even further from our grasp, the critical reaction of state and public opinion to the decision to use force against Iraq is indicative that the majority of the world will not necessarily accept this weakening and erosion.

Did the Iraq crisis of 2003 leave the Council hanging onto its role by a thread? Although it seemed to be business as usual after the adoption of Resolution 1483 and subsequent resolutions in post-conflict Iraq, it may be doubted whether the Council's authority could survive another crisis of the type witnessed in Kosovo and Iraq, when it successfully fulfilled neither its executive nor its diplomatic functions. Without change that thread may break and the Council's relevance will be much reduced. With change—which has to be driven by the permanent members limiting their right of veto, recognizing their responsibilities for peace wherever it is ruptured, and proposing resolutions and measures that accord with the Charter and fundamental principles of international law—it stands a chance of performing a central role in maintaining peace and securing justice.

The British government's attitude to the UN and its actions within the Security Council on Iraq were cynical and duplicitous. The government spent a great deal of effort building up the threat of WMD from Iraq from something that in reality was quite remote into something that was imminent and capable of striking at British targets. This evidence was primarily directed at convincing parliament to support the war: a parliament that became much more critical of the invasion after the event once it realized that it had might have been misled into voting for the war. It is doubtful whether the government would have lost the vote if the intelligence had been presented in a more balanced way, but the longer-term consequences of such behaviour have been corrosive.

Britain had clearly committed its forces to war against Iraq by the winter of 2002–3, and at this stage by threatening force without clear UN authority the British government was in breach of international law. It compounded its unlawful actions by going to war without clear authority, and compromised its legitimacy by indicating to Council members that it was not going to automatically use force. By misleading both the international community and its own polity, the government struggled to convince that its role in post-invasion Iraq was legitimate. Despite the fact that it had secured authority from the Security Council for post-conflict occupation, this did not serve to cure the illegality of the initial invasion and in a sense the government never overcame this obstacle. The domestic and international debate about the legality of the invasion burgeoned after the invasion, with the government facing a number of individually weak but nonetheless difficult instances of political accountability distracting it from dealing with the growing brutality in Iraq. In fact British influence (as well as presence) in post-invasion Iraq dwindled and all the major decisions were made by the United States. If there is going to be a peaceful Iraq, it will be an American-made one.

11

Democracy, Accountability, and Military Action

1. Introduction

Accountability is a central element of a democracy. In simple terms it means that those in power and making decisions should have to account for those decisions to their peers, to the electorate, and, if a crime or violation of law has occurred, to the courts. Given the huge consequences for soldiers and their families, as well as for Britain and the countries and region being subjected to military intervention, decisions to go to war should be subject to scrutiny and review. This chapter considers the breadth of accountability in the British political and legal system, and makes references to other democracies as well as to the international mechanisms of accountability, bearing in mind that decisions to go to war bring the UK into these wider contexts. Indeed, breaches of wider legal orders may have consequences in terms of accountability for the decision-makers as well as soldiers within the British legal and political system.

Rather than running through the different types and forms of domestic then international accountability, the chapter considers political forms of accountability at all levels. It assesses their effectiveness in challenging government decisions that seem to breach the international legal order. It considers the current reform debate over the role of parliament in the decision-making process. It then goes on to discuss the limited judicial forms of review that exist, and considers the arguments for greater judicial scrutiny of decisions to go to war at both national and international levels. Recent conflicts, especially those over Kosovo in 1999 and in Iraq in 2003, have given rise to a number of cases before British Courts, the European Court of Human Rights and the International Court of Justice. These and other judicial forms of accountability, including the International Criminal Court, are considered in this final chapter, which ends with recommendations for reform.

2. Accountability and Democracy

In a straightforward sense the concept of 'accountability' signifies 'the process of being called "to account" to some authority for one's actions'.[1] But the term

---

[1] R. Mulgan, 'Accountability: An Ever-Expanding Concept' (2000) 78 Public Administration 555.

has been deployed in a broader fashion over the past quarter of a century.[2] This is reflected in a widely cited definition of accountability proffered within the context of the UK:

[A] framework for the exercise of state power in a liberal-democratic system, within which public bodies are forced to seek to promote the public interest and compelled to justify their actions in those terms or in other constitutionally acceptable terms (justice, humanity, equity); to modify policies if they should turn out to have been ill-conceived; and to make amends if mistakes and errors of judgment have been made.[3]

While accountability is fundamental to the exercise of power in a liberal-democratic system, it is also becoming increasingly important for the exercise of power by public bodies in the wider international framework. As the International Law Association's Committee on the Accountability of International Organizations makes clear 'as a matter of principle, accountability is linked to the authority and power of an [organization]. Power entails accountability, that is the duty to account for its exercise'.[4] However, while accountability is at the heart of the liberal-democratic state, it is not inherent in the construction of many international organizations. For example in relation to the EU Carol Harlow has written:

The architecture of the EU was not originally constructed with openness or accountability in mind, nor was the EU modelled on parliamentary democracy. Its embryonic assembly was purely consultative, and the short history of the European Parliament has been one of clawing power back from other institutions.[5]

Nevertheless, the European legal order (including the European Convention and Court on Human Rights, as well as EU law and institutions) is becoming increasingly influential, especially in establishing judicial mechanisms and avenues of accountability where individuals can seek justice when national legal orders have failed.

Accountability takes many forms, financial, administrative, political (democratic) and legal, though the latter two will form the fulcrum of this chapter. Underpinning it all though is the concept of democratic accountability:

Democratic accountability is a term familiar in political science, and one with considerable resonance in western society. This is a simple definition of accountability in terms of suffrage: the principle according to which it is possible to replace the holders of

    [2] A. Arnull, 'Introduction: The European Union's Accountability and Legitimacy Deficit', in A. Arnull and D. Wincott (eds), *Accountability and Legitimacy in the European Union* (Oxford: Oxford University Press, 2002) 2.
    [3] D. Oliver, *Government in the United Kingdom: The Search for Accountability, Effectiveness and Citizenship* (Milton Keynes: Open University Press, 1991) 28.
    [4] Final Report of the ILA Committee on the Accountability of International Organizations (Berlin Conference, April 2004) 5–6.
    [5] C. Harlow, *Accountability in the European Union* (Oxford: Oxford University Press, 2002) 52.

political office through general elections. In this sense, accountability is the framework of government and precondition for all democratic rule.[6]

In this chapter a wider approach to democratic accountability is taken to include not only electoral mechanisms but also political or public mechanisms whereby holders of political office may be held to account, either by elected representatives or by other means. As summarized by Christopher Lord:

Effective democratic accountability requires all of the following: *administrative accountability* of bureaucracies to political leaders; continuous *parliamentary accountability* of political leaders to democratic actors; *electoral accountability* based on a radical simplification of voter choice by democratic intermediaries, such as political parties, and on opportunities for the public to sanction their political leaders, notably by removing them from office; and a system of *judicial accountability* that any citizen can access with a complaint that power-holders are seeking to evade or distort the rules by which they are themselves brought to account.[7]

In the first section of this chapter we will consider those mechanisms of parliamentary and international institutional accountability as regards decisions to go to war; while in the second section the analysis will turn to consider the possibility of independent review of the legality of those decisions by judicial bodies.

3. Political Accountability

Democracy is not just about the regular holding of elections. In fact, that is quite a crude method of holding the government of the day to account for its past decisions, since the electorate has to judge many issues, but is concerned about the next few years rather than the past. So individual decisions to go to war will not generally be the issue upon which the electorate decides the fate of the incumbent government. The re-election of the Labour government in 2005 shows this all too well. Furthermore, in the UK the opposition may not be strong enough or numerous enough (or both) to be able to offer a real challenge to the government of the day. Though executive accountability to the elected representatives of the people is a very important element in ensuring the health of the democracy between elections, there have developed a number of other methods of political or democratic accountability, especially the system of Select Committees in the UK. Though they consist of MPs and therefore reflect the politics of the day, they do serve an essential purpose of questioning the government's action in detail, something that parliament as a whole does not have time for. Occasionally too the Select Committees can produce reports that truly hold the government to

---

[6] Harlow, *Accountability*, 8.
[7] C. Lord, *Democracy in the European Union* (Sheffield: Sheffield University Press, 1998) 80.

account, albeit retrospectively, as did the Foreign Affairs Committee's Report of 2000 on Kosovo.

It must be borne in mind too that there are avenues of political accountability at the international level, by international organizations scrutinizing the actions of their member states for compliance with the rules of the organization and international law. While the British government's actions on human rights are regularly scrutinized by UN Committees created under a number of human rights treaties, there is very little such expert quasi-judicial review in the field of use of force. For this we have to rely on the political judgment of the international community on the uses of force by member states.

The international historian Paul Kennedy has written that:

It is quite possible to argue that the [UN General] Assembly, whose size has risen from the original 50 members in 1945 to 191 as we entered the twenty-first century, is the closest we are ever going to get to the parliament of man; and that it is an entirely representative body since ambassadors who are partaking in General Assembly debates and decisions have been appointed on behalf of their own sovereign nations (regardless, alas, of whether their governments were elected democratically).[8]

Kennedy could have strengthened his case by examining the increasing support for democratization within states coming from the General Assembly since 1989,[9] and the growing trend towards democratic governance in member states. It is true that the UN is open to all states, whether democratic or not,[10] but there is an undeniable upward trend in countries establishing democratic government often with UN assistance. If most governments in the UN are democratically elected then, at least in theory, there should be democratic accountability for their international policies within each of their domestic constitutional structures.

Indeed, during the Cold War the General Assembly did call the superpowers to account for a number of interventions when the Security Council was inevitably deadlocked by the veto. The main instances of this can be given. In 1956 the Assembly called upon the Soviet Union 'to desist forthwith from all armed attack on the people of Hungary and from any form of intervention, in particular armed intervention, in the internal affairs of Hungary'; further it condemned Soviet actions as a 'violation of the accepted standards and principles of international law, justice and morality'.[11] The Assembly condemned the 1979 Soviet intervention in Afghanistan.[12] In 1983 it deeply deplored the American armed intervention in Grenada, which constituted 'a flagrant violation of

---

[8] P. Kennedy, *The Parliament of Man: The Past, Present and Future of the United Nations* (Toronto: Harper Collins, 2006) 208.

[9] N.D. White, 'The United Nations and Democracy Assistance: Developing Practice within a Constitutional Framework', in P. Burnell (ed), *Democracy Assistance: International Cooperation for Democratization* (London: Frank Cass, 2000) 67.

[10] Art 4(1) of the UN Charter.

[11] GA Res. 1004 (ES-II), 4 Nov. 1956; GA Res. 1006, 9 Nov. 1956.

[12] GA Res. ES-6/1, 15 Jan. 1980.

international law'.[13] In 1986, it condemned the US bombings of Libya (when some of the US planes had been sent from bases in Britain) as a 'violation of the Charter of the United Nations and international law'.[14] Though not comprehensive in its condemnations (there was for example no condemnation of the Soviet intervention in Czechoslovakia in 1968), and with the majority in favour not always overwhelming, the Assembly's record during the Cold War was still creditable given the pressures on small and developing states to join one of the opposing camps.

In the case of interventions by Britain during the Cold War the General Assembly offered support for the operation in Korea. The fact that the operation had support from both the Security Council and the General Assembly is a reflection of the fact that the UN was western dominated at the time. The development of a coalition of the willing under UN authority was controversial at the time, but as we have seen in chapter four, has become accepted in practice. Indeed, the General Assembly's resolution supported strongly by Britain supplemented the Security Council's authority by recommending that 'all appropriate steps be taken to ensure conditions of stability throughout Korea', thus giving the green light to the UN forces to enter North Korea.[15] In the case of the disastrous intervention in Suez in 1956, the Assembly's criticism came in the form of recommending the sending of a UN peacekeeping force to ensure British and French withdrawal from the conflict zone. In the Assembly's resolutions it had to be careful not to cause offence to the UK and France in order to seek their withdrawal, but it did note that 'the armed forces' of the two states were 'conducting military operations against Egyptian territory'.[16] Britain was part of the UN force in Cyprus in the 1960s and in Bosnia in the 1990s, and therefore had the support of the Assembly, though that body was critical of the maintenance of the arms embargo (strongly argued for by the UK) against the whole of Yugoslavia, which seriously hampered Bosnia's right of self-defence.[17] In the Falklands dispute of 1982 the Assembly was silent during the conflict (the Security Council having condemned the Argentinian invasion) though soon after it was critical of the unwillingness of the UK to negotiate on the issue of sovereignty.[18]

With the end of the Cold War, political and economic pressures on the majority of states in the Assembly have, if anything, increased, so that criticism has been much more muted. No direct support was given to the Security Council authorized action to push Iraq out of Kuwait in 1991; though the Assembly condemned the invasion and the violation of the human rights of the Kuwaitis and third state nationals.[19] Indeed, the Assembly in the post-Cold War period has returned to one of its primary concerns under the UN Charter—the promotion

[13] GA Res. 38/7, 2 Nov. 1983.   [14] GA Res. 41/38, 20 Nov. 1986.
[15] GA Res. 376, 7 Oct. 1950.   [16] GA Res. 997 (ES-I), 2 Nov. 1956.
[17] GA Res. 47/121, 18 Dec. 1992.   [18] GA Res. 37/9, 4 Nov. 1982.
[19] GA Res. 45/170, 18 Dec. 1990.

and protection of human rights,[20] and has stayed clear of security issues. In 1998 during the period in the Kosovo crisis leading up to the NATO bombing of Serbia, the Assembly was very critical of Serbia's 'persistent and grave violations and abuse of human rights and humanitarian law in Kosovo'.[21] Like the resolution on Iraq in 1990 it did not mention any use of force against Serbia, but unlike Iraq in 1990 there was no enabling resolution from the Security Council. The majority of states condemned the practice of humanitarian intervention at a meeting of the G77 group of over 120 developing countries at its First South Summit held in Cuba on 10–14 April 2000 in no uncertain terms: 'We reject the so-called "right" of humanitarian intervention, which has no legal basis in the United Nations Charter or in the general principles of international law'.[22]

There has, however, been a lack of clear consensus on the invasions of Afghanistan in 2001 and Iraq in 2003. Though the Assembly did strongly condemn the 'heinous acts of terrorism, which have caused enormous loss of human life' in New York, Washington and Pennsylvania on 11 September 2001, it confined itself to calling for co-operation to bring the perpetrators to justice, and those that supported them to be held to account.[23] This resolution could not be said to support full-scale invasion of the country, but rather was suggestive of a criminal justice approach. But neither did it condemn the invasion when it occurred. The G77 too was silent on the matter at its annual ministerial meeting of 16 November 2001 held in New York,[24] as it was over the invasion of Iraq at its equivalent meeting on 25 September 2003.[25] However, the General Assembly did manage in 2004 to adopt a resolution introduced by the Non Aligned Movement 'reaffirming the central role of the United Nations in the maintenance of international peace and security'. Israel and the United States voted against the resolution and the UK along with forty-six other states abstained, though ninety-three countries voted in favour. The debate made it clear that those voting against and some of those abstaining were unhappy about the elements of the resolution that were clearly directed at the invasion and occupation of Iraq. Though the resolution did not mention Iraq by name it did express concern 'over any act or threat of foreign intervention or occupation of any State or territory in contravention of the Charter', and it called for measures 'to prevent the use of threat of force and the exercise of political pressure and coercion as a means for obtaining certain political objectives'.[26] This was sufficient to make the point that the majority of the world's states viewed the invasion as illegal.

Thus there is political accountability at the international level—it is not systematic nor necessarily impartial but the General Assembly does serve as the

---

[20] Art 55 of the UN Charter.   [21] GA Res. 53/164, 9 Dec. 1998.
[22] UN Doc. A/55/74, 12 May 2000, para 54.
[23] GA Res. 56/1, 12 Sept. 2001.
[24] UN Doc. A/56/647, 26 Nov. 2001.
[25] UN Doc. A/58/413, 7 Oct. 2003.
[26] GA Res. 58/317, adopted at 93rd plen mtg, 5 Aug. 2004.

conscience of those powerful states wishing to use force on the international stage. In the short-term it does not change the behaviour of the powerful states, whose desire to secure national goals outweighs any international criticism, but disapproval by the General Assembly does undermine the legitimacy of their actions in the long-term, as well as serving to uphold the fundamental principles of international law governing the use of force. It is a pity that the Assembly has lost that voice to some extent with the end of the Cold War, but its more abstract resolutions do still reinforce the basic rules on the use of force, though they do not directly hold individual states to account.

4. The Role of Parliament

Throughout the course of this book we have included an account of the role of parliament in scrutinizing, questioning, but in practice invariably supporting government decisions to go to war. If we consider the widely supported British deployment to the Gulf in 1990–1 in response to Iraq's invasion of Kuwait, we saw a very healthy series of debates (and votes) on the matter prior to the actual conflict, though after the troops had been sent. A similar scenario occurred in the much more controversial invasion of Iraq in 2003, with a substantive vote being taken before the invasion though after forces had been deployed.[27] The questioning and discussions on both occasions were fair but critical, though there was no question of the House attempting to undermine or reject the government's decision to go to war. It is very questionable indeed whether the government would have been politically wise to have prosecuted a war in the face of a negative vote, though constitutionally that was possible since the decision to go to war was based solely upon prerogative powers. As Prime Minister Tony Blair stated in January 2003 in questioning before Parliament's Liaison Committee in the lead up to the invasion of Iraq, but before the substantive vote in the House of Commons:

I cannot think of a set of circumstances in which a Government can go to war without the support of Parliament... I think you can get into a great constitutional argument about this, but the reality is that Governments are in the end accountable to Parliament,... and they are accountable for any war they engage in.... The question is, do you take one step further and get rid of the Royal Prerogative? I do not see any reason to change it, but I do really think that in the end it is more theoretical than real... Supposing in relation to any conflict Parliament voted down the Government over the conflict... it is just not thinkable that the Government would then continue the conflict.[28]

---

[27] But see the Prime Minister's statement that 'I decided to commit UK forces after securing the approval of the House on 18 March': *Hansard* HC vol 424, col 1769w, 16 Sept. 2004 (Blair). The invasion of Iraq was launched on 20 March 2003.

[28] Prime Minister's examination by the Liaison Committee, 21 Jan. 2003, q125, at <http://www.parliament.the-stationery-office.co.uk/pa/cm200203/cmselect/cmliaisn/uc334-i/uc33402.htm> (accessed 26 Jan. 2009).

However, the increasing deployment of troops to conflicts and post-conflict zones during the Labour governments of 1997 onwards, not all of them (neither Kosovo nor Afghanistan) approved by substantive votes in parliament, has led to pressure to reform the prerogative powers, with the suggestion that parliament be made part of the decision-making process.

This raises many issues: whether it would improve the accountability of the government since by making parliament part of the decision there is still the issue of a review of that decision, as well as problems of when such joint decision-making is to be invoked. An early proposal in this debate put forward in February 2003 was that 'Parliament shall have the opportunity to consider and approve the exercise of duties vested in ... Ministers to commit the United Kingdom's armed forces to hostilities abroad, or to a situation abroad where hostilities are likely', before such a commitment (where circumstances permit), otherwise within 20 days of deployment.[29] It can be seen how any proposal will create difficulties of application with endless debates over meanings of 'hostilities' (in the case of peace operations in particular); 'abroad' (in the case of the Falklands for instance); as well as the government not wishing to curtail the efficiency of deployment by seeking prior approval from parliament. Although the proposal would require the Prime Minister to report to parliament on the reasons for the deployment, there was no requirement that there must be a clear international legal basis for the military action; this would just be one of many factors that parliament might weigh up, and then it would be based upon the legal evidence presented by the government. While such proposals would strengthen domestic constitutional procedures, they do not ensure that the government respects the substance of international law.

Nevertheless, in March 2004 the Select Committee on Public Administration produced a report entitled *Taming the Prerogative: Strengthening Ministerial Accountability to Parliament,* which 'while recognising that such powers are necessary for effective administration, especially in times of national emergency, the report considers that they should be subject to more systematic parliamentary oversight'.[30] Some of the evidence given to the Committee suggested legislation along the lines of the US War Powers Act passed after the Vietnam War, which tried to ensure that the 'collective judgement of both Congress and the President would apply to future exercises of the war-making power'.[31] The Committee's principal reason for wanting to reform the prerogative on the issue of troop deployment was that 'the decision whether or not to consult Parliament' was dependent 'on the generosity or good will of government', so that a mere convention that

[29] P. Bowers, 'Parliament and the Use of Force', House of Commons Library, Standard Note SN/IA/1218, 25 Feb. 2003, 4.

[30] HC 422, 16 March 2004, 3.

[31] Ibid., 9 (Benn); but see 10 (Hague). For analysis of different democratic countries' constitutional processes on war powers see C. Ku and H.K. Jacobson (eds), *Democratic Accountability and the Use of Force in International Law* (Cambridge: Cambridge University Press, 2003).

parliament be consulted was 'not enough when lives are at stake'. Further, the 'increasing frequency of conflict in recent years is proof of the importance of ensuring that, when the country takes military action, Parliament supported the government in its decision'.[32] In a more general attack on prerogative powers the Committee stated:

The prerogative has allowed powers to move from Monarch to Ministers without Parliament having a say in how they are exercised. This should no longer be acceptable to Parliament or the people. We have shown how these powers can begin to be constitutionalised, and in particular how certain key powers can be anchored in the consent of Parliament for their exercise.[33]

The Draft Bill attached to the report would have required that 'Her Majesty's armed forces shall take part in armed conflict only if participation in it is approved by resolution of each House of Parliament', using the concept of 'armed conflict', found in the Geneva Conventions of 1949. Resolutions must be obtained before 'those armed forces participate in armed conflict' or if the government 'is of the opinion that such participation is necessary as a matter of urgency before such resolutions could be obtained, within seven days of the beginning of that participation'.[34]

Similar difficulties emerge from this proposal in that the concept of 'armed conflict' is perhaps no clearer that that of 'hostilities' with no clear definition in the Geneva Conventions or more generally in international humanitarian law.[35] There remains the problem of the government deploying troops and then seeking parliamentary approval, which would be difficult for parliament to refuse without causing a serious crisis. In resisting the recommendation to put prerogative powers under a statutory framework, the government pointed to the difficulties in definition and timing, saying on the latter that the existing arrangements which allow for British involvement in 'armed conflict to be debated and scrutinised by Parliament after the event are by no means unique to the UK'.[36]

Clare Short, MP for Birmingham Ladywood, who resigned from the Labour government in May 2003 over the invasion of Iraq, introduced a Private Members' Bill in 2005, which was based on the Public Administration Select Committee's Bill. The proposed norm was approval of both Houses before any participation in an armed conflict, with the exception being retrospective approval in matters of urgency. The Bill would also have required that in seeking approval from Parliament the Prime Minister present the reasons for the proposed participation, any legal authority, as well as the geographical extent, duration and the

---

[32] HC 422, 16.   [33] Ibid., 17.

[34] Ibid., 35–6. Draft Ministers of the Crown (Executive Powers) Bill prepared by Professor Rodney Brazier.

[35] Y. Dinstein, *The Conduct of Hostilities under the Law of International Armed Conflict* (Cambridge: Cambridge University Press, 2004) ch. 2.

[36] Government Response to HC 422, July 2004.

types and numbers of forces.[37] In introducing the Bill Clare Short spoke about the problems with the current system where the 'power to make war belongs to the Prime Minister and requires no approval from Parliament', so that in the case of the invasion of Iraq, 'he was entitled to do what he thought was right and then set out to persuade, in the way that he found best, the Cabinet, Parliament and country to support the decision that he had already made', with troops already committed.[38] Sir Menzies Campbell MP of the Liberal Democrats supported the Bill and stated that on the issue of the legal case for war the House would have to see a full legal opinion rather than an abbreviated one that presented the government's case in the best light.[39] Some of the discussion centred on the difference between the Gulf War of 1991 where a clear case was made based on international law and the 2003 invasion of Iraq when there was no clear legal basis,[40] which suggests that a clear international legal basis should be a prerequisite for approval.

The constitutional difficulty in making parliament co-responsible for decisions to go to war was pointed to by James Gray, Conservative MP for North Wiltshire:

The Prime Minister and the Government are of course accountable to the House. If they took us into some absurd war that did not have popular support, or did not have the support of this House, the Government would without question fall. That is the point about parliamentary scrutiny of the Executive: it is not about telling the Executive in advance what we want them to do but about examining what they have done and if it was unreasonable...it would result in the resignation of a Minister, or ultimately the fall of the Government. That is the nature of Parliamentary democracy. The whole reason for having an Executive is that the Executive carry things out. They do things and this place scrutinises what they have done. The Bill would remove the ability to be an Executive from the Government and makes it this place that made decisions about what the Government should do.[41]

Despite the possible constitutional weaknesses of the proposals being put forward, the House of Lords' Select Committee on the Constitution also produced a report in July 2006 urging reform. In *Waging War: Parliament's Role and Responsibility* the Committee considered the 'alternatives there are to the use of the Royal prerogative power in the deployment of armed force', in particular whether parliamentary approval should be required for any deployment of British forces outside the UK. It also considered whether the government should be required to explain the legal basis for any use of force, and so whether

---

[37] Armed Force (Parliamentary Approval for Participation in Armed Conflict) Bill, 22 June 2005.

[38] *Hansard* HC vol 437, cols 1085–93, 21 Oct. 2005 (Short).

[39] Ibid., col 1090 (Menzies-Campbell).

[40] Ibid., cols 1104–5 (Flynn, Menzies-Campbell, Short).

[41] Ibid., col 1108 (Gray). Though the Bill received 91 votes in its favour to 12 against, this was an insufficient number for it to proceed.

the courts would then have competence to rule upon the government's decision to use force.[42] It concluded that the prerogative 'is outdated and should not be allowed to continue as the basis for legitimate war-making in our 21st century democracy'.[43] According to the Committee, parliament's role in decision-making should be established by convention rather than statute, and that convention should include parliamentary approval for any proposed deployment of British troops outside the UK into actual or potential armed conflict. In seeking approval the government would have to indicate the objectives and legal basis of the deployment, and approval for any significant change in these should be sought. It also recommended that retrospective approval should be sought only 'for reasons of emergency and security', within seven days of deployment.[44]

Interestingly the House of Lords' Committee made the point that in the 'absence of legal restraint on the deployment power under domestic law, the rules of international law on the use of force take on an enhanced significance as the only apparent limitation on the prerogative'.[45] This book has shown though, that while international law has an influence on debates, it is not sufficiently determinate in the final decision to go to war. Serious doubts about the legality of war have not deterred the government from making such decisions in Suez in 1956 or Iraq in 2003, nor have they prevented parliament from supporting, or at least not undermining those decisions. However, if the government was required to obtain and publish clear, independent legal advice, and that advice was to the effect that any proposed war was unlawful under international law, it would be more difficult for parliament to agree with a decision to use force.

Simply insisting that the government bring its decision before parliament before troops are deployed, and requiring the government to clearly state the legal basis for the war on the basis of independent and impartial advice, would be compatible with a view that the executive must be properly accountable to parliament, without making the latter part of the decision-making process. Votes may be taken, including ones on censure as with the current parliamentary process, but such an approach would remedy the problems caused by coming to the House too late in the day when troops are already deployed or committed even though they might not be fighting yet, and would also prevent the misleading of the House on the legal basis of the operation.

The analysis in this book has shown that in the cases of self-defence, when the life of the nation is at stake, the executive must make rapid decisions and so should not be hampered by additional processes. But if it is a true case of self-defence as a result of an armed attack on the UK then parliamentary scrutiny is not going to question the decision to resist aggression, even if the attack is not against mainland Britain. The Falklands War of 1982 shows this. In the

---

[42] House of Lords, Select Committee on the Constitution, 15th Report 2005–6, 27 July 2006 (HL 236-I), para 3.
[43] Ibid., para 103.   [44] Ibid., paras 108–10.
[45] Ibid., para 30.

case of coming to the aid of another state that is under attack then the Korean War in 1950 and the Gulf War of 1991 show that parliamentary scrutiny is not going to undermine the decisions of the Executive when, as in those situations, they have authority from the UN for such actions. Even in the case of the action in Afghanistan in 2001, which was taken under an expanded version of collective self-defence of the US after it suffered the attacks of 9/11, and which did not have Security Council authority but did have endorsement from that body, parliamentary scrutiny did not undermine the government's decision.

It is mainly in those cases where there was a clear lack of international legal basis—Suez in 1956, Bosnia in 1994, Kosovo in 1999, and Iraq in 2003—that parliament should have taken a stronger role, not simply in terms of voting on the matter but in terms of questioning the decisions to go to war. Parliamentary scrutiny did occur but it was not strong enough to challenge the case for war. The votes in 2002–3 on Iraq supporting the government show that the problem of prosecuting unlawful wars is not going to be tackled by introducing votes alone, since in those instances the government won those votes and historically it always has done so, but rather by parliament adopting a far more critical response to decisions to go to war, using international law as a key reference point. It is true that the Attorney General's full advice was not before parliament in March 2003, but there was plenty of advice in the public domain that the war was not justified under international law, and politicians simply chose to ignore this. The tendency is for any criticism to be outweighed by the need to support British troops and not to be seen as appeasing aggressors or brutal dictators. Crudely put, criticism of decisions to go to war is portrayed as unpatriotic and most members of parliament are not prepared to risk their positions and challenge the government, particularly if they are part of the majority from which the government is drawn. Parliament is simply not independent enough nor, it seems, strong enough, to scrutinize the actions of the executive in matters of such importance as decisions to go to war.

Nevertheless, the main parties seem to be moving towards a consensus that parliament must approve of any decision to deploy troops, as found in other countries such as the Netherlands and Germany, but not in others where the decision lies with the executive (for example Australia, France, Italy, and Spain). The Conservative Party's Democracy Task Force produced a report (*An End to Sofa Government*) in 2006 in which a belief was expressed that a parliamentary convention should be adopted requiring the laying of a resolution in the House of Commons in order to commit British troops to any 'war, international armed conflict or peace-keeping activity' with retrospective approval reserved for situations of 'dire emergency'.[46] Before becoming Prime Minister in 2007, Gordon

---

[46] Conservative Democracy Task Force, *An End to Sofa Government: Better Working of Prime Minister and Cabinet* (2006) 8.

Brown had stated in January 2006 that a 'case now exists for a further restriction of executive power and a detailed consideration of the role of Parliament in the declaration of peace and war'.[47] This was in the context of the new Prime Minister's desire, in the words of the Commons Select Committee on Public Administration, 'to hold power more accountable', both to parliament and the people.[48] This would include a government proposal on the deployment of armed forces abroad that would balance accountability against the needs to be flexible and to maintain operational security.[49]

A consultation paper was drawn up by the Ministry of Justice in October 2007 summarizing the debate and putting forward different options for a 'more formal way of regularizing Parliament's involvement in decisions on the deployment of armed forces in armed conflict overseas'. These had common features of requiring the 'Government to seek authorisation from the House of Commons before participating in armed conflict overseas, or before committing armed forces to a situation where there is a real likelihood that they might become engaged in armed conflict'.[50] In March 2008 a draft House of Commons resolution was published in the Constitutional Renewal White Paper. By this the government has made it clear that 'while not ruling out legislation in the future', it 'believes that a detailed resolution is the best way forward'. In fact the proposed resolution, as explained in the government's White Paper, is a watered-down affair giving maximum flexibility to the Prime Minister as to timing in seeking prior approval, and requiring no retrospective approval when the operation is secret or urgent. On the timing for seeking prior approval the Prime Minister 'will have to consider the time required to give Parliament a real say in the decision'. Approval need only be sought from the House of Commons 'as the representatives of the people', and not from the House of Lords. Further, the proposal does not require that the advice of the Attorney General should be made available to Parliament, although it would be informed of the legal basis of the operation. The salient parts of the proposed Commons resolution would require that 'the approval of this House should be obtained for a conflict decision', which is a decision by the government 'to authorise the use of force by UK forces' outside the UK, the operation being regulated by the law of armed conflict. Further, 'it is for the Prime Minister to start the process in relation to approval', by setting out in a report both 'the terms of the proposed approval' and 'information about the objectives, locations and legal matters that the Prime Minister thinks appropriate in the circumstances'. The House of Commons must then 'give the approval

---

[47] House of Lords Select Committee on the Constitution, 15th Report of 2005–6, 27 July 2006, para 92 (HL 236-I).

[48] House of Commons Public Administration Select Committee, 'The Governance of Britain', First Special Report of 2006–7, 11 July 2007, para 1 (HC 901).

[49] Ministry of Justice, 'The Governance of Britain', July 2007, para 29 (CM 7170).

[50] Ministry of Justice, 'The Governance of Britain: War Powers and Treaties: Limiting Executive Powers', Consultation Paper CP26/07, 25 Oct. 2007, paras 96–7.

by resolving to approve the terms set out in the Prime Minister's report', for a decision to be made.[51]

The two Houses of Parliament then established a Joint Committee to examine the government's Draft Constitutional Renewal Bill, which covers not only war powers but also other matters including treaty-making powers. In its report of July 2008 the Committee largely agreed with the government's proposal for a detailed resolution, the content of which it was satisfied with except for a clearer definition of 'conflict decision'. It concluded that 'it is appropriate that the Executive should retain discretionary powers over such issues as the information provided to Parliament' and 'the timing of a vote', with the Prime Minister being in the 'best position to make an informed decision on such matters'. The Committee also agreed with the government 'that a retrospective approval process for conflict decisions is not desirable',[52] so that in emergency situations the government could deploy troops, then inform parliament without having to seek approval.

With neither of the main parties actively or at least consistently pursuing policies of non-intervention—evidenced in the survey in this book where a Conservative government launched military campaigns in Suez in 1956, the Falklands in 1982, the Gulf in 1991 and in Bosnia in 1994; while a Labour government deployed forces to Korea in 1950, Kosovo in 1991, Afghanistan in 1991 and Iraq in 2003—there is generally no overall opposition to any war, only individual MPs voicing concern and criticism. Following from this the current desire for reform of the decision-making process is unlikely to change government policy by making it less willing to commit troops, though greater clarity on the legal basis for war might make it more difficult to persuade parliament and the country that war is justified. However, the current proposal which seems to have sufficient support to be adopted, places the role of legal advice essentially under the control of the Prime Minister, with the prospect of re-runs of the controversies that surrounded the invasion of Iraq in 2003.

Furthermore, one of the objections to Clare Short's Bill was that the requirement of published legal advice would 'lead to court cases about the legitimacy or otherwise of political decisions'. In issues of war 'we cannot be governed by our judges; we must be governed by our sovereign Parliament—by the democratically elected representatives of the nation. I have a significant reservation about laying on the table legal justification and legal opinion, using that as a reference point and opening ourselves up to court cases that challenge the sovereignty of Parliament'.[53] One of the reasons why the government's reform proposal is in the form of a resolution rather than legislation is that a statute might give grounds for

---

[51] 'The Governance of Britain—Constitutional Renewal', March 2008, paras 215–23, and Annex A (Cm 7342-I).

[52] House of Lords, House of Commons Joint Committee on the Draft Constitutional Renewal Bill, Session 2007–8, 31 July 2008, paras 318, 332 (HL 166-I, HC 551-I).

[53] *Hansard* HC vol 437, col 1150, 21 Oct. 2005 (Grayling).

judicial review. As Sir Michael Wood, former Foreign Office Legal Adviser wrote in evidence to the Joint Committee on the Draft Constitutional Renewal Bill:

Unless the aim is to reduce the ability of the United Kingdom's armed forces to participate in overseas operations to the level of, say, those of Germany or Japan, great care should be taken not to judicialise the decision-making process. If matters of war and peace were to become justiciable in the courts of the United Kingdom, this would risk putting serious obstacles in the way of United Kingdom participation in United Nations, NATO, EU peace-keeping and other operations overseas, with the consequent diminution of our standing in the world. And it would risk involving the judiciary in highly political questions. Judges could find themselves having to second guess the Government, not only as regards the original decision to use armed force, but also as regards decisions to continue to use armed force, to use armed force in a certain way, and so on.... Ministers and military commanders would continually need to have regard to the judge over the shoulder. The distraction of court proceedings (which might well take place in the lead up to or during a conflict) ... would be considerable ... and there would be the prospect of legal proceedings dragging on for years thereafter.[54]

The objection to having independent scrutiny of the legality of decisions to go to war is due to the fact that the government of the day has to make rapid decisions and must weigh up a number of factors including, but not only, the legality of the proposed military action. However, most modern conflicts since the end of the Cold War in which Britain has been involved have had a relatively long lead-in period in which legal opinion could be given and tested before a court. Clearly in cases where a more rapid response is necessary, such as actions in self-defence, this cannot be the case, but then the issue may be one of true national defence during which the normal requirements of the rule of law may be suspended while the life of the country is in danger. Further, if the military action has a clear legal basis in either self-defence or by dint of Security Council authority, the government should have little to fear from the courts. The courts though are inherently reluctant to intervene in such decisions as the following analysis will show.

5. Accountability before the Courts

As related in chapter two, individuals have had little success in challenging the conflict decisions of the government before domestic courts. When in 2002 CND sought a declaration on the meaning of Security Council Resolution 1441 (2002) in relation to any decision by the government to go to war in Iraq on the basis of the Resolution, the Court, following a long line of precedents, refused to review the supremacy of the executive in the exercise of prerogative powers. The Divisional Court declined 'to embark upon a determination of an issue if to do so

---

[54] House of Lords, House of Commons, Joint Committee on the Draft Constitutional Renewal Bill, 2007–8, Volume II: Evidence, 12 Aug. 2008, 434–5 (HL 166-II, HC 551-II).

would be damaging to the public interests in the field of international relations, national security or defence'.[55] It is somewhat ironic though that in its reasoning the Court was dismissive of CND's claim that the government might go to war 'under a mistake of law'. Lord Justice Brown asked 'How real a risk is that?' He answers 'I am bound to say for my part that I think it no more than fanciful. Plainly the government has access to the best advice not only from law officers but also from a number of distinguished specialists in the field'.[56] As we have seen in the previous chapter, the legal advice given for the invasion of Iraq was far from convincing.

With direct access to judicial review of government decisions to go to war currently denied, it is necessary to look to the possibility of indirect review by the courts. It may be that cases brought on other grounds raise issues of the legality of a particular war. Courts Martial brought against soldiers do not directly put the government in the dock for its decisions to go to war, but the soldier may try to claim illegality of the conflict as some sort of defence. However, the courts have given short-shrift to any attempt to claim that a soldier's unlawful actions can be excused by reason of the alleged illegality of the conflict in which they are involved. When Flight Lieutenant Malcolm Kendall-Smith argued that he could not be obliged to go to Iraq to fight an illegal war, the Judge Advocate convicted him in 2007 for disobeying orders, ruling that the order was not unlawful since it was given after UN Resolutions had authorized the presence of the multinational force in post-invasion Iraq; but he also ruled that it was no defence that the defendant believed the order to be unlawful.[57]

When Margaret Jones claimed in her defence to a charge of criminal damage to military equipment (after breaking into an RAF base on 13 March 2003) that it was justified to prevent the commission of a greater crime—the crime of aggression against Iraq—the court dismissed her argument. Although the Law Lords found, without deciding whether Iraq was an illegal aggressive war, that aggression was a crime under international law, it was not a crime under English domestic law. Lord Bingham, without any sense of irony, stated that it was 'an important democratic principle' in Britain, 'that it is for those representing the people in the country in Parliament, not the executive and not the judges, to decide what conduct should be treated' as criminal under English law. Further, 'there are well-established rules that the courts will be very slow to review the exercise of prerogative powers in relation to the conduct of foreign affairs and the deployment of the armed services'.[58] Thus while democracy is important for

---

[55] *The Campaign for Nuclear Disarmament v The Prime Minister of the United Kingdom* [2002] EWHC 2777, para 47 (Brown LJ), relying on *Chandler v Director of Public Prosecutions* [1962] AC 763.

[56] Ibid., para 44.

[57] <http://news.bbc.co.uk/2/hi/uk_news/4905672.stm>, 18 Oct. 2007. Summarized in *R (Gentle) v The Prime Minister* [2006] UKHL 20, para 50 (Baroness Hale).

[58] *R v Jones* [2006] UKHL 16, paras 29–30.

determining the criminal law of the country, it is not important enough to restrict the executive's right to go to war.

Similarly, when Rose Gentle, the mother of a soldier killed in Iraq, claimed a right to have an independent inquiry into the wider circumstances surrounding the death of Fusilier Gordon Gentle and his comrades on 28 June 2004, as part of the British government's obligation to uphold the right to life under article 2 of the European Convention on Human Rights incorporated into English law by the Human Rights Act 1998, the Law Lords again were unwilling to become involved in upholding rights that would challenge the government's decisions to go to war. Lord Bingham gave a number of reasons as to why article 2 of the European Convention 'has never been held to apply to the process of deciding on the lawfulness of the resort to arms, despite the number of occasions of which member states made that decision over the past half century and despite the fact that such a decision almost inevitably exposes military personnel to the risk of fatalities'. First of all, 'the lawfulness of military action has no bearing on the risk of fatalities', giving the example of the Japanese surprise attack on Pearl Harbor, which, though illegal, minimized Japanese casualties. In any case Fusilier Gentle had been killed after 'Security Council Resolution 1546 had legitimated British military action in Iraq, so that such action was not by then unlawful even if it had earlier been so'. Finally, to allow such claims would mean that the courts would be 'drawn into consideration of issues which judicial tribunals have traditionally been reluctant to entertain because they recognise their limitations as suitable bodies to resolve them'.[59]

Though their Lordships exercised the traditional restraint on issues of 'high policy', the mention of the legitimating effect of Resolution 1546 does offer some crumbs of comfort for those seeking signs of a willingness to review. Stronger fare can indeed be found in the opinion of Baroness Hale who labelled the advice given by the Attorney General on the 7 March 2003 on the legality of the invasion of Iraq as 'very far from clear and unambiguous' with the revival argument within it—that Resolution 678 (1990) was revived in 2003—being 'controversial'. She expressed sympathy with the mothers of the dead soldiers: 'if the use of force was lawful, it would be of some comfort to know that their sons had died in a just cause. If it was not, there might at least be some public acknowledgment and attribution of responsibility and lessons learned for the future'. Baroness Hale went on to say that though she wished 'that we could spell out of article 2 a duty in a state not to send its soldiers to fight in an unlawful war', the House of Lords could not go that far given that 'the lawfulness of war is an issue between states, not between individuals or between individuals and the state'. Clearly Baroness Hale struggled with the issue but ultimately declined to suggest a move towards review stating that while the 'state that goes to war cannot and should not be the judge of whether or not the war was lawful

---

[59]   *R (Gentle) v The Prime Minister* [2008] UKHL 20, para 8.

in international law', 'that question can only be authoritatively decided, not by us or by Strasbourg, but by the international institutions which police the international treaties governing the law of war'.[60] The problem is that with the UK having a veto on the main body which polices the UN Charter, we have to look to other bodies such as the General Assembly, or the International Court of Justice to see if they can call the government to account for their illegal wars. As we have seen, the General Assembly, while willing to act as the conscience of the superpowers during the Cold War, has lost its voice after the fall of the Berlin Wall. The International Court of Justice is severely hampered by the fact that states must consent to its jurisdiction before it can hear a case.

Though the House of Lords has established that the European Convention does apply to places of detention in Iraq thereby allowing claims of human rights abuse to be brought by Iraqi detainees or their families against the government,[61] this falls short of reviewing the decisions to go to war themselves. Essentially, the English courts have refused to question the government's decisions to go to war; in effect they have refused individuals the right to call the government to account for waging allegedly illegal wars which have led to the loss of British lives. The courts' decision is not purely a legal one, though it is based on a traditional view of the constitution whereby such executive decisions cannot be challenged before the courts. However, the courts have expressed a willingness to review the use of prerogative powers in other areas.[62]

Turning to cases brought before international courts against the British government for violations of international law, including international and regional human rights law, the picture is no brighter. In fact the *Corfu Channel* case of 1949, dealt with in chapter two, is the main instance in the International Court's history of Britain being found to have violated international law in that case by despatching a minesweeping operation to Albanian waters. Even then the court spoke about unlawful intervention by the UK rather than the unlawful use of force.[63] Another occasion on which the UK has appeared before the court was as one of the respondents in cases brought by Serbia against the UK and nine other NATO countries in 1999 for their bombing of Serbia during the air campaign to stop Serbian repression in Kosovo. Ultimately the court did not find that it had jurisdiction to hear the case in 2004.[64] Though there may be cases

---

[60] Ibid., paras 47, 53–8.

[61] *R (Al-Skeini) v Secretary of State for Defence* [2007] UKHL 26. See discussion of the case of Baha Mousa in chapter two. See generally P. Rowe, *The Impact of Human Rights Law on Armed Forces* (Cambridge: Cambridge University Press, 2006).

[62] Most recently the House of Lords in *R (Bancoult) v Secretary of State for Foreign and Commonwealth Affairs (No 2)* [2008] UKHL 61.

[63] 1949 ICJ Rep. at 35.

[64] *Case Concerning the Legality of Use of Force (Serbia and Montenegro v UK) Preliminary Objections*, 2004 ICJ Rep. 1307. See also the case brought by relatives of those killed by NATO bombing of the Serbian TV station before the European Court of Human Rights in *Bankovic v Belgium*, ECHR Decision of 12 Dec. 2001 (Appl. No. 52207/99) at 9. The Court declared it did not have jurisdiction given that the right to life guaranteed by the European Convention did not

brought against Britain in the future, the fact that before the International Court states must consent to its jurisdiction[65] makes it unlikely, at least in any systematic sense. Thus the most controversial war, namely that prosecuted against Iraq in 2003, was not litigated before the International Court. Though the Court's jurisprudence on the use of force, in cases such as the *Corfu Channel*, reinforces and develops the rules, it is not equipped to be a regular and reliable mechanism of accountability.

There is though the prospect of indicting individual political leaders for their decision to go to war before the International Criminal Court (ICC). However, this will not happen until the state parties to the Rome Statute establishing the Court have agreed on a definition of aggression.[66] It is interesting to note that while German leaders were tried for crimes against peace before the Nuremberg Tribunal in 1946, there can, as yet, be no trial for the equivalent crime of aggression before the International Criminal Court though it is listed as one of the crimes.[67] Though the post-Cold War period has seen the international trial of a political leader of a country (President Milosevic of Serbia before the ICTY who died during the trial in 2006), and the request for an arrest warrant against another (President al-Bashir of Sudan in July 2008 by the ICC Prosecutor), the charges against them were for crimes against humanity and genocide, not aggression. Although there were attempts to persuade the ICTY and the ICC to indict Prime Minister Tony Blair for alleged crimes committed against Serbia in 1999 and Iraq in 2003, they singularly failed. More progress was made on the issue whether NATO had committed war crimes in relation to targeting issues during the Kosovo bombing campaign, when targets included bridges, roads, convoys and a TV station leading to several hundred civilian casualties. The jurisdiction of the ICTY extends to possible NATO crimes in Yugoslavia, article 7 of the tribunal's Statute stating that a political leader can be held individually responsible 'if he knew or had reason to know that the subordinate was about to commit such actions'. However, the Prosecutor ruled out any prosecution of individuals involved in the NATO operation on the questionable grounds that 'either the law is not sufficiently clear or investigations are unlikely to result in the acquisition of sufficient evidence'.[68]

---

extend to the applicants who were not within a state party to the Convention nor in an area under the effective control of such a party.

[65] Art 36(1) of the Statute of the International Court of Justice 1945.

[66] A Special Working Group on the Crime of Aggression was established in 2002 by the Assembly of State Parties to the Rome Statute, and is making progress towards a proposal to be put forward for adoption at the Rome Review Conference in 2009. For the latest Working Group Report see ICC-ASP/6/20/Add. 1 (June 2008).

[67] Art 5(1) of the Rome Statute of the International Criminal Court 1998.

[68] 'Final Report to the Prosecutor by the Committee Established to Review the NATO Bombing Campaign against the Federal Republic of Yugoslavia', June 2000, para 90 available at <http:www.un.org/icty/cases-e/index-e.htm> (accessed 26 Jan. 2009). For criticism of this decision see P. Benvenuti, 'The ICTY Prosecutor and the Review of the NATO Bombing against the Federal Republic of Yugoslavia' (2001) 12 EJIL 503.

6. The Dominance of Security Concerns before the Courts

We have seen that domestic courts have been unwilling to review decisions to go to war. An explanation of this is the reluctance of the courts to adjudicate on issues of national security, since this might compromise the nation's defence. We might expect international courts to be less influenced by this concern. In a wider security context, which includes non-forcible as well as forcible measures, this has led to the British government relying on the supremacy of Security Council resolutions before courts in order to prevent any review of its policies. If we look at the International Court's jurisprudence more widely to include cases in the area of peace and security involving Britain we can see an alarming trend in which the government in effect tries (often successfully) to hide behind Security Council resolutions. By consistently arguing that a combination of articles 25 and 103 of the UN Charter which between them provide that binding decisions of the Council prevail over any other inconsistent treaty obligation, the UK government has argued on a number of occasions, before domestic courts and regional courts as well as the International Court, that this means that it cannot be held to account for violations of its treaty obligations, including those arising under human rights covenants.

This argument has been made by the UK government when applying UN economic measures against countries and more recently individuals. It argues that Security Council economic sanctions imposed under chapter VII (article 41) of the Charter are binding by virtue of article 25 on all member states and therefore they must be applied against the target state or targeted individuals. Further, given that article 103 provides for the supremacy of Charter obligations over other treaty duties, the argument is that states are obliged to disregard any treaty duty (including one protecting human rights) that might prevent the successful application of the sanctions.

This argument was successfully used by the UK before the International Court of Justice in a case brought against it (and the US) by Libya in 1992. Libya had argued that by securing Security Council Resolution 748 of 1992 that imposed sanctions on Libya unless two Libyan individuals suspected of the Lockerbie bombing of 1988 were handed over, the UK (and the US) had violated the Montreal Convention of 1971. The 1971 Convention, to which all three of the litigant states were parties and which provided for the International Court's jurisdiction in case of dispute, covered the sort of terrorist offence committed over Lockerbie, and entitled the Libyans to prosecute the individuals themselves rather than hand them over to other states that claimed jurisdiction. In its provisional measures judgments of 1992, the Court upheld the British and American arguments and denied Libya's request for protection by declaring that the obligations imposed by Resolution 748 *prima facie* applied to all the parties and that this obligation prevailed over any other treaty obligation including those in the 1971 Convention by virtue of article 103 of the UN Charter.[69]

It is important to note that the judgment only accepted this contention *prima facie*, which led to speculation that the argument might not be accepted at the merits stage, speculation fuelled both by the separate opinions of several of the judges in 1992,[70] and by the fact that the court allowed the case to proceed to the merits. Ultimately the case was not decided as relations between the countries improved and the case was withdrawn from the court's docket in 2003. Despite these caveats the supremacy of Security Council decisions became accepted orthodoxy, and has been followed by both the English House of Lords and the European Court of Human Rights.

Although not a case involving economic sanctions, the *Al-Jedda* judgment of the House of Lords in 2007 raised similar issues of supremacy. The appellant (a British/Iraqi national) had been held since 2004 by British troops at detention facilities in Iraq. He complained that the detention infringed his rights under article 5 of the European Convention on Human Rights ('everyone has the right to liberty and security of person. No one shall be deprived of his liberty save in the following cases and in accordance with a procedure prescribed by law . . .'). Al-Jedda was not charged with any offence, and no charge or trial was in prospect. As explained by Lord Bingham in the judgment 'he has been arrested and has since been detained on the ground that his internment is necessary for imperative reasons of security in Iraq. He is suspected of being a member of a terrorist group involved in weapons smuggling and explosive attacks in Iraq'. 'These allegations are roundly denied by the appellant, and they have not been tested in any proceedings'.[71]

The courts below were faced with the issue of whether article 5(1) of the Convention was qualified by Security Council Resolution 1546, which was adopted under chapter VII of the UN Charter and which empowered the multinational force in Iraq to take 'all necessary measures to contribute to the maintenance and stability in Iraq . . . including by preventing and deterring terrorism'. The Resolution also endorsed a letter attached to the Resolution from the US Secretary of State (Colin Powell) which stated that measures included 'internment where . . . necessary for imperative reasons of security in Iraq'.

In upholding the government's argument that the obligations imposed by the Security Council prevailed, it is clear that their Lordships were uneasy. Lord Bingham was clearly of the opinion that the appellant's rights had been violated but felt that the court had to accept the overriding nature of the obligation

---

[69] *Questions of Interpretation and Application of the 1971 Montreal Convention Arising from the Aerial Incident at Lockerbie*, 1992 ICJ Rep. 114 at 126.

[70] See T.M. Franck, 'The Powers of Appreciation: Who is the Ultimate Guardian of UN Legality?' (1992) 86 AJIL 519.

[71] *R (Al-Jedda) v Secretary of State for Defence* [2007] UKHL 58, at para 2.

imposed by the Council. 'In the absence of some exonerating condition, the detention would plainly infringe his right under article 5(1)'.[72] In dismissing the appeal, the court was not prepared to challenge the security imperative behind the Resolution and strongly advocated by the British government. The clash between the duty to detain and the duty to secure the appellant's human rights could only be reconciled by ruling that the 'UK may lawfully, where it is necessary for imperative reasons of security, exercise the power to detain authorised by UNSCR 1546 and successive resolutions, but must ensure that the detainee's rights under article 5 are not infringed to any greater extent than is inherent in such detention'.[73] Though the court in *Al-Jedda* did try to reduce the harshness of detention powers granted, it is not clear that this was adequate to allay Lord Carswell's fears that 'internment without trial is so antithetical to the rule of law as understood in a democratic society'.[74]

The European Court of Human Rights has also addressed the supremacy of Security Council imposed obligations in the *Behrami* case of 2007, which involved the death and injury of the applicant's sons caused by unexploded NATO cluster bombs that had not been cleared in post-conflict Kosovo by French-KFOR troops.[75]

The judgment was a controversial one but turned on the issue of responsibility. Since it found the UN and not France responsible,[76] it was not necessary for the court to comment on the application of article 103. However, both the respondent states as well as the UK government in its representations to the court, argued the supremacy of Security Council obligations in Resolution 1244 (1999), which was the legal basis of KFOR and UNMIK in Kosovo.[77] In response to these arguments the court stated generally that 'the Convention has to be interpreted in the light of any relevant rules of international law applicable in relations between its Contracting Parties'.

[72] Ibid., para 27.

[73] Ibid., para 39. Lords Rogers and Brown agreed, as did a reluctant Baroness Hale saying the 'right is qualified but not displaced...the right is qualified only to the extent required or authorised by the resolution' (para 126). Lord Carswell adopted a similar line saying that the power to intern may lawfully be exercised by the UK but only in such a way 'to minimise the infringement of the detainee's rights' under the Convention (para 136). In particular he identified the following 'safeguards': 'the compilation of intelligence about such persons which is accurate and reliable as possible, the regular review of the continuing need to detain each person and a system whereby that need and the underlying evidence can be checked and challenged by representatives on behalf of the detained persons, so far as is practicable and consistent with the needs of national security and the safety of other persons' (para 30).

[74] Ibid., para 57. A further case is expected before the English courts on the detention of Iraqis by UK forces: see *R (Al-Saddoon and Mufdhi) v Secretary of State for Defence* being litigated before the High Court in November 2008 (<http://www.publicinterestlawyers.co.uk> (accessed 26 Jan. 2009)).

[75] *Behrami and Saramati v France, Germany and Norway*, ECHR Grand Chamber Decision as to Admissibility of Application No. 71412/01, and Application No. 78166/01.

[76] Ibid., para 33.

[77] For UK argument see ibid., para 113.

The court therefore had regard to the two complementary provisions of the UN Charter—articles 25 and 103 'as interpreted by the International Court of Justice'—citing the *Lockerbie* cases.[78] It went on to state that 'the primary objective of the UN is the maintenance of international peace and security', and that 'while it is equally clear that ensuring respect for human rights represents an important contribution to achieving international peace...the fact remains that the UNSC has primary responsibility, as well as extensive means under Charter VII, to fulfil this objective, notably through the use of coercive powers'.[79] This, according to the court meant that the Convention could not be 'interpreted in a manner which would subject the acts and omissions of Contracting Parties which are covered by UNSC Resolutions and occur prior to or in the course of such missions, to the scrutiny of the Court'. The court stated that 'to do so would be to interfere with the fulfilment of the UN's key mission in this field including...with the effective conduct of its operations. It would also be tantamount to imposing conditions on the implementation of a UNSC Resolution which were not provided for in the text of the Resolution itself'.[80]

This seems to accept the supremacy of Security Council resolutions and puts the obligations created by that organ over those under existing human rights treaties, including the right to life. The *Behrami* judgment is reflective of a growing tendency to accept the Security Council as increasingly omnipotent, especially when dealing with global threats such as al-Qaeda, so that a combination of articles 25 and 103 of the UN Charter will even override human rights.[81] In effect, supposedly constitutional provisions of the UN Charter (especially article 103)[82] are being used to override constitutional rights. This seemed to be the orthodoxy until the European Court of Justice's judgment in *Kadi* in 2008.[83] In the case the applicant sought to overturn Community legislation that implemented Security Council anti-terrorist resolutions (especially Resolution 1267 of 1999), on the basis that his listing by the Security Council had led, by dint of the obligation imposed by the Security Council, to the freezing of his assets, thereby denying his right to property and his right to challenge the freezing order. True to its arguments before the House of Lords in *Al-Jedda*, and the European Court of Human Rights in *Behrami*, the UK government strongly argued for the supremacy of Security Council imposed obligations in its representations to the European Court of Justice.[84]

---

[78] Ibid., paras 27 and 147.   [79] Ibid., para 148.
[80] Ibid., para 149.
[81] See, for example, J.E. Alvarez, *International Organizations as Lawmakers* (Oxford: Oxford University Press, Oxford, 2005) 207.
[82] See R. Bernhardt, 'Article 103', in B. Simma (ed), *The Charter of the United Nations: A Commentary* (2nd edn, Oxford: Oxford University Press, 2002) 1299.
[83] Judgment of the Court (Grand Chamber) of 3 September 2008, *Yassin Abdullah Kadi, Al Barakaat International Foundation v Council of the European Union and Commission of the European Communities* (Joined Cases C-402/05 P and C-415/05 P).
[84] Ibid., paras 86, 118.

At the outset of the *Kadi* judgment the European Court of Justice cited relevant provisions of the UN Charter (including articles 25 and 103), but also significantly mentioned article 24,[85] paragraph 2 of which states that the Council in carrying out its duties to maintain international peace and security 'shall act in accordance with the Purposes and Principles of the United Nations'. The purposes and principles contained in articles 1 and 2 of the Charter are broad but they include the achievement of international co-operation 'in promoting and encouraging respect for human rights and for fundamental freedoms for all without distinction as to race, language, or religion'. It is in fulfilment of this purpose that instruments such as the 1948 Universal Declaration of Human Rights were adopted by the General Assembly, embedding human rights in the UN system, and being the source of customary law and the inspiration for treaties both international and regional. Thus when article 103 speaks in terms of 'a conflict of obligations... under the present Charter and... obligations under any other international agreement', the matter is not a simple application of articles 25 and 103 to override any treaty obligation that might impinge on the most efficient method of implementing the sanction.

The court's reasoning in *Kadi* is compatible with a human rights approach to Security Council resolutions, though the judgment was limited to the issue of the implementation of regulations within the EU legal order. The court was very clear though on the fundamentals of the EU legal order which is based on the rule of law, and a legal order which contains a 'complete system of legal remedies and procedures designed to enable the Court of Justice to review the legality of acts of the institutions'.[86] There is no critique of the UN system by the court, but there is clearly a less developed legal order within the UN, to the extent that we can say that though lawmaking and judicial elements are present, it is not governed by the strict application of the rule of law, exemplified in the workings of the Security Council where judicial, legislative and executive powers are intertwined and almost completely subject to unaccountable political judgment. To give such a political body power to override human rights, even in the name of peace and security, would be to allow it to subvert the rule of law in domestic and regional systems.

The European Court of Justice in *Kadi* puts fundamental rights at the heart of the EU legal order drawing 'inspiration' from the domestic legal order of member states and from international instruments, especially the European Convention on Human Rights. Thus 'respect for human rights is a condition of the lawfulness of Community acts',[87] with the result that implementation of obligations imposed under the UN Charter within the EU legal order cannot undermine human rights.[88] At the same time the court accepted that its judgment did

---

[85] Ibid., para 4. Article 24 of the UN Charter is also mentioned at para 294.
[86] Ibid., para 281.   [87] Ibid., paras 283–4.
[88] Ibid., para 285.

'not entail any challenge to the primacy' of the Security Council's resolution in international law.[89] By allowing the Council of Ministers a brief period of time to fix the regulations 'to remedy the infringements found, but which also takes account of the considerable impact of the restrictive measures concerned on the appellant's rights and duties',[90] the European Court of Justice was in effect recognizing that targeted sanctions are lawful if they are imposed in such a way as to be human rights compliant.

Despite its limitations, the *Kadi* judgment does give some hope that the courts will be more willing to challenge the supremacy of Security Council resolutions. Though there remains little possibility of the International Court reviewing the legality of Security Council resolutions, this should not stop other courts assessing more carefully their effects. Countries like the US and UK are seeking Security Council authority for their actions not simply to enable them to wage war or to list suspected terrorists, but to argue that the authority granted to them in these resolutions effectively can override even the most important of obligations—those requiring states like the UK to protect human rights.[91] While the courts might not be able to challenge resolutions *per se*, they can at least mitigate the effects of them by recognizing that they do simply sweep aside any international obligation that might impinge on their effective implementation. It is interesting that the English Court of Appeal has in 2008 considered the implementation of targeted sanctions within the UK by orders made under the United Nations Act of 1946. While accepting the legality of these orders it did state that the applicant was entitled to have a merits based review of the basis of the listing, and if the court were to hold that the individual should not be listed then the government should take steps to delist him.[92]

None of this though enables the British or international courts to challenge decisions to go to war *per se*, especially if the decision is undertaken by dint of authority granted by the Security Council in a resolution authorizing 'necessary measures'. Though such a resolution cannot override the obligations of member states under humanitarian law if they act under the resolution,[93] it does exonerate them from their obligation not to use force in international relations, for as was stated in chapter two, acting under the authority of the Security Council is a clear exception to the prohibition on the use of force in the UN Charter. However, where there is no such resolution, international courts clearly have jurisdiction and domestic courts may decide at some future point that decisions to go to war

---

[89] Ibid., para 288.   [90] Ibid., para 375.

[91] Though it is not clear that the Security Council as a whole intends this: see SC Res. 1456 of 20 Jan. 2003 (Declaration on Combating Terrorism) which in part declares that states 'must ensure that any measure taken to combat terrorism comply with all their obligations under international law, and should adopt measures in accordance with international law, in particular international human rights, refugee, and humanitarian law'.

[92] *G v HM Teasury* [2008] EWCA Civ 1187.

[93] R. Liivoja, 'The Scope of the Supremacy Clause of the United Nations Charter' (2008) 57 ICLQ 583 at 589.

that are not clearly justified under international law should be within their power of review. Having said this, a comparative analysis of other countries shows that judicial review of such decisions is far and away the exception to the rule.[94]

With the International Court of Justice hampered by the fact that states must consent to appear before it, more pressure is on domestic and regional courts, which are at least more accessible, to take the initiative. Domestic courts have taken the approach that decisions to go to war are issues of high policy or are political questions, but this calls into question the very heart of democracies based on the rule of law. The *Lockerbie* cases before the International Court of Justice show the difficulty of obtaining a review of Security Council resolutions at the international level. At both domestic and international levels the rule of law is incomplete when considering decisions to go to war. At both domestic and international levels the executive will not be held to account before the courts for such decisions. At regional level, despite the judgment in *Kadi*, the European Court of Justice's lack of competence over the second pillar of the EU—concerning foreign and security policy—restricts its capability to review decisions on security issues except where they involve economic matters over which it has jurisdiction. Finally the European Court of Human Rights' competence is restricted to breaches of the Convention, which may only indirectly raise issues of war. Thus the prospect of developing a more than incidental form of judicial review of decisions to go to war is remote.

7. Conclusion

While criticism may be made of illegal interventions at the international level, principally by the UN General Assembly, this is not going to stop illegal wars from being prosecuted. This can only be done, at the current time, at the domestic level. The consensus in the UK seems to be that reform is necessary to require that parliamentary approval be given before troops can be deployed to any conflict zone. Though the proposal has been weakened over time, this would at least require the government's case to be made to parliament. The absence in the proposal of any requirement for impartial advice on the legal basis of the proposed military action is predictable but disappointing given that the major problems of legitimacy that the government has encountered with recent military interventions, especially in Iraq in 2003, are directly traceable to the lack of a sound legal basis of the military action. If the action has such a basis, as with a number of British military actions examined in this book—principally Korea in 1950, the Falklands in 1982, and Iraq in 1991—and others that seemed to be

---

[94] L.F. Damrosch, 'The Interface of National Constitutional Systems with International Law and Institutions on Using Military Forces: Changing Trends in Executive and Legislative Powers', in Ku and Jacobson (eds), *Democratic Accountability*, 57.

accepted at the international level as lawful (Sierra Leone for instance in 2000 and Afghanistan in 2001), then the government has little to fear. However, given that British governments, both Labour and Conservative, have a record of more dubious interventions—from the Corfu Channel incident in 1946, to Suez in 1956, as well as Kosovo in 1999 and Iraq in 2003, the unwillingness to release clear legal advice is understandable, but the concern of parliament should be to prevent illegal wars from being prosecuted.

With clarity about the international legal basis, the House of Commons ought to be more willing to challenge those decisions to go to war that are in breach of the rules governing the use of force. It might decide that in certain cases analogous to Kosovo the moral imperative is to take action though there is no clear justification in international law, but at least it will do so on the basis of clear legal advice. All this though depends on MPs freeing themselves from party discipline on such matters as war and peace as well as from what appears to be a fear of appearing weak, and overcoming the unwillingness of politicians to be perceived as undermining the morale of the armed forces. Criticizing the legal, political and military justifications given by the government should not be seen somehow as unpatriotic. MPs should take account of and give voice to the views of the people they represent. In addition, they should be open to the views of organized groups of pro as well as anti-war protestors, as well as any clearly identifiable public opinion on the legality, legitimacy and desirability of any proposed conflict.

The role of 'world opinion' in shaping political decisions is perhaps exaggerated, though there were widespread demonstrations against the Iraq war of 2003. The idea that all global citizens should be able to influence political decisions that affect them is an ideal that, if we consider the democratic deficit in international organizations, is a long way from being achieved. Cosmopolitan democracy may be a distant dream, but within democracies the arguments of this school of thought are persuasive. Daniele Archibugi has recently argued that 'popular control should restrain the executive from waging wars that jeopardize the life and welfare of its citizens'. However, the reality is that 'the incidence of wars waged by democracies is comparable to that waged by autocracies', a fact explicable by the strategy deployed by countries such as the US and the UK to use technology to limit their casualties as much as possible, epitomized by Operation Allied Force over Kosovo. Archibugi adopts a strong Kantian position that democracies should act abroad as they act within their own countries, rather than ignoring basic norms of behaviour as autocracies do. When abuses of international law are committed by democracies 'they violate the democracies' own constituent pact', thereby 'jeopardizing the very existence of the political community'.[95]

---

[95] D. Archibugi, *The Global Commonwealth of Citizens* (Princeton: Princeton University Press, 2008) 62–3, 74–5, 274–6.

Could greater review by independent courts be a part of the framework of accountability? The reluctance of domestic courts to concern themselves with such matters of high policy is understandable. For one thing there would be a great fear that embroiling the government in court cases would inhibit the efficiency of decision-making and therefore the effectiveness of response. But as has been argued the urgency to respond is great in situations of aggression or genocide, but not so in other situations where troops are deployed (for example in the case of breach of disarmament resolutions). Judicial intervention in these cases may not be detrimental to the effective prosecution of military action.

Given that decisions to go to war primarily have an impact in the international legal order between states it should be the International Court of Justice that has the capability of calling the government to account. The consensual basis of its competence severely restricts its impact as a mechanism of accountability, and there appears little prospect of it being reformed since it is clearly based on a traditional view of international law. The International Criminal Court, which paradoxically challenges the traditional approach to international law, will potentially have more impact as regards the potential criminal responsibility of political leaders for decisions to go to war once a definition of aggression is agreed by the state parties to the Rome Statute. Expectations might be higher of the European Courts especially after the *Kadi* case of 2008 challenged the competence of both the EU executive and indirectly the Security Council, but it must be remembered that this was a decision about non-forcible measures against individuals, not decisions to use force against states.

A strengthening of mechanisms of judicial review and accountability at the international level is the most that we can hope for, a process that might eventually lead to governments (and executives of international organizations) being held to account by courts for decisions to go to war in breach of international law. It will be argued by democratically elected governments that with current world instability, with armed conflict being all too commonplace, it is premature to subject political decisions to use military force to judicial review. However, the stronger argument must be that with war being increasingly waged by liberal democracies, the very democratic fabric of these countries is under threat, demanding greatly increased levels of democratic and judicial accountability for decisions to go to war.

Bibliography

BOOKS

Abass, A., *Regional Organizations in the Development of Collective Security* (Oxford: Hart, 2004)

Alvarez, J.E., *International Organizations as Lawmakers* (Oxford: Oxford University Press, 2005)

Archibugi, D., *The Global Commonwealth of Citizens* (Princeton: Princeton University Press, 2008)

—— and Held, D. (eds), *Cosmopolitan Democracy: An Agenda for a New World Global Order* (Cambridge: Polity Press, 1995)

Arnull, A., and Wincott, D. (eds), *Accountability and Legitimacy in the European Union* (Oxford: Oxford University Press, 2002)

Asrat, B., *Prohibition of Force under the UN Charter* (Stockholm: Iustus, 1991)

Austin, J., *The Province of Jurisprudence Determined* (London: John Murray, 1833)

Bailey, S.D., *Voting in the Security Council* (Oxford: Clarendon Press, 1969)

—— *The Korean Armistice* (London: Palgrave, 1992)

—— and Daws, S., *The Procedure of the UN Security Council* (3rd edn, Oxford: Clarendon Press, 1998)

Baylis, J., *The Diplomacy of Pragmatism: Britain and the Formation of NATO 1942–1950* (Basingstoke: Macmillan, 1993)

Bellamy, A.J., Williams, P., and Griffin, S., *Understanding Peacekeeping* (Cambridge: Polity, 2004)

Blokker, N.M., and Schermers, H.G. (eds), *Proliferation of International Organizations: Legal Issues* (The Hague: Kluwer, 2001)

—— and Schrijver, N. (eds), *The Security Council and the Use of Force* (Leiden: Martinus Nijhoff, 2005)

Bogdandor, V. (ed), *The British Constitution in the Twentieth Century* (Oxford: Oxford University Press, 2003)

Bowett, D.W., *Self-Defence in International Law* (Manchester: Manchester University Press, 1958)

—— *United Nations Forces* (London: Stevens, 1964)

Bradley, A.W., and Ewing, K.D., *Constitutional and Administrative Law* (12th edn, London: Longman, 1997)

Brownlie, I., *International Law and the Use of Force by States* (Oxford: Oxford University Press, 1963)

—— *Principles of Public International Law* (6th edn, Oxford: Oxford University Press, 2003)

Bull, H., Kingsbury, B., and Roberts, A. (eds), *Hugo Grotius and International Relations* (Oxford: Clarendon, 1992)

Burchill, R., White, N.D., and Morris, J. (eds), *International Conflict and Security Law* (Cambridge: Cambridge University Press, 2005)

Burnell, P. (ed), *Democracy Assistance: International Cooperation for Democratization* (London: Frank Cass, 2000)

Butler, R., *The Non-Use of Force in International Relations* (The Hague: Kluwer, 1989)

Byrd, P. (ed), *British Foreign Policy under Thatcher* (Oxford: Philip Allan, 1988)

Carlton, D., *Britain and the Suez Crisis* (London: Basil Blackwell, 1988)

Chandler, D., *Bosnia: Faking Democracy after Dayton* (2nd edn, London: Pluto, 2000)

Chandler, D.G., and Beckett, I. (eds), *The Oxford History of the British Army* (Oxford: Oxford University Press, 1994)

Churchill, W.S., *The Second World War: Volume I The Gathering Storm* (London: Cassell, 1949)

—— *The Second World War: Volume IV The Hinge of Fate* (London: Cassell, 1951)

—— *The Second World War: Volume V Closing the Ring* (London: Cassell, 1952)

Claude, I.L., *Power and International Relations* (New York: Random House, 1962)

Cohen, S. (ed), *Democracies at War Against Terrorism* (London: Palgrave, 2008)

Cordier, A.W., and Foote, W. (eds), *Public Papers of the Secretaries General of the United Nations: Volume I Trygve Lie* (New York: Columbia University Press, 1969)

Cot, J.P., and Pellet, A. (eds), *La Charte des Nations Unies* (Paris: Economica, 1985)

Cryer, R., *Prosecuting International Crimes: Selectivity and the International Criminal Law Regime* (Cambridge: Cambridge University Press, 2005)

Curtis, M., *The Ambiguities of Power: British Foreign Policy Since 1945* (London: Zed Books, 1995)

Dahl, R.A., *On Democracy* (New Haven: Yale University Press, 1998)

Daintith, T., and Page, A., *The Executive in the Constitution: Structure, Autonomy, and Internal Control* (Oxford: Oxford University Press, 1999)

de Smith, S., and Brazier, R., *Constitutional and Administrative Law* (8th edn, London: Penguin, 1998)

Delbruck, J. (ed), *Allocation of Law Enforcement Authority in the International System* (Berlin: Duncker and Humblot, 1995)

Dicey, A.V., *Introduction to the Study of the Law of the Constitution* (10th edn, London: Macmillan, 1959)

Diehl, P.F. (ed), *The Politics of Global Governance* (Boulder: Lynne Rienner, 2001)

Dinstein, Y., *The Conduct of Hostilities under the Law of International Armed Conflict* (Cambridge: Cambridge University Press, 2004)

—— *War, Aggression and Self-Defence* (4th edn, Cambridge: Cambridge University Press, 2005)

Dowling, K., Goodin, R.E., and Pateman, C. (eds), *Justice and Democracy* (Cambridge: Cambridge University Press, 2004)

Downs, G.W. (ed), *Collective Security Beyond the Cold War* (New York: University of Michigan Press, 1995)

Dyson, K.H.F., *The State Tradition in Western Europe* (Oxford: Robertson, 1980)

Eeckhout, P., *External Relations of the European Union* (Oxford: Oxford University Press, 2004)

Evatt, H.V., *The United Nations* (London: Oxford University Press, 1948)

Farrar-Hockley, A., *The British Part in the Korean War: Volume 1 A Distant Obligation* (London: HMSO, 1991)

Fletcher, G.P., *Basic Concepts of Criminal Law* (Oxford: Oxford University Press, 1998)

——, and Ohlin, F.D., *Defending Humanity: When Force is Justified and Why* (Oxford: Oxford University Press, 2008)

Franck, T.M., *Recourse to Force: State Action Against Threats and Armed Attacks* (Oxford: Oxford University Press, 2002)

Freeman, L., *The Official History of the Falklands Campaign: Volume II War and Diplomacy* (London: Routledge, 2005)

Freestone, D., and Davidson, J.S., *The Institutional Framework of the European Community* (London: Routledge, 1988)

Fukuyama, F., *The End of History and the Last Man* (London: Penguin, 1992)

Gans, H.J., *Democracy and the News* (Oxford: Oxford University Press, 2003)

Goldsworthy, J., *The Sovereignty of Parliament: History and Philosophy* (Oxford: Oxford University Press, 2002)

Goodwin, G.L., *Britain and the United Nations* (Oxford: Oxford University Press, 1957)

Gray, C., *International Law and the Use of Force* (2nd edn, Oxford: Oxford University Press, 2004)

Hardin, R., *Liberalism, Constitutionalism and Democracy* (Oxford: Oxford University Press, 2003)

Harlow, C., *Accountability in the European Union* (Oxford: Oxford University Press, 2002)

Harris, D.J., *Cases and Materials on International Law* (6th edn, London: Sweet and Maxwell, 2004)

Hastings, M., *The Korean War* (London: Michael Joseph, 1987)

—— and Jenkins, S., *The Battle for the Falklands* (London: Book Club Associates, 1982)

Heyman, C., *The British Army: A Pocket Guide 2006–2007* (Barnsley: Pen and Sword Books, 2005)

Higgins, R., *The Development of International Law through the Political Organs of the United Nations* (Oxford: Oxford University Press, 1963)

—— *United Nations Peacekeeping: Documents and Commentary: Volume 4 Europe 1946–1979* (Oxford: Oxford University Press, 1981)

Hill, J.R., *The Oxford Illustrated History of the Royal Navy* (Oxford: Oxford University Press, 1995)

Jennings, R., and Watts, A., *Oppenheim's International Law* (9th edn, London: Longman, 1992)

Jowell, J., and Oliver, D. (eds), *The Changing Constitution* (5th edn, Oxford: Oxford University Press, 2004)

Kant, I., *Perpetual Peace and Other Essays on History and Morals* (Indianapolis: Hackett Publishing, 1983)

Keir, D.L., *The Constitutional History of Modern Britain 1485–1937* (3rd edn, London: Blacks, 1938)

Kelsen, H., *The Law of the United Nations* (London: Stevens, 1951)

Kennedy, P., *The Parliament of Man: The Past, Present and Future of the United Nations* (Toronto: HarperCollins, 2006)

Kirgis, F.L., *International Organizations in their Legal Setting* (2nd edn, St Paul: West Publishing, 1993)

Ku, C. and Jacobson, H.K. (eds), *Democratic Accountability and the Use of Force in International Law* (Cambridge: Cambridge University Press, 2003)

Lester, L., and Oliver, D. (eds), *Constitutional Law and Human Rights* (London: Butterworths, 1997)

Lie, T., *In the Cause of Peace* (London: Macmillan, 1954)

Lillich, R. (ed), *Humanitarian Intervention and the United Nations* (Charlottesville: University Press of Virginia, 1973)

Lloyd, L., *Peace Through Law: Britain and the International Court in the 1920s* (London: Boydell, 1997)

Lord, C., *Democracy in the European Union* (Sheffield: Sheffield University Press, 1998)

Loveland, I., *Constitutional Law, Administrative Law and Human Rights* (3rd edn, London: Butterworths, 2003)

Luard, E. (ed), *The Evolution of International Organizations* (London: Thames and Hudson, 1966)

Lyon, A., *A Constitutional History of the United Kingdom* (London: Cavendish, 2003)

Mackintosh, J.P., *People and Parliament* (Farnborough: Saxon House, 1978)

Maitland, F.W., *The Constitutional History of England* (Cambridge: Cambridge University Press, 1931)

Malone, D. (ed), *The UN Security Council: From the Cold War to the 21st Century* (Boulder: Lynne Rienner, 2004)

Marks, S., *The Riddle of All Constitutions* (Oxford: Oxford University Press, 2000)

Matheson, M.J., *Council UnBound: The Growth of UN Decision Making on Conflict and Postconflict Issues after the Cold War* (Washington: The US Institute of Peace Press, 2006)

McDougal, M.S., and Feliciano, F.P., *Law and Minimum World Public Order* (New Haven: Yale University Press, 1961)

Mill, J.S., *Considerations on Representative Democracy* (New York: Liberal Arts Press, 1958)

Muir, R., *British History* (London: George Philip and Son, 1936)

Nozick, R., *Anarchy, State and Utopia* (Oxford: Basil Blackwell, 1974)

Nutting, A., *No End of a Lesson: The Story of Suez* (London: Constable, 1967)

O'Keefe, D., and Twomey, P.M. (eds), *Legal Issues of the Maastricht Treaty* (London: Chancery Law, 1994)

O'Neill, J.T., and Rees, N., *United Nations Peacekeeping in the Post-Cold War Era* (Abingdon: Routledge, 2005)

Oliver, D., *Government in the United Kingdom: The Search for Accountability, Effectiveness and Citizenship* (Milton Keynes: Open University Press, 1991)

—— *Constitutional Reform in the UK* (Oxford: Oxford University Press, 2003)

Rawlings, J., *History of the Royal Air Force* (London: Random House, 1985)

Reiter, D., and Stam, A.C., *Democracies at War* (Princeton: Princeton University Press, 2002)

Riley, J., *The Life and Campaigns of General Hughie Stockwell* (London: Pen and Sword Books, 2006)

Rodin, D., *War and Self-Defense* (Oxford: Clarendon Press, 2002)

Rogers, A., *Law on the Battlefield* (2nd edn, Manchester: Manchester University Press, 2004)

Ronzitti, N., *Rescuing Nationals Abroad through Military Coercion and Intervention on the Grounds of Humanity* (Dordrecht: Martinus Nijhoff, 1985)

Rose, M., *Fighting for Peace: Lessons from Bosnia* (London: Sphere, 1998)

Rosenne, S., *Developments in the Law of Treaties* (Cambridge: Cambridge University Press, 1989)

Rowe, P., *Defence: The Legal Implications* (London: Brassey's 1987)

—— *The Impact of Human Rights Law on Armed Forces* (Cambridge: Cambridge University Press, 2006)

Russell R.B. and Muther J.E., *A History of the United Nations Charter* (Washington: Brookings Institute, 1958)

Russett, B., *Grasping the Democratic Peace: Principles for a Post-Cold War World* (Princeton: Princeton University Press, 1993)

Saksena, K.P., *The United Nations and Collective Security* (Delhi: Sage, 1974)

Sarooshi, D., *The United Nations and the Development of Collective Security* (Oxford: Oxford University Press, 1999)

Schama, S., *A History of Britain: At the Edge of the World* (London: BBC, 2000)

Schermers, H.G., and Blokker, N.M., *International Institutional Law* (4th edn, Leiden: Martinus Nijhoff, 2003)

Schlesinger, S.C., *Act of Creation: The Founding of the United Nations* (Boulder: Westview, 2003)

Schmieding, H., *Europe after Maastricht* (London: Institute of Economic Affairs, 1993)

Shaw, M.N., *International Law* (5th edn, Cambridge: Cambridge University Press, 2003)

Shotwell, J.T., *War as an Instrument of National Policy* (New York: Harcourt, Brace and Co, 1929)

Simma, B. (ed), *The Charter of the United Nations: A Commentary* (2nd edn, Oxford: Oxford University Press, 2002)

Simms, B., *Unfinest Hour: Britain and the Destruction of Bosnia* (London: Penguin, 2002)

Singh, J.N., *Use of Force under International Law* (Baltimore: Johns Hopkins, 1994)

Stone, J., *Legal Controls of International Conflict* (London: Stevens, 1954)

—— *Aggression and World Order* (London: Stevens, 1958)

Tal, D. (ed), *The 1956 War: Collusion and Rivalry in the Middle East* (London: Frank Cass, 2001)

Taylor, P., *International Organizations in the Modern World* (London: Pinter, 1993)

Teson, F.R., *Humanitarian Intervention: An Inquiry into Law and Morals* (3rd edn, New York: Transnational, 2005)

Tomuschat, C. (ed), *The United Nations at Fifty: A Legal Perspective* (The Hague: Kluwer, 1995)

Trybus, M., and White, N.D. (eds), *European Security Law* (Oxford: Oxford University Press, 2007)

Turpin, C., *British Government and the Constitution* (5th edn, London: Butterworths, 2002)

Vattel, *The Law of Nations or the Principles of Natural Law*, Book III, 35 (3 Classics of International Law ed, C.G. Fenwick trans, 1916)

Verzijl, J.H.W., *International Law in Historical Perspective* (Leiden: Sijthoff, 1976)

Weart, S.R., *Never at War: Why Democracies Will Not Fight One Another* (New Haven: Yale University Press, 1998)

Weigall, D., and Stirk, P. (eds), *The Origins and Development of the European Community* (Leicester: Leicester University Press, 1992)

Weiss, T., *Humanitarian Intervention: Ideas in Action* (Cambridge: Polity, 2007)

Weller, M. (ed), *Iraq and Kuwait: The Hostilities and their Aftermath* (Cambridge: Cambridge University Press, 1993)

White, N.D., *Keeping the Peace: The United Nations and the Maintenance of International Peace and Security* (2nd edn, Manchester: Manchester University Press, 1997)

Wright, Q., *A Study of War* (2nd edn, Chicago: Chicago University Press, 1967)

Yoo, J., *The Powers of War and Peace: The Constitution and Foreign Affairs After 9/11* (Chicago: University of Chicago Press, 2006)

ARTICLES

Acheson, D., 'Response to Panel: The Cuban Quarantine—Implications for the Future' (1963) 14 ASIL Proceedings 14

Benvenuti, P., 'The ICTY Prosecutor and the Review of the NATO Bombing Campaign Against the Federal Republic of Yugoslavia' (2001) 12 EJIL 503

Blokker, N.M., 'Is Authorization Authorized? Powers and Practice of the UN Security Council to Authorize the Use of Force by "Coalitions of the Able and Willing" ' (2000) 11 EJIL 541

Blum, Y., 'State Responses to Acts of Terrorism' (1976) 19 GYBIL 223

—— 'Proposals for UN Security Council Reform' (2005) 99 AJIL 632

Byers, M., 'Terrorism, the Use of Force and International Law after 11 September' (2002) 51 ICLQ 401

—— 'The Shifting Foundations of International Law: A Decade of Forceful Measures Against Iraq' (2002) 13 EJIL 21

—— 'Self-Defence or Pre-emptive Actions? The Law and Politics of Normative Change' (2003) 16 Ethics and International Affairs 52

Carcano, A., 'End of Occupation in 2004? The Status of the Multinational Force in Iraq after the Transfer of Authority to the Interim Iraqi Government' (2006) 11 JCSL 41

Cassese, A., 'Ex Inuria Ius Oritur: Are We Moving Towards International Legitimation of Forcible Countermeasures in the World Community?' (1999) 10 EJIL 23

—— 'The *Nicaragua* and *Tadic* Tests Revisited in the Light of the ICJ Judgment on Genocide in Bosnia' (2007) 18 EJIL 649

Charney, J., 'The Use of Force against Terrorism and International Law' (2001) 95 AJIL 835

Cockayne, J., and Malone, D., 'United Nations Peace Operations: Then and Now' (2003) 9 International Peacekeeping: The Yearbook of International Peace Operations 1

Dupuy, P.-M., 'The Constitutional Dimension of the Charter of the United Nations Revisited' (1997) 1 MPYBUNL 20

Egan, P.T., 'The Kosovo Intervention and Collective Self-Defence' (2001) 8 International Peacekeeping 39

Farer, T.J., 'Beyond the Charter Frame: Unilateralism or Condominium?' (2002) 96 AJIL 359

Fassbender, B., 'All Illusions Shattered? Looking Back on a Decade of Failed Attempts to Reform the UN Security Council' (2003) 7 MPYBUNL 183

Franck, T.M., 'The Emerging Rights to Democratic Governance' (1992) 86 AJIL 82

—— 'The Powers of Appreciation: Who is the Ultimate Guardian of UN Legality?' (1992) 86 AJIL 519

—— 'Terrorism and the Right of Self-Defense' (2001) 95 AJIL 839

—— 'What Happens Now? The United Nations After Iraq' (2003) 97 AJIL 607

Gill, T.D., 'Legal and Political Limitations on the Power of the UN Security Council to Exercise its Enforcement Powers under Chapter VII of the UN Charter' (1995) 26 NYBIL 57

Goudling, M., 'The Evolution of United Nations Peacekeeping' (1993) 69 International Affairs 451

Gray, C., 'From Unity to Polarization: International Law and the Use of Force Against Iraq' (2002) 13 EJIL 1

Greenwood, C., 'International Law and the Pre-Emptive Use of Force: Afghanistan, Al-Qaida and Iraq' (2003) 4 San Diego Intl L J 7

Grieco, J.M., 'Anarchy and the Limits of Cooperation: A Realist Critique of the Newest Liberal Internationalism' (1988) 42 International Organization 485

Hansen, O., Ramsbotham, O., and Woodhouse, T., 'Hawks and Doves: Peacekeeping and Conflict Resolution' (Berghof Research Centre for Constructive Conflict Management, 2004)

Happold, M., 'Security Council Resolution 1373 and the Constitution of the United Nations' (2003) 16 LJIL 593

Jennings, R.Y., 'The Caroline and McLeod Cases' (1938) 32 AJIL 82

Johnstone, I., 'Treaty Interpretation: The Authority of Interpretive Communities' (1991) 12 Michigan J Intl L 381

—— 'Security Council Deliberations: The Power of Better Argument' (2003) 14 EJIL 437

Kirgis, F.L., 'Pre-emptive Action to Forestall Terrorism' (2002) ASIL Insights

—— 'Security Council Resolution 1441 on Iraq's Final Opportunity to Comply with Disarmament Obligations' (2002) ASIL Insights

Koskenniemi, M., 'The Place of Law in Collective Security' (1996) 17 Michigan J Intl L 455

Krisch, N., 'Unilateral Enforcement of the Collective Will: Kosovo, Iraq, and the Security Council' (1999) 3 MPYBUNL 59

Kunz, J.L., 'Individual and Collective Self-Defense in Article 51 of the Charter of the United Nations' (1947) 41 AJIL 872

Lavalle, R., 'The Law of the United Nations and the Use of Force under the Relevant Security Council Resolutions of 1990 and 1991 to Resolve the Persian Gulf Crisis' (1992) 23 NYBIL 3

Liivoja, R., 'The Scope of the Supremacy Clause of the United Nations Charter' (2008) 57 ICLQ 583

Lillich, R.B., 'Humanitarian Intervention through the United Nations: Towards the Development of Criteria' (1993) 17 Heidelberg L Rev 563

Lobel, J., and Ratner, M., 'Bypassing the Security Council: Ambiguous Authorizations to Use Force, Cease-Fires and the Iraqi Inspection Regime' (1999) 93 AJIL 124

Marston, G., 'Armed Intervention in the 1956 Suez Canal Crisis: Legal Advice Tendered to the British Government' (1988) 37 ICLQ 773

McCoubrey, H., 'Kosovo, NATO and International Law' (1999) 14 International Relations 34

McDougal, M.S., 'The Soviet-Cuban Quarantine and Self-Defense' (1963) 57 AJIL 597

Morris, J., 'UN Security Council Reform: A Counsel for the 21st Century' (2000) 31 Security Dialogue 265

Mulgan, R., 'Accountability: An Ever-Expanding Concept' (2000) 78 Public Administration 555

Musson, J., 'Britain and the Recognition of Bangladesh' (2008) 19 Diplomacy and Statecraft 125

Myjer, E.P.J., and White, N.D., 'The Twin Towers Attack: An Unlimited Right to Self-Defence?' (2002) 7 JCSL 5

O'Connell, M.E., 'The Myth of Preemptive Self-Defense' (2000) ASIL Task Force Papers 3
—— 'Evidence of Terror' (2002) 7 JCSL 19

Oliver, D., 'The Scott Report' (1996) Public Law 357

Paris, R., 'International Peacekeeping and the "Mission Civilisatrice"' (2002) 28 Review of International Studies 637

Perry, G., 'Security Council Resolution 242: The Withdrawal Clause' (1977) 31 Middle East Journal 413

Quigley, J., 'The United States and the United Nations in the Persian Gulf War: New Order or Disorder?' (1992) 25 Cornell Intl L J 28
—— 'The Privatization of Security Council Enforcement Actions: A Threat to Unilateralism' (1996) 17 Michigan J of Intl L 271

Ratner, S., 'Ius ad Bellum and Ius in Bello after September 11' (2002) 96 AJIL 906

Reisman, W.M., 'In Defence of World Public Order' (2001) 95 AJIL 833

Rostow, E.V., 'Until What? Enforcement Action or Collective Self-Defense?' (1991) 85 AJIL 506

Schachter, O., 'United Nations Law in the Gulf Conflict' (1991) 85 AJIL 459

Scheffer, D., 'Beyond Occupation Law' (2003) 97 AJIL 842

Scott, K., 'Commentary on Suez: Forty Years On' (1996) 1 JACL 205

Seymour-Ure, C., 'British "War Cabinets" in Limited Wars: Korea, Suez and the Falklands' (1984) 62 Public Administration 182

Shapira, A., 'The Six Day War and the Right of Self-Defence' (1971) 6 Israeli Law Review 65

Simma, B., 'NATO, the UN and the Use of Force: Legal Aspects' (1999) 10 EJIL 1

Simpson, G., 'The Death of Baha Mousa' (2007) 8 Melbourne J of Intl L 19

Taft, W.H., and Buchwald, T.F., 'Pre-emption, Iraq and International Law' (2003) 97 AJIL 557

Thirlway, H., 'The Law and Procedure of the International Court of Justice' (1996) 67 BYBIL 29

Tsagourias, N., 'The Shifting Laws on the Use of Force and the Trivialization of the UN Security System: The Need to Reconstitute It' (2003) XXXIV NYBIL 55

Villiani, U., 'The Security Council's Authorization of Enforcement Action by Regional Organizations' (2002) 6 MPYBUNL 535

Waldock, C.H.M., 'The Regulation of the Use of Force by Individual States in International Law' (1952) 81 Recueil des Cours 455

Wartentin, C., and Mingst, K., 'International Institutions, the State, and Global Civil Society in an Age of the World Wide Web' (2000) 6 Global Governance 237

Wessell, R.A., 'Revisiting the International Legal Status of the EU' (2000) 5 EFAR 507
—— 'The State of Affairs in EU Security and Defence Policy: The Breakthrough in the Treaty of Nice' (2003) 8 JCSL 265

White, N.D., 'From Korea to Kuwait: The Legal Basis of United Nations' Military Action' (1998) XX International History Review 600

—— 'The Legality of Bombing in the Name of Humanity' (2000) 5 JCSL 27

—— 'The Will and Authority of the Security Council after Iraq' (2004) 17 LJIL 645

Willetts, P., 'From Consultative Arrangements to Partnership: The Changing Status of NGOs in Diplomacy at the UN' (2000) 6 Global Governance 191

Wilmshurst, E., 'The Chatham House Principles of International Law on the Use of Force in Self-Defence' (2006) 55 ICLQ 963

Wood, M.C., 'The Interpretation of UN Security Council Resolutions' (1998) 2 MPYBUNL 73

Index